Ralph Harris in His Own Wo.
the Selected Writings of Lord Harris

Ralph Harris in His Own Words, the Selected Writings of Lord Harris

Ralph Harris

Edited with an Introduction by Colin Robinson

Emeritus Professor of Economics, University of Surrey, UK

With a Foreword by Lord Howe of Aberavon

In Association with the Institute of Economic Affairs

Edward Elgar
Cheltenham, UK • Northampton, MA, USA

Published by
Edward Elgar Publishing Limited
Glensanda House
Montpellier Parade
Cheltenham
Glos GL50 1UA
UK

Edward Elgar Publishing, Inc.
William Pratt House
9 Dewey Court
Northampton
Massachusetts 01060
USA

ISBN 978 0 255 36621 2

Typeset by Cambrian Typesetters, Camberley, Surrey
Printed and bound in Great Britain by MPG Books Ltd, Bodmin, Cornwall

Contents

Abbreviations

CBI	Confederation of British Industry
CPS	Centre for Policy Studies
EEC	European Economic Community
EU	European Union
IEA	Institute of Economic Affairs
IRA	Irish Republican Army
LSE	London School of Economics
MPS	Mont Pèlerin Society
NCB	National Coal Board
NEDC	National Economic Development Council
NEDO	National Economic Development Office
NHS	National Health Service
NIESR	National Institute of Economic and Social Research
TUC	Trades Union Congress

Acknowledgements

I wish to acknowledge the considerable help of Lady Jose Harris, who allowed me to look through the papers of Lord Harris, and of Paul Lennon, who searched through the pages of *Hansard* to discover the speeches and other contributions to debates in the House of Lords by Lord Harris and then organised them into a form in which they could be used in this book.

Part III 'House of Lord Speeches', Parliamentary material reproduced with the permission of the Controller of HMSO on behalf of Parliament.

The Times obituary by George Lucas by kind permission of The Times, N.I. Syndication.

The Daily Telegraph obituary, Friday 20 October 2006 by kind permission.

The Economist obituary © The Economist Newspaper Limited, London, 4 November 2006.

The Independent obituary 'Lord Harris of High Cross' by Russell Lewis, 21 October 2006 by kind permission of Independent Newspapers.

The *Financial Times* obituary by Martin Wolf, 20 October 2006.

I would also like to acknowledge:

The Institute of Economic Affairs (IEA) for allowing the reproduction of 'An independent station', 'Now for "planning"', 'Market versus state' and 'Behind enemy lines' first published in *Towards a Liberal Utopia*, ed. P. Booth, London: IEA, Hobart Paperback 32, 2005; 'No Prime Minister! Ralph Harris against the consensus', IEA Occasional Paper 94, 1994; 'No Minister! (Early House of Lords Speeches)', IEA Occasional Paper 71, 1985; 'Adam Smith: revolutionary for the third millennium', *Economic Affairs*, **22**(3), September 2002, Blackwell Publishing.

The Centre for Policy Studies for allowing the reproduction of 'The challenge of a radical reactionary', East Sussex: Strange the Printer, March 1980 (pamphlet) and 'Morality and markets', London: G. Donald & Co., December 1986 (pamphlet).

Foreword

Geoffrey Howe

Ralph Harris and I were not quite contemporaries – and from rather different backgrounds: his was London and a scholarship to Tottenham Grammar and mine was South Wales and an exhibition to Winchester. But we both ended up with Cambridge degrees: mine in Law and his (First Class) in Economics – the launch-pad of his meteoric academic career.

Quite soon, however, we had both taken to politics – each, in our first intervention, supporting the Liberal Unionist cause. And by 1955 we were both Conservative candidates for Parliament – Ralph in Edinburgh and myself in Aberavon.

But never again, thereafter, was Ralph tempted to act as a politician himself. On the contrary, he was increasingly inclined to dismiss us all, in Adam Smith's harsh phrase, as 'that insidious and crafty animal, vulgarly called a statesman or politician, whose councils are directed by the momentary fluctuations of affairs'. Yet by 1960, Ralph and I often found ourselves actively campaigning alongside each other – Ralph, in his third year in charge of the deliberately non-political Institute of Economic Affairs, and myself, as editor of the deliberately Conservative (but independent) *Crossbow*, also in its third year.

And very often – much more often than not, indeed – we were striking identical notes. My own second pamphlet, for example, calling for the abolition of rent control, appeared in the same year as the Institute's (by Norman Macrae) with almost identical titles.[1] More than twenty years later, my abolition (as Chancellor of the Exchequer) of pay, price, dividend and exchange control seemed to secure me almost eternal reverence in Institute circles. I was honoured to be recruited by Ralph as one of the very few politician members of the Mont Pelerin Society.

And so it remained, almost literally until the day Ralph died, with one huge, exceptional item, alas: our (sharply divergent) views of Brussels and all that went with it – a possible subject for another book, that will never be written! Ralph was certainly right, when setting out with Antony Fisher to establish the IEA, and later, in his pivotal role in promoting the birth of so many similar units around the world, in insisting that they should be absolutely independent and wholly free from the encumbrance of any party political pursuit of short-term electoral expediency. There can be no doubt that this manifest political independence of the various institutions helped enormously to secure academic and other acceptance – almost world-wide – of fundamentally new (or long unrecognised) truths and policies.

All this I was delighted to witness, as I made my own way forward in the avowedly political field – for the most part with very similar objectives, and not infrequently achieving them. But I bridled from time to time (right to the end, indeed) when I heard or read Ralph occasionally denouncing – even sometimes, as Colin Robinson puts it in the Introduction to this excellent book, 'castigating' politicians almost *en masse*, as an inclusive group, for our failure to tackle (let alone to complete) his agenda. To be fair, I must acknowledge that there have been occasions when I have myself been disappointed for the same reason.

It is this dilemma which identifies for me the principal reason for absorbing this hugely inclusive book. Much of Ralph Harris's formidable agenda has indeed been achieved in the real world in which we live today. But much has not. Why is that? Is it because of the absence of any sufficient bridge of sympathy and understanding between the policy analyst – the person who thinks policy problems through – and the politician – the person who has to put that policy into practice in a democratic society?

We all understand the purpose, and the value, of a democratically elected system of government – even if only as a means of 'chucking the blighters out'. But that is not always the issue and it is seldom, if ever, the only one. It was Bagehot who first said, at the time of the 1867 Reform Act, that he could think of nothing more corrupting than for two groups of rich and intelligent men to present themselves to the working man, asking what it is that he would like them to do, and then to compete for the right to do it. But that is exactly how the market works – and how you sell (or purport to sell) what the customer would like. But not so often what the customer (still less the nation) actually needs.

Items that had long been on the Harris agenda were transformed into practice for a diversity of reasons, and in response to the efforts of a wide variety of people. Not many did so simply because the intellectual argument had been won. The abolition of retail price maintenance, by Edward Heath, was one such. The ending of rent control was another – when New Labour was finally persuaded, in 1997, to exclude from its manifesto, for the first time ever, any pledge to reintroduce it. In other cases – for example, pay, price and dividend control, even trade union privilege – the discarded policies were being, already in practice, tested literally to destruction.

But despite the scale of Ralph's achievements, much remains to be done. We have, for example, fallen far short of real success in our struggle to staunch the flow of new legislation, even to get rid of much of the dross, by

which we are all still encumbered. Small wonder that politics is so often
defined as the art of the possible.

So how do we make possible the necessary – desirable even – but difficult?
Britain's experience suggests that this can only be done when the electorate
realises that, in Margaret Thatcher's words, 'there is no alternative'. She, and
probably Winston Churchill, were the only two Prime Ministers in recent
history lucky enough to be confronting a nation which realised that it was in
the last chance saloon. It was that which enabled us, in the Thatcher years, to
'sell' many of the policies which Ralph Harris (and others) had argued were
inescapably right. But not those which they regarded as equally desirable, but
difficult, and which would hugely improve our society but could not easily, or
at all, be politically marketed as such. The educational voucher system is one
example.

This analysis of the wide-ranging agenda, exposed and explored in this
mammoth collection of thoughts of my old friend Ralph Harris, will help to
identify the questions, which the reader should be asking him or herself, while
skipping a way through this treasure-house of wisdom.

Can politicians, for example, be expected to tackle really difficult, but
necessary, policies, if they are repeatedly denounced for concentrating on the
hunt for votes – without which they will never be in a position to introduce
those policies? How can the desirable, but difficult, be made electorally
acceptable? How can we best enable Ralph Harris to win all the contests that
still lie ahead?

NOTE

1   The IEA paper was Norman Macrae, *To Let?*, Hobart Paper 2, 1960

Editor's introduction

Colin Robinson

When Lord Harris of High Cross (Ralph Harris) died, on 19 October 2006, at the age of 81, all Britain's major newspapers (and many overseas publications) carried tributes to him as one of the 'men who changed Britain'. Friends and opponents alike acknowledged that Ralph, in his role as General Director of the Institute of Economic Affairs (IEA) and in partnership with his friend, Arthur Seldon, had been instrumental in providing the ideas and the intellectual entrepreneurship that sparked the 'Thatcher revolution' of the 1980s. That revolution had transformed the British economy, turning it from one of the worst performers among developed countries to one of the best.

This volume is intended to provide a flavour of Ralph's writings by selecting from his considerable *opus*. Part I is about his work at the IEA and related activities; Part II includes some of his papers on markets and freedom; Part III contains a selection from his large number of speeches in the House of Lords. Part IV departs from the rest of the book in not containing Ralph's own writings: it consists of five of the many obituary notices.

In the spring and summer of 2006, Ralph had been considering the publication in one volume of some of his past works, several new pieces he had written and a selection of his speeches in the House of Lords. He had discussed with me, as possible editor, the contents of such a book (apart from which House of Lords speeches should be included which he felt that the editor should decide). This book is therefore largely Ralph's own choice of the writings that best represent the ideas he had espoused and the views he had advocated from the late 1950s to the early years of this century.

PART I

The first part of the volume begins with three papers that Ralph described as 'ramblings', written in the last couple of years of his life and not previously published, that he particularly wanted to appear in his selected works.

To start the volume, the most appropriate paper has to be one about Ralph's relationship with Arthur Seldon. In 'Living with Arthur', Ralph describes his long and fruitful relationship with Arthur Seldon, both as a working colleague and as a close friend. The complementary nature of the Harris–Seldon relationship emerges vividly from this brief paper. Ralph, as always, acknowledges Arthur's enormous contribution in the 'engine room' – thinking up ideas, finding authors and editing their work – while Ralph was the ideal 'front man' – publicising the work of IEA authors, raising funds for the Institute and speaking and writing himself. Like most of the best things in life, their division of labour was not consciously planned: it evolved as the two men worked together in what – judged by results – was one of the most successful partnerships of the twentieth century. The 'Gilbert and Sullivan' analogy which Ralph uses, in recognition of that other great partnership, is indeed apt.

Next is 'Watch out for the "Peter Principle"', another previously unpublished article, in which Ralph applies to his own life the well-known and powerful idea that we all tend to rise to the level of our own incompetence. Temptations were placed in his way on numerous occasions: to stay in the academic world where he worked when he was young, to move to the United States to head a 'development office', to head a government think-tank, to become a government minister. Thankfully he resisted all of these, recognising that his own strengths and weaknesses fitted him much better for the role of intellectual entrepreneur at which he excelled. Not until he was offered a peerage in 1979 did he, after much soul-searching (as his article explains), accept a role that allowed him another platform from which to proclaim his views on markets and freedom while retaining his position at the IEA. It was fortunate he did accept, because otherwise we would not have had the powerful contributions to the debate about ideas (some of which are reproduced in Part III) that his position in the House of Lords allowed him to make.

Buckingham University was one of Ralph's great projects during his time at the IEA. In the next article, also previously unpublished, he explores the question of 'Who invented Buckingham?'. He lists various contenders for that honour – Harry Ferns and Arthur Seldon as 'joint inspirers', Sir Sydney Caine, Donald Denman, Lord Tanlaw, Ralph Yablon and Max Beloff – before settling on Beloff as the one with best claim as 'creator'. One obvious omission from the article is that Ralph, though he mentions his own fund-raising efforts for Buckingham, modestly overlooks his own claim to be regarded as one of the prime inventors. Certainly, it is hard to believe that without his great driving force – undeterred by all the barriers that were placed in the way by the authorities and by the sheer difficulty of funding such an enterprise – Britain's only university independent of the state would ever have been established.

The last four articles in Part I – 'An Independent Station', 'Now for Planning', 'Market versus State' and 'Behind Enemy Lines' – were all first included in an IEA volume published to celebrate the Institute's fiftieth anniversary. They give a first-hand account of the battles that had to be fought from the Institute's early days onwards and how Ralph Harris, in partnership with Arthur Seldon, went about winning them. It is hard now to put oneself in the position of these two pioneers of free market ideas who, faced with a political and economic establishment that was, with very few exceptions, completely hostile to market ideas, had the determination to persist with views they knew to be correct. Not only did they persist, but, despite the unpropitious environment, in the end they triumphed. By 1979, when a prime minister who turned out to be a political ally had been elected, the groundwork had been prepared by the IEA in the sense that an intellectual framework of liberal ideas had been established and broad lines of policy had been drawn. The stage was therefore set for a bold politician to put into practice the ideas that had been pouring out of the IEA over the previous two decades. The approaches to economic and social policies espoused by the IEA in that period, under Ralph's leadership and with Arthur's intellectual contribution, are now in the mainstream of political and economic life. They are, in principle, accepted by the two major British political parties, even if their execution (particularly in terms of welfare state reform), still has a long way to go.

PART II

Part II includes some of Ralph's papers about markets and freedom. It begins with two speeches which Ralph gave abroad. Both demonstrate the inspiration Ralph derived from famous classical liberal economists. The first is a speech given in Prague in 2001 when the Czech language edition of *The Wealth of Nations* was published. In the speech, Ralph sets out the main features of Adam Smith's great work and explains how revolutionary Smith's ideas were when they first appeared. Indeed, he argues, the idea central to Smith – that the economy is 'an integrated system of voluntary co-operation through competition' – is still a model from which 'many, perhaps most governments in this imperfect world could learn valuable lessons, not least about globalisation'.

An article on Hayek, the 'arch radical reactionary', follows. This lecture, previously unpublished, given at the University of Chicago in 1999, like the one on Adam Smith, shows how Ralph traced his own thinking back to earlier classical liberals, though in this case to an economist he had known well and who had inspired the creation of the IEA. He discusses the main contributions of Hayek – the inherent problems of planning, the errors of socialism, the importance of property rights, competition as a process of discovery, the significance of individualism – and, as an ex-Conservative candidate, sympathises with Hayek's views about why radicals can only go so far with conservatives who are defenders of the status quo and lack the courage to let change run its course.

These two speeches are followed by two earlier papers published by the Centre for Policy Studies (famously described by Arthur Seldon as the 'infantry', as compared with the IEA role as the 'artillery'). In these papers, Ralph explains his own views about the benefits of markets and also about the moral aspects of markets. In these, as in his other writings, he was greatly concerned to counter the view that only socialists have a moral basis for their views. On the contrary, he argues, there is no virtue in doing good with other people's money, whereas markets will reflect whatever is the underlying morality of the people who compose the market. Bishops, in particular, come in for sharp criticism as purveyors of the conventional wisdom who make pronouncements on economic issues without understanding the basis on which markets operate.

The final section of Part II reprints an IEA Occasional Paper (*No, Prime Minister!*) which collects together thirty of Ralph's short articles, from newspapers and elsewhere, which capture the essence of his views. It begins with his own favourite short piece ('Cheer up! Things are getting worse'), a prophetic article from 1975 which argued that the economy was in such a parlous state that the argument for a market economy 'has gained the intellectual ascendancy' in terms of morality and freedom as well as efficiency and that political change must come. The articles cover the years 1965 to 1993 and deal with all the main issues of those years, demonstrating Ralph's ability to catch his audience's attention with witty phrases which go to the heart of complex economic issues and to set out the case for using markets to deal with the problems that then seemed so difficult. Politicians, civil servants, bishops, EU bureaucrats, planners of all kinds are castigated for their inability or unwillingness to understand simple economic truths that would save Britain from the ruinous economic and social policies that were then being pursued. Towards the end of the book, a more optimistic note creeps in as in a 1990 article he reviews the years in which Mrs Thatcher showed she had the courage to challenge the previously 'dominant collectivist sentiment'; nevertheless, Ralph warns, there is still much to do.

PART III

The rest of the book is devoted mainly to Ralph Harris's speeches in the House of Lords, of which he made over 200 (mostly full speeches, though including a few questions). Each speech is a brief, self-contained discussion of some significant economic or social issue which invariably points out the key role that markets can play in any policy to deal with it, while gently and humorously rebuking the would-be centralisers and planners who seem to be in the majority in both Houses of Parliament.

Part III begins with a reprint of a 1985 IEA Occasional Paper (*No, Minister!*) in which Arthur Seldon edited a selection of Ralph's early speeches in the House of Lords (between 1981 and 1984). These speeches range over the principal matters that then exercised politicians, grouped under three heading: unions and unemployment, cases for repeal, and markets, taxation and equality.

It is clear from these early speeches that the House of Lords provided Ralph with a near-ideal platform. With his gift for simplifying complex issues and his humour, he immediately mastered the art of speech-making in the Lords, where the speaker has to be brief and must capture the attention of his audience from the beginning. The Lords allowed Ralph to discuss and analyse contemporary issues, while making sure that his audience – usually in danger of becoming enmeshed in detail – distinguished the wood from the trees. He constantly brought to the attention of the House and his wider audience the fundamental economic principles that he was so adept at expounding: planning does not work, markets are far superior and, by and large, people are best left free to make their own decisions and their own mistakes from which they (and others) learn. Arthur Seldon's description of Ralph, in the Preface to 'No, Minister!', wonderfully captures Ralph's gifts as a speaker and debater, especially in the context of the Lords speeches: 'I think of him as a football centre-forward deftly picking up passes, thinking fast on his feet, outwitting the opposing fullbacks by clever dribbling, and distracting goalkeepers with jokes while shooting straight into the goal'.

Over the remaining 22 years of his life, Ralph Harris made about 150 speeches in the House of Lords. A selection of these is reprinted in the rest of Part III. They are reproduced here without editing, so that all the references to other speakers, the asides and other essential elements of speeches in the Lords are revealed. On reading through all of these 150 speeches, an editor's first reaction is that none of them can be excluded from a book of Ralph's writings because there is not one in which he fails to convey, in compressed form, some important insight about markets and freedom – whether it is about planning, or socialism, or competition, or rent control, or a minimum wage, or Sunday trading, or regulation, or restrictions on freedom (including smoking bans), or (increasingly in the later speeches) the problems caused for Britain by membership of the European Union. But, of course, space constraints mean that a selection has to be made and so the difficult task of choosing 21 speeches for inclusion had to be undertaken. Reading these speeches will, it is to be hoped, provide readers with an appetite for going to *Hansard* to see more of Ralph's penetrating and timeless observations on economic and social issues.

PART IV

Although this is a volume of Ralph Harris's writings, it seems appropriate to end it with some of the tributes, in the form of obituary notices, paid to him just after he died in the autumn of 2006. Of the many of these, from all round the world, five obituary notices – all from British newspapers – have been selected for inclusion in Part IV. These obituaries, which set out how he helped to provide an intellectual framework that was turned by politicians into a platform for radical political action, demonstrate not only how great were his achievements but in what affection he was held for his perpetual good humour and his generosity towards friends and colleagues. This book describes and explores that intellectual framework, in terms of his own writings, showing that economics need not always be a 'dismal science': economic analysis was, in the hands of Ralph Harris, deployed to great effect in plain language and with a wit and a wisdom that made it fun.

PART I

Papers on IEA-related activities

Living with Arthur*

I say 'living' rather than working with Arthur Seldon as conveying a truer picture of the nature of our partnership at the Institute over 30 years. To the outsider, we might have appeared an unlikely, even ill-assorted pair, very different in appearance and no less so in personality. On slight acquaintance in the early days, Arthur struck many as reserved and shy. Always thoughtful, he spoke slowly, occasionally pausing over a word that wouldn't easily come out. By contrast, I was more often described as 'ebullient', quickly getting onto terms with new people and treating anyone who would listen, whether friend or foe, to a torrent of words. If over the years my ready bonhomie helped bring Arthur out of his shell, his deeper qualities certainly had a subtle but profound influence on my whole approach to the IEA's work, so that earlier differences in approach became less marked. This was especially true in my approach towards party politics.

GOING STRAIGHT

Arthur was drawn towards the Liberal Party in the 1930s. Having been brought up in the East End of London and witnessed street parades by [Oswald] Mosley's Black-shirts, he identified the Tories with appeasement of Hitler's national socialism. At the LSE [London School of Economics] after 1934 his outstanding classical liberal teachers, led by Lionel (later Lord) Robbins and F.A. ('Fritz') Hayek, had also alerted him to the protectionist/interventionist policies pursued by the Conservatives under [Stanley] Baldwin and [Neville] Chamberlain.

I owed my own induction into politics to my favourite uncle Horace who, having left school at 13, taught himself about literature, history and current affairs. Though an admirer of [Herbert] Asquith's Liberal government, by 1940 when he took my education in hand, he had become a strong supporter of our great war-time liberator whose battle cry for peace to 'set the people free' was anyway far more congenial to me than Labour's austere, even alarming, appeal, as I saw it, to conscript the entire nation into 'planning for peace'.

---

* April 2005.

At Cambridge, mercifully before the self-appointed 'Keynesians' under Joan Robinson finally brought down the iron curtain and took over pretty well the whole of the economics faculty, I readily fell under the influence of the senior University lecturer, the tall, stooping, scholarly, gentle but intellectually robust Professor D.H. Robertson of Trinity College. Since my own Queens' College had no economists among its fellows, I had the good fortune to be farmed-out for supervision, first to the combative Stanley Dennison of Gonville and Caius who introduced me to *The Road to Serfdom* and other powerful writings of Hayek, then to the more austere market analyst, Alan Prest of Christ's College. Our solid standard textbooks were Alfred Marshall's trenchant *Principles of Economics*, which was sufficiently comprehensive almost to justify the quip that 'it's all in Marshall', and [Arthur] Pigou's later *Economics of Welfare* which nicely brought the quip into question with a major extension into the social impact of free market transactions. From these diverse liberal sources, I enjoyed as thorough an innoculation against conventional collectivism in all its guises as Arthur had enjoyed at LSE, despite its reputation as left-wing due largely to the party political antics of Professor Harold Laski.

My growing anti-socialist conviction was powerfully reinforced by my first job on graduating from Cambridge in 1947. In preference to offers from Unilever and ICI – both at starting salaries around £350 a year, read off from a fixed scale depending on age and without regard to my proud possession of a first class honours degree – I joined the newly established Conservative Political Centre at £500 a year as one of ten regional education officers. These were envisaged as an elite corps of graduates recruited by 'Rab' Butler to inject some intellectual stuffing into the stolid Tory rank and file. Switching to university teaching at St Andrews in 1949, I had easily found time to stand as a 'Liberal Unionist' candidate for the hopeless parliamentary seat of Kirkcaldy (the birthplace of Adam Smith) in the 1951 general election when I lost, much as expected, by 10,000 votes. In 1955 I stood for Central Edinburgh where I only narrowly escaped being elected, this time by a margin of less than 1,000 votes.

In truth, much as I had enjoyed the warm comradeship of party workers, I had begun to find politics rather intellectually cramping with its repetitive emphasis on the party's manifesto and exaggerated claims of past 'achievements'. Likewise, despite the attraction of teaching lively young men and women students at the charming, historic University of St Andrews, after seven good years and with an established family I was ready for a change. Accordingly, at Easter 1956, anticipating a firm offer by my prospective patron, Antony Fisher, to give effect to his brainchild Institute of Economic Affairs (IEA), I gave the University a term's notice and filled in six months as a leader writer with *The Glasgow Herald*. There I took over the desk vacated by Alastair Burnet (later editor of *The Economist* and distinguished pioneer

TV newscaster) who had gone to the United States on a Commonwealth Fund scholarship.

I first met Arthur a few months after being set up in a City office near the Stock Exchange as 'General Director' (and sole employee!) of the IEA in January 1957. Antony Fisher had suggested our first publication might be on pensions and Arthur's name was proposed as author by a rather austere Liberal peer named Lord Grantchester whose interest in the subject arose from being chairman of the prestigious London & Manchester insurance company. It was a dull winter afternoon when I found my way to a rather gloomy office in Dean's Yard, in the corner opposite Westminster Abbey, where Arthur worked as economic adviser to a group of leading brewers with famous brand names. He later explained his job as warning mostly old-fashioned family companies that the low price of their shares at a time of dividend restraint made the site value of their pubs vulnerable to take-over bidders like Clore who was then much in the financial news. He was also predicting a spread of wine-drinking which threatened the acceptability of their 'spit and sawdust' public bars, especially to an emerging clientele of women and families. I was to learn that his earlier job had been as editor of a leading retail journal which prepared his mind for the revolution in shopping which was to become a significant theme of IEA Papers under his visionary direction. He readily agreed to write a paper on pensions which I later discovered drew on his research into the 'problems of the aged poor' for a Liberal Party committee.

Nevertheless, I was mightily impressed when a little later he spent a weekend at the Reform Club and emerged with an almost illegibly handwritten manuscript which was magically transcribed and swiftly published as 'Pensions in a Free Society', with the Tassie medallion of Adam Smith on the front cover. Thereafter, we maintained regular contact, with Arthur becoming, first editorial adviser when the Institute moved from Austin Friars to a basement in Hobart Place with a staff of three in 1958, and then fully-fledged editorial director when we moved to Eaton Square in 1960 to accommodate double that number.

Within two years of our joining forces, my lingering Conservative loyalty was finally abandoned when Harold Macmillan casually acquiesced in the resignation of his distinguished Treasury team ([Enoch] Powell, [Peter] Thorneycroft and [Nigel] Birch) on the key issue of government spending. Both Arthur and I unerringly saw it as the triumph of Supermac's 'middle way' over the Party's liberal wing. Prompted by a generous donor named Sir Robert (later Lord) Renwick, we thereupon agreed that I should seek out Enoch Powell at the House of Commons and invite him to write a Paper drawing on his experience at the Treasury. Although the result was not exactly what we had hoped, it made a fascinating study which we published promptly as 'Saving in a Free Society' in 1960.

From those early days, Arthur stood ready to warn me gently against any political backsliding – usually with some such words as: 'Come off it Rafe, tuck in your Tory shirt'. He also invented the quip, which I quickly made my own, that after a serious flirtation with politics I was now 'going straight!'. I responded to his quips rather feebly by recalling, in bantering style, his own more modest political apprenticeship served on the fringes of the Liberal Party, contributing to reports on pensions and ownership for all, with the encouragement of his special LSE mentor, Arnold Plant. More earnestly, I used to tease him about the misnomer 'Liberal' for such a wishy-washy 'me-too' Party, whereupon he would take refuge in such giants as [Richard] Cobden and [John] Bright, but offer little excuse for such contemporary – now long forgotten – leaders as Clement Davis, though when the lively-minded Jo Grimond took over we both privately clung to the diminishing hope for better things. Whenever we discussed politics, Arthur never tired of recalling his early antipathy to pre-war Toryism with its appeasement of socialism as well as of Hitler in his student radical days.

'Living with Arthur' almost exactly conveys the way that within very few years of meeting in 1957, we grew closer together than either of us was to anyone else outside our respective families. He once confided that he'd had three slices of outstanding luck in his life: first meeting and marrying Marjorie, second his family upbringing (by a devoted, widowed adoptive mother), and third joining up with me at the IEA. I could honestly have said almost precisely the same for the three personal elements that shaped my own life. Perhaps that helps explain how two such strong-minded men, both of us capable of strenuously arguing our corners and equally preferring to have our own way, lived together in a harmony undistracted by a single serious row in 30 years. We had our share of differences and periodic tensions, but it was never conceivable that we should separate.

DIVISION OF LABOUR

One of many advantages of a small enterprise such as the IEA was that, sharing adjoining offices and lunching together most days with or without company, we were in almost continuous communion. There remained plenty of scope for strong differences in judgements on other people, office arrangements and, perhaps most persistent, on eking-out our tiny financial resources. We could both be stubborn and I was sometimes aware of infuriating him, as he did me. I pride myself on being highly sensitive in detecting the danger signals in personal relationships. With Arthur, a firm tightening of the lips, direct eye contact and slight lowering of the head meant time for me to yield, compromise or suggest postponing a decision.

On choice of topics or authors for new Papers, he was always scrupulous in consulting/informing me at every stage from commissioning through to page proofs But he explained early on that he 'worked best on a loose rein' and I never needed telling a second time. As a former journalist, first with *The Glasgow Herald* and then free-lancing with the *Director* to supplement the initially meagre IEA salary, I was encouraged to write press releases and invent eye-catching titles, such as 'The Price of Blood', 'Not Unanimous', 'Paying for Parking', 'Radical Reaction', 'Could Do Better', 'Ancient and Modern', 'Rome or Brussels?', 'Politically Impossible?', 'Not From Benevolence', 'The Vote Motive'. On content, understanding how he prized untrammelled independence and authority over publications, I avoided pushing rare doubts too far and was happy in public to adopt his judgement absolutely as my own, as on the education voucher which I thought second-best to an increasing element of direct parental payment for schools of choice. Only on the vexed European issue did we quietly stick to our respective views.

He would certainly periodically bridle at my reluctance to spend money, whether on extra staff, promoting sales, or on our own salaries and expenses, though in retirement, I have never ceased to be grateful that, eight years my senior, he persuaded me to give early attention to adequate provision for occupational pensions. But, remembering our early day-to-day financial struggles, and witnessing the ceaseless effort I put into building up a modest reserve of income, he always deferred absolutely, if not always cheerfully, to my ultimate financial veto. Thus did a natural division of labour grow up between us: his job was chiefly to 'produce the goods' and keep our shelves well stocked with path-breaking Hobart and other Papers from what he took to calling 'the engine room', while I 'kept the shop', raised the finance, and promoted our brand by cultivating businessmen and 'travelling' leading universities lecturing and debating. We shared the critical task of engaging the interest of leading journalists, both as likely reviewers or authors and as outlets for periodic articles based on the IEA's work, especially in the *The Daily Telegraph*, *The Times*, and *The Spectator*.

From the early days we got into double harness as joint authors of half a dozen books. Thus in 1958 hire purchase erupted into public debate as responsible for fuelling inflation by encouraging improvident consumer spending. Since we could find no academic authority to commission as author, Arthur and I, together with a forceful and shrewd City writer named Margot Naylor, spent six months of research to compile *Hire Purchase in a Free Society* which ran to a third edition by 1961. In brief compass it combined history, practice and law to make a textbook that demonstrated the value of consumer credit in spreading the cost of domestic 'investment' in 'consumer durables' over the lifetime of fridges, TV sets, washing and washing-up machines, to say nothing of motor cars, all of which were emerging from being the preserve of the rich to catering for a mass market.

Then again the following year, in the wake of burgeoning commercial television, advertising had come under fire, not only from the socialist economist [Nicholas] Kaldor as inflating costs but also from [John Kenneth] Galbraith as inciting and distorting demand and thereby aggravating the evils of the 'affluent society'. Once more, in complete, spontaneous agreement, Arthur and I devoted another six months in 1959 to writing *Advertising in a Free Society*, analysing its role as an essential tool of competitive marketing of both mass-produced necessities and luxuries through media carefully selected to reach well-defined, potential customers. The book's commercial success encouraged us to compile case studies for *Advertising in Action* three years later. Both these substantial pioneering studies had an additional, uncovenanted advantage for the infant IEA. They drew our work to the attention of the top practitioners in advertising agencies and the leading companies marketing branded products for growing markets, which proved not unhelpful in attracting wider financial support for our research and educational work.

Over the next 20 years the remorseless growth – and disappointing results – of government spending on the welfare state provoked us to join in writing three reports under my challenging title of *Choice in Welfare*, based on professional national surveys of attitudes towards public and private education and medical care. These were followed by *Not From Benevolence* in 1977 summarising IEA findings over 20 years (which I recall Margaret Thatcher particularly liked), and *Over-ruled on Welfare* in 1979. In each case our collaboration was based on briskly settling the contents page, allocating chapters equally between us, and then exchanging first drafts of one chapter every week or two. I can still remember the excitement of receiving Arthur's successive instalments, with their meticulous analysis and fastidious prose always with new words to express old truths.

DISTRACTIONS

One issue that could periodically have threatened more seriously to disturb the even tenor of our working relationship was the priority I would, apparently impetuously, give to some distracting development on the fringe of our main work. For example, hardly had we settled into our Lord North Street office in 1968 than the death of Harold Wincott prompted Graham Hutton and me to establish a foundation in the name of this gentle yet courageous FT [*Financial Times*] columnist and IEA ally. I immediately threw myself into the task of raising a fund of £100,000 (well over a million pounds in today's depreciated money) to perpetuate his example by granting awards for financial journalism, research and annual lectures. Without extra staff, the work of drawing-up lists of possible donors and writing begging letters took up more office time than I could have bargained for and, not unreasonably, Arthur would politely, patiently but pointedly complain that some weeks he couldn't get my full attention for the day-to-day problems of the office.

About the same time, I became heavily involved as an Enfield parent helping my old friend, Ross McWhirter of *Guinness Book of Records* fame, lead a campaign against the local Labour-controlled authority's plan to transform all local schools into what we regarded as 'make-shift' comprehensives. That was the beginning of a drive – indelibly associated in my mind with the names of Tony Crosland and Shirley Williams – to close down grammar schools and impose a 'progressive' educational revolution that led to the drastic decline in teaching standards from which we still suffer more than 30 years later. Arthur's barely concealed impatience with this further distraction was sharpened by a subtle objection. He feared that piece-meal amelioration of the inevitably baneful effects of politicisation in state education would simply postpone the only lasting solution – which, for him and his formidable wife Marjorie, was to enfranchise parents directly by means of education vouchers. Having, partly for the sake of argument, long advocated direct payment based on parental income, I have come to accept Arthur's voucher as the nearest we have to a practical panacea for the failing state system.

A similar diversion was created by my sudden enthusiasm in the early 1970s for setting up Churchill Press with Dr Rhodes Boyson, a former Labour councillor whom I met as a fellow contributor to the Black Papers on Education. Provoked by disillusionment with Ted Heath's feeble Conservative Government, we joined in setting up the Constitutional Book Club as an independent campaigning publisher of popularised versions of IEA Hobart and other Papers. And again in 1975, the ruthless assassination by the IRA of Ross McWhirter stung me into a renewed bout of fund-raising. For several weeks on end, I set less pressing business aside to join Norris McWhirter and Lord Boyd in raising another £100,000, this time for a foundation to commemorate Ross's inspiring example of active citizenship and personal courage in combating lawlessness and terrorism. But most prolonged and disruptive of our normal IEA working arrangements was the project to establish an independent university which absorbed a great deal of my time throughout the early 1970s. Luckily, this was a project of which Arthur not only wholeheartedly approved, but has some title to be acclaimed as the original inspirer.

Whenever the call for seed money inevitably took me back into the fund-raising business, I acknowledged my debt to another old friend of the McWhirter twins and mine from Enfield, Dr Michael Hooker. As the pioneer of professional fund-raising for British charities, especially in education and the church, he freely imparted the practical lessons he had learned in creating

Hooker Craigmyle. The essence was to decide a realistic target for the appeal, delay the public launch until at least a quarter was raised in advance pledges, breaking the balance into manageable sums, identify patrons and potential donors of modest, medium and major donations, before devising appeal letters and brochures.

Throughout this middle period (1965 to 1975), my major continuous distraction from the daily work of the IEA was as secretary of the international Mont Pèlerin Society which Hayek had set up back in 1947, in effect to explore the way back from his bleak vision outlined in *The Road to Serfdom*. Its annual conferences in places as scattered (and attractive) as Oxford, Cambridge, St Andrews, Paris, Turin, Salzburg, Vienna, Berlin, Venezuela, Hong Kong, regularly brought together 150 to 300 or more academic members and guests to study the theory and practice of free markets to stem the tide of collectivism. For me as secretary, each conference called for laborious negotiation of the programme, speakers, travel, accommodation and (again) fund-raising, followed by intensive supervision of the week-long proceedings. Luckily, Arthur was already an equally dedicated member of the MPS, becoming later its first Honorary Fellow. He not only, like my wife and me, treated the meetings as part of his and his wife (and fellow member) Marjorie's, annual holidays, but exploited this unique international gathering of classical liberal scholars as a heaven-sent recruiting ground for new IEA authors.

There followed a swelling stream of celebrated IEA Papers by overseas academics like Hayek, [Milton] Friedman, [George] Stigler, [James] Buchanan, [Gordon] Tullock, [Herbert] Giersch, [Roland] Vaubel, [Israel] Kirzner, [Friedrich] Lutz and many more. Often Arthur did not so much recruit authors as conscript them, as with Gordon Tullock who was reluctant to write *The Vote Motive* and even more nervous about my suggested title for his powerful exposition of the economics of politics, which he later acknowledged to be his single most influential endeavour to spread understanding of 'public choice' around the world in its umpteen foreign translations.

If I felt free to get on with these varied extra-curricular activities, safe in the knowledge that Arthur would keep up the stream of publications, it says much for his growing confidence in me that he offered so little objection. After all, until the coming of Margaret Thatcher in 1979, the IEA was still on trial and confronted by an alien consensus that alternated between tolerant dismissal of us as academic cranks and bitter hostility as threatening their precarious consensus. For example, when we dared entitle one of our early studies (1961) *A Market for Labour*, it provoked uncomprehending protests that our author was treating people like goods to be bought and sold – as under slavery! Our intellectual adversaries not only ignored or scorned markets, as at best 'politically impossible', but went on seeking statist solutions to the problems caused by state sponsored trade unionism, state industries, state welfare, and state inflation.

We had special reason to oppose inflation. Until the 1970s the IEA, as a tiny educational charity, lacked any substantial endowment and looked to 7-year covenants and annual donations mostly from businesses. Accordingly, our income was specially vulnerable to the alternating depredations of business recessions and, worse, accelerating inflation which Heath's disastrous monetary excesses in the 1970s pushed first above 10 and then 20 and 25% a year. I had come to feel I was on a financial treadmill, running ever faster just to keep the show on the road. The only consolation was that I could more easily resist periodic demands for more staff to ease mounting pressures. Passing from infancy in the 1960s to maturity in the 1980s, our full-time staff never rose much above a dozen. I used to emphasise to business men that this was a mere fraction of the tax-financed 'macro-men' of the NIESR and the National Economic Development Office set up in the unrealised hope of curing the 'British disease' – which had to await the arrival in Downing Street of Margaret Thatcher. All such stresses and strains acted as a cement to the partnership between Arthur and me. Just as he appreciated my success in keeping our income above expenditure, I knew it was his exciting publications and the increasing attention they attracted which made my success possible.

THE OFFICE

In 1968, a special fund-raising drive conceived by an avuncular volunteer named John (G.E.) Blundell and 'fronted' by George (Lord) Cole, formerly chairman of Unilever, enabled the Institute to move from four spacious rooms on the third and fourth floors of an elegant late Victorian pile on a corner of Eaton Square, to our own self-contained office. I remember Professor Harry Johnson of LSE and Chicago claiming an extra glass (or two!) of whisky to celebrate, but warning against moving too close to the seat of government in Westminster for fear of contamination. Our new offices, on the corner of Lord North Street and Great Peter Street were almost across the road from the House of Lords. They comprised a dozen mostly cramped rooms on three floors, plus basement and attic, in what had been a charming eighteenth century gentleman's residence beautifully modernised by Haslemere Estates under Fred Cleary, who I later discovered wanted, deserved but, alas, never received a knighthood. Closer to the City and Fleet Street as well as Parliament, our new headquarters provided an altogether more congenial setting with a boardroom in which to lunch company chairmen, bankers, editors, and the few politicians, who by the 1970s had awakened to the impact of our relentless stream of challenging, unconventional thinking.

Looking back on the unpredictable trials of these often tumultuous, crisis-ridden years of inflation, strikes, over-work, I can better acknowledge how far my harmonious partnership with Arthur depended on the total dedication and unquestioning loyalty of Joan Culverwell as my secretary, personal assistant, protector, as well as office manager, from 1959 to 1986. Patient, cheerful, conscientious and dependably efficient, it made it easier for me that she got on well with Arthur. Further stability for our small office was provided by the unswerving commitment and loyalty of Mike Solly, in proud charge of printing and production since the earliest days in the Hobart Place basement, chivvying-up printers and meticulously correcting proofs; Ken Smith who joined us as librarian in 1968 but cheerfully found himself covering all the office chores that fell between the rest of us; and finally, George Laxton as the resourceful accountant who kept our growing, though still hazardous finances in perfect order before the days of spread-sheets. Our dozen staff by 1980 was completed by five or six all-purpose secretaries and copy typist/telephonists, forever pounding-out second and third drafts of much amended letters and manuscripts in those far-off days before the joy of word processors and automatic copying machines.

REMEMBER GILBERT AND SULLIVAN!

For all the smooth running of the office, it is only in leisurely retrospect that I can appreciate how much I under-estimated the strain my succession of new enthusiasms placed on Arthur's shoulders, despite the amiable readiness of John Wood and the earlier John (G.E.) Blundell to take over from me specific office tasks after they joined us at Lord North Street in 1968. Indeed, my close friendship with John Wood dating back to Cambridge more than a decade before I met Arthur, provided a separate strain on Arthur's patience. Arthur had come to know and respect John Wood since he stepped into the breach as a temporary Trustee after 1960 while still working as economic adviser to Oliver Lyttleton (Lord Chandos) at AEI [Associated Electrical Industries] in Grosvenor Gardens, conveniently close to our earlier Eaton Square office. On coming down from Cambridge, he had worked with Richard Fry in the Fleet Street City office of the Manchester Guardian – before it dropped Manchester from its title and classical liberalism from its columns. He had then worked at the premier merchant bank of Lazards, which happened to be round the corner from the IEA's first office, the other side of the Stock Exchange in Austin Friars.

Arthur and I agreed that the move to larger offices in Lord North Street provided a good opportunity to bring in a third director. We also had no doubt that JBW [John Wood] shared our devotion to liberal market economics and that his practical experience in journalism, the City and industry would provide a valuable complement to our more narrow academic backgrounds.

But we couldn't know in advance precisely where he would fit into the scheme of things so we settled for the provisional title of 'Deputy Director'.

From the first day we were not disappointed in our enjoyment of his sharp intelligence, casual wit and total dedication to the IEA's mission. But I soon detected in Arthur a certain impatience with John's more leisurely, even lethargic, mode of work, an anxiety which I came increasingly to share. For example, although John was a bachelor without our family distractions, he never took manuscripts or other work home in the evenings or even at week-ends, as both Arthur and I regularly did as a matter of course. Instead, he preferred music lessons (he was an accomplished French horn player), entertaining and eating out with his wide circle of sophisticated friends. But a contribution to our team effort which was easily under-rated was John's utterly dependable, continuous attention to the demands of the office when both Arthur and I took to working on papers from home on a different day each week.

Nevertheless, Arthur began to express regret about the ambiguity of John's title as Deputy Director which he thought suggested to outsiders that John was deputy to me as General Director and therefore superior to Arthur as 'only' Editorial Director. Although I took every opportunity in private to emphasise that concern over titles and status was misplaced and that everyone familiar with the IEA acknowledged Arthur's intellectual leadership, I remained sensitive to Arthur's feelings. However well-concealed, he and I were both state-educated, working-class lads who could feel gauche in the company of effortlessly, self-confident public school men like Oundle-educated John. Of course, John never put on airs. But he had an easy grace we never quite acquired and, coming from the City (with Lord Brand at Lazards) and industry (with Lord Chandos), he seemed from the start often more at home with top company chairmen who regularly graced our private lunches, especially when conversation turned to the stock market, or as Arthur privately mocked to 'the short end of the long gilts'. In fashionable restaurants around Chelsea, where he ran a comfortable bachelor establishment in Cheyne Row, he was even known to wave back wine as 'corked' or 'not cooled'.

The first time Arthur seriously raised the John Wood question, I drew on the classic story of my favourite Gilbert & Sullivan. 'Arthur', I urged most earnestly, 'so long as those two marvellous prima donnas enjoyed the mutual stimulation of working together harmoniously, with D'Oyly Carte in the background, they went from strength to strength. But once they fell out, supposedly over a comparative trifle of expenditure, neither ever again achieved equal success'. I acknowledged that it was not a precise model if only because as Editorial Director he might be said to write both the words and music, but it had its effect. Thereafter, whenever he dwelt overlong on a complaint about John Wood's dilatoriness – or my meanness with IEA money – a whisper of 'Gilbert & Sullivan' worked to defuse tension in a shared chuckle.

On several occasions I summoned up courage gently to urge John as my old Cambridge friend to spend less time mulling over ephemeral newspapers (I never opened the *Financial Times*) or tidying-up files (my papers were generally in a muddle), and instead throw himself energetically into a specific piece of research or writing. His hesitant response almost suggested a lack of confidence, yet on three occasions he took heed with results displayed in some of our best-written and cogent IEA Papers. Two provided lucid exposures of bogus statistics (on 'unemployment' and 'inequality of wealth') and the third urged the case for abolishing exchange controls only months before Geoffrey Howe as Chancellor took courage to do just that as one of the first radical reforms of the Thatcher administration in 1979. Perhaps significantly, the last two were written in harness with younger, more energetic, joint authors, respectively George Polanyi (son of the legendary Michael) and the ever studious Robert Miller.

Whenever Arthur and I, with our wives, fell to discussing John's apparent diffidence in writing more, we always came back to thinking it had something to do with his being unmarried, as well as more comfortably-off through inheritance from his father who was a prosperous country solicitor in Parbold, Cheshire – which enabled me to tease him cheerfully as 'a lad from Wigan'. I inclined to the view that, lacking a wife and family, bachelors were busier shopping, cooking, attending to laundry – and perhaps seeking compensating pleasures forbidden to the happily married! Arthur, with the example before him of Marjorie's unfailing support for his work, regretted simply that comfortably-off bachelors appeared to lack the goad of financial pressures and wifely encouragement to fan their ambition to earn more and succeed better in their chosen work.

THE TRUE BOND

Fom our first days together in 1957 I recognised and deferred to Arthur's intellectual pre-eminence as the essential ingredient in the growing reputation won by the IEA, not least among the ranks of Tuscany which he was earlier than me to cultivate. All the more, I saw my peerage in 1979 as a possible threat to our flourishing partnership. It was not, as Arthur first feared, that I should find it difficult to resist the temptation of throwing myself into yet another distraction – speaking in the Lords – to the neglect of the office. Rather, I felt, and have to this day continued to feel an acute sense of the gross inequity of being thus singled out for recognition of so conspicuously shared an achievement. Recalling, not least, Marjorie's active work in publicising the merits of a voucher for education, it still angers me that these two incomparable champions of all that was best in Thatcherism should never have received the full public acknowledgement they both so richly merited. I count it not the least of my blessings that our long friendship has survived and deepened, despite this potentially divisive contrast of unequal recognition.

During almost 15 years of active retirement, there is no couple my wife and I have more enjoyed visiting most weeks than Arthur and Marjorie at their charming Thatched Cottage deep in the countryside near Sevenoaks. Especially on such occasions, I often find myself reflecting on how two of Graham Hutton's 'awkward squad', with somewhat contrasting temperaments and styles, could have got on so famously together. For what it's worth, and at the risk of smugness, I have identified three or possibly four sources of mutual respect and admiration, maturing into deep affection.

For me, the first *sine qua non* is that intimate, daily observation gave me the highest conceivable admiration for the unique talents and industry Arthur restlessly applied to every aspect of his work for the IEA. His example taught me more about writing English than was ever dinned into me by boring old 'Nelly' Nelson at the Tottenham Grammar School. For 30 years I never wrote an article, prepared a speech nor drafted an important internal memo without submitting my 'first shot' to Arthur, double-line spaced to leave ample room for amendment. When he asked: 'Rafe, do you want my opinion or my approval?', unless it was urgent, I'd always opt for 'the full treatment'. The same day or overnight at the latest, the copy would be returned, meticulously annotated with copious scribbled suggestions on substance, style, grammar and punctuation. Not least, he was a masterly wordsmith. My favourite example was his own choice of the striking title for one of his papers as 'Corrigible Capitalism, Incorrigible Socialism', which went to the heart of the philosophical choice before us. As I got better at anticipating the Seldon 'treatment', he would smother the margins of my drafts with ticks, an occasional 'bravo' or 'nice' and sometimes even add 'alpha' at the top! And if the admiration was mutual, his gratitude to me was for providing the financial wherewithal for him to enjoy unfettered freedom for the independent exercise of his unique talents.

The unvarnished truth is that Arthur was a quite exceptional teacher and I positively revelled in my good fortune for 30 years to be his favoured, perpetual pupil. More objective IEA authors, as varied as Austro-British Hayek, American Buchanan, and Lancastrian [Jack] Wiseman declared themselves better served by his deft editorial guidance than by anything in their previous literary experience. So, as a matter of self-preservation alone, I had the strongest possible incentive to cherish and, where necessary, indulge such an indispensable colleague. Furthermore, as an economist, I found his subtle exposition of the unsuspected light shed by theoretical analysis filled in gaps left by my abbreviated two-year post-war degree at Cambridge. When the least doubt about some aspect of our lonely free market mission flickered across my mind, it did not survive what can only be described as my continuous seminar

with Arthur. He could hardly have realised how far he was carrying my education forward – at the office, over lunch, at the Reform Club, discussing a draft
Hobart Paper, even on modest antique shopping expeditions with our wives at
week-ends. Never off-duty, he was always ready with fertile, unwavering
answers for every challenge thrown at us.

A second reason our collaboration flourished was that, if I lacked his scholarly subtlety and breadth of economic knowledge, I had from childhood on my
mother's testimony always been 'quick on the uptake'. As a student, with an
indifferent memory, I had developed a more practical knack for sorting out
useful, central ideas from what I judged pernickety refinements or more
abstract theoretical qualifications which I was content to leave academics to
dispute. So it was particularly helpful that Arthur would constantly refer me
back to the literature of classical liberalism. with treasured quotes from Adam
Smith, the Austrian school, [Lionel] Robbins, [W.H.] Hutt, and especially
'Fritz' Hayek whose range was even wider than our other favourite, Milton
Friedman. It was easy to dismiss the latest short-term manoeuvres of [Harold]
Macmillan, [Harold] Wilson, [Edward] Heath when Arthur was at hand to
recall the ageless wisdom of [Eugen] Böhm-Bawerk that in the long run what
Arthur called 'elemental market forces' would prevail over the puny pranks of
petty party politicians.

The third, more objective bond, was our spontaneous, unwavering, single-
minded, intellectual, even missionary dedication to the IEA's unique mandate
and method which calls for no further elaboration here. It need only be added
that almost from our very first meeting at Arthur's drab office in Deans Yard,
this powerful compact was sealed by our shared, palpable sense of isolation in
the teeth of what I liked to call the 'Keynesian-collectivist consensus' which
we daily, cheerfully, even cheekily, devoted ourselves to challenge.

I have occasionally wondered whether such purely intellectual bonds could
have sufficed to draw our working, waking and week-end lives so closely
together without some emotional or sentimental underpinning. In the changed
world of the 21st century, that final seal may strike mutual friends, though not
Arthur himself, as surprising, but I believe it stems from our common origins
among the aspiring working classes of North and East London. Certainly, my
intense admiration for Arthur was strengthened as I learned more of his
upbringing by poor, immigrant, Russian-Jewish adoptive parents, and we used
periodically to tease each other privately about which of us had the better
working-class credentials, him with a cobbler for father in the East End of
London or me with an LPTB [London Passenger Transport Board] bus inspector on a bleak council estate a few miles further north? So it came about that,
on good days or bad, I increasingly found myself looking on Arthur as a
second brother with whom it would be inconceivable to fall out very seriously
or for very long.

Finally, such warm family sentiments became more natural as I got to know Marjorie, from a very different social background (hence their pronunciation of my name to this day as 'Rafe'), and as my wife and she also became the most intimate of friends. A crowning bond was, no doubt, that both Arthur and I have had the good fortune to enjoy the stability of happy marriages for well over 50 years with wives prepared to endure the earlier strains of inadequate income and uncertain futures, and the subsequent certainty of excessive workloads.

Throughout our working lives together, Arthur and I, supported always by our wives, cheerfully withstood our share of problems and anxieties, and more than our share of opposition. All the more did the four of us enjoy the compensating pleasure and privilege of meeting some of the outstanding champions of freedom in the diverse worlds of economics, politics, and journalism. Prominent among them were the incomparable Milton and Rose Friedman who in 1998 (after over 60 years of marriage) wrote an extended joint memoir running to 600 pages and entitled 'Two Lucky People'. If Arthur and I could have matched their remarkable industry and he had looked to me as usual to suggest possible titles for a joint memoir on our 30 years together, my customary short list might at least include: 'Four Lucky People', though he would have probably have rejected it – on grounds of sentimentality and smugness rather than substance.

Watch out for the 'Peter Principle'*

I don't remember who wrote the book or even its title[1] but, as so often, I must have flicked through a review that told me all I needed to know without the fatigue of reading the book. Its message for me was that many able people come a cropper and ruin promising careers by accepting a job just one notch above their level of competence. The warning was I think especially directed against companies that promoted a first-class number two to the top job. A moment's reflection suggests plenty of examples, not least in politics where Anthony Eden, John Major and Iain Duncan Smith look like post-war cases of decent, sincere, even courageous, politicians who were clearly over-promoted to leadership of the Tory Party, as were Michael Foot and Neil Kinnock among Labour leaders.

HEALTHY SELF-DOUBT

Ambition is a fine thing, but requires to be tempered by knowledge of your own limitations if the natural vanity which most of us have is to be kept within bounds and not to land you in terrible trouble. Part of my good fortune in coming from a modest working-class family was that nothing remarkable was expected of me, either by my family or by myself. Although having first shaken off an early marked inferiority complex by success in Higher Schools Certificate (today's A levels), deep down and for some time thereafter I never felt quite as self-confident as I managed to appear. Indeed, at Cambridge on my way to first class honours in both parts of the economics tripos, self-doubt led me six months before the final exam in 1947 to consult Stanley Dennison as my supervisor about whether it was too ambitious for me to persevere with the two-year degree permitted for ex-servicemen. I was encouraged by his immediate reassurance, but did not let it lead to any relaxation of my customary routine of daily swotting.

My first serious test came almost ten years later. In the Spring of 1956, my seventh year as a lecturer at the delightful University of St Andrews, I decided to resign in preparation for returning to London on the hope of starting up the Institute of Economic Affairs the following year. The most amiable head of the

* 16 March 2004.

'political economy' department, Professor James Wilkie Nisbet, did his best to persuade me to stay, hinting that when Dundee College across the Tay was promoted to full university status, I would be in the running for a chair. Having held my own as a university teacher and enjoyed working with the Scottish staff and the more mixed, lively student body, I was duly flattered that 'the Prof' should entertain such high hopes for me. Yet modesty or self-doubt was sufficient protection against my giving more than a moment's thought to with-drawing my resignation. After all, although the IEA opening was not completely certain, I would sooner have returned to my family in London than stay in Scotland. But that moment of thought was enough for me to conclude that, even if the Dundee job were offered me on a plate, I would have turned it down. In 1957 it was still possible to cling to the illusion that professors should all be scholars like [Dennis] Robertson at Cambridge or [Lionel] Robbins at LSE on an elevated pedestal, and I could not imagine I would ever be qualified for such rarefied academic distinction. So 'Professor Harris' was never put to the test of the Peter Principle, which I remain convinced was just as well.

WANT A BETTER JOB?

It was a little over a decade later, in the early 1970s, when I was firmly estab-lished in my work at the IEA and had successfully arranged our move from Eaton Square to Lord North Street, that my next test presented itself. A tele-phone call came through from an outstanding American professor named Henry Manne whom I had got to know through attendance at meetings of the international Mont Pèlerin Sociey, founded by Hayek in 1947 of which I was then secretary. He told me he had just moved, his academic base, I think from Chicago to Florida, as a step in his life-long mission to spread the teaching of law combined with economics as a fruitful single discipline of which he was an early pioneer. His question was whether I would consider throwing my lot in with him to help build up this new venture. He promised me a hefty advance on whatever salary I was getting, as well as an improvement on the English weather. My task would be to run the 'development office', an American euphemism for fund-raising which had, after all, been a major part of my work in 'developing' the Institute from nothing in 1957.

Flattered as I was to be 'head-hunted' in this way, I did not really have to apply the calculus of the Peter Principle. Not only had I three children settled in schools and university, but I had discovered through hard experience that success in fund-raising depends chiefly on knack, style and contacts, none of which was transferable to the very different culture of America. Above all, in the IEA I had a job which I thoroughly enjoyed and which I was supremely

confident I could do as well as anybody. But I was anxious to avoid repaying
the Professor's confidence with the abrupt refusal that was on the tip of my
tongue. Accordingly, I patiently explained these three reasons and, knowing
the transAtlantic assumption of 'get-up-and-go' mobility, I laid special emphasis on the probability that my 'investment' in success with fund-raising in
Britain was not a skill that could easily be transported. So my polite rejection
of Florida was put down to English modesty, and did not interfere with a
transAtlantic friendship which has blossomed.

Before the end of the 1970s, three more substantial 'Peter' temptations
were to come my way in unnervingly rapid succession and the only one I fell
for, only after much anxious thought and with some trepidation, was the totally
unexpected offer of a life peerage a month or two after the spring general election which brought Margaret Thatcher to power in 1979.

The first arose in 1978 when Keith Joseph, whom we came to refer to as
'KJ', phoned to ask how soon we could meet to discuss an 'important proposition' which could not be discussed on the telephone. It turned out to be an
invitation to consider taking over control of the Central Policy Research Staff
(CPRS) which Ted Heath in technocratic mode had set up after he won the
1970 general election. Its purpose was to help the cabinet shape its priorities
and programme. Scrupulous as ever, KJ pointed out that a Conservative
victory at the forthcoming election was by no means certain, nor perhaps even
merited. But if the Conservatives did win, the new government would want a
new director in whom they had confidence. He was not briefed to say what the
salary would be but supposed it would be significantly higher than the IEA
could afford though, again scrupulously, he added there would be less security
of tenure. Anticipating my obvious doubt whether I would be generally
thought to carry the rank for such a senior, high-profile appointment, he hinted
that suitable recognition would be conferred on me to carry the necessary
authority. (The previous heads had been Lord Rothschild and Sir Kenneth
Berrill, both big shots in the mild Leftist establishment.)

Again, I didn't need the promptings of the Peter Principle, nor of my
colleague Arthur Seldon, to decide it was not the job for me. As a matter of
personal preference, I was never very interested in the nuts and bolts of public
policy but in the broad philosophy of the free society, marked by a strictly
limited range of duties for government that left politicians and civil servants
to work out the details. On the issue of personal competence I had by 1979
grown to be perfectly comfortable and confident in economic discussions with
such high-powered scholars as Hayek and Friedman whose ideas I fully
shared. But I would be completely out of sympathy, and I suspected ill-at-ease
and therefore less effective, in dealing with politicians who were consumed by
an itch to lay down the law and relished every opportunity to manipulate nominally independent official bodies like the CPRS for their purposes. I thought

to return KJ's warm personal confidence by expressing serious doubts but agreeing to give his offer further thought.

Much as I always wished to oblige KJ, if only in return for his unfailing courtesy and early recognition of the pathfinder value of the IEA going back to 1964, I lost no time writing regretfully to decline his invitation, offering the excuse suggested by Arthur Seldon that my sudden departure from the IEA would risk disrupting its work just as it was being taken more seriously and not only by members of his own party. I did not need to spell out that I had always been fundamentally sceptical of the typically technocratic Heathite notion of an official 'think tank' as a hybrid of academic, business and civil service know-alls. To soften my refusal I suggested a number of better-suited but like-minded professors who might even have salvaged the CPRS: Harold Rose of the London Business School, an established IEA ally, whom I commended as 'a vigorous 55 as impressive in manner as profound in matter'; Max Hartwell of Oxford, whose 'tough Australian mettle is overlaid by a geniality that is almost Pickwickian'; and Sir Hugh Ford of Imperial College whose rare mix of entrepreneur and engineering don had led him to invite me regularly to lecture his students on market economics and who joined with his colleague, the Nobel Laureate Sir Ernst Chain, to sponsor the embrionic, independent university at Buckingham. In the event I rejoiced when Mrs Thatcher abolished the CPRS in 1983 and doubt if anyone missed it.

HOW ABOUT THE LORDS?

Potentially the most severe risk of falling foul of the Peter Principle came with the offer of a life peerage in 1979. Although Arthur had once speculated privately about what might happen to 'our Institute' if a future Tory government 'had the sense to put you, Rafe, into the Lords', I had thought the prospect too remote a threat to our partnership to be worth even discussing. Accordingly, my surprise can only be imagined when a few weeks after the 1979 general election I received the following letter from the new prime minister:

> I have it in mind on the occasion of the forthcoming list of Birthday Honours to submit your name to the Queen with a recommendation that her Majesty may be graciously pleased to approve that the dignity of a Barony of the United Kingdom for Life be conferred upon you. I should be glad to know if this would be agreeable to you. I shall take no steps until I have your reply.

The letter had come as a bolt from the blue, seeming all the more unreal because my wife and I were sunk in deep private mourning over the accidental death of our elder son, Simon, three months earlier at the age of 26, following a struggle, since his last year at Haberdashers School, against drugs and drink which he had at last shown signs of winning. Not surprisingly, therefore, my wife hardly seemed to take in the news as we read our letters over her customary morning cup of tea in bed. Her rather bemused attitude was that presumably this was something to be automatically accepted and she was plainly puzzled when I talked of consulting friends about what my answer should be.

Yet the letter had been marked IN CONFIDENCE and I dimly recalled the story of a Labour MP who, receiving such a communication, had innocently alerted his constituency agent to the prospect of a by-election. Alas, the news got into the local paper and the offer of a peerage was never confirmed. After all, the PM only 'had it in mind' and if she were to have second thoughts, I should prefer they were prompted by my doubts or deliberate delay rather than by a leak. The more soberly I reflected, the clearer it became that acceptance of what would obviously be seen as political preferment could threaten serious effects on the perception of the IEA's independence which was vital to its continued influence, let alone its charitable status.

I swiftly concluded that I could not seriously consider accepting the elevation without the full approval of my closest colleagues, Arthur Seldon and our patron, Antony Fisher, who as founder and chairman of trustees from the beginning, was the nearest we had to an employer. Happily, with John Wood, they were my most trusted confidants. Not only could they be relied upon to keep my secret to themselves, but neither would hesitate to tell me bluntly what they thought. Both readily agreed such an honour reflected credit on the work of the IEA and would encourage our friends in the 'awkward squad' to stick to their guns. Arthur further suggested it would also impress our businessmen subscribers and so help with fund-raising. It was Arthur again who emphasised the key consideration that, if I sat on the crossbenches, any charge of politicking would be blunted if not wholly avoided. I was later to find it also freed me from the attention of party whips who – even in the House of Lords – have a variety of unpleasantnesses for any of their flock who seriously stray from the party line.

CROSSBENCHES IT WAS

Nevertheless, the final decision had to be mine and the Peter Principle compelled me to ponder deeply whether this might prove the dreaded step beyond my level of competence. It would certainly, as they say, offer a new platform for my still unfashionable views, and we already had a sprinkling of potential allies there, such as Lionel Robbins on the crossbenches, Douglas Houghton as a senior Labour backbencher, and my old Cambridge friend, John Vaizey, who had gravitated from Labour to the Tory benches. And there was the prospect of recruiting new allies in the more favourable climate created by Margaret Thatcher's bold promise of radical economic reform. Having no whips to 'encourage' attendance, I could also choose when to drop in. The IEA was less than a five minutes' stroll from the Lords' main entrance, well within the division bell area if there was the prospect of an important vote. This thought reminded me uneasily that when the Institute moved from Eaton Square to Westminster back in 1968, Harry Johnson, a genius among the front rank of economists who late in the day had become a genial IEA stalwart, once quipped that proximity to Parliament might prove to herald the end of our jealously-guarded political incorruptibility. My usual response to such doubters was to say how much easier for that other radical, Guy Fawkes, if he had lived in our cellar off Lord North Street.

Looking back to 1979, I can hardly claim that my decision to accept the peerage was particularly well-informed. As a debating chamber, Lionel had often commended the 'Upper House' as justifying this name by its debates which were superior to 'the other place'. This I was to discover, was largely thanks to the weaker whipping than in the Commons where it extends to expulsion from the party and withdrawing official support at future elections, which is invariably equivalent to a political death sentence. Although I had occasionally sat in the gallery of the House of Commons, I had never seen the Lords in action and cannot remember ever reading a Hansard of its debates.

CONTINUED DOUBTS

Worse still, remembrance of Robbins's commendation of speeches in the Lords, rather sharpened doubts about my competence. Of course, I'd had plenty of experience in public speaking during 30 years of talking both to political and academic audiences, and on my day could give a good account of myself – especially if my wife was present to warn against my natural tendency to speak too quickly, almost to gabble. But I was uncomfortable with a prepared text, always being tempted to ad-lib, lose my place and go on too long. So I early calculated that I would have to school myself to making meticulously prepared speeches just short of 1,000 words to allow time to refer briefly to other speakers. But could I hold the attention of the House even for such reliably brief interventions?

Having heard pompous would-be peers say they felt they 'had a contribution to make', I am just a little embarrassed to admit that, in weighing up the pros and cons of membership, I readily accepted Arthur's view that I would have something distinctive to say on economic and social policy by drawing on a lengthening catalogue of IEA titles, with expert authors for up-to-the-minute briefing by telephone. But would I ever sufficiently overcome the initial nervousness of holding forth in the presence of Hansard shorthand-writers taking down a verbatim report? In the event, I never did until the running debates on the Maastricht Bill which found me making a dozen interventions in as many days, with no time to compose polished texts.

Looking back, I can see it was even more of a gamble to accept the peerage than I realised in 1979. What if I had not quickly been able to make new friends in most parts of the House, especially Michael Spens, Ian Orr-Ewing, David Renton, Bill De L'Isle, Ivan Monson, Alan Rugby and, above all, the splendidly ebullient Jean Trumpington, whose husband, Alan Barker, had, before his sad premature death, been a prominent independent school headmaster and advocate of the education voucher. These were among my ready allies in the non-party Repeal Group which I rather boldly set up in 1981 to get rid of illiberal, outdated, or obstructive restrictions, starting with the nonsense of the Shops Acts, and followed by the more ancient Truck Acts, the opticians monopoly of selling spectacles, not forgetting rent control. Nor could I have known in 1979 how staunch an ally my old mentor Lionel Robbins would prove, both in and outside the Chamber. In short, I really had no way of judging in advance how well it would all turn out.

It may after all be that my wife was right all along and there was never much question of turning down the peerage. Perhaps after all the Peter Principle is more of a gamble than appears with hindsight so that people most often fall foul of it because they cannot know in advance enough of the risks to resist the natural temptation to accept advancement.

ACCEPTANCE

So for good or ill, entirely without relish and with some foreboding, I decided to accept the peerage. My mood, almost of resignation, may be conveyed by the following letter to the Prime Minister, which in retrospect might be thought rather cheeky:

> I feel greatly honoured that you should consider my name suitable for recommendation as a life peer. If such invitations were transferable (as in the market!), I could venture to nominate a number of more senior colleagues of individual freedom like Hayek, Jewkes, Hutton, Beloff, whose example I have simply tried to emulate. But in direct reply to your question, I am pleased to signify agreement that my name should go forward if you so decide.

Once the die was cast, it immediately struck me that some of my wide circle of friends and supporters might have other views about the wisdom of accepting the peerage, fuelled partly by their fear that it might risk changing settled personal relationships. Of course, when the news was published on the first

Saturday of June, hundreds of congratulatory messages started arriving. Most were warm, hand-written, excessively flattering notes, although one rather lofty hereditary peer named Lord Drogheda, with whom I'd crossed swords on the Financial Times and Wincott Foundation, could not resist a jibe: 'What a good idea! Why don't you take over running the entire government?' It struck me as unlikely that he was the only one to harbour the thought that I was getting above myself.

. . . EVEN BY FRIEDMAN

But I couldn't help wondering whether some of my special American friends would feel their republican sentiments outraged by all this flummery, snobbish-sounding stuff. With that in mind I scribbled at the bottom of a circular letter to Milton Friedman the following carefully phrased question: 'If you were a British subject and were offered a peerage, would you feel obliged to refuse?'. His reply was such a characteristic blend of principle tempered by commonsense, served up with winning wit that it is worth reproducing *in extenso*:

> In reply to your pencilled note, if I were British and were offered a peerage, I would certainly not feel obliged to refuse. That does not mean I would necessarily accept. That would depend on the circumstances of the offer. I can well conceive that specific circumstances might be such as to lead to refusal, but I see no reason on grounds of principle to refuse. As an American, I believe the United States is well-off not having a system of peers. I believe our founding fathers were very wise indeed to rule such titles out of court in the Constitution. However . . . the traditions and values and beliefs in Britain are very different. A peerage is an essential element of the social and political structure of Britain. Conceivably, if I were an Englishman, I might be opposed to the institution of the peerage. But even if I were, I do not see that would carry over to my refusing to accept a peerage given that the institution exists. Is that any different from my living in a rent-controlled apartment even though I object to the existence of rent control?

NEVER AGAIN!

The third and final Peter temptation threatened a few months after the peerage, with which it was directly connected. It loomed without warning at a celebration party arranged by my old Cambridge chum and IEA colleague, John Wood, with characteristic generosity and style in the garden of his modernised barn in West Dean, East Sussex. Prominent among the guests was the exceedingly jolly and highly intelligent local Tory MP and staunch IEA ally, Ian Gow, whom we all congratulated on his well-deserved appointment as parliamentary private secretary to the new Prime Minister. In the midst of the noisy jollifi-cations, Ian solemnly took me aside, his usual wide smile replaced by a rare expression of earnest intensity. 'The boss' had asked him to sound me out on whether I would be available for a ministerial job on the government front bench in the Lords. He pointed out she had so few personal adherents in the 'Upper House' that she was looking for people to bring in and create as 'instant ministers'. One advantage of me was that I was already there.

I could see he was waiting eagerly for my answer as I struggled to regain my composure. This time I did not need to consult Arthur or John or anyone else. Nor did I have to ponder deeply on the Peter Principle. Adopting a seri-ous expression to match his own, I managed to say politely but emphatically: 'No doubt I should thank you for such a flattering proposition, but it is absolutely out of the question'. For avoidance of doubt, as lawyers say (Ian was a solicitor), I immediately added, 'I'd be no good at a political job and I beg you to convey my hope that such an alarming question is never again allowed to put our valued friendship at risk'. Nor was it, though Ian regularly continued enthusiastically to ask me down to Eastbourne to explain Thatcherism to his mostly adoring constituents.

It was almost exactly ten years later, that he persuaded my wife and me to buy a sea-side flat there when I retired from the IEA on reaching 65. It is a decision in which we still rejoice, but one of the greatest personal sadnesses of our lives remains to this day that he was assassinated by the IRA six months later outside his charming family home a mile or two away.

NOTE

1. The book is *The Peter Principle: Why Things Always Go Wrong*, Laurence J. Peter and Raymond Hull, William Morrow & Company Inc., New York, 1969.

Who invented Buckingham?*

For 25 years I seldom missed the annual graduation ceremony of the University College at Buckingham, which received its royal charter in 1983 to become the University at Buckingham. It was always in February and on a Friday or Saturday, which timing was doubly unwelcome for me as involving my wife in a wintry drive by motorway and then through rather featurelesss countryside, as well as sacrificing our regular week-end at the invariably more sunny Eastbourne. But from the earliest days of 1976, it provided for me a not-to-be-missed, informal reunion with the select handful of academics and business men who in their prime had played their part, under the initial aegis of the IEA, in establishing 'our' independent university.

An added poignancy in the earlier years was that these get-togethers might bring together no less than four of us having my rather unusual christian name: Sir Ralph Bateman, the chairman of Turner & Newall with a mild manner that concealed a rare enthusiasm which spread from the IEA to embrace Buckingham; Ralph Yablon, a down-to-earth Jewish entrepreneur with an appealing, soft Yorkshire accent; and a local 'squire', whom I knew less well, named Sir Ralph Verney who hovered on the fringes of action and, like Ralph Bateman pronounced his name the upper-class way as 'Rafe'. An episode I cherish that caught the light-hearted mood of our reunions was when someone took a photo of the first three of us and mounted it with the light-hearted caption: 'Buckingham's three Rs'.

ENTREPRENEURIAL HISTORY

Year after year, I would watch them jostling around the modest buffet table for lunch in the Old Mill before donning academic robes to process into the vast church of St Peter and St Paul which served as our great assembly hall for such occasions. Again and again, I would run my eye over them and ask myself which among them had the best claim to be regarded as the true founder of this remarkable enterprise.

Of course there was no clear-cut answer. At successive stages quite different contributions were to prove decisive. After the first conception and

* February 2004.

formulation came the patient exploration of alternative structures and possible locations. There followed the crucial need for finance, perhaps new buildings, construction of courses, no less than of skeleton administration, the academic leadership necessary to attract high quality staff, and finally the all-important recruitment of students.

When the full story comes to be told, it should form a more than usually instructive chapter in that fascinating branch of study known as entrepreneurial history. Any new business plainly requires a combination of talents and resources. It is generally thought necessary from the outset to identify a gap in the market before specifying and then devising a product or service that would meet the unsatisfied demand. But we started with nothing more substantial than an original, even revolutionary, gleam of an idea. When an inventor seeks commercial advice on developing his idea, the first question marketing men ask is: what is the unique selling proposition (USP)? Is it the novelty or special utility of what is being offered, or its superior quality or convenience, or its low price compared with the competition, or what?

Establishing a new university – from scratch? Even if start-up capital were abundant, a brand new academy could not swiftly – nor even slowly – rival the academic appeal to good staff or students of the great established foundations. Speaking of which, there was an even more formidable obstacle. All the best potential students could already choose between a growing number of state universities offering 'free' places, which automatically qualified them for local authority maintenance grants, subject admittedly to a parental means test. Since, however, our aspiring founders began without a penny piece of endowment, the appeal of our USP might be parodied as:

> Prospective students are hereby invited to find their way into the sticks of run-down Buckingham (which no longer has even a functioning railway station), for the unproved prospect of a 'licence' (before a royal charter was granted to issue degrees) which will cost you or your parents several thousand pounds a year, and may not be recognised as a qualification for professional examinations or for post-graduate study in the state sector!

Looking back, it seems clear the founders complacently assumed the student body would be largely drawn from the independent ('public') schools and when a majority turned out to come from the Commonwealth countries where English was not their first language, the founders simply displayed their enterprise by laying on intensive courses in English as a foreign language!

DISGRUNTLED INTELLECTUALS

In short, there was no research into the potential market for such a far-fetched

– many would say crazy – idea. There was only a shared commitment to independence from political control felt passionately by a handful of brave spirits, allied to the belief – or vague hope – that Britain was big enough and prosperous enough to supply the modest numbers of students necessary to bring their dream to fruition at least on a modest scale. In the event, the money and staff were to come from Britain while, because of 'unfair' competition from state-financed universities, a majority of students came from abroad.

Our secret weapon, we hoped, was that independence would allow us to break away from the medieval pattern of a three-year degree course with three months summer vacation for young men to help with the harvest. Instead of three years, each with three terms of 8 to 10 weeks, part of our USP was to be the option of a degree course of two years, each of four longer terms, giving at least as many weeks tuition as conventional universities in three years, thereby allowing our graduates to start work and earning a year earlier.

If the founders had been practical, prudent business men of similar liberal persuasion, they might have met for a slap-up dinner at the Reform Club, agreed in deploring the oppressive influence of state finance over higher education in the post-Robbins euphoria, raised their voices in regretting that nothing could be done about it, before breaking up at best with the resolve to get round to writing a letter to *The Times*. But our impractical would-be entrepreneurs were of a far more determined and dangerous breed. They were disgruntled intellectuals with a mission, mercifully lacking forewarning or experience of the harsh requirements of competitive business and therefore innocent of the difficulties that were shortly to beset the embryonic planning board. All the more can we see that their success was to prove a tribute to Samuel Smiles's big word: determination.

ENTER PAULLEY AND FERNS

As it happened, this project did start with a letter to *The Times*. It was from a then unknown physician in Ipswich, Dr John Paulley, who wrote in May 1967 to express concern at the growing political influence over British universities inseparable from state finance. Having just returned from New York on a Harkness Commonwealth Fund scholarship, he had been impressed by the great private American universities and his letter asked: 'Is it not time to examine the possibility of creating at least one university in this country on [their] pattern'. By a remarkable coincidence, this precise question had been occupying the thoughts of a little-known Canadian political scientist named Professor H.S. Ferns of Birmingham University, who had written an article for the *Political Quarterly* entitled 'A Radical Proposal for the Universities', which was published a month after *The Times* letter. Not only did Ferns seek out

Paulley, but even more significantly the ever-watchful Arthur Seldon sought out Ferns and asked him to elaborate his thinking for an IEA Occasional Paper. Only after the usual thorough editorial treatment was the draft published at the beginning of 1969 with my optimistic title: 'Towards an Independent University'.

Since, prima facie, Harry Ferns appears to have the best claim to have fathered Buckingham, it is worth pondering what an unlikely candidate he was for the role of founder. He was not an easy person to get to know. At first meeting, an amiable teddy-bear of a man peering back through thick glasses and leaning forward to turn his best ear to catch your conversation, he was hardly in the mould of those tough Canadian pioneers who forced a railway through the Rockies to link the Pacific with the Atlantic coast. Rather, he appeared a shy, thoughtful, emollient academic. But like many political scientists he was not lacking in deep convictions and on closer acquaintance could become assertive, forceful, even passionate. It was only in 1992 when I came to write his obituary that I discovered his children, to whom he was plainly devoted, used to call him 'old exploder' and I still recall the shy chuckle with which over pre-lunch drinks at Lord North Street around 1980 he confided how he had graduated to what he called 'the IEA camp' from what I liked to call 'the ranks of Tuscany' if not, playfully, 'the forces of darkness'.

By the 1970s there was no longer any novelty in academic economists breaking out of the Keynesian–collectivist consensus to write radical liberal tracts for the IEA. But here was a Canadian, Christian academic confessing that as a post-graduate student at Cambridge before the war he had operated as 'a Marxist missionary' among the students. Since then, he had become an authority on Argentina and had learned how Perón's socialism had brought that lush country from pre-war prosperity into poverty and almost perpetual crisis, from which it has not yet recovered. Having moved to Britain in 1950, he had watched, with an academic's detachment, how the collapse of Harold Wilson's milder brand of collectivism had brought Britain low and had debased the idealism of the founders of the Labour Party. Ten years later, in a paper entitled 'The Disease of Government', Ferns was to urge the phasing-out of government subsidies to the entire university sector.

SELDON DOES HIS STUFF

Without Ferns's IEA Paper there would have been no Buckingham. But without Arthur Seldon there would, in a manner of speaking, have been no Harry Ferns. Not only did our editorial director give the verbose draft his 'full treatment', but he had the shrewd idea of including as an appendix a Declaration on the Urgency of an Independent University drafted largely by Professor Max Beloff of Oxford. Between us we recruited approaching 50 signatories from among our authors, leading dons and headmasters, including some heavy-weight Fabian types such as Mark Blaug, the distinguished historian of economic thought. Their purpose was to indicate the breadth of anxiety about dependence on 'public' finance which had brought increasing *political* influence and control that threatened independent scholarship and inhibited experimentation and non-conformity in courses and teaching methods, as well as in methods of finance, including student loans. It was Seldon's genius to convert an eccentric 'cranky' idea into a serious academic movement. Support for this project went much wider than the signatories whom we managed to enrol in a few weeks, since it took a good deal of spirit, even courage, for academics to associate themselves publicly with such a bold challenge to prevailing political orthodoxy, especially at a time of student unrest.

WILLIAMS VERSUS THATCHER

Evidence that socialist prejudice against university independence was deep-seated and long-lasting presented itself some years later when the more reasonable-seeming ideologue, Shirley (now Baroness) Williams, displayed a totally unexpected hostility. In 1977 one of the first generation of graduates of the new University College at Buckingham expressed the wish to enrol in the army as an officer cadet for which a university degree was an essential qualification. When the War Office raised doubts whether a Buckingham degree would be acceptable, Beloff, as first vice-chancellor, was confident his friend Mrs Williams, as Labour's education minister, could be persuaded to recognise the degree which, thanks to the drawing power of Beloff's prestige, was supervised by a distinguished academic advisory board, marked by external examiners and accepted by leading universities for post-graduate study. When he presented this powerful case to the minister, he was astounded to find that it completely failed to prevail against the intellectual Left's blind hostility to independence in education.

It may be worth recounting the attitude of another prominent political lady towards our project, which was marked by the sharpest possible contrast. Thus before Buckingham had even been selected as the site of our new university, the planning board thought it prudent to invite informally the view of the Conservative secretary of state for education, Margaret Thatcher, on our project. When we arrived by appointment at the department's highly unimpressive, rather drab office in Curzon Street, it was explained that an emergency cabinet meeting on the Middle East had detained the secretary of state whose place would be taken by a junior minister, William van Straubenzee. He grandly motioned Beloff, [Sir Sydney] Caine and me to armchairs arranged in a semi-circle and took his seat facing us.

As he was about to embark on his welcoming speech, the door flew open and, behold, the lady herself entered in her outdoor clothes, complete in those days with a stylish hat. Perching on the edge of a spare chair, handbag on lap, she breathlessly explained that she particularly wished to meet us but had got away from Downing Street for only a few minutes, and beckoned to her junior minister to continue with the meeting. His opening words were to assure us there was 'no fundamental opposition in the department to this interesting project'. He got no further before the lady interrupted: 'William, I think it would be truer to say there is a positive welcome . . .'. Getting into her stride Mrs Thatcher congratulated us on our bold initiative, but made it clear that the best way government could help was not by financial support, which would detract from our independence, but by not getting in the way and removing any bureaucratic obstacles that might make our development needlesssly diffi-cult. That heartening meeting explains why we invited her, as no more than an opposition shadow minister, formally to address the opening ceremony at Buckingham in 1976. It was then her Government in 1983 which granted a charter to the fully-fledged University of Buckingham, of which she later became a most conscientious as well as decorative, Chancellor in succession to her former cabinet colleague Lord Hailsham. So who was the more liberal politician: Margaret Thatcher, often scorned as arch conservative, or Shirley Williams, who was later to be crowned as leader of the Liberal Democrats in the House of Lords? The latter revealed herself as hardly democratic, and certainly not liberal.

PLANNING BOARD GOES INTO ACTION

If there would have been no Buckingham without Harry Ferns, not even his most fervent admirers would have supposed him capable of running even a bookshop, let alone a university. Following his Paper, we had arranged a couple of private conferences at which selected signatories were invited to carry forward discussion of ways and means to develop the Ferns project from conception to actual birth. Among these forerunners was Sir Sydney Caine with whom we felt very much at home since he had only recently retired from being Director of the LSE, the home of at least half of early IEA adherents. Outraged by the student violence which had overtaken his successor for no better reason than that he had been recruited from Rhodesia, the gentle, even diffident Sir Sydney Caine agreed to act as chairman of a provisional planning board, which had been the instrument for the creation of all the post-Robbins new universities. Not for the first, nor the last time, Arthur, now joined by John Wood as the third IEA director, allowed me to devote a large slice of my atten-tion to a parallel task, that of acting as honorary secretary to the planning board until a permanent secretariat was established in an attic at Lord North Street under John MacCallum Scott, an able and most amiable retired publisher whom Max Beloff had somehow conjured up from their earlier shared Liberal Party connections.

Although by 1969 I had got used to hobnobbing with senior academics, servicing the planning board proved quite a testing experience. In addition to Ferns, Caine and Paulley, they comprised a marvellous mixture of formidable scholars, including the dominating Max Beloff, the studious Hugh Lloyd-Jones (Oxford Professor of Greek), the exotic Sir Ernst Chain (Nobel scientist from Imperial College, married to Beloff's sister and looking like a cheerful Toscanini), the mild-seeming Michael McCrum (headmaster of Tonbridge, later of Eton and Master of Corpus College, Cambridge), the ever-cheerful though slightly crippled George Lehmann (chairman of the commercial language college of Linguaphone), the ebullient Donald Denman (Professor of Land Economy, Cambridge), the charming Barbara Shenfield (formerly Bedford College, London and later, as Dame Barbara, national chairman of the WRVS [Women's Royal Voluntary Service]), and the shy, scholarly Colin Clark (former Fabian, agricultural economist at Oxford and pioneer of national income statistics). In the background there was the tough-minded Fabian economist, Professor Mark Blaug (London Institute of Education) who produced impressive calculations on the returns for graduates on their investment in university education which justified student loans repayable from their increased life-time earnings. All these and others had distinctive contributions to make towards our shared vision of independence, drawn from their widely varied experience and specialisms in many British and overseas universities.

CASTLES IN THE AIR?

Looking round the oval board-room table which Antony Fisher had originally bought from Harrods for the Eaton Square office, I never ceased to marvel that such a diverse group of scholars should be devoting so much time to our initial, wide-ranging, often inconclusive discussions, which seemed at best little more than building elaborate castles in the air, to the possible neglect of their books, college port, and in the case at least of George Lehmann, Sir Ernst Chain and Donald Denman, their well-paid consultancies. Meetings were mostly cheerful, though not always exactly a load of fun. Lehmann was the only natural joker, although MacCallum Scott and Sydney Caine were capable of lofty chuckles at political obstruction from the likes of Shirley Williams that had Beloff, Chain and me almost choking with anger and impotent indignation. From Beloff, I can recall nothing stronger than a fleeting, frosty smile over some donnish quip at the expense of politicians or other conventional opponents. But then the agendas I dutifully produced for every meeting always included the awkward topic of finance, which was naturally less to the taste of five-star academics than endless, animated discussion of degree syllabus, teaching methods, student enrolment and relations with other universities.

At one meeting I recall an enthusiastic discussion on the need for a large financial provision for expenditure on a well-stocked library being interrupted by a discreet cough from Professor 'Ash' Wheatcroft, a law professor at LSE, who gently but firmly observed that contemplating early commitments without the financial wherewithal would not be strictly in conformity with the highest standards of business that he was sure we would wish to uphold! Library ambitions were a repeated source of argument, in which I led the case for initial caution. On a later occasion when they were drawing up estimates of budget requirements, on which they looked to me for guidance in fund-raising, my customary doubts about the scale and priority of library provision provoked an angry snort from Beloff who ceremoniously collected together his papers scattered on the table, pushed back his chair and threatened to leave the meeting if he had any more of these cheese-paring economist's objections.

At the outset of the deliberations of the planning board, I had an uneasy feeling that the moment thoughts turned to fund-raising eyes would turn in my direction. In 1969 the IEA had just moved into a converted Georgian residence on the corner of Great Peter Street and Lord North Street, splendidly refurbished by Haslemere Estates, a property company developed by Fred Cleary which led the way in demonstrating that profit-making need not be at the expense of amenity and sensitive environmentalism. We must have appeared to academics from cash-strapped universities to be flush with funds. But ever since starting up the IEA in 1957, I had found the effort to keep our income a bit ahead of expenditure on our growing programme of research and publications was an unending treadmill of letter-writing and meetings. We certainly had no cushion of spare resources to divert to the university project which had sprung from our publication of the Ferns paper but was not central to our broad objective of improving public understanding of economic affairs.

NOT JUST YET ANOTHER UNIVERSITY

Nevertheless, from tiny beginnings I had built up what might be called fruitful personal links with the chairmen or managing directors of many of the top companies in the land. So I now thought it should be easy at least to put our claims on their further generosity to an early test by discreet personal canvassing. My first hope was Unilever which had strongly welcomed our early pathbreaking study of the serious economic role of advertising on which their business relied more than most. I had heard from an insider that the firm made a practice of giving £25,000 a year (say £250,000 today) under covenant to the rash of new universities launched after the Robbins Report. Alas, I was soon to discover that many such companies thought they had already done their stint and even felt disenchanted by the antics of the National Union of Students and the sporadic campus disorders under the leadership of such reckless fire-brands as the younger Jack Straw. Others did not share our dedication to university independence and argued that voluntary endowment was simply filling a gap that should be bridged by the old incantation of 'public finance'.

We tried to turn this backlash to our advantage. It was the powerful, genial former Fabian, but then city editor of *The Sunday Telegraph*, who ingeniously invented the slogan: 'Buckingham is the university for donors who don't like universities'. That certainly encapsulated a central part of our unwritten unique selling proposition, which was that our paying students would be strongly motivated to behave very differently from the minority of trouble-makers at LSE, Warwick, Essex and elsewhere. Whatever else we initially disagreed about, the planning board were united that our prospectus would start from the need for payment of student fees to cover running costs (though not capital investment) with the help, where necessary, of a loan scheme and student bursaries. We would also welcome mature students in their 20s and 30s, without formally insisting on A levels so long as they could satisfy the admissions Dean by interview, or by written application if from overseas, that they were likely to benefit from our distinctive teaching, which would give special emphasis to tuition in small groups. We would also offer the option of a two-year degree course, a broad range of compulsory topics including verbal competence in a foreign European language, plus scientific and statistical method, together with a choice between more 'useful' main subjects, such as law, economics, finance, later computer science, as well as history.

Yet even this more practical proposition proved impossible to sell to most of our business friends. Indeed, our project might never have survived the gestation period to see the light of day without the encouragement of a few discerning entrepreneurs such as Sir Richard Dobson of BAT [British American Tobacco], Sir John Reiss of Associated Portland Cement and Sir Ralph Bateman of Turner & Newall. With such initial support we scraped along and kept the project alive until fortune favoured us with a succession of benefactors capable of major gifts without having to gain approval from necessarily mixed boards of directors.

WHY BUCKINGHAM?

Before we could seriously appeal for major gifts, we had to have a better idea about the physical form and geographical location of our proposed university.

Colin Clark from Oxford had the most original suggestion, favouring a central London site like the deserted dockland buildings, with plenty of space for cycle racks to enlarge our catchment area for day students, thereby avoiding the need for student residences. Another inventive suggestion which also avoided the high cost of building residential accommodation, was to set up in a large holiday resort on the south coast with plenty of empty boarding houses at times that almost exactly matched customary university terms.

The issue was resolved by a chance conversation at the Carlton Club between one of our academic supporters from Cambridge, Professor Donald Denman, and an old friend named Fred Pooley who was the planning officer for Buckinghamshire – one of the few remaining counties without a university. It transpired that Buckingham, the former county town which had been supplanted by Aylesbury, was intent on restoring its declining fortunes and a university might be just the thing to attract people, spending power and employment. Even better, the extensive site chosen for development included a number of fine but fading Georgian buildings, including the former drill hall of Bucks Yeomanry, the commander's stylish house, some attractive cottages, plus a spacious dairy research laboratory about to be deserted by Unigate.

The die was cast shortly after, when I was called out of an IEA fund-raising lunch at the IEA to be asked on the telephone if I could urgently identify the source of £40,000 which was necessary to acquire the first of these buildings to come on the market. It sounded like a make-or-break opportunity, As it happened, one of the guests at lunch was Ralph Yablon, who was among our prime prospects for a sizeable donation. On the spur of the moment, I told my caller to hang on while I put our luck to the test by calling my lunch guest from the table and asking if he felt able to make a decision on the spot. Looking back, it was perhaps when that other Ralph smilingly nodded his assent that the corner was turned on the road to establishing our university at Buckingham.

From then on, at least in retrospect, everything seemed to fall into place, though it didn't feel quite like that at the time. Out of the blue, MacCallum Scott produced a mild-seeming friend named Lord Tanlaw who in turn cheerfully produced the munificent sum of one million pounds (today nearer £10m) towards our independent university. I still savour the impish chuckle with which MacCallum Scott said it was especially welcome because if this gift had not been given to us it might have gone to the Liberal Party of which Lord Tanlaw had been a supporter until he had lost confidence in their wishy-washy attitude towards private education.

THE INCOMPARABLE MAX WINS THE PALM

Undoubtedly, that million inspired all the members of the planning board to believe that they were at last seriously in business. But it was far from the end of the road. The acquisition of buildings was no guarantee that a single student would be attracted into the comparative wilds of Buckingham. That required staff of the highest quality who could be attracted from life-tenured posts elswhere only by the assurance of unquestionable academic standards, which in turn required recruitment of a high level academic advisory council to vouch for the teaching, and external examiners to guarantee the quality of Buckingham degrees. In all this essential academic construction the contribution of Max Beloff was absolutely indispensable.

Personally, I have to admit I always found him one of the least easy close colleagues with whom I have ever had to deal. But I recognised in him a quite exceptionally clever, powerful, tough-minded, intellectual heavyweight. Then and now I have never ceased to marvel that he should have abandoned the pinnacle of academia, represented by All Souls, Oxford, for the comparative backwater of Buckingham. But then, throughout my experience at the IEA, I have found the admirable awkward squad present a stubborn challenge to the simple rule of economic maximisation which governs too many eventually unfulfilled – or incompletely fulfilled – lives.

It might be added that in addition to an exceptional combination of academic distinction, forceful personality and unwavering perseverance, Max Beloff had sufficient modesty or self-knowledge to recognise an important deficiency. When the practical challenge of running such a novel institution exposed his administrative shortcomings, he did not hesitate to enlist the services of capable, even formidable allies, such as Caryl Ramsden and Charles Vereker, to whom he would on occasions more gracefully defer.

So who invented Buckingham? The candidates for that distinction must certainly include Harry Ferns as its intellectual or spiritual parent and Lord Tanlaw as its early mainstay. The role of honour must also include Sir Sydney Caine who gently kept the mettlesome steeds on the planning board pulling together in the early days of slim hopes, not forgetting the enthusiastic Donald Denman who identified Buckingham as an almost ideal location. But these and other important players would never have been brought together without Arthur Seldon's decision to commission and edit Ferns's draft for publication as an IEA Occasional Paper and then to cap it with the inspired idea of including that Declaration which rallied many other academics to our cause in the first place. So while I would award the palm as *creator* of the university to the incomparable, though austere and touchy, Max Beloff, I would nominate my no less incomparable but more agreeable colleague, Arthur Seldon, together with Harry Ferns, as the joint *inspirers* of the enterprise. But implementation of their hopes might have been indefinitely delayed without the munificent, disinterested but enthusiastic personal generosity of Simon Tanlaw.

An independent station*

Fifty years ago the outlook for the newly formed IEA was hardly promising. The post-war Labour government under Attlee had been followed by the Conservatives under Churchill, followed briefly by Eden and then Macmillan. Between them, the political stage was already being set for the long-running drama of the 'mixed economy', with the mixture, like Scotch on the rocks, becoming less and less Scotch and more and more rocks. The prospectus was never clearly set out. Policy was improvised on the remnants of wartime planning and high taxation, on to which Labour had grafted an ill-prepared programme of extensive nationalisation. Both parties broadly accepted the proposals for a comprehensive welfare state set out in the Beveridge Report to the wartime coalition government.

It did not take long to discern the emerging pattern of inflation, balance-of-payments crises and recession that were the beginnings of the boom-and-bust cycle that was to plague the British economy with widening swings for more than three decades. The first of Labour's two post-war devaluations occurred in 1949. Before his resignation as Chancellor, following a careless budget leak, Hugh Dalton, formerly a lecturer at the London School of Economics, had coined the description of inflation as 'too much money chasing too few goods'. Commentators began talking of an 'over-loaded economy' and looked for cuts in public spending. In 1950 the new Chancellor, Sir Stafford Cripps, reluctantly felt driven to impose charges for NHS prescriptions, thereby provoking a political crisis and the resignation of Aneurin Bevan.

By 1958 continuing anxieties about inflation had prompted the Treasury, now under the Tories, to propose a similar token cut in budget spending. The patrician Harold Macmillan rejected the proposals, thereby provoking the resignation of Peter Thorneycroft and his complete Exchequer team, including Enoch Powell. That 'little local difficulty', as Macmillan described it, can be seen in retrospect to have been the last stand of the old orthodoxy. The next two decades saw the era of Butskellism (named after the Conservative and Labour Chancellors, respectively Rab Butler and Hugh Gaitskell). What I came to call the 'Keynesian collectivist consensus' allowed little scope for

* First published in *Towards a Liberal Utopia*, London: Institute of Economic Affairs, Hobart Paperback 32, 2005.

fundamental change in economic policy right up until the Callaghan government was reluctantly forced to accept the inevitability of change in 1976.

Against such entrenched all-party opposition, the prospect for the fledgling IEA seemed hardly stronger than that for the British economy. Although our founder, Antony Fisher, had first voiced his dream of a kind of independent 'anti-Fabian' society to raise the banner of a free society ten years earlier,[1] building-up his Buxted Chicken enterprise necessarily took first priority. It was not until 1955 that he felt able to register the IEA as an educational charity, and a further two years before he took the plunge with my appointment as part-time general director in January 1957.

Looking back, it may seem that we embarked on our great adventure with no 'road map', nor even a business plan. We simply had start-up capital of about £1,000 and ran our budget on a monthly cash-flow basis, holding back printing bills to pay my retainer of £50 a month and the £3 a week rent for a tiny shared office in the City. If we were ever to find authors to write for us, it would certainly not be for the money.

Once Arthur Seldon joined me as editorial director, becoming full time in July 1961, we found that in reality we had a sheaf of road maps. These took the form of the luminous writings of the great classical liberal economists going back to Adam Smith and David Hume, enriched by Mill, Marshall, Cannan, Robbins and the neglected Austrian school of Böhm-Bawerk and Mises. Miraculously, both Arthur Seldon and I, having proceeded to university from state grammar schools, had enjoyed a powerful inoculation against fashionable collectivism: he from the LSE, home of Hayek and Lionel Robbins, and I from the Cambridge of Dennis Robertson and Stanley Dennison before the Keynesian curtain descended on independent scholarship. Furthermore we had both had our fill of party politics: he with the shadowy remnants of the Liberal Party under Clement Davies, and I with the Conservative Party under Churchill's call to 'set the people free'. At last, in our first basement office together at Hobart Place, we had what Fisher, himself a disillusioned Conservative, liked to call, quoting Aristotle, 'an independent station'. If I showed the slightest political backsliding, Arthur Seldon was at my side to warn me, like a freed prisoner, to 'keep going straight'.

That he issued such a warning was just as well since the IEA was a charitable trust and therefore forbidden from conducting anything approaching political propaganda. We also came to see independence as expedient as we learned that party politicians were more or less impotent to reverse policies in the face of the hostile climate of opinion that confronted those sharing our classical liberal conception of the free society in the post-war years.

IN THE WAKE OF KEYNES – AND HAYEK

So, with slender resources, how could we hope to spread a better public understanding of the true contribution that a study of economics might make to
public affairs? The answer, surprisingly, was first provided by Keynes. In the
last paragraph of *The General Theory of Employment, Interest and Money*, he
explained why he anticipated that his revolutionary doctrine would pass into
general acceptance:

> the ideas of economists and political philosophers, both when they are right and
> when they are wrong, are more powerful than is commonly understood. Indeed the
> world is ruled by little else. Practical men, who believe themselves to be quite
> exempt from any intellectual influences, are usually the slaves of some defunct
> economist . . . the power of vested interests is vastly exaggerated compared with the
> gradual encroachment of ideas . . . soon or late, it is ideas, not vested interests,
> which are dangerous for good or evil.[2]

With equal confidence in the eventual acceptance of our own very different
ideas, we had this passage framed and displayed prominently on our board-
room wall.

This confidence was mightily reinforced by Hayek's more penetrating elaboration of the same thesis in his impressive 1949 essay 'The Intellectuals and
Socialism', in which he wrote: 'It is no exaggeration to say that once the more
active part of the intellectuals has been converted to a set of beliefs, the
process by which these become generally accepted is almost automatic and
irresistible'.[3]

Hayek explained that intellectuals are not generally original thinkers and
may not even be particularly intelligent. In fact, he lumped together teachers,
journalists, broadcasters, priests, commentators and other communicators as
'professional second-hand dealers in ideas'. There is a further passage in this
essay which inspired us at the IEA in difficult times:

> We must make the building of a free society once more an intellectual adventure, a
> deed of courage . . . Unless we can make the philosophic foundations of a free soci-
> ety once more a living intellectual issue, and its implementation a task which chal-
> lenges the ingenuity and imagination of our liveliest minds, the prospects of
> freedom are indeed dark . . .[4]

HARRIS AND SELDON BEGIN THE FIGHT BACK

We had an early opportunity to put to the test both the relevance of our shared
liberal heritage for contemporary policy, and also our personal compatibility
in working together on practical projects. As we settled into our first shared

worthy of public discussion. We were in effect entering the market for student texts once largely monopolised by the Fabian Society, but without its enfeebling constraint of having to conform to a party political agenda. We were therefore enormously encouraged when, within a decade, a Fabian Tract with the explicit title *The New Right: A Critique* was published in 1968 (Fabian Tract 387). The author was David Collard, who later joined our list of authors, and the tract devoted itself mainly to an earnest, respectful discussion of IEA publications as the 'most coherently expressed' samples of that genre. The author expressed his worry that the left was being successfully outflanked by the New Right.

Many authors will still remember, some ruefully, their first encounter with Seldon as what might be called a 'hands-on' editor. In addition to circulating guidance notes on length of manuscripts, house style, layout with side headings and the all-important question of timing, he required discussion of the literature, including alternative views, and forthright conclusions for policy without the least deference to what was conventionally regarded as 'politically possible' or even 'administratively feasible' – on neither of which could economists claim special authority. As an incomparable wordsmith, he would often pepper first drafts with suggestions in the margin on content, language and punctuation, and frequent one-word questions: 'source?' or 'evidence?'. He also had an ear for music and the rhythm of good prose which led him occasionally, when words failed him, to scribble in the margin: 'ugh'. When printer's proofs arrived, he would eagerly seize them from our colleague, Mike Solly, who worked with us from the early days as production manager, hand me a copy and invite comments. But I never forgot his early, emphatic warning that he worked best 'on a loose rein'.

His skill was not only in identifying topics but in matching them with authors who could draw on their existing work to produce a 10,000-word text for a Hobart Paper within a few months. He scoured the universities and journals to discover authors, not excluding civilised left-wingers, who understood the power of standard market analysis and could apply it to their special subjects. As members of the Mont Pèlerin Society, we were able to extend our search for authors to America, Europe, Australia and Hong Kong, among the distinguished fellow members of Hayek's informal international academy, formed in 1947 explicitly to bring scattered but like-minded scholars into regular communion every year or two at week-long conferences on almost every continent.

Our authors were attracted less by the modest fee, which in the early days might be 50 or 100 guineas for 10,000–12,000 words. More important was getting their distinctive views into print promptly and the growing evidence that publication by the IEA impressed more scholarly colleagues and was certainly no barrier to academic promotion.

RECRUITING AMONG THE AWKWARD SQUAD

Nevertheless, in the early years we found some more established academics understandably reluctant to become too closely associated with a new, untried institute which our enemies regularly sought to dismiss as outdated, 'right wing' or worse. In retrospect it is easier to forgive those university teachers who privately shared our doubts on the ruling collectivist consensus but chose to keep their heads below the parapet out of anxiety about how talk of market forces would go down in the common room or among radical students, confused by the Keynesians or bemused by the Galbraithians. All the more credit is due to those early, mostly junior, academics whom our lively early patron, Graham Hutton, taught us to value as fellow members of the 'awkward squad' who positively relished acting as early path-finders for our educational mission. From them Arthur Seldon coaxed a stream of challenging studies on an almost bewildering range of topics such as the role of trade unions (Ben Roberts of LSE), the incurable flaws of the NHS (Dennis Lees of Nottingham), the case against farm subsidies (Eric Nash and Richard Howarth of Aberystwyth), the abolition of resale price maintenance (B.S. Yamey of LSE), the folly of rent control (Norman Macrae of *The Economist*), the potency of monetary policy (Alan Walters of LSE and Victor Morgan of Swansea), the case for education vouchers (Alan Peacock and Jack Wiseman of York), paying for parking and self-financing roads (Gabriel Roth, who had studied this subject while researching at the University of Cambridge), liberalising road transport (Gilbert Ponsonby of the LSE and John Hibbs of Birmingham), and the inevitable decline of British coal (Colin Robinson of Surrey). Arthur Seldon and I were both proud of having won places from grammar schools to leading universities and therefore took satisfaction in the fact that the majority of our most robust authors came from similarly unprivileged backgrounds. So far from enjoying 'gap years', quite a few of us had an enforced spell as wage-earners before moving into higher education.

Many more senior academics were to follow, including internationally famous names such as Hayek, Friedman, Buchanan, Stigler, Meade and Hicks, all of whom were to be crowned Nobel laureates,[5] and the legendary Harry Johnson (of LSE and Chicago), whose untimely death deprived him of the chance to achieve that distinction.

But it was no use publishing lively studies unless we could get them distributed and read. In the absence of salesmen to travel round bookshops, we depended on getting our papers reviewed by journalists in the right quarters or indeed in any quarters. We started with a number of allies, mostly among old-style City editors – before the days when every newspaper had at least one 'economic correspondent'. The allies included such heavyweights as Harold Wincott (*Financial Times*), Oscar Hobson (*News Chronicle*), William Clarke (*The Times*), Richard Fry (*Manchester Guardian*), Paul Bareau (*Statist*) and Andrew Alexander (*Yorkshire Post* and later *The Daily Mail*). *The Daily Telegraph* rarely missed welcoming the latest publication from the IEA, by many outstanding writers, such as Colin Welch, Maurice Green, John O'Sullivan, Peter Utley and later the powerful former Fabian, Patrick Hutber. Our deepest disappointment was the invariable neglect of IEA publications by *The Economist*, which we had expected to give special attention to our revival of classical liberalism, but which, in the early days of the IEA, adopted a conventional Keynesian viewpoint.

Within the office, which moved from 66a Eaton Square to 2 Lord North Street in 1969, the ceaseless flow of publications, meetings, monthly Hobart lunches[6] and special events came to rely on the total dedication and unquestioning loyalty of a compact staff headed by Joan Culverwell as my secretary, personal assistant and protector, as well as office manager, from 1959 to 1986. Further office stability was provided by the unswerving commitment of Mike Solly, also dependable and in proud charge of the printing and production of our handsome papers since the earliest days in the Hobart Place basement back in 1959; by the energetic Ken Smith, who joined us as librarian in 1968, but cheerfully found himself covering all the office chores that fell between the rest of us; and finally, as accountant, the ever patient George Laxaton, who kept our growing, though still hazardous, finances in perfect order before the days of spread-sheets. Marketing was greatly enlivened when John Raybould returned from Canada in 1975 to devote his experience and rare enthusiasm to extending sales and subscriptions for our dozen or so new titles each year. Our dozen-strong staff was completed by the gentle Sheila Shah working on subscriptions, and three all-purpose secretaries and copy typist/telephonists, forever 'bashing out' second and third drafts of much-amended letters and manuscripts in the days before the joys of word processing and photo-copying machines.

In 1969, pressure on Arthur Seldon and me was eased when John Wood joined us from Associated Electrical Industries (and earlier Lazards) as deputy director, to help with fund-raising, industrial contacts and general office oversight, as well as writing or contributing to half a dozen seminal studies, on subjects including the distribution of wealth, the measurement of unemployment and the evils of exchange control. I had first met John at Cambridge in 1945, when we were both supervised in economics by Stanley Dennison of Caius College, and so saved from the fashionable statism of Joan Robinson. Professor Dennison thought himself amply rewarded by becoming a dedicated trustee of the IEA in the 1970s and 1980s.

AND THE WORLD SAID . . .

In the early days, it was little comfort to identify other intellectual allies if they felt inhibited from proclaiming the missionary truths we shared with most of our authors. Indeed, their failure to speak out lent credence to critics who were more easily able to mock the brave minority who did as a remnant of outdated, fringe cranks intent on returning to a vanished past. The superficial plausibility of such early dismissals prompts me to conclude this first chapter with a selection from the growing flood of tributes which gave us all the more satisfaction for being often from unexpected sources.

> These new radicals are Jacobin inegalitarians, the sea-green incorruptibles of the Institute of Economic Affairs, who combine irreverence and power of analysis with a certain political naivety
>
> (Brian Walden, Labour MP, 1969)

> Ten years ago the IEA with its devotion to Adam Smith, free market economics and guidance of the economy by the money supply . . . was still regarded as a bit of a joke. Today, helped by the pressures of real life, it has shifted some of the best known economic writers in its direction . . . the analysis of Hayek and Friedman has taken on a new relevance to Chancellors and shadow Chancellors
>
> (Ronald Butt, *The Times*, 1976)

> The IEA for many years has been dismissed as a crank outfit . . . its ideas now have much wider currency. In large parts of the Press they are the new orthodoxy and the Labour Government is by no means immune from them
>
> (*Labour Weekly*, 1976)

> Most of the axioms of economic Thatcherism are still intact. Consider some of them: the need to liberate the economy; the need to reduce central control and planning; the assertion that incomes cannot be regulated by laws; the belief in efficiency and competitiveness as absolute priorities; the contention that public spending must be paid for by productive output; and the sacred incantation that there is indeed no such thing as a free lunch
>
> (Hugo Young, *The Guardian*, 1985)

> The long uphill struggle of the IEA, which I stupidly wrote off as an amusing collection of cranks only 15 or so years ago, will surely come to constitute a vital part of any serious history of late-20th century Britain
>
> (Joe Rogaly, *Financial Times*, 1988)

NOTES

1. The full story of the creation of the IEA is well recounted in *Antony Fisher: Champion of Liberty* by Gerald Frost, Profile Books, London, 2002; see also John Blundell, *Waging the War of Ideas* (2nd edn), IEA Occasional Paper 131.

2. J.M. Keynes, *The General Theory of Employment, Interest and Money*, Macmillan, London, 1936, p. 383.
3. *University of Chicago Law Review*, spring 1949; reprinted by the IEA Health and Welfare Unit in 1998, p. 13.
4. Ibid., p. 26.
5. Douglass North later wrote for the IEA and Coase, Becker and Vernon Smith all contributed to our mission in other ways.
6. Hobart lunches were named after Hobart Square, one of the IEA's early homes. This was to make clear the essential detachment from the day-to-day deliberations conducted across the road from our current home in the Houses of Parliament.

Now for 'planning'*

It is easy with hindsight to see where post-war governments of all parties went wrong, leading to the incalculable damage of ever rising inflation, recurrent sterling crises, industrial unrest and flagging standards of living. Their combined effect was to bring Britain from the peak of international prestige as leading liberators of Europe in 1945 to the status of 'sick man of Europe', suffering from 'the British disease'. What can be claimed for the IEA is that, from its earliest days, under the editorial selection, direction and orchestration of Arthur Seldon, our growing band of authors consistently diagnosed the errors and pointed to remedies that were largely ignored – even mocked – until the election of Margaret Thatcher in 1979 following 'the winter of discontent'. Yet we had no access to special information, let alone the many millions of pounds of taxpayers' funds that should have conferred a huge research advantage on the NIESR, the National Economic Development Council (NEDC) and of course the Treasury, with its army of mostly Keynesian-trained economists. Nor would we, or our authors, have claimed to possess superior talents to all those 'clever sillies' trapped in the Keynesian collectivist consensus. The two critical advantages we enjoyed were a thorough grounding in classical market analysis and an independent station, which left us wholly free from the encumbrance of the party political pursuit of short-term electoral expediency.

Misled by the apparent success of wartime planning – with a comprehensive apparatus of coercion wholly inappropriate to a free society in times of peace – and a single national vision, the Labour Party after 1945 assumed there were no limits to the power of good intentions to solve every economic problem. Hence their reckless promises, not only of full employment, but of bigger and better welfare benefits, rising standards of living, a strong pound and stable prices. Despite Churchill's instinctive call to 'set the people free', the Conservatives before 1979 shrank from a head-on confrontation with unpalatable collectivism and settled for an unprincipled 'mixed economy'. It was the predictable failure to resolve these inherent contradictions which shifted the policy mixture cumulatively towards an increasing measure of confused collectivism.

---

* First published in *Towards a Liberal Utopia*, London: Institute of Economic Affairs, Hobart Paperback 32, 2005.

ON TO 'GROWTHMANSHIP'

In addition to the distortionary effects and inequity – I would say fraud – of continuous depreciation of the value of money, inflation was used, as we have seen, to justify ineffective incomes policies and ever more piecemeal government expedients that were dignified by the name of 'planning'. A particular source of long-run damage was the increasing subsidisation of nationalised industries in the hope of holding down their prices. Such expedients had the unintended effects of removing the spur to efficiency, financing unearned wage increases and raising taxation to cover the resulting deficits, without keeping inflation in check. So if governments were not prepared to stop the 'too much money' which was 'chasing too few goods' for fear of violating the sacred cow of full employment, the soft option appeared to be to go flat out to increase the supply of goods.

Thus did the leading aim of policy shift to the single-minded cultivation of a new sacred cow, namely that of economic growth. Having nationalised the 'commanding heights of the economy' only to find they became bottomless pits for taxpayers' money, ministers set ambitious targets for their output. Instead of repeated failure bringing such expedients into question, it led to ever more strident demands for more or 'better' planning. It was a Conservative government which first launched a 'national exercise' by setting up the NEDC in 1961. The Chancellor, Selwyn Lloyd, was briefly able to bask in the euphoric support of the CBI, the TUC, the NIESR and what passed as the 'responsible' press and broadcasting commentators. In place of piecemeal planning, the big idea was an essentially corporatist attempt to bring together representatives of government, industry and trade unions to help guide the economy on to an agreed 'path' of faster economic growth, principally through Andrew Shonfield's superficial panacea of increased investment. Even before the NEDC had produced its first projections, Arthur Seldon had invited an internationally renowned economist from Oxford, Dr Colin Clark, to review the prospects.

The result was an outstanding Hobart Paper (10) published in 1961 with the simple title of *Growthmanship* and the author's subtitle: 'A Study in the Mythology of Investment'. He offered a damning definition of growthmanship as: 'An excessive preoccupation with economic growth, advocacy of unduly simple proposals for obtaining it, and the careful choice of statistics to prove that countries with a political and economic system which you favour have made exceptionally good economic growth'.

That characterisation is worth pondering as the verdict of a leading economic statistician whose pioneering *Conditions of Economic Progress*, written 20 years earlier, had become a widely acknowledged student classic. In addition, sceptics might bear in mind that Clark was a former Fabian and his hint at statistical skulduggery is especially significant from a scrupulous analyst who was respected as a devout Roman Catholic. Rather than parade his superior technical skill, he identified the principal factors in economic growth as being not material but human qualities, including knowledge, effort, skill, organisation, education and enterprise. His list of recommendations consti- tuted a radical programme of liberal reform, ranging from freeing competitive markets by reducing both union and business restrictive practices, to cutting taxation, imposing commercial criteria on state industries and encouraging the distribution of profits rather than ploughing them back. Above all, he scored a bull's-eye by warning against trying to force growth by means that created inflation, thereby distorting efficient investment that was the professed aim of the whole exercise.

BEHOLD: THE NATIONAL PLAN

So far from heeding such strictures from a former planning assistant to the austere socialist Sir Stafford Cripps, the Labour government that came to power under Harold Wilson in 1964, following his appeal against 'thirteen wasted years of Tory misrule', went hell for leather to create a whole new Department of Economic Affairs free from what Keynesians scorned as the cautious 'Treasury view'. Its senior minister – as full secretary of state, no less – was the trade union MP George Brown. His speciality was persuading and cajoling trade union and business leaders into paying at least lip-service to a fully fledged, comprehensive National Plan. This document was duly assem- bled on the basis of dubious company answers to a national questionnaire on such issues as production capacities and demands for labour and strategic materials, not forgetting corporate hopes for expansion. The imposing-looking document duly mocked nature by having a gestation period of one year followed by a frenetic life of only nine months before collapsing amidst yet another economic crisis. The whole charade was masterminded by the NEDC, which acquired the user-friendly nickname of 'Neddy'. Recalling the *Shorter Oxford* definition of a mule as 'the off-spring of a he-ass and a mare', I used to parade one of my favourite quips that Neddy, like the mule, 'had neither pride of ancestry nor hope of progeny'.

But the Conservatives in opposition were not to be left out of the launching celebrations. Proof of the all-party commitment to such nonsense was provided by a great Conservative swell and old Etonian baronet named Sir Edward Boyle, who joined enthusiastically in supporting a House of Commons motion welcoming the National Plan, adding the sneer that every- one now supported planning except the Oxford professor Jewkes. No doubt this well-bred Oxford man singled out Jewkes not only as an opponent of the truly egregious socialist Oxford don Thomas Balogh, but also as author of a brilliant exposure of wartime economic management published back in 1947 under the title *Ordeal by Planning*. Knowing John Jewkes well as a delightful, gentle, modest IEA trustee, I was not surprised by how hurt he was to have been exposed to public mockery.

DOES PLANNING NEVER WORK?

The abject failure of the National Plan was predictable, and was indeed predicted. Several months before it was unveiled, portentously as ever by George Brown in September 1965, the IEA published an Eaton Paper (having moved from 7 Hobart Place to 66a Eaton Square) with the same title, exposing the emptiness of the sterile questionnaire to businessmen on which it purported to be based. The author, John Brunner, was another old Etonian, modest, scholarly and wholly free from party political delusions, but with good 'leftist' credentials, having worked for the BBC and the Treasury, before joining *The Observer*, from where he had helped respond to the Department of Economic Affairs questionnaire. That experience persuaded him how unreliable industry's answers would be as a guide to future investment and employment, based as they must be on a mixture of sheer guesswork, pious crystal-ball-gazing and optimistic hopes by companies of increased production, without any certainty of being able to sell the projected output. He warned against fabricating a statistical straitjacket for British industry and concluded: 'The more everything is reconciled with everything else, the worse the confusion when a particular forecast is confounded.' This verdict brings to mind a similar warning by Hayek in *The Road to Serfdom* that 'the more the State plans, the more difficult planning becomes for the individual'.

George Brown certainly took his Plan very seriously indeed, and we at the IEA positively relished the accolade of being denounced by him as 'weary willies'. We took more tangible satisfaction from Brunner's Paper going into three editions in as many years. Even *The Economist*, on this occasion, welcomed 'a corrosive examination of the ponderous questionnaire that the DEA sent to businessmen to help it prepare its plan'. Alas, John Brunner was so disenchanted with Mr Wilson's government that he emigrated to Western Australia, where, he said, politicians did not indulge in endless rhetoric about growth but rather created the freer market conditions that encouraged growth to happen.

However trenchant we may judge John Brunner's lucid Paper to have been, it cannot be claimed to have contributed to the collapse of the National Plan since such a mountain of make-believe did not require outside help to fail of its own absurdities. Suffice to report that by mid-1966 a renewed balance-of-payments crisis jolted the shell-shocked Mr Brown into declaring: 'Britain no longer has a Plan', and the economy limped on planlessly towards Labour's second unplanned devaluation in 1967.

So far from being discouraged by the apparent indifference of politicians to our warnings, Arthur Seldon's reaction was to redouble his search for authors in order to produce a positive barrage of high-powered literary shells against the entrenched position of the planners in government and academia. On the recommendation of Professor Jewkes, we appointed as staff researcher the industrious George Polanyi (son of the legendary polymath Michael), who drew on his experience as an economist in the gas industry to prepare a report published as *Planning in Britain: The Experience of the 1960s* (1967). Notice that, just as we produced our National Plan before the original was actually published, we could not wait until the end of the decade before pronouncing our requiem on the 1960s. Polanyi's exhaustive documentation and meticulous analysis left no room to doubt the failure of the NEDC and the Department of Economic Affairs to escape from the go-stop cycle. Most compelling was his demonstration that planning offered no rational criteria to guide investment and other decisions between alternative lines of production. In short, planning provided no substitute for 'the price and profit signals' of competitive markets.

Not content with such demolition, Arthur Seldon threw himself with gusto into assembling more and more economists to expose the fallibility of planning and forecasting in steel, electricity, nuclear power, science, medicine, imports, exports, national income (GNP) and even the revised estimates of population changes by no less an authority than the Registrar General. Again and again, the errors were caused by extrapolating past trends, without allowing sufficient margins for unexpected changes. Always, the planners were backward-looking. The official forecasters were further inclined to incorporate an undisclosed element of wishful thinking in which the planners were encouraged to persist longer, so that eventual adjustments had to be all the more drastic and disruptive.

. . . EVEN IN FRANCE

Frustrated by economic crises at home, the 'clever sillies' took refuge in *la planification française* of M. Jean Monnet, which prompted our masterful editorial director to commission an appraisal by Dr Vera Lutz, an English economist living in Switzerland. Her meticulous report, published for us by Longmans in 1969, was called *Central Planning for the Market Economy* and showed that French planners were not immune to wide discrepancies between targets and outcomes. Dr Lutz's scholarly analysis identified the fundamental problem as nothing more than 'the prevalence of uncertainty and limited knowledge about the course of human affairs'. As an anonymous joker has said: forecasting is always difficult, especially about the future. The decisive merit of a market economy is that it acknowledges a central role for risk-taking and mitigates the problem of ignorance by dispersing judgement and initiative among entrepreneurs using their own or their shareholders' money.

When the failure of planning drove Galbraith and Shonfield to propose the great 'new' idea of a convergence between the collectivist and competitive models, Dr Lutz argued powerfully that compromise was impossible between the rival logic of two utterly distinct conceptions. Instead, the best prospect of progress was by purging such distortions as inflation, excessive taxation, bureaucracy and restrictive practices; and ending the political denigration of the profit motive.

Among further papers that followed in the 1960s, the persistent Professor John Heath followed Professor B.S. Yamey's earlier classic (and successful) demolition of resale price maintenance with Hobart Paper 11, entitled *Still Not Enough Competition*, in 1961. The wise economic historian Professor G.C. Allen wrote Occasional Paper 14, entitled *Economic Fact and Fantasy*, published in 1967, celebrating how vigorously competitive enterprise persisted in the teeth of inappropriate and inconsistent state interventions. In Research Monograph 5, *Private Enterprise and Public Emulation*, published in 1966, a young Italian journalist named Mario Deaglio compared another of Labour's pet ideas, launched with the usual fanfare of trumpets as the Industrial Reorganisation Corporation (IRC), unfavourably with its more thorough-going Italian model, renowned as the Industrial Reorganisation Institute (IRI). In more constructive mode, Professor Harold Rose of the London Business School drew on his combined experience in business and academia to launch in 1963 our new series of Eaton Papers with *Disclosure in Company Accounts*, which called for more information more frequently to enable shareholders, takeover bidders and managements themselves to assess the efficiency with which all aspects of their business were conducted. An interesting proposal, echoed by other IEA authors, was that companies should distribute profits to shareholders for reinvestment or spending, rather than retaining them for investment as the directors decided, which too easily led to 'the survival of the fattest' rather than of the fittest.

NOT FORGETTING FREE TRADE

The lessons of both Dr Deaglio and Professor Rose were reinforced in 1970 by Dr Brian Hindley's Hobart Paper 50, *Industrial Merger and Public Policy*, which urged freer competition, including from imports, through tariff reduction. Against the meretricious fashion of growth through planning, many IEA authors consistently argued for the stimulus of international competition through free trade. In Research Monograph 17, entitled *The Shape of Britain's Tariff* (1968), Dr Sidney Wells attacked protectionism, which is after all a patchy form of partial planning. In Hobart Paper 17, *UK, Commonwealth and Common Market*, 1962, another of our Nobel laureate authors, James Meade, welcomed the prospect of removing trade barriers while strongly opposing the Common Agricultural Policy and import levies, and warning of the possibility of the EEC becoming 'a tight parochial, European bloc'. Nevertheless, at that time the comparative success of post-war European economies appeared to offer disillusioned Keynesians and planners in all parties an escape from go-stop in Britain by joining the 'common market', as the European Economic Community (later EU) was then called.

To test this new fashion, Arthur Seldon commissioned Russell Lewis as a liberal economist and a 'good European' who had represented the Brussels Commission in London. His Hobart Paperback 3 shrewdly analysed the Treaty of Rome as incorporating the free market principles of Adam Smith, but operating through a strong bureaucracy in the form of an unelected Commission. My chosen title, *Rome or Brussels . . . ?* (1971), exactly conveyed the author's anxiety that the benefits from widening competitive markets could be swamped by bureaucratic regulation from an overactive Commission. We can now see how that fear was realised by the nomination of a French corporatist, Jacques Delors, as President of the Commission. Instead of implementing the Single European Act to open up the market through 'mutual recognition' of national products, the Commission imposed crude standardisation in the name of 'a level playing field', which is no more than a textbook example of flat earth economics, since trade depends on differences rather than uniformities of products. It is primarily that collectivist impulse which explains why market economists have almost universally turned against such an apparently liberal project.

THE VERDICT ON 'PLANNING'

Looking back on the prolonged collectivist experiment of those three post-war decades, the saddest reflection for an economist concerned with public as well as personal economy is the truly incalculable waste of time, talent and resources devoted to the project of planning the British economy. Is there anyone not personally caught up in these tortuous proceedings who would in retrospect dispute my verdict that it was all along an intellectually disreputable project? Despite the apparent sophistication of the civil servants, businessmen, leading commentators and at least some of the politicians involved, it amounted to nothing more than a succession of desperate expedients in a determined effort comparable to making water flow uphill. It is a wry reflection that most of the guilty men, especially from the Treasury, will by now be blissfully retired, some with knighthoods and all with comfortable pensions, the values of which were thoughtfully indexed on the very eve of Heath's reckless inflation after 1972!

Against such a sorry background of profound intellectual confusion and bewilderment, a mere handful of MPs stand out all the more memorably for their courage and clear thinking. Among Conservatives, such exemplars would include Enoch Powell, whose sophisticated advocacy of free market forces put his colleagues to shame, the young Geoffrey Howe from the Bow Group, who became one of our most principled and perceptive regular subscribers, and the scholarly Keith Joseph, who was conscientiously fighting his way from early agnosticism to crusading champion of competitive enterprise. All three were regular students of IEA papers and periodic visitors to Eaton Square and Lord North Street. For a brief interval we had hopes of intellectual support from a brooding Welsh Labour MP, Desmond Donnelly, who broke away from his party to launch an independent, anti-Wilson campaign for freedom of choice, which abruptly collapsed in the 1970 general election. The only Liberal MP from whom we drew the least indication of interest was its dashing leader for a while, Joseph Grimond, who totally failed to carry support among any of his followers.

It was not until the early 1970s, with the abject failure of Heath's latest version of 'economic planning' plain to all except Wedgwood Benn and a handful of hard Left MPs and trade union leaders, that we at the IEA detected unmistakable signs of keen interest among an emerging band of high-flying Tory MPs. Led by Margaret Thatcher, Geoffrey Howe and Keith Joseph, they now included a younger trio of lively economic journalists (Nigel Lawson, David Howell, Jock Bruce-Gardyne), a thoughtful stockbroker (John Biffin) and a delightful, sparky solicitor (Ian Gow). Both Arthur Seldon and I, impatient as ever for the anticipated awakening, might be forgiven for thinking it had seemed a long and lonely wait.

Market versus state*

The 'clever sillies' were perhaps at their silliest in their lofty scorn for 'market forces'. It is hardly too harsh to say that many sophisticated academic leaders of the Keynesian collectivist consensus never really got the hang of market pricing.[1] They seemed stuck in the early chapters of elementary textbooks that start from the highly abstract formal model of 'perfect (atomistic) competition' and go on to denounce such real-world 'imperfections' as consumer ignorance, salesmanship, branded products and other 'monopolistic' practices. The trouble was less with the real world than with their wholly unrealistic parody of perfection.

INCORRIGIBLE SOCIALISM

This is a large subject, but the assumption that every market 'imperfection' can be remedied by political intervention depends on the elementary non sequitur of perfect government. The best demolition of this fallacy was a masterly Occasional Paper by our editorial director, Arthur Seldon himself, for which, with his rare verbal felicity, he chose the title *Corrigible Capitalism, Incorrigible Socialism*. It was published as Occasional Paper 57 in 1980. It compared 'the relative perfectibility of competitive private enterprise and monopolistic government production'. Not only does competition disperse and diversify decision-making, its faults are 'largely incidental and removable', whereas the faults of monopoly government production are 'essentially integral and irremovable'. That argument followed his old LSE mentor, Lord Robbins, who taught that the market was more democratic than government because it provided a process of election[2] in which consumers vote daily with their own money for the goods and services that best satisfy their (developing) individual preferences. Even imperfectly competitive pricing thus widens consumer choice and gives full representation to minority tastes.

Rather than joining the elaborate theorising of the 'clever sillies' on monopolistic competition, oligopoly and other variants, Arthur Seldon constantly sought out authors who could assemble and analyse empirical evidence from

---

* First published in *Towards a Liberal Utopia*, London: Institute of Economic Affairs, Hobart Paperback 32, 2005.

the practical operation of markets and non-markets in a wide range of goods and services both at home and abroad. Thus one of the earliest Hobart Papers, entitled *To Let?*, published in 1960 as Hobart Paper 2, by Norman Macrae of *The Economist*, showed how rent control exacerbated the housing shortage by increasing the demand and reducing the supply of rented accommodation, exactly as would be predicted by the elementary, commonsense theories of supply and demand. Similar lessons from other distorted markets were taught by, among others: Hallett and James in *Farming for Consumers* (Hobart Paper 22), published in 1963; a succession of devastating exposures of the contradictions and contortions of politicised fuel policy by Professor Colin Robinson, starting with *A Policy for Fuel* (Occasional Paper 31) in 1969; and from the different world of commodity markets in *Prices for Primary Producers* (Hobart Paper 24) in 1963 by Sir Sydney Caine, who drew on his unrivalled early experience in the colonial service to show the advantages of freer trade and market pricing.

When the spread of car ownership began to exacerbate road congestion, a transport economist named Gabriel Roth was discovered to write *Paying for Parking* (Hobart Paper 33, 1965), which showed how such then unheard-of devices as parking meters worked in other countries to check the problem of congestion. The following year, the same author produced Research Monograph 3 entitled *A Self-financing Road System*, which went well beyond tolls in charging for the use of scarce road space. The IEA's last Research Monograph (59) before this volume was published, *Pricing Our Roads: Vision and Reality*, by Stephen Glaister and Daniel Graham, also tackled this issue of road pricing. The politicians are catching up with sensible free market economics: but only slowly, with minor road pricing and private road schemes having been developed in London and around Birmingham! Turning to the supply side, John Hibbs was invited to write Hobart Paper 23, entitled *Transport for Passengers* (1971), in which he dismissed talk of excluding private cars from cities and urged freer, unsubsidised competition between roads, minibuses, so-called 'pirate' operators and rail transport to serve passengers. A major, early contribution to another debate that has since exploded – that of how to deal with environmental problems in a market economy – was Hobart Paper 66, *Pricing for Pollution* (1975), by Oxford professor Wilfred Beckerman.

WHAT ABOUT THE UNIONS?

Evidence of the priority we gave to trade unions – as anti-market, rather than non-market, institutions – in the diagnosis of the British disease was the invitation in 1959 to Ben Roberts, Reader in Industrial Relations at the LSE and a former research scholar at Nuffield and lecturer at Ruskin, to write *Trade Unions in a Free Society*. His broad sympathy with the aspirations of the British labour movement informed this review of the history, organisation, law and economic consequences of trade unions. All the more weighty were his proposals, which, in addition to advocating the abolition of the closed shop and more local wage bargaining, went to the heart of the role of wage demands in the causation of inflation. Rejecting a 'central wages policy' as unenforceable in a free society, he challenged the Keynesians head-on by suggesting 'a more reasonable definition of full employment than an excess of jobs over persons available to fill them'. If that single, seasoned academic insight had been heeded, the boom-and-bust inflation of the following two decades under both Labour and Tory governments could have been avoided.

Two years later, another challenge was thrown down in Hobart Paper 12, entitled simply *A Market for Labour*. The author, Dennis Robertson, dared to analyse the labour market 'as a market and not as some kind of social institution'. It is indicative of the intellectual climate of those days that one reviewer was so shocked that he asked rhetorically whether the author was harking back to slave markets. Others expressed milder surprise that an economist should apply to human beings the same analysis of supply and demand that seemed more appropriate to groceries! Many later authors were to direct even more pointed analysis at the restrictive working practices of trade unions (as in *The Restrictive Society*, 1967, by John Lincoln, an assistant to Beveridge on his wartime reports, with a foreword by ex-Labour minister Sir Hartley (later Lord) Shawcross), and the abuse of 'peaceful picketing', by which these monopoly suppliers of labour routinely enforced strikes to support wage demands and closed shops.

Hayek and other IEA authors repeatedly called for repeal of the Trade Disputes Act of 1906, which, together with union closed shops, strengthened these labour monopolies and gave them immunity from claims for damages caused by their disruption of production. Most persistent was the irrepressible Professor W.H. (Bill) Hutt, an academic from Cape Town University, whose scholarly Hobart Paperback 8, published in 1975, *The Theory of Collective Bargaining 1930–75*, contested the popular view that unions were necessary to overcome the disadvantage of workers in bargaining with powerful employers and argued that restrictive practices kept wages down by discouraging investment in new technology – as forced on the print unions after the long-delayed reforms of union law in the 1980s. In 1975, when Ted Heath was asked what he thought of the usurpation of political authority by the unions, Hutt quoted him as accepting it as 'the reality of industrial life'.

That craven acceptance of impotence by a former British prime minister on an issue of such decisive importance for the survival of a free society stands in stark contrast to the persistence of IEA authors acting on the editorial injunction to 'think the unthinkable'. It also explains the reliance of the

Keynesian collectivist consensus on mounting exhortation and successive incomes policies in a doomed effort to check continuing wage inflation accommodated by the Keynesian neglect of monetary policy. Indeed, wage inflation was aggravated by a rigged market in which the supply of labour was constrained by trade union restrictions while demand for labour was increased by a Keynesian full employment policy.

IEA authors hammered away on the advantages of competitive pricing in goods and services as varied as agricultural products, postal services, blood banks, foreign currencies, air transport, television, sport, telephones, water and local government services. An interesting experiment in 1967 suggested that some students had a firmer grasp of market realities than many of their teachers. Thus Arthur Seldon arranged a school essay competition in the name of a Labour MP of liberal economic views, Evan Durbin, who had died in tragic circumstances. The product was *Essays in the Theory and Practice of Pricing* (Readings 3, 1967), which included discussion of metering water supply, charging for private beaches and varying electricity tariffs by time of day to even out peak loads. The cumulative result was a powerful reaffirmation of the power of open markets to harness the energies of competing producers in the service of individual consumer choice.

WHY NOT WELFARE?

There is insufficient space here to do justice to the enormous volume and variety of IEA studies of market alternatives to state services, especially in health and education. In both areas, the collectivist consensus in policy, though less so in public sentiment (see below), has prevailed with few, mostly superficial, concessions to the preferences of consumers, who, as taxpayers, continue to be required to pay the ever higher cost of 'free' services. The full extent of government failure has been brought home to me from my vantage point on the cross-benches in the House of Lords where, even after 1979, I have watched dozens of full-blown statutes on education and health forced through by the party whips, each purporting to provide lasting cures for the acknowledged failures of previous 'remedies'.

The failure of what Richard Cockett called Margaret Thatcher's 'counter-revolution'[3] to have any significant impact on the lingering dinosaurs of state medical care and education cannot be explained by any failure of IEA authors to demonstrate their need for radical reform. Indeed, one of our earliest Hobart Papers (14), *Health through Choice* (1961), by Dr Dennis Lees of Nottingham University, might be singled out as a classic model of diagnosis and prescription. Ponder deeply the following luminous extracts from Lees's conclusions in the light of all that has since transpired:

The fundamental weaknesses of the NHS are the dominance of political decision, the absence of built-in forces making for improvement and the removal of the test of the market. These defects bring dangers for the quality of medical care that cannot be removed without far-reaching reform. (p. 60)

My verdict would be that a monolithic structure financed by taxation is ill-suited to a service in which the personal element is so strong, in which rapid advances in knowledge require flexibility and freedom to experiment, and for which consumer demand can be expected to increase with growing prosperity.

Rather than offering a detailed alternative blueprint, which has become the fashion for the multiplying number of modern 'think tanks', Dr Lees was modestly content to indicate lines of reform. His aim was 'to diminish the role of political decisions and to enlarge the influence of consumer choice'. Methods should include, first, moving away from taxation and free services to private insurance and fees, helped by tax concessions for those who can provide for themselves and direct assistance to the dwindling minority who cannot; and second, part-payment for the cost of prescriptions with special provision for life-saving drugs and patients with low incomes.

On the other major, failing pillar of state welfare, *Education and the State* (1965) by E.G. West provided a no less powerful intellectual demolition of the case for political control. The author's meticulous study of nineteenth-century developments led him to the remarkable conclusion that in 1870, before compulsory state education was introduced, over 95 per cent of fifteen-year-olds were literate. Little wonder that Dr West's study prompted the generally aloof *Times Educational Supplement* to offer a rare eulogy: 'If his arguments cannot induce us to abolish state provision, they can surely open our eyes to the urgent need, on grounds of human dignity, for more parental choice'.

The same 'undemocratic' lack of choice and failing standards led a brace of heavyweight professors from the University of York, Alan Peacock and Jack Wiseman, to write Hobart Paper 25, entitled *Education for Democrats* (1964). With scrupulous analysis, they urged financing by loans for university students and, for schoolchildren, full-cost education vouchers paid to parents as taxable income so as to recoup part of the subsidy from better-off families.

Many more specialist studies amplified and reinforced the case for moving away from state monopoly of welfare services, to remedy the obvious defects of inadequate finance, poor quality and suppression of family choice and responsibility. With the welfare state accounting for a third or more of all public spending, the commonsense argument was repeated over and again: that rising incomes made possible direct payment by the majority in return for lower taxation, with more subsidy to the declining minority in need. To demonstrate the spread of support for radical reform, Arthur Seldon assembled a study group of a dozen academics, doctors and journalists, whose report was published as *Towards a Welfare Society* (Occasional Paper 13, 1966). The authors proposed a reverse income tax in place of means testing and offered evidence from opinion polls that a change in direction on health and education was 'politically possible' and, from foreign examples, also 'administratively feasible'.

A new opportunity presented itself with the resignation from Harold Wilson's government of a former, highly independent trade union leader, Douglas (later Lord) Houghton, who for two years had served as minister with special responsibility for coordinating social policy. He marked the occasion with a typically challenging speech which our watchful editorial director immediately sought his permission to publish as Occasional Paper 16 under the unassuming but radical title *Paying for the Social Services* (1967). His bold proposal of charges for the NHS was so startling from a serving Labour MP that his reasons deserve quotation as being even more valid 40 years later: 'What is in doubt is whether we in Britain will ever give medicine the priority given to it in some other countries (and America is not the only one) so long as it is financed almost wholly out of taxation'. Then came the blunt reason:

> While people would be willing to pay for better services for themselves, they may not be willing to pay more in taxes as a kind of insurance premium which may bear no relation to the services actually received . . . we are now getting the worst of both worlds. The government cannot find the money out of taxation and the citizen is not allowed to pay it out of his own pocket.

Alas, almost forty years later the Chancellor, Gordon Brown, is attempting to paper over the gap by lavishing huge sums of taxpayers' money on creating an ever larger state monolith.

PUBLIC CHOICE

Politicians brush aside the painful, pervasive and perpetual failures of state welfare and other services by appealing to the holy grail of 'representative government'. A policy may not turn out well or may fall victim to the law of unintended consequences by achieving results different from, even opposite to, what was intended, but they say: 'It's what the people want', or at least 'what they voted for'. It becomes subsumed in that most question-begging of all phrases: 'the public interest'. But, as Robbins first asked, how can a single vote every four or five years, between two or three parties giving away a monstrous ragbag of several hundred assorted services listed in cunningly compiled political manifestos, stand comparison with the 'daily referendum' of competitive markets? None of the individual promises can be voted on separately, except by referendum. None indicates costs. None carries the money-back guarantee increasingly offered by leading producers or retailers.

Politicians at elections say, in effect, 'a vote for me means a vote for every item in my party's programme'. In the economic analysis of business, it is called 'full-line forcing' and is branded as an anti-competitive practice that prevents consumers comparing costs and values for separable elements of the product mix.

It has taken the development of 'public choice', more descriptively known as 'the economic analysis of politics', to expose how representative government has been transformed into misrepresentative government, catering not for broad majorities but captured by organised, often small, minorities. Thus doctors, teachers, nurses, other public sector workers, farmers, motorists, cyclists, conservationists and hundreds of other groups, sharing a cohesive, common (sometimes arcane) interest, can each organise themselves to lobby MPs for subsidies or other special privileges. As many IEA authors have pointed out, their success depends on their members having a larger, more concentrated stake in gaining their ends than the widely dispersed individual taxpayers or consumers have in resisting (even noticing) the costs.

Leaving aside the European farm lobby's racket of the EU Common Agricultural Policy, examples from social policy would certainly include the defeat of Keith Joseph's effort to introduce student loans or education vouchers in the 1980s, and Michael Howard's recent opportunistic opposition to university top-up fees, all in deference to organised lobbying by the unions of teachers and students, backed up for good measure by the self-serving bureaucrats in the national and local education establishments.

It was another example of the genius of Seldon that he was among the first in Britain to spot the importance of this new American academic development of public choice, associated with two fellow Mont Pèlerin Society members, James Buchanan and Gordon Tullock. His first major blow was to publish an exposition by Tullock in Hobart Paperback 9, entitled *The Vote Motive*[4] (1976), which compared the politician's drive to maximise votes with the businessman's aim to maximise profits. He then organised the first seminar in Britain on the subject and assembled a symposium of British, American and European academics, publishing their lectures as an IEA Reading entitled *The Economics of Politics* (Readings 18, 1978). A general conclusion was that the democratic process does not merit the widespread presumption of moral superiority over the economic marketplace. Elsewhere, Arthur Seldon has summed up the operation of the political market by rewriting Lincoln's definition of democracy as: 'Government of the Busy, by the Bossy, for the Bully'.[5]

A related editorial initiative was to combine the businessman's market research with the politician's opinion polling to discover people's preferences between state and private provision of health and education. The party men like to quote periodic polls showing large majorities in favour of the ('free') NHS, and to point to the small minorities who chose to support BUPA or private schools, as proving satisfaction with state provision. The twin fallacies in all such arguments arise from conveniently neglecting two facts: first, that approval of state services ignores their (unknown) 'price' both in terms of alternatives forgone and the high taxes levied even on families with low incomes; and, second, that private provision paid for out of net income involves double payment, in insurance or fees on top of taxes for the state service they do not use.

Accordingly, we had lengthy discussions with a leading professional market researcher to find out whether he could compile a questionnaire that would present a more balanced choice between public and private health and education services. The result was a series of four reports published between 1963 and 1979[6] on employing the device of the voucher. *The Economist* at last redeemed itself in my eyes by printing a well-aimed review of the last of these reports: 'the ideas adumbrated so readably in this book do have the most plausible application . . . The IEA's splendidly anti-bureaucratic principles are an invaluable antidote to public sector Toryism as much as to socialism'.

In bald summary, a national quota sample of some two thousand men and women of working age were invited to say whether they would accept vouchers for education and medical care amounting to two-thirds or one-third of the (stated) cost and add the balance to make up the full cost of private provision. The number accepting the larger voucher was in both cases naturally higher than those accepting the smaller, and rose for education to just above 50 per cent in 1978 and for medical care to 57 per cent. Even allowing for the standard margin of error of around 3 per cent, these and other findings of our *Choice in Welfare* researches left little doubt that the universal provision of 'free' tax-financed welfare was very far from satisfying the public's underlying taste for choice in medical care and education.

It must be admitted that our repeated findings of wide support for radical reform in welfare have so far foundered on the misplaced prejudices of the modern 'levellers': if all cannot have the best, none shall have better. They ignore the evidence from everyday markets that competition works ceaselessly to transform today's minority luxuries into tomorrow's necessities – videos, CDs, DVDs, mobile telephones . . . Instead of welcoming such creative competition, Labour and Tory spin masters now engage in offering make-believe competition within the public sector, both sides shrilly claiming to have solved the illusion of conjuring real choice for parents and patients from the unyielding, entrenched, monopoly bureaucracies of state education and healthcare.

NOTES

1. Their visceral hatred of market forces was vividly revealed by T. Balogh's confident but

premature obituary on Erhard's post-war miracle in Germany, mockingly entitled *An Experiment in 'Planning' by the 'Free' Price Mechanism*, Basil Blackwell, Oxford, 1950.
2. *The Economic Problem in Peace and War*, Macmillan, London, 1947.
3. *Thinking the Unthinkable: Think-tanks and the Economic Counter-Revolution 1931–1983*, HarperCollins, London, 1994.
4. Editor's note: this title was the inspired choice of Ralph Harris himself. Gordon Tullock once said that *The Vote Motive* did more to spread public understanding of public choice economics than any other single publication as a result of its multiple editions and twelve translations.
5. *Capitalism*, Basil Blackwell, Oxford, 1990, p. 235. Although it is not published by the IEA, I commend it as an unsurpassed exposition of the anti-statist case from a combined economic, political and ethical standpoint.
6. *Choice in Welfare*, 1963, 1965 and 1970; and Harris and Seldon, *Over-ruled on Welfare*, Hobart Paperback 13, 1979.

Behind enemy lines*

How can any observer under the age of 50 recapture the hostile, even intimidating, intellectual atmosphere of the post-war national debate on British political economy? The reigning Keynesian collectivist consensus, though less oppressive than the KGB, scornfully dismissed dissenting opinion and, albeit with diminishing confidence, prescribed what passed as 'sophisticated' discussion of public policy. Those of us who dared persist with stubborn doubts only gradually overcame what I might call a shared sense of isolation. A little fancifully, I have, in retirement, come to liken my experience travelling round the country to address some unknown student audience – say at Essex University at the time of student unrest – to that of a wartime British agent infiltrating hostile territory in the vanished era of Attlee, Macmillan, Wilson, Heath. With few exceptions, most notably *The Daily Telegraph*, the mainstream media, including the BBC and commercial television, paid little attention to critics of the new collectivism. Even the prestigious *Financial Times* confined itself to a brief note on most of our Papers but, with the exception of individual writers such as Harold Wincott and later Samuel Brittan, never rose to an expression of approval in its staid leaders. Elsewhere, critics of the received wisdom were regarded as lacking in patriotism, even as engaged in mildly treasonable activities.

Throughout the 1960s and into the 1970s, whenever the general run of commentators deigned to notice our Hobart and other papers, they invariably described us as 'the right-wing IEA', whereas the National Institute of Economic and Social Research – which was both government -funded and Keynesian-inspired – was always respectfully referred to as 'the independent NIESR'. We consoled ourselves by privately mis-naming them the 'National Institute of Economic and Social*ist* Research'.

COOL RECEPTION

The reception for IEA speakers was distinctly cool when addressing audiences of people who accepted the prevailing economic opinion of the age. There was

---

* First published in *Towards a Liberal Utopia*, London: Institute of Economic Affairs, Hobart Paperback 32, 2005.

of course little chance of convincing a conference of earnest social workers in my favourite Cambridge one overcast Saturday morning that increasing unconditional cash benefits for the unemployed must risk actually increasing unemployment so long as income tax was levied on earnings below benefit levels. Here was another example of the law of unintended consequences. Elementary market economics predicts that the higher you pitch social benefits, especially for families with children, the more you risk making benefits more attractive than net take-home pay from a full week's work. Yet to meet their swollen budgets Chancellors of both parties thought nothing of starting to levy tax on incomes below social benefits paid to families with children. I recall press gossip of beneficiaries saying they could not afford to take a job – unless it was in the 'cash' economy. And how could I hope to get the secretary of the Engineering Employers' Federation to grasp that successive incomes policies were no shield against an inflation stoked up by monetary excess?

As for a trade union audience in Tunbridge Wells of all places, no fallacy was too crude for some hecklers to deploy in favour of ever-rising wages. But then the likes of such trade union barons as Jack Jones and Hugh (later Lord) Scanlon never tired of telling their members that wage increases could actually increase employment – by raising the public's spending power and thereby stimulating demand for unemployed labour. Such myopic Keynesianism was blind to the effect of higher wages (unmatched by higher output) in raising unit costs so as to cancel any stimulus from monetary demand and pricing marginal workers out of jobs.

Then again, was I wasting time travelling to Oxford for a seminar – presided over by Roger Opie, who was a dashing leader in the Keynesian collectivist consensus? Could his students really be expected to display much sympathy for my warning against the neglect of monetary discipline against inflation, when Opie had long preached the opposite? In the event I found I had not entirely wasted my journey when two or three students quietly sidled up after the meeting to express interest in what I had said and to enquire about the work of the IEA.

Again and again at such meetings, the chairman would read a formally polite introduction – Cambridge economist, double first, general director of the IEA, author, etc. – before I found myself rising to confront an impassive audience. To break the ice, I would ring the changes on endlessly repeated opening quips against the whole tribe of economists: 'Six economists, six opinions – or seven if Keynes was present'; 'If all economists were laid end to end, they would still reach no definite conclusion'; 'Economists, those chaps who know the price of everything and the value of nothing'. I would ask rhetorically how many economists – or for that matter politicians – would be prepared to back their confident forecasts with their own money, or even with that of their spouses. These and rather better topical jests would often be received in frozen silence, and I would soon be running a practised eye along the rows of impassive faces for the odd trace of a nod or knowing smile.

PLANNING AGAIN

There seemed no escape from hostility. I remember welcoming at last the prospect of allies in addressing a sober audience of business economists on the folly of George Brown's 1965 National Plan. Here was no parachute drop into enemy territory. These were, after all, people paid to think about future changes in their companies' markets and the impact of government policies on them. They should have been the first to grasp the dangers of centrally planning the entire economy by official extrapolations of past trends. They should have been especially wary of such Keynesian macro-magnitudes as total demand, investment, employment and, most elusive of all, forecasts of the vagaries of foreign trade. Among what I supposed to be friends, I launched into my demolition of national economic planning by inviting the audience to agree that all such exercises were backward-looking, 'like steering a ship by its wake' while calling for full speed ahead. This analogy came into its own when, as Chancellor of the Exchequer, Jim Callaghan (a former naval man) used to boast that he would avert the next sterling crisis by a timely 'touch on the tiller'.

But surely an audience of business economists might be expected to be highly receptive to my commonsense warning against unforeseeable rocks in an uncharted future? Alas, most of them appeared no more perceptive than those CBI worthies whom I later came to upbraid for accepting the routine incantations about a mixed economy without foreseeing that inevitable setbacks would risk progressive dilution of the mixture by more party politics and less private enterprise.

It was this perennial phantom of central planning or 'better planning' to which the Keynesian collectivist consensus endlessly appealed, despite mounting evidence of economic disorder and failure. Picture me being ushered into a bare sixth-form classroom for a debate on the National Plan, some time in the brief interval between its enthusiastic launch in September 1965 and its collapse in June 1966. My opponent on this occasion was a large, imposing, pukka public school man, like me in his early forties. He had been seconded, by a top firm, to the NEDC with a specific brief to promote George Brown's National Plan. Almost forty years later I have not forgotten his opening sentences along the following lines: 'The purpose of the Plan is to raise economic growth to four per cent a year in the gross national product and associated parameters. And I would add, as a practical businessman, how proud I am to be using this kind of technical language'. Practical businessman?!

Technical language?! Bah! What was I, as a mere academic economist, to say? I suppressed the wicked retort that some businessmen who had been seconded to the NEDC were duds the sponsoring companies were glad to see the back of.

My adversary was eventually to vanish whence he came, but at that school debate I was momentarily encouraged to detect that the sixth-form audience were not much impressed by his pompous, pseudo-technical mumbo-jumbo. My cheerful response had attempted to explain the crucial difference between a central plan devised by party politicians to impose a single, fixed blueprint for action on everyone, and a business plan that is shaped by competitive market realities ('price signals') but remains sufficiently flexible to accommodate prompt revision in the light of ever changing relative costs and prices, consumer demand, foreign trade, advertising, new products and, not least, new entrants into the market. Even a rather dim 'practical businessman' could hardly dispute there was something in that distinction.

Though short lived, the long-forgotten National Plan provided plenty of opportunities for me to advertise the IEA's teachings on the role of the entrepreneur. A favourite theme was the ubiquity of uncertainty in the rapidly changing post-war world, especially for Britain, with almost a third of national output devoted to the vagaries of foreign trade. As an old *Glasgow Herald* leader writer with a penchant for a good headline, I liked to commend the guidance of business investment decisions by 'profits' rather than by 'prophets'. So when invited to address the Ashridge Management College on the subject of planning, I waxed lyrical on the contribution of the entrepreneurial drive to the transformation of our well-equipped kitchens and centrally heated and carpeted homes, no less than to widespread motoring and foreign holidays. It went down well enough, but I was astonished when the director of the college wound up thanking me especially for introducing the word 'entrepreneur' for the first time he could remember in his years at Ashridge. For some time thereafter I feared the worst about the new fashion of 'management training'.

ENTER *BÊTE NOIRE* SHONFIELD

One of my most miserable memories in the Wilson years was of an encounter in a cramped BBC radio studio with no room to sit down and – more serious – no 'hospitality room', where victims were introduced to each other over a welcome drink. My antagonist turned out to be one of my least favourite *bêtes noires*, Andrew Shonfield, then economics editor of *The Observer* and author of an influential Penguin Special called *British Economic Policy since the War*, published in 1958. I recognised him as an outstanding *FT* journalist and found him an even more fluent talker, who pontificated impressively with an unmistakable aura of authority. The interviewer shuffled forward deferentially and addressed Shonfield by his Christian name as an old friend before briefly turning to me and reading my name from his script. The subject was incomes policy, which gave Shonfield the opportunity to hold forth magisterially on the important role of trade unions and the need to win their leaders over to moderation in their ceaseless demands for higher wages. When my turn came, I got no farther than beginning to explain how market forces must in the end set limits to the level of wage increases that could be afforded without causing either inflation or unemployment. With barely concealed impatience, the interviewer cut me short and turned back to Shonfield, who almost pityingly dismissed talk of market forces as 'laissez-faire extremism irrelevant to the real world'. I remember crawling home and vowing to avoid, whether on radio or television, any further such unequal encounters, which allowed no time to develop a coherent argument. It was a vow to which I resolutely stuck thereafter, preferring a live audience whose reactions, favourable or not, I could see and judge and respond to as I went along.

For all his reputation as a savant, Shonfield's Penguin paperback revealed an almost religious faith in political intervention to boost economic growth. His universal panacea for policy, guided by something he dignified with the title of the 'capital–output ratio', appeared always to require more and yet more investment, although, in the absence of the despised profit motive, without any clear guidance about what exactly the new machines and equipment were supposed to produce. His ideal was later mocked in *The Daily Telegraph* by Colin Welch, a marvellous literary writer with no pretensions of economic expertise beyond what he had learned from the IEA. He summed up Shonfield's panacea as: 'investment in machine tools, to produce machine tools, to produce machine tools'. It was a turn of phrase I used to good effect in many subsequent lectures.

Shonfield loved to mock concern about the Bank Rate as primitive worship of a totem pole to appease the gods of the City of London. He displayed the standard Keynesian preference for continued inflationary pressure, rather than using interest rates to moderate the booms. It was no mere technical dispute about alternative economic theories. Not only did the go-stop cycle severely disrupt industrial production and investment, it led to wildly fluctuating inflation from between 1 and 10 per cent a year in the 1950s to 25 per cent in the 1970s. In addition to cheating people living on pensions and other fixed incomes, the erratic rises in price undermined national budgeting as well as good domestic housekeeping. Above all, they created the new post-war practice of annual trade union wage demands, the escalation of which provoked a succession of incomes policies leading to the further disruption of strikes and civic disorder. The final indictment of the Keynesian era is that so far from inflation warding off unemployment, the jobless total rose remorselessly over the economic cycle from a peak of around 300,000 after the war to above a million in the early 1970s, before hitting 3 million in the early 1980s.

Such was the price, or part of the price, paid for the appalling hubris of the 'clever sillies'.

ET TU, WILLIAM!

At least I knew of Shonfield as a deeply committed socialist intellectual, super-confident in the power of planning to transform Britain's flagging fortunes. But what was I to expect when, around 1970, a Conservative women's organisation invited me to share the platform at Caxton Hall with William Rees-Mogg, whom I then knew of only as the rather aloof, highbrow editor of *The Times*. He had a reputation for studious sophistication of manner combined with a quiet profundity of matter which had already carried him effortlessly from president of the Oxford Union to chief leader writer of the *Financial Times* and City editor of *The Sunday Times* before becoming succes- sively political and economics editor then deputy editor and finally editor of *The Times* in 1967. In those days the 'top people's paper' was still a touch too Establishment-minded for my taste, but I was attracted by the topic, which was 'The Responsible Society', and looked forward to a constructive exchange of views in a friendly atmosphere. I might have been warned when 'madam chairman' greeted Rees-Mogg warmly by his Christian name and turned to me, briskly announcing that I would speak first.

I recall setting out my standard case that a free society founded on a market economy gave the widest scope for individual and family freedom and respon- sibility, which, I always added, was thrice blessed by economic, moral and political advantages. If governments would turn from dispensing universal free benefits, they could provide more generous support for the declining minority in poverty. When Rees-Mogg's turn came, he was formally perfectly polite but made no reference to my arguments, beyond saying that although he had thought of a number of possible interpretations of the term 'responsible society', the case I presented had not been one of them. How was that for a lofty put-down? There followed an eloquent exposition of the paternalist case for the welfare state with plenty of references to compassion and other civilised values.

This story is worth telling only because a very few years later Rees-Mogg, and *The Times* under his direction, was among the leading apostles of the best of the ideas that came to be known as 'Thatcherism'. Indeed, in 1974, after the collapse of the Heath government, he wrote a marvellous slim volume assail- ing the evils of inflation under the title of *The Reigning Error*, which he exposed as a manifestation of the pervasive human tendency to push every-thing, including the money supply, to excess. His nicely chosen word was 'inordinacy', which I have since often pressed into service to drive home argu-ments against excessive government (I like to believe he would now agree that the neglect of individual responsibility has been carried to inordinate lengths in the welfare state, as in many other paternalistic policies).

KEEP SMILING

I sometimes began to wonder why I should expose myself to such mostly hostile encounters. But of course it was an essential part of my chosen work at the IEA, as a kind of missionary in a pagan land preaching the gospel accord-ing to such intellectual giants as Adam Smith, Hayek and Friedman. After all, our Keynesian tormentors were hardly to be feared as dangerous cannibals. Furthermore I could often work up my notes into articles for *The Daily Telegraph*, the *Director* or *The Spectator*.

But beyond economic motives, I must admit I mostly came to enjoy such jousts and increasingly encountered allies and, most rewarding of all, new younger converts, especially at my alma mater of Cambridge, and even at Oxford, the home of so many lost Labour intellectuals. My favourite meetings were undoubtedly at St Andrews University, where I had earlier spent seven years lecturing in the political economy department. Despite the long journey, involving an overnight stay, I seldom refused an invitation to return to address the students and was amply repaid when *The Scotsman* reported that they received every new Hobart Paper as 'an additional chapter of the Bible'. It was an added reward when that beautiful medieval university produced two very modern, enterprising graduates, Eamonn Butler and Madsen Pirie, who in 1977 created the lively Adam Smith Institute, whose work in spreading the free market message was very much complementary to that of the IEA. St Andrews also produced half a dozen young Conservative MPs to support Margaret Thatcher's free market crusade, including the outstanding Michael Forsyth, who became an impressive Secretary of State for Scotland under John Major.

Lighter relief was regularly provided in the 1970s and 1980s by debates at the Oxford and Cambridge Unions, to which circuit I came to be regularly invited. Once I had witnessed how casually the ayes and noes were sometimes counted at Oxford, I took less interest in the final vote, which was just as well since, in the pre-Thatcher era, the announced verdict usually went against my free market side. Instead, I came to relax and enjoy the high-spirited student rough-and-tumble, with constant good-natured interruptions and often hilari-ous 'points of order'. From the handbills of debates that I have kept, I am reminded that other participants over the years included a succession of trade union leaders, including Ray Buckton, Alan Sapper and David Lea. There were also plenty of livelier adversaries, including Tariq Ali, Peter Shore, Bernard Williams and Lord Soper, and a growing list of doughty allies, including Kenneth Minogue, William Hague, Geoffrey Howe, Norman Lamont, Bill Deedes, Lord (David) Young, Patrick Cosgrave, Sir Ian McGregor and John Wakeham.

The first Oxford Union debate that brought hope that the IEA view was coming into the ascendancy was the year before Margaret Thatcher won the general election of 1979. The terms of the motion could not have been more explicit: 'That a return to a free market economy would be the best solution to the British crisis'. I immediately took heart when I saw that the bumbling Lord Balogh was the main speaker on the other side, but could hardly believe the vote when it was announced by the president as: 230 in favour and 128 against. Even if the counting tended to be a little irregular, there was no disputing our overwhelming victory. From Cambridge, among the many outstanding allies I best remember were David Prior, the charming son of one of my most jolly but sceptical sparring partners, James (now Lord) Prior, and Simon Heffer, since author of many fine political biographies as well as star columnist of the *Daily Mail*.

HONOURABLE DEFEAT

Another enduring memory was of a less happy encounter with students at Exeter around 1968, though it had a happier twist some years later. After a cold train journey from London with the prospect of returning after midnight, I had to propose the motion that 'economic planning is a form of necromancy'. After verifying the dictionary definition of the key word as 'prediction by means of communication with the dead', I had leapt at the chance to instruct serious students in my established view that national planning was essentially backward-looking, being based on extrapolating past trends, and was doomed to fail. Instead of the anticipated victory, I was comprehensively trounced by around twenty-odd votes to nearer two hundred. It was an honourable defeat in so far as my tormentor was an exceptionally persuasive debater, a trained barrister, and unfailingly pleasant to boot. He was the youthful Dick (later Lord) Taverne, then a confident, well-briefed Treasury minister under Harold Wilson.

The memory of that defeat is softened by recalling my next encounter with the still-youthful Dick Taverne around 1980, when he had accepted an invitation to lunch at the IEA. Greeting him ceremoniously at the door, I cheerfully confessed shame at the memory of my total defeat at his hands. His smiling reply was along the lines of: 'No, there's no need for shame. I won the vote, but I now see you won the argument'. It is also worth noting that he coura-geously resigned and fought his constituency as an independent candidate. When freed from the Commons, he was able to do far more good, first build-ing up the Institute for Fiscal Studies, then developing the Social Democratic Party, becoming a director of many businesses, and finally joining the Lords. My only lingering regret is that, instead of joining me and the other mixed bag of independent peers on the cross-benches, he joined the Liberal Democrats, who have always struck me as not particularly liberal and too inclined to look to government as the answer to every problem.

VALEDICTION

From comfortable and contented retirement, these hard-fought battles over Keynesian inflation and collectivist planning seem a vanished era. In 1995 Tony Blair won the leadership of a 'new' Labour Party under the brave banner of 'a dynamic market economy', which even some of Margaret Thatcher's more Tory followers might have found a touch stark. In 1997 they swept John Major's government from power. Today, both main parties vie with each other in lauding choice, competition, enterprise and avoidance of higher income tax, though not (yet) lower total taxes. It is now accepted that lower inflation, though not (yet) stable money, comes before reducing unemployment. It is perhaps less widely understood that its recent achievement has depended entirely on restoring to the Bank of England the very control over monetary policy which Labour had recklessly swept away after their electoral victory in 1945.

Since the Thatcher counter-revolution, the central economic battleground has shifted – first, to the extent of Westminster and Brussels regulation and control compatible with Blair's 'dynamic economy'; and second, to the abil-ity of the British government to manage effectively its inflated range of func-tions, and to finance the mounting cost of developing welfare services, on top of a host of new 'initiatives'. The smallest budgetary setback must now risk still higher direct, indirect, central and local (and concealed) taxation that would further weaken and distort incentives to individual effort and enterprise.

As a non-economist without business experience, Tony Blair may be forgiven neglecting the probability (I would say 'certainty') that the gargan-tuan NHS, even under the masterful direction of John Reid, will eventually prove impossible to adapt to ever changing opportunities and requirements – for some of the same reasons that recently prompted Bill Gates to question whether Microsoft will survive another ten years of ceaseless global competi-tion. Likewise, rising incomes and frustrated parental aspirations are likely to overwhelm the ill-performing state schools, presided over by a combination of self-serving teachers' unions and a complacent and bloated educational bureaucracy. Like the drab council housing into which I was born almost 80 years ago, the welfare state must fail increasingly to satisfy what Adam Smith diagnosed as: 'The uniform, constant, and uninterrupted effort of every man to better his condition', and, I would add: to better the condition of his family, community and other freely chosen causes.

It is central to my philosophy that no one can be certain about the precise direction of the changes ahead. This uncertainty prompts two further questions that overhang our future: first, the pace and scale of this transformation, and second, whether its progress will be eased or obstructed by what passes as modern representative government, which finds such difficulty in restraining its incessant itch to interfere.

Meanwhile, debate has moved away from the clear-cut issue of dispersed versus centralised initiative, which has been largely won – at least in principle though not yet in practice. We are still faced with the crucial judgement of how much government regulation is consistent with continuing economic success in a global economy faced with totally unprecedented economic, social and political change. Having watched the interplay between professed political idealism and crude electioneering since 1945, I have been repeatedly reminded of Adam Smith's description of: 'that insidious and crafty animal, vulgarly called a statesman or politician, *whose councils are directed by the momentary fluctuations of affairs*' (my emphasis). And that was written in 1776, long before MPs turned professional!

We can now appreciate the huge benefit of removing monetary policy from the opportunistic control of party politicians. The signal success of this bold act of depoliticisation demonstrates the urgent need to remove schools, universities, health services, pensions and other social benefits from the present unchecked, daily electoral vote-grubbing. Since government controls inevitably grow like Topsy and bring with them more party political administration, I believe experience will increasingly demonstrate that the less we have of both the better for the true welfare of our families, the flexibility and vigour of the economy, and the health of British democracy, with individual freedom at its heart.

PART II

Papers on markets and freedom

Adam Smith: revolutionary for the third millennium?*

The full title of Adam Smith's great masterpiece is *An Inquiry into the Nature and Causes of the Wealth of Nations*, usually abbreviated as the *Wealth of Nations*. I believe it could more accurately be expanded into 'An Inquiry into the Nature and Causes of the EVER-INCREASING Wealth of Nations'. Although full of historical information, Adam Smith's study was no static or backward-looking analysis. Certainly, he explains how a British labourer in the 18th century might live better than princes in other lands and better even than kings in earlier times. But, writing at the dawn of Britain's industrial revolution, he offers the first comprehensive explanation of the continuing human forces and conditions making for what he calls 'the progress of opulence', which we would term rising standards of prosperity. Of course, we have to remember that some of his most seminal insights, however surprising to his contemporaries, might strike us today as commonsense observations. For example, in his day, free trade was regarded by a protectionist world as pure heresy.

A socialist today – if there are any still about – would certainly be astonished to hear me describe Smith as not only a progressive, but as almost a revolutionary. Yet he challenged the then prevalent mercantilist system of pervasive state control in 1776, even more fundamentally and boldly than Margaret Thatcher in 1979 confronted its contemporary manifestation 200 years later. In addition, Smith has a surprise in store for those who think of economics as a narrow materialist business. They will discover that he combined the insights, not only of world-wide history – from China to Peru, East Indies to North America, as well as ancient Greece and Rome, not forgetting the Tartars and Hottentots. He also drew on his voracious reading of philosophy, ethics, psychology, law and politics.

If that were not enough, he was an acute observer of life around him, starting among merchants in the thriving entrepôt trade of Glasgow, which was also home to one of the foremost universities of Europe. It was there that he

*   Lecture given in Prague, 1 November 2001, to celebrate the publication of the Czech language edition of *The Wealth of Nations*. Previously published in *Economic Affairs*, **22**(3), September 2002, Blackwell Publishing.

became Professor of Logic in 1751 at the age of 28 and took the Chair of Moral Philosophy the following year. His intellectual horizons were extended in 1764 when he accompanied a rich young Duke as tutor on a tour of France where he met the leaders of the Physiocrat school who believed in an uneasy combination of agricultural primacy and free trade.

Of course Smith drew on the existing literature and followed leads suggested by [David] Hume, [Francois] Quesnay, [Anne Robert Jacques] Turgot and others. But the celebrity widely accorded to Smith, even by critics, is sufficient acknowledgement of the unrivalled grandeur and comprehensive sweep of his vision.

I shall rely on extensive quotation to convey the main teachings of Adam Smith which I judge of most relevance for public policy today – in the year 2001 – and indeed for this new millennium.

DIVISION OF LABOUR

I start with the opening words of his Introduction to Chapter 1, which challenges head-on the ruling mercantilist fallacy. Remember, they thought that hoarding gold and silver was the best road to national wealth. Not so for Smith:

> [T]he annual labour of every nation is the fund which originally supplies it with all the necessaries and conveniences of life which it annually consumes, and which consists always either in the immediate produce of that labour, or in what is purchased with that produce from other nations.[1]

Thus from the very beginning, Smith lifts his eyes from the narrow nationalism of mercantilism to foreign trade and the first, early glimmerings of today's global economy.

So for Smith, the increase in national wealth therefore depends on improving the productivity of human work by the division of labour. It is a process which had developed spontaneously since the earliest days of hunting and gathering, and was discussed by Plato. But Smith gave the division of labour primary importance. He showed that industrialisation would bring ever more scope for its refinement. And so we are led to his famous illustration from pin-making. Here was a trade divided into 18 distinct operations, thereby enabling 10 men to produce an average of 4,800 pins a day, where if each laboured independently: 'they certainly could not each of them have made twenty, perhaps not one pin in a day'.[2]

Not only did each specialist worker develop great skill and dexterity, but machines could be invented to help them perform their separate, simple tasks. From such practical observation of the multiplication of output, Smith deduces two important lessons. First, the division of labour depends on the extent of the market, both domestic and overseas; and second, it promotes ever-extending trade between the products of the differing specialists. Thus with remarkable foresight, he declares that the discovery of America opened up: 'a new and inexhaustible market to all the commodities of Europe [permitting] new divisions of labour and improvements of art which, in the the narrow circle of the ancient commerce, could never have taken place'.[3] How very obvious today, but a startling vision 225 years ago.

A more remarkable prediction has been drawn to my attention by the leading American economist, Milton Friedman:

> Such has hitherto been the rapid progress of America in wealth, population, and improvement, that in the course of a little more than a century, perhaps, the produce of American might exceed that of British taxation. The seat of the empire would then naturally remove itself to that part of the empire which contributed most to the general defence and support of the whole.[4]

Friedman reports that America overtook Britain just about 100 years later.

GAINS FROM TRADE

Just as the division of labour develops spontaneously, under a system of natural liberty, without central direction, so does the consequential growth in trade. Smith then lays heavy emphasis on the mutual gains from trade between a willing buyer and a willing seller. Trade is not a zero sum game where one side benefits at the expense of the other. In all voluntary exchange, both buyer and seller must derive additional satisfaction from parting, respectively, with their money or supplies. However, this spontaneous system of social co-operation through trade, is mutually beneficial only so long as competition prevails among suppliers. After all, a central precept of Smith's system – again in contrast to producer-dominated mercantilist regimes – would carry support from every shopper:

> Consumption is the sole end and purpose of all production; and the interests of the producer ought to be attended to only so far as it may be necessary for promoting that of the consumer. The maxim is so perfectly self-evident that it would be absurd to attempt to prove it.[5]

Marxist critics of Smith as the lackey of capitalists, must have missed his repeated, trenchant attacks on monopoly. He never tires of emphasising that monopolists seek to restrict supply so as to raise prices. He talks of the 'mean rapacity, the monopolising spirit of merchants and manufacturers', and offers one of my favourite quotations as follows: 'People of the same trade seldom meet together, even for merriment and diversion, but the conversation ends in a conspiracy against the public or in some contrivance to raise prices'.[6]

From this follows his radical proposals to end all monopoly privilege and establish free, unfettered markets, including the market for labour. It was not capitalists that Smith defended, but open, competitive markets.

SELF-INTEREST

But what is the motive power that drives this division of labour and the resulting extension of trade? Smith here asserts the indispensable driving force, the lack of which goes far to explain the poverty of backward societies – like dare I say, Afghanistan:

> The uniform, constant, and uninterrupted effort of every man to better his condition, the principle from which public and national, as well as private opulence is originally derived, is frequently powerful enough to maintain the natural progress of things towards improvement, in spite both of the extravagance of government and of the greatest errors of administration.[7]

This is the famous self-interest or maximising principle which is the mainspring of individual motivation. It is easily mocked by critics as selfishness or greed, and gave rise to the caricature of 'economic man' as little more than a belly on two legs. Yet is not self-interest simply a reflection of the truism (voiced, I think, by [John Stuart] Mill) that we all generally prefer a larger to a smaller gain? Self-interest is not to be dismissed as narrow selfishness. An individual may work harder 'to better his condition' principally in order to benefit his family, his church, his neighbourhood, or any other good cause or charity he favours. Rather than 'self-interest' as the ruling motive, a better phrase which I strongly commend is 'self-chosen purposes'.

Before launching *Wealth of Nations* in 1776, Adam Smith had written a companion volume drawn from his lectures on ethics and theology. It was entitled *The Theory of the Moral Sentiments* and was published in 1759. Two brief quotations must suffice to convey its flavour: 'to feel much for others, and little for ourselves . . . to restrain our selfish, and indulge our benevolent affections, constitutes the perfection of human nature'.[8] Then, the Scotsman comes down to earth:

> The administration of the great system of the universe, however . . . is the business of God . . . To man is allotted a much humbler department, but one much more suited to the weakness of his powers, and to the narrowness of his comprehension; the care of his own happiness, of that of his family, his country . . .[9]

Scholars have debated the apparent conflict between the motive of self-interest in *Wealth of Nations* and the benevolence or sympathy of *Moral Sentiments*. The reconciliation is that most people are capable of acting from both motives, depending on the circumstances. Thus in personal dealings, fellow-feeling or benevolence may play a large, even dominant part, whereas buying and selling in the marketplace is a matter of impersonal exchange. This difference is most succinctly conveyed in *Wealth of Nations* where Smith declares that mankind: 'stands at all times in need of the co-operation and assistance of great multitudes, while his whole life is scarce sufficient to gain the friendship of a few persons'.[10]

Thus from 'the humbler department' of the *Wealth of Nations*, Smith offers one of his most celebrated supporting pronouncements:

> It is not from the benevolence of the butcher, the brewer or the baker that we expect our dinner, but from their regard to their own interest. We address ourselves, not to their humanity but to their self-love, and never talk to them of our own necessities but of their advantages.[11]

Again, how obvious!

PROPERTY RIGHTS

Of the three great forces making for prosperity (what Smith calls 'the progress of opulence'), we have discussed two: the division of labour and the individual's effort to better his condition. The third, essential ingredient is saving and investment. Indeed. Smith's emphasis on the role of capital accumulation in promoting economic progress has been described as his greatest innovation. Yet again he starts from an obvious fact that saving for investment must precede the extension of the division of labour. The key question, therefore, is how can people be encouraged to save and lend for future production? Smith's answer should hardly astonish us: 'the equal and impartial administration of justice which . . . by securing to every man the fruits of his own industry, gives the greatest and most effectual encouragement to every sort of industry'.[12]

Here is the elementary logic of secure property rights.

> The property which every man has in his own labour, as it is the original foundation of all other property, so is the most sacred and inviolable . . . to hinder him from employing his strength and dexterity in what manner he thinks proper is a plain violation of this most sacred property.[13]

Living in the great era of smuggling, Adam Smith knew that beyond some limit, taxation leads to evasion – sometimes called underground, submerged, or informal economy, or plain black markets. Naturally, the private investor will use his capital to get the best return for himself, but note carefully the following quotation:

> [H]e is in this, as in many other cases, led by an invisible hand to promote an end which was no part of his intention ... By pursuing his own interest he frequently promotes that of society more effectually than when he really intends to promote it. I have never known much good done by those who affected to trade for the public good ... [14]

In other words, that 'effort of every man to better his condition' in a competitive market, operates spontaneously to serve the public interest.

Milton Friedman has two brief quips. The first is: to do well for yourself, you have to do good for others. The second is the obverse: the Founding Fathers went to America to do good, and ended up doing well!

BEWARE OF POLITICIANS

The alternative to private investment would be to look to government – in which Smith had no great confidence, as you may judge from this quotation:

> The statesman who should attempt to direct private people in what manner they ought to employ their capitals, would not only load himself with a most unnecessary attention, but assume an authority which could safely be trusted, not only to no single person, but to no council or senate whatever, and which would nowhere be so dangerous as in the hands of a man who had the folly and presumption to fancy himself fit to exercise it.[15]

The private investor, protected by the rule of law, also takes a longer view than the short-sighted politician, whom Smith scorns as: 'that insidious and crafty animal ... whose councils are directed by the momentary fluctuations of affairs'.[16]

Evidence of this mistrust abounds throughout the *Wealth of Nations*:

> It is the highest impertinence and presumption in kings and ministers, to pretend to watch over the economy of private people ... They are themselves, always and without any exception, the greatest spendthrifts in society ... If their own extravagance does not ruin the state, that of their subjects never will.[17]

So Smith is led to recommend the abandonment of almost all mercantilist restrictions on investment, employment, production, foreign and domestic trade: That left what he upholds as:

[T]he obvious and simple system of natural liberty [whereby] every man, so long as he does not violate the laws of justice, is left perfectly free to pursue his own interest in his own way, and to bring both his industry and capital into competition with those of any other man . . . The sovereign is completely discharged from a duty, in the attempting to perform which he must always be exposed to innumerable delusions, and for the proper performance of which no human wisdom or knowledge could ever be sufficient . . .[18]

Forgive that long quotation, but it is one that should be deeply pondered at leisure. It anticipates Hayek's insight that relevant knowledge is so fragmented and widely dispersed that it can be fully brought into play only through open competitive markets. Smith, as a practical Scotsman, did not believe that his 'simple system of natural liberty' would ever be fully established this side of Utopia. He accepted, for example, that those 'insidious and crafty animals' called politicians would keep getting in the way. His optimism, nevertheless, sprang from the power of markets to overcome such obstructions: 'But though the profusion of government must, undoubtedly, have retarded the natural progress of England towards wealth and improvement, it has not been able to stop it'.[19]

He goes on:

That security which the laws in Great Britain give to every man that he shall enjoy the fruits of his own labour is alone sufficient to make any country flourish, notwithstanding . . . a hundred impertinent obstructions with which the folly of human laws too often incumbers its operations . . .[20]

Today, he would give a similar, mixed verdict on the European Union whose 'insidious and crafty' *fonctionnaires* never cease imposing thousands of 'impertinent' regulations in a dozen languages on both labour and capital. For a classical liberal like me, the special attraction of Smith's doctrine is that it presents freedom and economic growth as complementary. They go together hand-in-hand. We don't have to choose which to enjoy. Not that he deserves the accusation of supporting *laissez-faire*, which has been mocked as 'the nightwatchman state'. Indeed, in commending the 'simple system of natural liberty', he concludes by specifying three important functions for government. The first is national defence, which he declares 'is more important than opulence'. The second is the administration of justice: the duty of protecting, as far as possible, every member of the society from the injustice or oppression of every other member of it'.[21] Smith would have warned our Russian friends in 1990 that free markets don't work in a vacuum, but require a strong legal framework to guarantee safety of person and property against force and fraud.

The third duty is the provision of public works that could not be supplied privately at a profit, like roads or bridges unsuitable for toll charges. A more interesting example he suggests elsewhere is support of schools to offset the narrowing effect of boring, repetitive work under the division of labour. But, interestingly enough, while he thinks some charge on taxation would be justified for education, he specifies that part of the cost should be contributed by the family of the pupils.

SOME LESSONS FROM ADAM SMITH

Before turning to the lessons for today from *Wealth of Nations*, I must acknowledge having omitted considering more than half of Adam Smith's great work. I have said nothing about his extensive discussions of the theory of value, money, public expenditure, taxation, rent of land, which have been overtaken by later writers. But I hope I have said enough to indicate how Adam Smith's masterpiece for the first time presented a comprehensive picture of an orderly yet self-adjusting, dynamic, economic system in which rising production, employment, investment and trade were linked spontaneously together by voluntary exchange in open markets. In a sentence that Hayek liked repeating: it is the result of human action but not of human design. The economy was, in short, an integrated system of voluntary co-operation through competition. It provides, to this day, a model from which many, perhaps most, governments in this imperfect world could learn valuable lessons, not least about globalisation.

If freedom of domestic and international trade offers such promise of increasing prosperity, why can anti-globalisation protesters point to the poverty of large parts of the world? Smith's prescription of the division of labour plus every man's effort to better his condition, seems simple enough to be grasped even by the rulers of the most backward of countries. So why does the formula not work its magic in large parts of Africa and the Middle East?

The plain answer is the total absence of secure property rights. So long as a peasant or even a rich man in Afghanistan or Palestine has no assurance of safety for his person, his family or their possessions, how can he be expected to apply himself to work, save or invest for the future? The contrasting model is Hong Kong. Here a barren rock, with no natural resources, has developed from providing wages of a bowl-of-rice-a-day to providing a European standard of living to a population that has grown more than ten-fold within my lifetime. Similar success has been reaped by secure property rights and free markets in the other 'tiger economies'. Taiwan, for example, with an identical workforce to mainland China, provides a standard of living ten, twenty, or more times as high.

Free trade is the nearest we have to a panacea for world poverty – by spreading access to the uneven bounty of what I persist in calling God's creation. Any country with a stable government that can guarantee foreign investors a safe haven will not long lack a flow of inward investment. If backward countries wish to accelerate the process, let them also keep taxes low and attract multinational companies to come and educate their workforce for the division of labour, as enlightened capitalists did in 19th century England.

Therefore, let the anti-global demonstrators return home and shout at their own governments, preferably giving their backward politicians a copy of this lecture! All that is necessary, in modern terminology, is to move towards a competive market economy, with limited government which will enforce a legal framework designed to guarantee property rights and personal safety, enforce contracts and prevent force or fraud.

Unfortunately, against the ignorant slogans of the anti-capitalist demonstrators, capitalism does not have effective public relations officers. Worse still, many European governments understand so little that they appease their consciences by increasing their foreign aid budgets without requiring the recipient governments to help themselves by turning towards the market. That is simply a short-sighted policy of subsiding continued backwardness forever.

FREE TO CHOOSE

Since the end of the last great war in 1945, the search for economic growth has driven developed and developing countries to reduce tariff and non-tariff barriers to imports by up to 90%. On one calculation, the resulting 20-fold increase in world trade has been the motor for an 8-fold increase in global wealth.

Consider some of the boons of the global economy as follows. One-tenth of the world's population now travel between two or more countries every year. In five years, the time spent on international telephone calls more than doubled from half a billion hours to over one billion hours. In constant 1990 prices, the cost of a 3-minute call from New York to London fell from almost $250 in 1930 to nearer $50 in 1960, to 1/3rd of a dollar in 1999.

The increase in world trade masks a massive change in its content. So far from the developed world raping the less developed countries of their raw materials, in 1965 85% of exports from LDCs were commodities, while 30 years later, 70% were manufactured goods. Where did they get the capital? By 1997, foreign direct investment leapt to $400 billion, which was 14 times the amount in real terms 20 years earlier.

Anti-capitalist agitators like to dwell on remaining poverty. Alas, there are no such precise ways of measuring the transformation in the diets, education, health, homes of that growing part of the world's population which has brought itself within what I would call the irrigation system of international trade based on Adam Smith's domestic and geographical division of labour.

And this benign process is far from ended. Above all, trade brings people and nations together in free and peaceful association, as indicated by my final quotation from Adam Smith: 'Were all nations to follow the liberal system of free exportation and free importation, the different states into which a great continent was divided would so far resemble the different provinces of a great empire'. [22]

My final words are a brief, constructive warning to the Taliban's successors, and all similar regimes in Asia, the Middle East and Africa. They all have a clear choice. Of course, the prospect of economic development must threaten disturbance, even the disruption of prevailing modes of life. Adam Smith understood that back in 1776 when he urged that free trade should be introduced by 'slow gradations' so as to ease the discomfort. But if countries – or groups of individuals – or religious sects – freely choose to persist with ancient ways, they must not blame anyone else that the 'Wealth of Nations' will continue to pass them by.

NOTES

1.   *The Wealth of Nations,* Everyman's Library, Introduction, p. 1.
2.   Ibid., Book I, chapter I, p. 5.
3.   Ibid., Book IV, chapter 1, p. 392.
4.   Ibid., Book IV, chapter VII, pp. 560–61.
5.   Ibid., Book IV, chapter VIII, p. 594.
6.   Ibid., Book I, chapter X, p. 116.
7.   Ibid., Book II, chapter III, p. 306.
8.   *The Theory of the Moral Sentiments,* Part I, section II, Adam Smith Institute online edition.
9.   Ibid., Part VI, section II.
10. *The Wealth of Nations*, Book I, chapter II, p. 13.
11. Ibid., Book I, chapter II, p. 13.
12. Ibid., Book IV, chapter VII, Part 3.
13. Ibid., Book I, chapter X, p. 109.
14. Ibid., Book IV, chapter II, p. 399.
15. Ibid., Book IV, chapter II, p. 399.
16. Ibid., Book IV, chapter II, pp. 410–11.
17. Ibid., Book II, chapter III, p. 309.
18. Ibid., Book IV, chapter IX, p. 620.
19. Ibid., Book II, chapter III, p. 309.
20. Ibid., Book IV, chapter V, p. 479.
21. Ibid., Book IV, chapter IX, p. 620.
22. Ibid., Book IV, chapter V, p. 477.

Hayek: the arch radical reactionary?*

It is no conventional courtesy to declare my sense of the double honour, first, in coming as a pilgrim to this internationally-acclaimed academy, and second, in helping to celebrate the life, learning and influence of F.A. Hayek. In a half-century of acquaintance with leading economists I have gathered a goodly half-dozen to my private pantheon of personal heroes. They are – apart from Milton Friedman – naturally English-born friends: Lionel Robbins, John Jewkes, Stanley Dennison, Graham Hutton, Arthur Seldon, Ronald Coase. But none I believe would grudge my giving pride of place to a naturalised Briton, known best to us all as Fritz Hayek, as mentor and model. He was a hero truly worthy of hero-worship. He was not just a man of the century, but like Adam Smith, he was a giant for all times. Expect from me, therefore, no clinical, academic assessment of his extensive library of publications. Instead, I offer the reflections and recollections of a modest disciple.

HAYEK, INTELLECTUALS AND SOCIALISM

I envy the student who comes for the first time to Hayek's seminal essay 'The Intellectuals and Socialism', first published half a century ago in *The University of Chicago Law Review* (Spring 1949). Its central lesson was the crucial influence of intellectuals in shaping public opinion and policy. In part, it echoed the closing words of his great antagonist, J.M. Keynes:

> [T]he ideas of economists and political philosophers, both when they are right and when they are wrong, are more powerful than is commonly understood. Indeed, the world is ruled by little else. Practical men, who believe themselves to be quite exempt from any intellectual influences, are usually the slaves of some defunct economist . . . The power of vested interests is vastly exaggerated compared with the gradual encroachment of ideas. (*The General Theory of Employment, Interest and Money*, New York: Macmillan, 1957, p. 383)

Hayek's judgement on ideas a dozen years later was remarkably similar: 'It is no exaggeration to say that, once the more active part of the intellectuals has

---

* Lecture given at the University of Chicago, November 1999, to celebrate the centenary of Hayek's life: 1899–1999.

been converted to a set of beliefs, the process by which these become generally accepted is almost automatic and irresistible'. ('The intellectuals and
socialism', *University of Chicago Law Review*, Spring 1949, p. 421)

In Hayek's more penetrating analysis, intellectuals are not generally original thinkers. They need not even be particularly intelligent. In fact, for reasons
he diligently analyses, he lumps together teachers, journalists, broadcasters,
preachers, commentators and other motley opinion-formers as 'professional
second-hand dealers in ideas'. Where Keynes was obsessed with short-term,
superficial, political panaceas for unemployment, Hayek's life-time's work
was to win the allegiance of the leading ideas merchants for his permanent
vision of spontaneous co-operation between free individuals.

'The Intellectuals and Socialism' was published in 1949 when Hayek was
already 50. It is no exaggeration to say that the next four decades of Hayek's
long life were single-mindedly, almost daily, dedicated to showing that the
market provided a method that worked better than planning because it alone
could harness all the energies and knowledge of free, creative men and
women. Through his writings, the founding of the Mont Pèlerin Society in
1947, and inspiring the creation of the Institute of Economic Affairs in 1955
as the first of his 'think tanks', he led a counter-revolution to spread this
elevated conception of a society of free individuals founded on an open,
competitive economy. His battle plan ignored the pessimists who feared that
democracy made a free economy no longer possible. His war aim was nothing
less than making politically acceptable what was then thought to be politically
impossible.

After his earlier abstract writings on capital theory and the trade cycle, *The
Road to Serfdom* can now be seen as Hayek's opening barrage in a battle for
intellectual converts. It remains his most celebrated work, though, by design,
not the most sophisticated. It was a challenging, polemical tract dedicated
provocatively: 'To socialists of all parties'. Published in London in March
1944 (and the following year by Chicago University Press), it was an immediate best-seller. Half a century later, it will still be familiar to some of you
here as a powerful, urgent, war-time warning that socialism is not only inefficient in production, obstructive of economic progress, and based on a
misjudgement of human nature; but, above all, it is of necessity lethal to individual freedom. Furthermore, however well-intentioned its practitioners – in
all parties, remember – socialism is driven increasingly towards the abyss of
totalitarianism.

Winston Churchill was so impressed by the powerful analysis that he
opened the general election campaign in 1945 with a radio broadcast warning
voters that socialism is 'inseparably interwoven with . . . the abject worship of
the state'. He concluded that, if Labour won, it would need 'some form of
Gestapo, no doubt very humanely directed in the first instance'. The Labour

leader, the mild Clement Attlee (whom Churchill had described as 'a sheep in sheep's clothing') made a dismissive reply placing heavy stress on 'von Hayek' to emphasise Hayek's foreign origins – although he had adopted British citizenship in 1938. Labour's most brazen reply was that national planning had won the war and was now necessary to win the peace. Alas! the Conservatives lacked the wit to draw on Hayek to explain that war provides the over-riding criterion – that of fighting capacity – to guide the allocation of resources; and at the same time war justifies the use of conscription, direction of labour, rationing of food, confiscatory taxation, and the suspension of civil liberties. War, indeed, is the true model of a socialist economy.

It was all too much for the British public, basking in victory over Germany and accustomed to regard communist Russia as their ally, along with capitalist America. The result was that not only did the Tories lose the election, but Hayek lost his scholarly reputation, and many teachers were led to ignore altogether his more academic works. In retirement years later in *Hayek on Hayek*, he recalled the 'incredible abuse' he experienced, before summing up: 'In the middle-1930s – I suppose this sounds very conceited – I think I was known as one of two main disputing economists: there was Keynes and there was I. Now Keynes died and became a saint; and I discredited myself by publishing *The Road to Serfdom* . . .'.

For those who can't wait for happy endings, let me add that by the time Hayek spoke those words, Keynes had been, not so much discredited, as more or less forgotten; while Hayek had been awarded the Nobel Prize in economics in 1974, and lived to see his central critique dramatically vindicated by the collapse of what he called 'hot socialism' and the lifting of the iron curtain. Nevertheless, it was not only for students with socialist preconceptions that Hayek could be painted an arch 'reactionary'. His credentials as the Prince of Darkness can be found scattered through his extensive writings and published conversations. It would be crudely selective but hardly a travesty to say that Hayek championed private property rights while opposing trade union monopoly; he was unenthusiastic about 'democracy' but cheerfully supported what are called 'inequalities' of income and wealth. Not least, he rejected absolutely 'social justice', favoured low taxation and opposed the welfare state.

I recall Hayek in action at the St Andrews University meeting of the MPS in 1976 to mark the bicentenary of *The Wealth of Nations*. I vividly recall this mild, scholarly, stooping figure rising from the audience to announce – with one of his wintry smiles – that he had taken up the study of economics in Vienna in 1918 because he shared the prevailing Fabian hope of thereby finding answers to the haunting questions of poverty. With the chairman's permission, he invited a show of hands and smiled more expansively when it revealed quite a number of senior MPS members prepared to confess to a similar, youthful, socialist indiscretion. Students familiar with *The Fatal Conceit* (1988) should hardly be surprised by Hayek's confession of early hopes and subsequent apostasy. In *The Fatal Conceit*, he analyses the warm social instincts deeply embedded in our psyche, which hark back to primitive tribes of hunter-gatherers where co-operation and sharing was necessary for collective security and individual survival. With the spontaneous development of the 'extended market order' – depending on the division of labour, international trade and remote impersonal relationships – the trouble is that: 'our daily lives and the pursuit of most occupations, give little satisfaction to the deep-seated, altruistic desires to do visible good'.

Perhaps Hayek here did not sufficiently allow that the growing preoccupation with commerce in 18th and 19th century Britain did not prevent the truly remarkable, spontaneous upsurge of philanthropy in private schools, hospitals, almshouses, etc., which has since been partly crowded-out by the heavy hand of taxation and the welfare state.

Nevertheless, there remains on Hayek's showing in most human breasts an innate hankering after what his LSE colleague, Lionel (later Lord) Robbins once mocked as 'the joys of tribal unity'. It helps to account for the distaste even capitalists sometimes express for capitalism. It helps to account for the common schizophrenia which induces guilt feelings among the rich, so that even the most hard-boiled of market men can feel a warm, self-indulgent glow of satisfaction in making a generous gesture of support for some dubious project in the – equally dubious – name of 'public interest'. It is certainly not only socialists who may wish – in more reflective moods – that there existed a gentler alternative to what critics relish denouncing as 'cut-throat competition'.

I challenge anyone to show me a passage in Hayek which commends the competitive market, the central feature of capitalism, as an intrinsically attractive institution. He acknowledges that efficient incentives and rewards often offend our sense of justice. Compared with the clamour of the derivatives market or a contested take-over, or the need to 'downsize' the labour force, who would not prefer the relaxed fellowship of the golf club or competitive sports to a tough, competitive market? The devil of it is that while such amiable, face to face cooperation has an indispensable place in what [Wilhelm] Röpke called 'the humane society', it cannot be effectively harnessed to direct and energise a complex modern economy – Hayek's 'extended market order'.

I'm inclined to surmise that Hayek discarded his youthful socialist sentiments with the same reluctance he plainly evinces in rejecting his parents' religion. In both religion and socialism he sympathises with believers and readily acknowledges their good intentions. But while he dismisses socialism on grounds of logic – that it is demonstrably wrong – he takes refuge in suspended judgement on religion until, he says, someone can 'give a reasonable explanation of what is meant by the word "God" '. In *The Fatal Conceit*, the Introduction is headed: 'Was Socialism a Mistake?'. Hayek's case is that socialism must fail not because particular plans are imperfect, but because it is predicated on what he calls a 'factual error', namely the assumption that even the most perfect plan could ever conceivably embody and integrate the comprehensive, dispersed, up-to-the-minute data necessary for success. We are back to 1936 and his seminal Presidential Address to the London Economic Club, entitled 'Economics and Knowledge', reinforced by his various essays on the impossibility of 'socialist calculation'. His valediction on socialism may be thought chilling: 'despite being inspired by good intentions and led by some of the most intelligent representatives of our time, [it] endangers the standard of living and the life itself of a large proportion of our existing population'.

Is that judgement too cataclysmic? It's one thing to say socialism reduces standards of living, but does it really end up increasing the death rate? Let doubters dip into the extensive writings of Hayek's friend from the LSE, Peter (Lord) Bauer, who analyses the chronic disasters caused by the suppression of price and choice by socialist planning in the undeveloped economies of Africa. If that smacks too much of theory, I have in a manner of speaking proof from beyond the grave. It comes from the obituaries on Julius Nyerere, the former President of Tanzania. He appears to have been an unusual politician, one of transparent integrity and honesty, as befitted a devout Roman Catholic. Yet the headline in the London *Daily Telegraph* described him as the man who 'with the best intentions brought his country to its knees by imposing socialism'. From being a prosperous exporter of food, Tanzania was reduced to starvation and abject dependence on foreign aid by Nyerere's collective farms, state marketing boards and wholesale nationalisation. His political legacy was a one-party state, a corrupt political elite, the suppression of strikes, suspension of habeas corpus and imprisonment of opponents without trial. It was the African fulfilment of the socialist road to serfdom.

How much poverty, starvation and death might have been avoided if Nyerere had been advised by the wisdom of Hayek rather than by the conventional macro-muck of 'development economists' like the Swedish Gunnar Myrdal. The bitter irony was that when Hayek was named Nobel Laureate in 1974, he shared the honour with none other than Myrdal. The presumed reason was that the Swedish judges wished to honour one of their own countrymen, and thought to divert suspicion by including his ideological opposite. Bearing in mind that they were later to anoint [Milton] Friedman, [James] Buchanan, [George] Stigler, [Ronald] Coase, [Gary] Becker, it is more plausible that they chose Hayek on his undoubted merits but threw in a left-wing Swede to dilute political criticism. That grim example of Tanzania sharpens Hayek's verdict on markets as a 'discovery procedure' which are even more important in backward countries, where it has been inactive, in order 'to discover yet unknown opportunities'.

THE MEANING OF COMPETITION

Under the malignant influence of Joan Robinson and others, critics of markets were obsessed with what they saw as the ubiquitous problem of monopoly. Let me confess that at my alma mater of Cambridge, England after 1945, many able students of economics left full of elementary textbook nonsense about 'perfect competition' versus monopoly, duopoly, oligopoly, among other now forgotten phantoms. From my student recollection, pretty well everything was either 'assumed' or 'given'. Thus all industries were composed of a large number of single-line firms, producing a homogeneous product, with unchanging techniques, for consumers with known and unchanging preferences. It was by appeal to this abstract model that enemies of private enterprise were able to scorn such competitive realities as advertising, marketing, product development and differentiation.

None of this mischievous nonsense could survive exposure to Hayek's lecture at Princeton on 'The Meaning of Competition' (reproduced in *Individualism and Economic Order*, 1949). This is vintage Hayek, deploying intricate and subtle analysis to support such simple, commonsense conclusions as the following:

> [T]he state of affairs assumed by the theory of perfect competition . . . would not only deprive of their scope all the activities which the verb 'compete' describes, but would make them virtually impossible . . . In fact, this moving force of economic life is left almost undiscussed.

So far from being able to rely on given and constant data, 'The solution of the economic problem of society is . . . always a voyage of exploration into the unknown . . . because all economic problems are created by unforeseen changes'.

There follows a foretaste of his revelatory essay on 'Competition as a Discovery Procedure': 'the starting point of the theory of competitive equilibrium assumes away the main tasks which only the process of competition can solve'. Indeed, Hayek's 'discovery procedure' is the precise opposite of given data.

Finally, come some robust digs at supporters of so-called 'public enterprise':

> Enthusiasm for perfect competition in theory and support of monopoly in practice

are, indeed, surprisingly often found to live together . . . The current tendency in discussion is to be intolerant about the imperfections and to be silent about the prevention of competition . . . Much more serious than the fact that prices may not correspond to marginal cost is the fact that, with entrenched monopoly, costs are likely to be much higher than is necessary.

I sometimes plagiarise Hayek in patiently explaining that our main difference with collectivists in all parties is their claim to know answers which we believe can be established only through the ceaseless exploratory processes of competitive markets. Take *Fatal Conceit* (1988) – which I have described, with I hope pardonable hyperbole, as Hayek's crowning work – the very title more or less says it all. There's the conceit:

- 'that man is able to shape the world around him according to his wishes . . .';
- 'that only those moral rules are valid which reason endorses';
- that no single intelligence can grasp the complex phenomenon of the 'extended order' which depends on the evolution of moral rules handed on by tradition, including private property, contract, exchange, honesty, trade, etc.;
- that 'such rules spread, not by reason, but because they enabled those practising them to survive and flourish'.

For Hayek: 'all evolution rests on competition; and continuing competition is necessary even to preserve existing achievements'. It is this conceit – this 'pretence to knowledge' – by socialist intellectuals which prevents them from acknowledging any limits to the rule of reason.

One of Hayek's favourite maxims, drawn from Smith's contemporary, Adam Ferguson is that: 'The market is the result of human action but not of human design'.

Here and elsewhere, Hayek induces in perceptive readers a sense of wonderment at how much the prosperity and order we take for granted owes to the spontaneous operation of even imperfect markets. I have repeatedly shocked Bishops in the Anglican church by repeating – as a humble second-hand dealer in ideas – something along the lines that the laws of supply and demand are the nearest we have in the social sciences to the God-given laws of gravity and motion in the physical sciences. Pondering the 'extended order', I have come increasingly to assert that a country's prosperity depends little on indigenous supplies of natural resources, labour or capital, but on unfettered freedom to work and invest within a framework of law based on evolved morals. Given security of person and property, including safety from excessive depredations of taxation, all the remaining requirements for development can be 'bought in', so to speak, by international trade, migration and global capital markets. Where barren Hong Kong, bereft of natural resources, has developed the right framework for prosperity; not even the best endowed African country has approached its success.

HAYEK AND CONSERVATISM

After Hayek's assault and battery against socialism, we can understand why he is easily characterised as a conservative, if not the full-blown reactionary of my provocative title. I now turn to showing that any such picture is not merely lop-sided but a caricature of his elegant philosophical equilibrium. The evidence is best paraded in a beautiful essay: 'Why I am not a Conservative', first published as an appendix to the *Constitution of Liberty* in 1960. No doubt it spoke especially powerfully to me since as a young university lecturer in 1951 and again in 1955 I stood for Parliament on a Liberal–Conservative platform. Mercifully, I failed both times and by 1960 was struggling to go straight developing with Arthur Seldon the Institute of Economic Affairs, as an independent, not-for-profit 'think tank'. To this day, I still encounter residual resistence to accepting the full, austere rigour of Hayek's pure liberal or, as he prefers, 'Whig' heterodoxy.

While Hayek is prepared to make common cause with conservatives in opposing socialism, his decisive divergence from them is that they have little vision beyond defending the status quo, including the established authorities, against the uncertain impact of change. In contrast, liberals cannot be content with preserving things as they are, when what is required in most countries is 'a thorough sweeping-away of the obstacles to free growth'. In magisterial style, Hayek declares: 'the chief need is once more, as it was at the beginning of the nineteenth century, to free the processes of spontaneous growth from the obstacles and encumbrances that human folly has erected'.

In this work of demolition, our radical reactionary does not despair of winning support from those who by disposition are 'progressives'. After all, unlike many conservatives, their minds are at least open to the need for change. True, conservative philosophers have celebrated the spontaneous growth of such institutions as language, law, morals and conventions, but their admiration for free growth generally applies only to the past. They lack the courage and confidence to welcome further undesigned developments – 'to let change run its course'. Not for them Hayek's trust that in the economic sphere the self-regulating forces of the market will: 'somehow bring about the required adjustments to new conditions, although no one can foretell how they will do this in a particular instance'.

For conservatives wedded to familiar ways, Hayek must appear, not so much a radical, as a reckless revolutionary, prepared to embark on uncharted seas. Such a leap in the dark would be unthinkable for traditional European Continental conservatives with their customary devotion to security and authority. This acceptance of freedom as a governing principle means tolerating things we dislike. It means, even on issues we regard as fundamental, allowing others to pursue different ends. It follows that neither moral nor religious ideals are proper objects of coercion; that conduct of which we disapprove – so long as it does not directly interfere with what he calls 'the protected sphere of others' – does not justify prohibition. The acid test of liberalism is 'opposition to all arbitrary power'; its aim the minimisation of coercion.

It has to be said that Hayek professes no exaggerated belief in democracy, beyond its ability 'to vote the rascals out'. He acknowledges that the extension of the franchise has led to the danger of unlimited government. At the risk of special pleading as a full-frontal, self-confessed pipe-smoker – like Hayek in his middle years – I would underline a passage from 'Individualism: True and False' where he names as 'one of the most important questions' for political theory, that of finding: 'a line of demarcation between the fields in which the majority views must be binding for all, and the fields in which . . . the minority view ought to be allowed to prevail'.

Turning back to 'Why I am not a Conservative', Hayek insists that the true evil is not democracy but unlimited government. Then comes an unusually optimistic sentence: 'I do not see why the people should not learn to limit the scope of majority rule . . . in order to secure the advantages of democracy as a method of peaceful change and of political education'. At first, I was tempted to scoff. But is it, I wonder, so fanciful to think that even since Hayek's death in 1992, the 'invisible hand' of globalisation is already beginning to reverse the previously unchecked growth of government?

My ever-fertile colleague, Arthur Seldon, argues there are already half-a-dozen escapes from over-government. The black, or underground, or – more neutral – 'parallel economy' has long obscured the difference between 'avoidance' and 'evasion' of tax – into what he has christened 'avoision'. In his recent *The Dilemma of Democracy*, Seldon elaborates how the 'rejection of government' is being increasingly facilitated by major developments. First, there's rapidly rising high incomes which permit more consumers to choose private services in preference to so-called 'free' state education and health care. Then there's the new 'domestic system', that is the return to working at home, and the spread of less controllable self-employment and small businesses. And finally, there's the spectacular explosion of electronic money, and the approaching infinity of the internet, with its ultimately ungovernable, because untraceable, world-wide, private contacts and transactions.

Yet for all his radicalism, Hayek claims respectful kinship with [Alexis de] Tocqueville, [Edmund] Burke, [Lord] Acton, whom many card-carrying

Conservatives like to claim as their own. And so we come to Hayek's true love affair with these giants as Whigs – or to be more precise 'Old Whigs' – a name which the sometimes unworldly Hayek seriously toyed with reviving to describe supporters now variously called 'conservatives' (in America), 'liberals (with a small 'l' in Britain), 'Austrians' outside Austria, or – for younger, bolder apostles – 'libertarians'. Such was Hayek's veneration for Acton and Tocqueville that in 1947 he proposed giving their joint names to what became the international Mont Pèlerin Society.

Perhaps my favourite Hayek quotation from *Individualism: True and False* (1945) runs as follows:

> The main merit of the individualism which Adam Smith and his contemporaries advocated is that it is a system under which bad men can do least harm. It is a social system which does not depend for its functioning on our finding good men for running it, or on all men becoming better than they now are, but which makes use of men in all their given variety and complexity, sometimes good and sometimes bad, sometimes intelligent and more often stupid. (p 11–12)

Here Hayek quotes Acton: 'The danger is not that a particular class is unfit to govern. Every class is unfit to govern. The law of liberty tends to abolish the reign of race over race, of faith over faith'.

In conclusion, I return briefly to my opening discussion of the role of ideas in 'The Intellectuals and Socialism'. There can be no doubt of the decisive influence on Margaret Thatcher – both at first and (through Keith Joseph) second-hand – of Hayek's teaching, powerfully complemented by the unique wit and wisdom of merry Milton Friedman. In the busy task of liberalising the sclerotic British economy, Margaret Thatcher found time to recommend his name to the Queen for the rare distinction of Companion of Honour. Then on his 90th birthday in May 1989, she wrote to him in Freiburg: 'None of it would have been possible without the values and beliefs to set us on the right path . . . The leadership and inspiration that your work and thinking gave us were absolutely crucial and we owe you a great debt'.

Nevertheless, for all the transformation wrought by Margaret Thatcher in the 1980s, Hayek's goal remains far from fulfilled even in Britain, especially in state welfare and regulation. He would urge that the case against state monopoly supply and captive consumers is as strong in education and health care as it would be in, say, computers and holidays. Few can doubt that, as incomes continue to rise, expanding demand for welfare must burst the shackles of state finance before the new millennium is far spent. Long-run market forces are undoubtedly on our side. Socialism must eventually lose to individual self-fulfilment. Scholars who wish to speed that day might pause in their multiplication of footnotes, and periodically refresh themselves and their students with the idealism of Hayek's original call to arms in 'The Intellectuals and Socialism': 'The main lesson which the true liberal must learn from the success of the socialists is that it was their courage to be Utopian which gained them the support of the intellectuals and therefore an influence on public opinion'.

In even more stirring terms, he wrote in the *Chicago Law Review* half a century ago: 'we must be able to offer a new liberal programme which appeals to the imagination. We must make the building of a free society once more an intellectual adventure, a deed of courage'.

Back to Hayek's faithful missionaries at the Institute of Economic Affairs, in the published collection of essays to which my colleague Arthur Seldon and I gave the bold title *Radical Reaction*, we argued that a healthy approach for classical liberals was: 'To be conservative about the principles of a free society, but radical about the measures necessary to ensure its dynamic operation and continuing evolution'.

The challenge of a radical reactionary*

Although I sit on the cross-benches in the Lords, I am delighted to appear on a platform sponsored by the Centre for Policy Studies. As I understand it, the Centre's purpose is to enliven the pragmatic Conservative tradition by exposing it to intellectual fermentation. If you think some of my strictures rather pointed, don't take them too personally. Imagine I am addressing some high Tory paladin to whom I might refer from time to time symbolically as, say, Perry.

The Centre was created in 1974, not before time, on the morrow of the well-merited collapse of Mr Heath's Government. Tory apologists for convenient compromise have long loved to denounce theory as ideology, dogma, or even theology. Its ancestral voices prefer to boast of practical judgement, realism, deciding issues on their merits, maintaining balance, defending the mixed economy, dare I say the middle way?

NEGLECT OF INTELLECTUALS

Yet the Conservative Party – or its Whig predecessors – were not always hostile to intellectuals. Witness the influence of Edmund Burke, David Hume and Adam Smith on the nineteenth century policies of both parties. Over the past century suspicion of intellectuals may be more understandable: the dominant trend was set by Marxists, Fabians, pseudo-Keynesians, Beveridgeites or other carriers of collectivism. Lacking any distinctive theory of economic or social policy, Conservatives failed to join the intellectual battle and fell back into a rear-guard action of slowing the pace of unwelcome socialism. More shamefully, the nominally Liberal Party, especially after 1905, abandoned its historic role as guardian of the classical philosophy of individual freedom in a vain effort to ingratiate itself with the emerging trade unions, leaving no principled opposition to the cumulative encroachment of state power over the lives, liberties, incomes and property of the citizens.

The progressive victory by intellectuals of the Left which accelerated after 1945 bears testimony to Keynes's judgement that it is ideas rather than vested

* First published by the Centre for Policy Studies, East Sussex: Strange the Printer, March 1980.

interests that rule the world: 'Practical men who believe themselves exempt from any intellectual influences are usually the slaves of some defunct economist'. In a reference that would seem to anticipate Wedgwood Benn, Keynes continued: 'Madmen in authority, who hear voices in the air, are distilling their frenzy from some academic scribbler of a few years back'. He concluded: 'I am sure that the power of vested interests is vastly exaggerated compared with the gradual encroachment of ideas'.

Please note, my dear Perry, the argument is not that Conservatives should defer to intellectuals because that motley crew possess special scholarship, knowledge or even intelligence – in all of which some of them are sadly deficient. Intellectuals are not predominantly seminal thinkers, like Adam Smith, Keynes himself, Hayek or even Marx. They are mostly what Hayek called 'second-hand dealers in ideas'. Their importance stems simply from their roles as writers, teachers, preachers, broadcasters, producers, in spreading ideas until they come to dominate popular opinion.

Yet it is not surprising that the general run of intellectuals has been drawn towards collectivist ideas. Teachers and journalists are recruited from people who preferred not to go into trade or industry. You may recall the quip: Those who can, do; those who can't, teach!

For such unworldly people, at least until recently, visionary speculations about transforming society were bound to have a stronger appeal than appearing to defend the establishment or, at best, seeking piecemeal reform. The less detailed knowledge a teacher or writer or artist has, the more easily he will fall for 'planning', social engineering and specious proposals for restructuring industry – or indeed the world.

There are two less reputable reasons why intellectuals have erred towards collectivism. The first is that the tightening grip of government control naturally holds less terror for most elites who see themselves as controllers rather than controlled. The second reason is that it takes more subtlety and more humility to grasp the Smithian concept of spontaneous coordination through the market system – or the Hayekian insight of the market as a discovery procedure – than to suppose that order and progress can be imposed by able and well-meaning people – such as they imagine themselves to be.

CONSERVATIVE COLLECTIVISM

We should not therefore be surprised that Conservative leaders since Baldwin have most often scorned intellectuals – usually lumped together as 'socialist intellectuals'. This myopia helps explain an otherwise baffling paradox. As collectivist ideas have increasingly shaped policy and institutions under Liberal, Labour and Conservative administrations since, at least, the early years of this century, Conservatives have found themselves drawn deeper and wider into defending socialist collectivism as part of the established order.

In other words, as the collectivist cancer took stronger hold on the mixed economy, the consensus broadly upheld by all 'serious' politicians, moved even further to the Left – until it seemed natural to all but cranks at fringe meetings that governments made up of people who have never run a whelk stall should casually dispose at weekly cabinet meetings of more than half the national income.

The Conservative Party's unprincipled compromise with collectivism was aided by several strands in the Tory tradition. In the first place, all good Tories believe as you and I do Perry – in *strong* governmental authority. This desideratum of effective administration is too easily confused with *big* government – which is quite different, and beyond some point in conflict with strong government. Secondly, Tories believe – as we do – in national strength and patriotism. Alas, as with the mercantilists, though with less reason, Conservatives have often confused national power with protectionism and planning, which weakens economic efficiency and progress on which power and influence abroad ultimately depend. Finally, Tories traditionally incline – as you do Perry – towards paternalism. This well-intentioned self-indulgence makes it easy to confuse a generous disposition towards personal, voluntary charity, with a state-enforced duty to pay for so-called social welfare by taxation that lacks the moral merit of free will and undermines individual self-help and responsibility.

PRIVATE PROPERTY IS NOT ENOUGH

It remains true that Conservative rhetoric has always preferred 'private enterprise' to state industry. But more acquaintance with economic theory would have taught them that there is no social virtue in privately-owned firms unless they operate in a competitive market economy. It is the market which gives the consumer sovereignty, and competition which acts as an invisible hand to convert private profit-seeking into a search for better ways of serving the general interest of consumers.

Conservatives have suffered electorally by being branded as defenders of the profit system. Yet they have often been prevented – are you there Perry? – by snobbish contempt for trade from championing the market economy as the only system that can be relied on to benefit both the producer and the customers. Why would willing buyers and willing sellers come together in voluntary exchange unless there were mutual gains to be had from trade? In a competitive economy there is no conflict between 'production for profit' and 'production for use': profitability is the measure of the usefulness of social output judged by individuals spending their own money.

Although Conservatives defend private property – rightly – as buttressing political independence, they lack an economic theory of property rights. Yet the classical theory is available to show how a competitive market economy can provide the structure of incentives and penalties that will check the possible abuse of the power that private property confers.

Nor is it only Conservatives who have failed to understand and exploit the truth that the most extensive property right is not capital, land or even home ownership but labour. Ponder the eighteenth century periods of Adam Smith:

> The property which every man has to his own labour, as it is the original foundations of all other property, so it is the most sacred and inviolable . . . to hinder a man from employing his strength and dexterity in what manner he thinks proper without injury to his neighbour is plain violation of his most sacred property.

Had Conservatives grasped that central truth, they could hardly have waited so long before attempting to redress the gross privileges of trade unions that have shifted the property rights in labour so far away from the worker and towards those leaders who exercise the corporate power of the union for their own political or personal interests.

FALLACY OF CONSENSUS AND MIXED ECONOMY

Conservatives have often been led by national sentiment to claim that cooperation and consensus are preferable to competition and conflict, and have sometimes even flirted with corporatism – collusion between Government and what Keith Middlemas[1] called 'oligarchic interest groups' such as the CBI and TUC. They have failed to see that fashionable consensus is no more than a complicity of ruling elites in growing government, taxation, bureaucratic trade union power that the majority resent or reject. They have failed to grasp that a market economy is the only method by which complex societies can practise fruitful cooperation between millions of free consumers and hundreds of thousands who serve them in competing for their custom, guided spontaneously and harmoniously by changes in relative prices (including wages) established in a competitive market economy.

So my dear Perry, I come to the main burden of my charge against the Conservatives: intellectual failure. Lacking any coherent, distinctive economic theory, too many Conservatives have failed to understand that the mixed economy is not a stable equilibrium that will obligingly stay put while the two parties dispute who can run it more efficiently. Since 1900 there has been a cumulative progressive shift away from dispersed private initiative and individual responsibility.

The danger for you Conservatives who generally feel more at home with conventional orthodoxy is that you begin to defend the mixed-up economy compounded of conflicting principles as though you really believed in it. The trouble with social democracy is not that it is half right but that it is all wrong. It is wrong, not least, in its belief that government can have the power and knowledge to shape the economy and society to its benign purposes, without mounting coercion that threatens democracy itself. That is why Wedgwood Benn is logically driven towards the Eastern European model of 'people's democracy'.

Let me admit that the Conservatives have been at a disadvantage in combating the ratchet effect of ever-increasing socialism. For example, in two of the worst afflictions of our economy – rent control and state industry – Labour opportunism in opposition can paralyse Conservative reform or make it more difficult by threatening to reverse decontrol or denationalisation – perhaps without compensation when they return to power.

Yet Churchill – whom I would claim as a Liberal-Tory of the better kind – introduced commercial television which Labour threatened to reverse, but never did. His success was partly due to implementing the change in good time for people to enjoy before the 1955 election. If the present Government has learned from that lesson, they might have followed Peter Walker in letting council tenants get their hands on the title deeds of their houses without waiting five years for ownership of the equity after the next election.

THE LAST BRAVE STAND

But before considering tactics and strategy, we must get our thinking straight. My central criticism is that, with such notable exceptions as Enoch Powell in olden times and Sir Keith Joseph more recently, too few Conservatives have started by deciding what is economically or socially desirable before resorting to feeble compromises over what is thought for the time being 'politically possible'. A more secure grasp of classical economic analysis might have prevented Conservative leaders from establishing the NEDC in 1961, welcoming Labour's National Plan in 1965, launching the Industry Act, becoming embroiled with incomes policy in 1972 (complete with Price Commission, profit and dividend control), writing off their share of £25,000m in subsidies to nationalised industries since 1960, and pumping up the money supply in 1972–73.

The last brave stand – until Mrs Thatcher came to power in 1979 – was in 1958, when Peter Thorneycroft and his two Treasury colleagues tried to stop the remorseless subordination of taxpayer and private economy to the insatiable demands of state spending – and were driven by failure to resign from

Mr Macmillan's Government. It was 'Butskellism' that prepared the way for 'Bennery'.

I thought that had the Conservatives grasped the decisive role of intellectuals and their ideas, they would have added another dimension – an independent ivory tower – to Conservative Central Office, in effect by creating the CPS almost twenty years earlier than they did. I recall writing to R.A. Butler and Iain Macleod along those lines at the time. They might have been in time to prevent the post-war consensus from congealing into the Keynesian-collectivist mould that now makes Mrs Thatcher's task of radical reform appear so much more contentious and difficult than it should have been.

REACTIONARY ON PRINCIPLES . . .

But by 1958 I had broken loose from the Conservative Party and started up the Institute of Economic Affairs where, with Arthur Seldon and growing numbers of others, we tried to practise what I am now preaching. So I stand before you as a humble unattached intellectual to commend the approach of *radical reaction*. This vantage point was described (in an IEA book of that title in 1961) as 'being *conservative* about the principles of a free society but *radical* about the measures necessary to ensure its dynamic operation and continuing evolution'.

There is no such thing as an objective, value-free economic theory or policy. All economists should be asked to come clean about their guiding principles or prejudices. How do they rank efficiency, growth, amenity, equality, variety, choice? For my money, the over-riding principle, about which I feel passionately conservative – even reactionary – is the preservation of maximum freedom of choice for all my fellow men and women as individuals, as both producers and consumers – the maximum freedom consistent with safeguarding the like freedom of others.

I personally uphold individual choice even more on moral and political than on economic grounds. Of course, the market economy is more efficient than central direction because we are all generally more ready to put forth our best exertions for causes we choose for ourselves than for what others declare to be the 'national interest'. Of course, market economy and individual economic freedom provide the indispensible under-pinning for intellectual, political and civic liberties. But towering above such economic and political calculations is the *moral* merit of acknowledging the unique individuality of our fellow men and, therefore, the desirability of leaving the reins of their destiny so far as possible in their own hands. On this issue I find myself in almost complete agreement with T.E. Utley's recent Research Department Paper, *Capitalism, The Moral Case*.

But before anyone invokes the ghost of *laissez-faire*, let me emphasise that freedom of choice is not possible in a vacuum. First, there must be a framework of laws and institutions to prevent the rule of force and fraud; that much was acknowledged by Adam Smith in 1776. Secondly, there must be a guaranteed minimum income for people who, through no fault of their own, cannot maintain a civilised standard in the market economy. This has nothing to do with the phoney 'compassion' of social democracy but dates back, at least, to the 1601 Elizabethan Poor Law.

Finally, government has to provide a number of services which cannot be supplied by competing producers catering for consumer choice. Again, there is no debt to socialism. This duty follows from the existence of a technical category of public goods, like national defence and law and order, which governments must provide. The reason is not that they are 'important', since food, shelter, clothing are no less essential but can be supplied in the market to people who pay their money and take their choice. True public goods provide indivisible services: they are consumed collectively or not at all and can therefore be supplied and financed only on a collectivist basis from compulsory taxation.

So the *reactionary* will stubbornly defend individual freedom of choice except where it must be over-ruled by government coercion in deference to such specific requirements of an orderly society as I have touched upon. Individual freedom can be enjoyed only under the rule of law common to all citizens; as Hayek has taught, it requires a system of general law that safeguards private property and does not confer privileges or income on any politically-favoured groups of producers.

. . BUT RADICAL IN POLICY

All reactionaries in my sense must soon become radical when they reflect how far we have strayed from such a conception of limited government and, therefore, how extensive are the reforms necessary to reduce the coercion of individuals by state control, regulation and taxation, to cut government down to the modest scale required to maintain a free society.

I certainly pay tribute to the present Conservative government for making a courageous start with radical reform – by abolishing exchange control, reducing income tax, repealing pay and price policy, and making a start with denationalisation in road transport, airways, aerospace, ferries, docks, buses and North Sea oil.

But by 1979 the State had come to spend more than half the nation's incomes and to employ between a quarter and a third of the labour force; and so far Conservatives have failed to make any net reductions in total expenditure from the volume left by Labour. They have rightly shifted more spending towards such true public services as defence and police, but most of the so-called 'cuts' about which Labour complains are in the spiralling plans for future years cooked-up for the election by Mr Healey.

Why can't you see, Perry, that Mrs Thatcher has inherited a vast range of central and local government services which are not public goods – but could be better provided in the market if consumers paid lower taxes and rates and had more to spend by choice on, for example, all forms of education and personal medical care, libraries and art galleries, swimming pools and other sports facilities, marinas and motorways. Can it be that Conservatives are more fearful of change or of public opinion than they are of over-government and the politicisation of life leading to tension, conflict and even collapse?

ALTERNATIVES FOR CHOICE

A large part of the IEA's research and educational work since 1957 has been devoted to examining ways of shrinking this bloated public sector. The prize to be gained by reducing government spending and taxing would be nothing less than spreading throughout welfare and local government services that boon of free choice we all take for granted when spending our own money on food, clothing, kitchen equipment, motor cars, hobbies, holidays, home ownership, insurance, hi-fi and fashion gear, not forgetting, my dear Perry, fancy waistcoats.

There are a variety of alternative policies available for Conservatives who are prepared to join the swelling ranks of radical reactionaries. 'Free' services for all are not necessary to help the declining minority who cannot pay their own way in welfare. A better approach would be a reverse income tax, that is, cash subsidies to top-up low incomes to the minimum necessary to enable recipients to pay the market price for essential welfare and other services of their choice.

Why should choice in welfare – including your favourite public school – be confined to people who can afford to pay twice: once in taxes for state services they don't use and then, again, from net income for the private services they prefer? Why not allow contracting-out? What's wrong with insurance? When will Britain join most other mature countries by allowing young people the freedom and responsibility of financing their own investment in university education by some variant of student loans?

There is no time to formulate similar questions on nationalised industries. I would simply assert that such as BR [British Rail], NCB [National Coal Board], BSC [British Steel], and PO [Post Office] mail services have long-since ceased to serve their customers, to satisfy their employees or to pay their way. Only the deepest-dyed conservatives in the antique trade union movement or the out-dated Labour Party can suppose that these state services will be cossetted to survive indefinitely in their present debilitated form.

ADVANTAGES OF THE MARKET

A determined move towards more limited government would bring many advantages:

- it would replace state monopoly, in nationalised welfare no less than industry, by competing suppliers who would offer innovation, value for money and choice;
- it would weaken over-powerful unions that have fastened like leeches onto the carcass of misbegotten public services;
- it would return responsibility to individuals, parents, families, for choices in personal goods and services where preferences differ and uniformity has no more place than in food, clothes and homes;
- it would extend diversity, pioneering and voluntary charity that are among the glories of a mature free society;
- it would assist government in mastering inflation by removing the ever-present temptation to provide more services than the public will pay for in taxation – which has provoked tax 'avoision' by the victims and inflationary printing of money by their oppressors.

In the past, the imperfections of the market provided a plausible pretext for politicians to extend government power. Yet we now find that government is even more imperfect and its apparatchiks even less capable of performing all the tasks laid upon them. Blemishes that economics textbooks call 'market failure' are dwarfed by the monumental failure of political education, medical care, nationalised industries and local government services.

Perhaps most serious of all for democracy, politicians of both parties have discredited themselves by trying to do what markets could do better. By extending their powers beyond their competence, they have appeared impotent or incompetent to discharge the essential tasks of government which should be their over-riding responsibility and which cannot be made good by markets if government fails.

It's no use, Perry, saying: 'This may be all very true, but radical reform is politically impossible'. Conservatives who share any of these radical–reactionary ideals must raise their voices and join the intellectual battle. Recall Hayek's now encouraging view: 'once the more active part of the intellectuals have been converted to a set of beliefs, the process by which they become generally accepted is almost automatic and irresistible'.

We are well on our way. Where have such spent intellectual forces as [Thomas] Balogh, [Nicholas] Kaldor, [John Kenneth] Galbraith, [Andrew] Shonfield, [Michael] Shanks, [Anthony] Crosland, gone? And from where came such recruits as Sam Brittan, Peter Jay, Paul Johnson, Bernard Levin, Brian Walden, Lord Vaizey, Lord George-Brown, Sir Richard Marsh, Reg Prentice, Jo Grimond – even former-socialist Rhodes Boyson and shortly, perhaps, Frank Chapple?

CONSERVATIVES INTO BATTLE

At last there are signs that Conservatives are rejoining this intellectual battle. In September 1980, the CPS published a notable talk to the Bow Group by Nigel Lawson. Entitled *The New Conservatism*, it was a scarcely-concealed critique of his colleagues who have denounced ideology without realising they are guilty of elevating the mixed economy into a new vogue. Mr Lawson put his finger on the central error of Tories who may be said to have a high humidity count:

> In the nineteenth century Conservatives could afford to disavow theory and affect a disdain for abstract ideas and general principles, for the simple reason that the theories, ideas and principles on which Conservatism rests were the unchallenged common currency of British politics. The rise of social democracy has changed all that.

Hence his call for Conservatives to 'fight the battle of ideas'. Plainly, it is not the present mixed economy that we ought to conserve. What urgently requires conserving is the underlying principle of the free society which this mixed-up economy threatens. The danger to freedom comes from the excessive power of the State and its entrenched bureaucracies over our incomes, jobs, family and social life. It is not a matter of ideology but of economic logic that *limitless* pressures on *limited* governmental resources can be relieved only by shedding functions politicians do not have to perform and have increasingly mismanaged.

How much longer before Conservative waverers, who pride themselves as realists – or even romantics, my dear Perry – recognise that overblown government cannot be cured by marginal tinkering or re-re-organisation of public agencies – any more than obesity can be cured by tightening belts or redesigning corsets? If we wish to restore credit and credibility to party politics, we must reverse almost a century of unprincipled and unsustainable growth in government. We now have to speed the climb back to reality by contemplating more radical measures to return the larger part of state industry and social welfare from centralised coercion – and the political manipulation witnessed last week at Labour's Blackpool conference – to dispersed initiative, competitive markets and wholesome freedom of choice.

NOTE

1. *Politics in Industrial Society*, 1979.

Morality and markets: gospel of an economist*

I am speaking here at St. George's House, Windsor, not as an amateur theologian but as a professional economist concerned with moral values.

Allow me to start by asserting ten missionary truths, which I shall lay down with the utmost boldness, and without apology.

TESTAMENT

1. We do not in Britain enjoy the benefits of a market economy; rather we suffer (like most of Europe outside Switzerland) from a corruption of confused collectivism.
2. To praise the market economy is not to call for the absence of government, but nor is it to countenance government deploying compulsion to spend half the nation's income.
3. Government is essential for the provision of collective services, such as defence, police, judiciary, monetary order and minimum standards of living (including income support for the poor – in cash rather than in kind).
4. The massive expansion of government this century has not been guided, or justified, by intellectual analysis or the 'public interest' but by electoral expediency driven by political competition for votes and power.
5. The resulting growth in government taxation, regulation and spending, especially on so-called 'social welfare', has not removed (but rather inflamed) the grievances that were its original justification.
6. Competitive markets do not work perfectly; but government, resting on competitive policies, is even more incurably flawed.
7. Behind the rhetoric of government as guardian of the public interest, lurks the reality of rival politicians appealing to private sectional interests to win or retain a majority.

* First published by the Centre for Policy Studies, London: G. Donald & Co., December 1986. The text follows that of a speech, delivered at a consultation on The Church and Social Policy which was held in the autumn of 1986 at St George's House, Windsor Castle, under the joint aegis of St George's House and the Centre for Policy Studies.

8. Within a legal framework which punishes force and fraud, competitive markets limit the evil bad men can do, whilst unlimited government opens the door to big and little Hitlers, Stalins, Khomeinis, Nyereres and lesser tyrants and tormentors.

9. The standing temptation of unchecked political power is chronic over-spending to buy votes, leading to mounting inflation followed by high unemployment.

10. Disillusion with overblown government has provoked a world-wide reaction towards the freeing of individual enterprise, even by socialists in countries as different as Australia, New Zealand, Hungary and China.

BIAS AGAINST MARKETS

I now turn to illustrate my charge against what passes as Christian economic argument by a couple of quotations from the Bishop of Liverpool, which I think may help to focus the discussion. Both my texts are taken from his recent socialist testament *Bias to the Poor*. First in his chapter entitled 'A Crisis for Capitalism', on page 136 he complains of the free market that: 'it is not only the inefficient that go to the wall; so do efficient industries which happen to be operating in areas from which the market has shifted away'.

The second quotation comes in the final chapter entitled 'Can the Church Bear Good News to the Poor?' where he writes on page 219:

> There is no more painful matter in Church life than pastoral reorganisation which involves closing churches . . . . Yet it is right to go through the painful processes of making some churches redundant in areas where the population has drastically reduced.

He goes on to explain:

> If we keep too many church buildings, we trap small congregations into putting all their energies into maintaining the buildings and justifying their existence by running Church organisations to use them.

If we substitute 'coal-mines' or 'steel-mills' for 'churches', we have a powerful vindication of Ian McGregor's recent activities with the BSC [British Steel Corporation] and NCB [National Coal Board]. My reason for recalling these passages is certainly not to mock one of the most attractive leaders of the Church to which I am sometimes proud to belong. It is to emphasise that much of the lofty moral criticism directed at the market economy and its practitioners is misconceived, where it is not plain humbug.

The Church is as much part of the market as the Coal Board, BL [British

Leyland] or, say, the brewers (who occasionally close pubs). Bishops have to close churches, not for the fun of it, but because resources are scarce. They have to weigh up their costs against the proceeds of selling old sites and investing in new buildings. They have to live within budgets, mostly derived from voluntary payments by customers who are free to choose rival brands of salvation or to buy quite different goods and services. Churches necessarily engage in advertising, packaging, display, product differentiation, and even – to judge from certain heretical Bishops – product development, if not outright switch-selling. The fact that their leading 'product' is intangible in no way distinguishes it from many subjective satisfactions offered by commercial producers (such as comfort, cures, confidence and cosmetics).

Indeed, not only are the churches part of the market economy: their ability to compete for the public's money and allegiance rests on the same freedom that allows consumer choice in more humdrum goods and services. It is a truism that religious freedom is severely curtailed in the countries of Eastern Europe because they lack the dispersed initiative and private property rights that are the cornerstones of a market economy. Yet the priceless boon of freedom is taken for granted by Bishops and others in Britain, while the system which guarantees that freedom is given no credit, but held up to moral obloquy.

The significance of such episcopal criticisms is that they typify so much hostility to the market as being unworthy, selfish, materialistic, money-grubbing, profit-seeking. As with so much purely party-political abuse, hostility springs from judging the great issue of economic freedom by reference to motives rather than results. Thus even critics of private enterprise may acknowledge its powerful productive impulses; but like many practitioners of capitalism, they nourish doubts about reliance on self-interest as the ruling incentive to effort, economy and investment.

INTENTIONS VERSUS RESULTS

The first answer to such criticism is that good intentions are no guarantee of good results. If we supposed politicians were motivated exclusively by their conception of the 'public interest', would we have to approve of the havoc they have unintentionally wrought through the debasement of our currency to less than one-twentieth of its pre-war value, with the attendant inequity and impoverishment of millions living on savings or fixed incomes? And what about the evil consequences of other well-intended, compassionate policies like rent control that have destroyed millions of lettings and worsened the plight of the homeless? Since 1906 'liberals' have preened themselves for conferring on trade unions exceptional legal privileges, which have contributed inadvertently but decisively to the tragic decline of British ship-building, steel, coal, motor cars, docks and printing. 'Do-gooders' may mean well, but they often turn out to be do-badders. The proof of public puddings is in the eating, not in the professed pure intentions of the amateur cooks, spiritual or political.

It is true that inventors and entrepreneurs may be driven on – against many discouragements – by material ambitions. But if they are successful, by far the larger part of the benefit is spread among millions of consumers in better or cheaper products and services. More prosaically, such firms as M&S, Boots, ICI, Beecham, do not aim directly at doing good, but at doing well, i.e. making bigger profits. But, so long as competition is not impeded, the law of the market is that they will continue to succeed only by doing better for their customers than alternative suppliers. Thus spake Adam Smith in the *Wealth of Nations* over 200 years ago: 'It is not from the benevolence of the butcher, the brewer or the baker that we expect our dinner, but from their regard to their own interest'.

MIXED MOTIVES

The second answer to those who damn the market by deriding self-interest and profit is that they are in truth damning – and often damning falsely – the mixed motives of ordinary people as producers, workers and consumers who operate in the market. Most of God's creatures are a mixture of the divine spark and the devil's streak. How can the fat man in a restaurant blame his own obesity on the waiter? In truth the market is neutral; it will supply what consumers want, from prayer books and communion wine to pornography and hard liquor. Within the law, competition will offer whatever incentives are likely to move people to work, save, invest, innovate.

It is true that differential monetary rewards are the most common forms of inducements to effort in modern economies. But few people are activated, like cash registers, exclusively by ready money. In choosing a job, for instance, people will give differing weights to less tangible features like training, long-run prospects, job satisfaction, location, vocation, social esteem, comfort, challenge, length of holidays or amount of overtime. No-one is obliged to work for the highest pay.

Likewise as consumers, people will not always choose the cheapest product, or spend all their income indulging their appetites. Most people have mixed motives. Take the prototype economic man, who sells his labour in the highest market and always shops around for bargains: even he may be redeemed by sharing his surplus income with charities, poorer members of his family, and what Bishops would approve as other good causes.

The merit of the market is that it harnesses individual effort, economy and thrift to maximise present and future social output, *not* by the narrow incentive of self-interest, but by the widest opportunity for everyone to pursue his own *self-chosen purposes*.

LIFT UP OUR EYES

If bishops and other critics of the market economy don't like the goals pursued by fallen man, they are not alone. But they have a special duty which should make them redouble their effort to elevate our conduct by preaching, teaching and personal example. If we object to people's tastes and appetites we must try to convert them by persuasion. It is no remedy for human weakness and fallibility to extend the coercive power of government, for this simple reason: we will have done nothing thereby to transform the conduct of politicians or voters. Instead we simply transfer the same self-seeking propensities in human nature to the political power-seeking process where their scope for corruption is wider, and the risks of damaging freedom and economic advance greater. As Keynes warned:

> [D]angerous human proclivities can be canalised into comparatively harmless channels by the existence of opportunities for money-making and private wealth, which if they cannot be satisfied in this way may find their outlet in cruelty, the reckless pursuit of personal power and authority, and other forms of self-aggrandisement. It is better that a man should tyrannise over his bank balance than over his fellow-citizens (*The General Theory of Employment, Interest and Money*, New York: Macmillan, 1957, p. 374)

I would add only that people who tyrannise over their fellow-men in the political arena seldom neglect to attend to their personal bank balance as well.

The Bishop of Liverpool capped his chapter 'A Crisis for Capitalism' with what he called 'a challenge to Socialism to produce the same energy, imagination, profitability and efficiency in a public enterprise as an entrepreneur brings to his own business'. He looked for 'more efficiency not go-slow protection of jobs'. Tell that to Mr Scargill and Mr Buckton. Tell it to the other Luddites in the so-called 'public' service. Tell it to the marines! As with so much unworldly denunciation of economic freedom, present imperfections are compared with hypothetical perfection. Stubborn, deep-seated human frailties and inadequacies are thus verbally vanquished by nothing more than wishful thinking and a lapse into empty exhortation. This emotional bubble was best pricked by an American philosopher, Professor William Barrett:

> I think I can say, with some degree of assurance, of every intellectual I have known personally who was a committed socialist, that the Socialist ideal represented a

displacement of moral and religious values which had not found their outlet elsewhere and here came to distorted expression.

In the socialist tradition you can scarcely disentangle specific social protest from
a metaphysical rebellion against, or evasion of, the human condition itself.

We certainly need to elevate our daily conduct, above all by more direct,
daily, unadvertised, personal caring and thought for others. Meanwhile, we
might look for wider agreement in purging our present institutions of avoidable 'moral hazard' which positively encourages individuals and families to
neglect self-reliant and responsible behaviour. I have a long agenda for radical
reform which would mostly require a progressive limitation rather than an
indefinite extension of government. The state has functions indispensable to a
healthy social order. But on my analysis, the worst disorders have come from
excessive and misdirected political intervention which has perverted the
market, for example by inducing the alternation between the moral and
economic abominations of inflation and unemployment.

HEAR THE PROPHETS

Let me cap what I regard as the misplaced idealism of collectivists by offering
a panegyric of competitive markets as indispensable for rational behaviour in
a free society, drawing on some of our great thinkers.

Lionel Robbins taught that the market is like a daily referendum where individual consumers are free to vote with their money between a wide range of
competing suppliers. (One deduction is that market democracy is more efficient and sensitive in serving diverse tastes than political democracy.)

F.A. Hayek has taught that in a complex and changing world no central
board can have the knowledge necessary to plan an industry, much less an
economy. Socialism is based on 'the pretence of knowledge'. Because knowledge is widely scattered, competition wins as 'the optimal discovery procedure'. (The NHS monopoly has suppressed improvements in health care
pioneered in the USA.)

Adam Smith taught that the 'wealth of nations' is derived from 'the effort
of every man to better his condition.' We have the authority of Shakespeare
(Henry V, Act II, scene IV) that 'Self-love, my liege, is not so vile a sin as self-
neglecting'. (Political appeals to 'public interest' or ' the Dunkirk spirit' do not
work except in dire emergencies.)

John Jewkes has taught the advantages for freedom, efficiency and
economic progress of dispersed initiative compared with central direction –
which was highly wasteful even in war-time planning. (Hence the general
superiority of private enterprise over nationalised–politicised industry, including education and medical care.)

Neo-classical economists have taught that market prices act as signals of changes in the relative scarcity of human and material resources. Changes in prices – rents, interest, wages, salaries – provide at once the information and the incentive for action to adjust both the supply and demand for goods, accommodation, savings, labour. (If you increase the relative reward for not working by raising benefits and taxing low earnings, you will increase the supply of unemployed people. That is one reason why the official 3.2m unemployed is, mercifully, a myth.)

Milton Friedman has taught that individual choice through the market maximises consent, whereas even if government were truly representative, it rests on coercion. Thus in a competitive market both buyer and seller gain from trade, whilst all government over-rides the preferences of minorities, if not of the majority. (Pushed too far, state taxes and regulation increase the temptation for normally honest people to resort to what is variously called the informal, submerged, underground, or black economy.)

David Friedman has taught that there are only three motives for getting people to put forth their best efforts: love, fear, or self-interest. Love is a scarce resource and is incorporated in the market, through the family, voluntary service, charity, mutual/cooperative enterprises. Fear depends on coercion which is necessarily the ultimate sanction of all government. So if we prize individual freedom, we are left with self-interest (or self-chosen purposes) as the widest incentive for effort, economy, thrift, honesty and risk-taking.

[James] Buchanan and *[Gordon] Tullock* from Virginia have taught that most advertised 'compassion' in the political market is little more than buying votes with other people's money.

Peter Bauer has taught that foreign aid has helped to impoverish African 'developing' countries by underwriting state policies that destroy peasant agriculture and displace commercial investment.

Hayek, again, has taught that 'social justice' is a will o' the wisp since there is no objective criterion for settling relative rewards unrelated to market incentives. Pressed too far, redistribution of income will blunt incentives and reduce total income. Our concern should not be with income differences (so-called 'inequality') but with topping up low incomes to avoid poverty.

[Ludwig von] Mises taught that without market pricing to indicate changing relative scarcities, rational calculation is impossible even in the simplest economy.

[Wilhelm] Röpke taught that even if the competitive market were not the most efficient social organism available, it would be morally preferable to collectivism as affording the poorest individual maximum freedom to shape his own life and destiny. Above all, freedom of action is linked with personal responsibility for the outcome, whereas so-called 'collective responsibility' by politicians is the pretext for all kinds of irresponsible mischief.

I BELIEVE ...

Like Professor Denis Robertson, I do not think economists are equipped to handle the keys to the kingdom of heaven. The 'market' is nothing more than men and women cooperating for mutual advantage to serve their own values – which, alas, are not those of which Christians or other moralists would always approve. Much as I rejoice in the variety of God's creation, I deplore some of the tastes exhibited by others – and occasionally by myself. But I deplore even more strongly the relapse of good men and women who seek to impose their will on others by coercion – or outright violence.

I take my stand with the IXth Article of Religion that 'man is far gone from original righteousness and is of his own nature inclined to evil. . . This infection of nature doth remain, yea in them that are regenerated'. I observe that original sin operates in both the economic and the political markets.

I believe that around the world the worst manifestations of evil in cruelty, oppression, exploitation, persecution of minorities, disregard of human life, and contempt for the sanctity of individual freedom, come from powerful governments or from those who seek to capture the power of governments to enforce their values or interests on others.

I conclude that it is easier to check or discipline evil through the voluntary processes of the market under a regime of limited government, than by concentrating economic and political power in the grasping hand of the State.

No, Prime Minister! Ralph Harris against the consensus*

FOREWORD

Writing short articles in newspapers and elsewhere is an extremely effective way of communicating ideas to a large and influential audience – provided the author has the gift of wit to catch his audience's attention, and the ability to make complex ideas simple. Ralph Harris, once a leader writer on *The Glasgow Herald* has that gift and that ability. To celebrate his seventieth birthday in December 1994 and as a tribute to the exceptional influence which he has had on the intellectual climate in Britain and around the world, the Institute of Economic Affairs has assembled this selection from his hundreds of short articles.

Selection was a difficult task. We have tried, using thirty articles, to set out a representative collection of his thoughts. There was, at least, no doubt with which piece this tribute to him should begin. In 1975 he wrote an article which he called 'Cheer up! Things are getting worse' which, he tells friends, is his favourite among all his short pieces.

The article begins with a neat nine-paragraph summary of British post-war economic history, complete with character sketches of the leading politicians – that 'clever man Harold Wilson', 'dynamic George Brown', 'that nice Tony Barber', 'tough Ted', 'that smart Peter Walker' et al. As a result of their efforts, in 1975

> The welfare state is a seething mass of grievances, nationalised industries brought to the verge of insolvency, public spending above 55 per cent of GNP, the pound going under for the third time, foreign debts mortgaging our future, unemployment mounting towards one million, inflation roaring above 20 per cent and national bankruptcy staring us in the face.

But what does national bankruptcy mean? – certainly not exhaustion of the skills and resources of the British people which 'have survived the assault and battery of government mismanagement'. The blame lies squarely with

---

* A selection of the shorter writings of Ralph Harris on the occasion of his 70th birthday. IEA Occasional Paper 94, 1994.

government, with the politicians and civil servants who have pretended they could solve Britain's economic problems: 'What is being bankrupted before your eyes is the post-war, all-party mythology that bigger and bigger government can solve any problems'.

Fasten your safety belts, says Harris, for 'the rudest awakening of all time is at hand': the argument for a market economy 'has gained the intellectual ascendancy – on grounds of morality and freedom, even more than efficiency'.

This prophetic article, written four years before Mrs Thatcher's first government achieved office, captures the essence of Ralph's writings and speeches. By 1975, he and Arthur Seldon and the academic authors they mustered had spent almost twenty years working up to a crescendo of criticism of overweening governments whose actions encroached more and more on the freedom of citizens – and in the process led to an economy wasteful in its use of resources. Inflation, unemployment and sterling crises were the symptoms of a deeper malaise afflicting Britain. Their words were beginning to fall on receptive ears and, as yet another crisis loomed, Ralph sensed correctly that Britain was on the verge of radical change.

Although a small collection of articles cannot do justice to the range of Ralph's ideas, it can remind readers of his great talent for entertaining them with radical views, expressed robustly, yet all the time grounded firmly on sound economic principles. Most of his favourite targets figure in this selection which, after 'Cheer up!', reproduces the articles in the order in which they first appeared.

Naturally, politicians and civil servants head the list. From early in the post-war period, he identifies their problem as dependence on the views of defunct economists. They have failed to read and understand Adam Smith, Hayek and (later) Friedman. Consequently, they are bound by the ideas of 1930s Cambridge, over-impressed not just by Keynesian demand-management but believing, following Joan Robinson, that 'imperfections' in markets justify any and every government intervention. Attempts at planning, incomes policies and the other favoured remedies of the 1960s are effectively and vigorously attacked, and the advantages of 'imperfect' competition are demonstrated, in four early articles reprinted here, written between 1965 and 1968 when he and Arthur Seldon were voices in the wilderness. In another early article, from the *Swinton Journal* in 1970, he points out that had Hayek been an 'apostle of collectivism' his seventieth birthday in 1969 would hardly have gone, as it did, virtually unnoticed by the BBC and other organs of opinion.

At the same time that he chastised the politicians, Ralph produced compelling arguments, quite against the conventional wisdom of the day, for the moral superiority of capitalism over socialism. For example, in *The Times* in September 1970 he argued: 'the first need for our moral health no less than our material well being is drastically to reduce central power to the minimum that politicians must discharge for security, order and the avoidance of poverty'.

In the early 1970s, Ralph was using short articles in *The Daily Telegraph, The Times* and *The Spectator* to explain that high unemployment results not from deficient demand but from the welfare system, from over-powerful trade unions, from minimum-wage provisions and from rent control. And, as the IEA, brought to British readers the ideas of Milton Friedman, Ralph spread them to a still wider audience through his newspaper articles. In a *Crossbow* article in 1977, for instance, he asks 'How many billions of pounds of lost output and thousands of unemployed might have been avoided?' if Chancellor Barber had grasped Friedman's point that inflation is always and everywhere a monetary phenomenon and had refrained from inflating the money supply.

As one would expect of a liberal economist, other targets which came under attack were protectionism (a 'costly form of economic warfare that impoverishes all'), the National Economic Development Council (Neddy should be 'carted off to the knacker's yard') and foreign aid (which 'provided incompetent governments with a soft option'). In 1983, impressed by his experience of the legislative process in the House of Lords, in a *Times* article Ralph turns to the need to make government less complex, confining it to 'the barest minimum of functions' and restoring 'politics to a part-time job suitable for gentlemen and lords, that is for unpaid amateurs'.

One of Ralph's most prolific periods for short articles was in 1988 when he was writing primarily for *The Sunday Telegraph*. Eight of these articles are reproduced here. They are classic Harris – witty, full of radical ideas and often based on contemporary IEA publications. The bishops are provided with an Easter offering: people should repent of looking to the government for special favours and do competitively as they would be done by. Student loans should be substituted for a large part of the student grant. Education vouchers should be introduced to encourage parent power in schools. Money should be denationalised to avoid political mismanagement.

In these articles, Ralph also returned to deeper philosophical issues. 'Public' services are mostly doomed to failure: self-government in the market-place is inherently superior and caters much better for minorities. 'Do-gooders' are generally destined to do harm, especially in the social welfare field where they increase dependence. Tobacco abolitionists who encourage intolerance are a 'more lethal threat to the sum of human welfare than the worst smoking can do to any of us'.

Hayek and 'Austrian School' discovery processes are never far from his mind and are mentioned in many of his papers. In November 1988 he returned specifically to Hayek (in this case, *The Fatal Conceit*), suggesting that his readers ponder 'the miracle of the economic order'. *The Fatal Conceit* was featured in another *Sunday Telegraph* article in February 1991 when he pointed to the dangers of the 'social market' concept then being adopted by 'closet collectivists'.

Mrs Thatcher's achievements were reviewed in *The Independent* in March 1990 – she owed 'a large debt to ideas' but she 'alone took courage to prick the bubble'. In Europe she stood against creeping socialism *(The Sunday Telegraph*, April 1989): others, with less courage, would 'hide behind her skirt and keep quiet, confident in the knowledge that in the last resort she will use the veto'. On the eve of Maastricht in December 1991, with Mrs Thatcher gone, Ralph urged Mr Major not to be 'stampeded into signing up for political and monetary union'. He could see no reason to enter on 'political and monetary experiments' which went far beyond freeing trade and factor movements. In June 1993, he pointed again to the dangers of Maastricht and, in particular, to 'the obsession with an irreversible monetary union [which] threatens to reduce economic self-government to empty ceremonial'.

Others have explained the influence on ideas which Ralph Harris and Arthur Seldon exerted through their work in the IEA. In this volume, our purpose is to remind Ralph's many admirers of the significant individual contribution which he made to overcoming the collectivist consensus through a series of entertaining, lucid and perspicacious short articles in which he clung tenaciously to classical liberal ideas when nearly all around him believed in various forms of 'planning'. For many years he swam against the tide. But then, remarkably, he helped to make the tide turn. For that, we are all in his debt.

As in all Institute publications, the views expressed in this Occasional Paper are those of the author, not of the IEA (which has no corporate view), its Trustees, Directors or Advisers.

November 1994   COLIN ROBINSON
Editorial Director, Institute of Economic Affairs;
Professor of Economics, University of Surrey

RALPH HARRIS: A PERSONAL NOTE

To understand the impact of Ralph's life's work one needs to understand many things about his times, his colleagues, the strategies they adopted and the resources they had at their command. Let me here mention just three matters, one a piece of history, the other two, some little known aspects of his work. They are little known to his fellow countrymen but well recognised overseas.

First, one has to have a sense of the intellectual atmosphere of the post-World War Two era which Ralph Harris and Arthur Seldon, at the bidding of the late Sir Antony Fisher, set out to change. Planning was in; markets were out. The People's War (so called because so many had been involved) had indeed become the People's Peace. As in war, so in peace, the government would run everything. Talk of markets was akin to swearing in church. And when Antony recruited Ralph (who in turn through Lord Grantchester soon found Arthur) the big joke of the day was that Antony had hired 'Britain's last two free-market economists'. They set out to stop a seemingly overwhelming tidal wave, a tsunami even of anti-market thinking, and their success is now well-documented in Richard Cockett's mistitled *Thinking the Unthinkable: Think-Tanks and the Economic Counter-Revolution, 1931–1983* (HarperCollins, 1994). I say 'mistitled' because his history stops not at 1983 but at 1993.

Second, one has to think of their creation, the IEA, not as a narrowly British institute, but rather as an international institution which just happens to be based in London. Its books are sold in over 90 countries every year now and every few days a permission to reprint or translate is issued to an overseas publisher. On a recent visit to the IEA, Gordon Tullock, the world-renowned economist and co-founder (along with 1986 Nobel Laureate James M. Buchanan) of the Public Choice or Virginia School of Economics, commented to me that his IEA Hobart Paperback (No. 9), *The Vote Motive* (1976), was without doubt the single most successful piece he had ever written in terms of bringing Public Choice insights to an international audience. It is about to go into a second revised and expanded IEA edition after two printings of the first edition, but more importantly it has been translated at least five times including French, Spanish, Italian, Swedish and Korean editions.

Finally, one has to appreciate Ralph's role as a mentor and role model (or 'hero' as I say whenever I have the pleasure of introducing him to audiences) to the growing family of 'IEAs' around the world – there are now about 100 such institutions in nearly 60 countries. Fisher, having made his fortune with Buxted Chickens, had lost nearly everything in Mariculture Ltd., the Cayman Turtle Farm after so-called 'environmentalists' had its products banned in the USA. But about the mid-1970s businessmen and academics around the world, sensing the IEA's growing impact, started turning to Fisher and Harris for advice: how do we copy the IEA?

Fisher, aged 59 by now, embarked on his fifth career. From fighter pilot, to farmer, to chicken king, to turtle saviour, he now became the world-wide institute entrepreneur, finally creating the Atlas Economic Research Foundation to raise start-up funds and act as a focal point for budding Harrises and Seldons. I followed Fisher as President of that Foundation for five years (1987–91) and continued his practice of involving Ralph as closely as possible in our mission of establishing IEAs all round the world. He was, more often than not, the keynote speaker at our many workshops. More important, he was always available to counsel our fledglings, even at times having them in residence at the IEA for a period to learn the ropes of our business.

As we salute Ralph with this selection from his many columns on the occasion of his achieving threescore and ten, let us not forget:

- the enormity of the task he, Arthur and Antony took on;
- the broader international role of the IEA; and
- Ralph's pivotal role in the birth and growth of so many new 'IEAs' the world over.

So, Happy Birthday, Ralph. Those of us around the world who strive to emulate and build on the success of your work are very much in your debt.

November 1994   JOHN BLUNDELL
General Director,
Institute of Economic Affairs

THE AUTHOR

Ralph Harris was born in 1924 and educated at Tottenham Grammar School and Queens' College, Cambridge. He was Lecturer in Political Economy at St Andrews University, 1949–56, a leader writer on *The Glasgow Herald,* and was General Director of the Institute of Economic Affairs from 1957 to 1987, when he became Chairman from 1987 to 1989 and subsequently (with Arthur Seldon) Founder President and an Honorary Trustee. Apart from his newspaper and other short articles, he has written for the IEA (with Arthur Seldon) *Hire Purchase in a Free Society, Advertising in a Free Society, Choice in Welfare, Pricing or Taxing?* (Hobart Paper No. 71, 1976), *Not from Benevolence . . .* (Hobart Paperback No. 10, 1977), *Over-ruled on Welfare* (Hobart Paperback No. 13, 1979), and *Shoppers' Choice* (Occasional Paper No. 68, 1983). His essay. 'In Place of Incomes Policy', was published in *Catch '76 . . .?* (Occasional Paper 'Special' (No. 47), 1976). He contributed the Epilogue. 'Can Confrontation be Avoided?', to *The Coming Confrontation* (Hobart Paperback No. 12, 1978); and his most recent IEA titles are *The End of Government . . .?* (Occasional Paper No. 58, 1980), *No, Minister!* (Occasional Paper No. 71, 1985), and *Beyond the Welfare State* (Occasional Paper No. 77, 1988).

He is a Trustee of the Wincott Foundation and the Atlas Economic Research Foundation (UK), a member of the Political Economy Club, former President of the Mont Pèlerin Society, and a former Council Member of the University of Buckingham. He is Chairman of the Advisory Council of the IEA Health and Welfare Unit, Chairman of the Trustees of the CRCE [Centre for Research into Post-Communist Economies] and British Co-Chairman of ICRET [International Centre for Economic Transformation], Moscow.

Ralph Harris was created a Life Peer in July 1979 as Lord Harris of High Cross.

ACKNOWLEDGEMENTS

The Institute acknowledges with appreciation the help of the following newspapers, journals and other organisations which gave permission to reproduce articles by Lord Harris they had originally published.

The Daily Telegraph
The Glasgow Herald
The Independent
The Sunday Telegraph
The Times
Crossbow
The Spectator
Swinton Journal
Yesterday, Today and Tomorrow
The British Institute of Management
Confederation of British Industry

Each article carries a note of the original source of publication and the date.

1   CHEER UP! THINGS ARE GETTING WORSE[1]

'What is being bankrupted before our eyes is the post-war all-party mythology that bigger and bigger government can solve any problems.'

It may not look easy to be an optimist in Britain in 1975. You have to work at it, but it's worth the effort.

You have to start by trying to remember Major Clement Attlee. After 1945 he was all set to usher in the New Jerusalem – welfare state, full employment and all that. 'We will never devalue', said Sir Stafford Cripps, shortly before putting the £ down from $4 to $2.80 in 1949.

By 1951 the electorate turned for relief to 13 years of Tory welfare state, full employment . . . There were some little local difficulties, especially with 'stop–go'. But super-Macmillan was always ready: first with 'three wise men', then a national incomes commission, and finally NEDO which would surely put everything right – once and for all. Butskellism and the middle-way for ever?

The voters seemed to twig that all was not well and decided in 1964 that the other socialist party should be given another chance – under that clever man Harold Wilson, bathing in the white heat of a technological revolution. But even if his 'first 100 days' did not actually solve any of the problems, it prepared the way for dynamic George Brown and his National Plan. True, that happened to come unstuck, but there was that young Wedgwood Benn with his IRC (Industrial Reorganisation Corporation] which was going to fix Leylands, Upper Clyde . . . the 100 days grew into 1,000 days – and nights – which just brought us up to the devaluation of 1967. 'Fine-tuning' and 'Finger Tip Control of the Economy' were not doing the trick. But that resourceful Mr Wilson was always ready with his freezes, norms, nil-norms, ceilings – just to show our foreign creditors that we could lick inflation.

By 1970 – with prices rising above 5 per cent and unemployment topping 500,000 – the voters thought it was tough Ted Heath's turn. He really knew what he was up to with all that talk about restructuring our economy, society and what-have-you. 'We will have nothing to do with incomes policies', said tough Ted.

So when the going got rough in 1971, that nice Tony Barber hit on the ingenious plan of spending our way at last to the New Jerusalem: 'go–go' would replace 'stop–stop' and GROWTH would solve all our problems – once and for all.

Ignoring those rude 'monetarists' and their alarmist talk of inflation, handouts and subsidies were squirted in all directions. In 1972 'We-will-never-devalue' Barber floated the pound – which promptly started to sink. As for inflation, Tough Ted was ready with – why, bless you, with an incomes policy to solve all problems – once and for all.

In 1973 that smart Peter Walker announced that all was going splendidly – except for raging inflation, the sinking pound, and mounting debts abroad. There must be some mistake . . .

Luckily, clever Mr Wilson was still available in 1974 with the final solution. It was so simple. In return for doing everything the TUC wanted, the unions would show us – once and for all – how socialism could really be made to work . . .

So by 1975 we can at last sit back and contemplate the wondrous New Jerusalem. Behold! The welfare state is a seething mass of grievances, nationalised industries in turmoil, companies brought to the verge of insolvency, public spending above 55 per cent of GNP, the pound going under for the third time, foreign debts mortgaging our future, unemployment mounting towards one million, inflation roaring above 20 per cent and national bankruptcy staring us in the face.

'Bankruptcy' – of what? Not of the skills, resources, enterprise of the British people. They have survived the assault and battery of government mismanagement. What is being bankrupted before your eyes is the post-war, all-party mythology that bigger and bigger government can solve any problems. If we are ready, 1975 should give those of us who never believed it a chance to prove our case. The Adam Smith, Hayek, Friedman argument for a market economy has gained the intellectual ascendancy – on grounds of morality and freedom, even more than efficiency.

'Oh yes,' say the pessimists, 'but the masses will never learn except by experience'. Very well, fasten your safety belts and cheer up: the rudest awakening of all time is at hand.

2   MARKETING PHARMACEUTICAL PRODUCTS[2]

Extracts from a paper presented at a British Institute of Management Consultation on Pharmaceutical Marketing

The younger generation of academic economists developed the idea of 'imperfect competition' from a technical concept to a kind of moral judgement that implied a departure from some ideal. If competition was 'imperfect' ought we not make every effort to identify and remove the blemishes? The hunt was on and a succession of otherwise sensible men began to assail advertising, packaging, branding and above all the wicked differentiation of products. The impracticable absurdity of the exercise would scarcely merit comment were it not that confusions about 'imperfect competition' continue to inflame and distort discussion of economic structure, activity and policy.

The Case for 'Imperfect' Competition

The fundamental error of much modern economic discussion is the assumption that we now know what assortment of goods should be produced – or that we (or the National Economic Development Council) can find the people who do know and get them to tell us once and for all. But by definition a dynamic economy involves change: economic growth has never meant simply turning out larger numbers of *given* products: more bread, more Model T Fords, more bar soap and scrubbing boards, more quill pens, more fly-papers, more poultices, senna pods, or aspirin B.P. The paths of progress in products old and new are various, but an awful lot boils down to something akin to what in medicine is often criticised as 'molecular manipulation'. What is the latest Rolls-Royce but the old Model T in 'elegant form and vehicle'!

It is because none of us has perfect knowledge about the present (let alone infallible foresight) that we need an open system for pooling intelligence, judgement and hunch to discover the best ways of improving the assortment of products and techniques, all the while testing new ways of catering for the variety of consumer conditions, resistances and preferences. This pooling is best achieved by competition and competitive marketing which is itself a continuing process of empirical research about improved products, techniques, and forms of consumption. It is the imperfections in our knowledge and understanding that argue most strongly for open-ended competition, involving endless experimentation and accompanied by the wastes that are inherent in finding better (but still 'imperfect') ways of achieving our purposes and discarding methods which only by competition can be proved less efficient.

The general lesson I draw from all this is that whilst we should be vigilant to identify and remove avoidable, man-made obstacles to competition, we should, as Hayek has said:[3] 'worry much less whether competition in a given case is perfect and worry much more whether there is competition at all'.

Marketing – the Hub of Competition

All the economic processes of competition come to a focus in the market-place, just as in political democracy the highly imperfect competition between two or three brands of salvation come to a focus in the ballot booth (once every four or five years, be it noted). However well a firm's techniques of manufacture have developed (in competition with others, needless to say), it must decide what and how much to produce *in anticipation of demand,* not in response to a 'given demand'. All the earlier calculations about research, investment, manufacturing methods, formulation are put to the test, or if you like put to the vote of consumers, in the act of marketing. The outcome must always be to some extent uncertain, since even in basic industries conditions of supply or demand are never static, as Lord Robens and Dr Beeching have painfully discovered. But in modern, emerging industries, where product innovation and obsolescence occur at a rapid and totally unpredictable rate, the uncertainties attending the marketing of new products (or even old products in competition with new) stand out in the sharpest possible contrast to the relatively predictable processes of factory production.

In these circumstances the decisive risk-taking, risk-reducing function which earlier economists entitled the 'entrepreneurial' function, comes to be exercised above all in the sphere of marketing. The economic centre of gravity in industries generally has moved forward from production to marketing as the economy has progressed to cater for the more varied, refined, sophisticated, individual, specific requirements and preferences of consumers with an increasing element of discretionary income. In short, the entrepreneurial function coincides ever more closely with the marketing function, and the marketing function moves from middle to top management.

3   PLANNING BY PROFITS OR PROPHETS?[4]

Belief in central planning implies a certain knowledge of the true aims and priorities of economic activity yet this certain knowledge and foresight do not exist. Obviously we must plan. 'The intelligent question is whether economic planning is best performed by a single central authority or dispersed among many individuals and groups, including public and private authorities, within some general institutional framework that will dovetail together these separate but related plans.'

It is easy to make fun of Mr Wilson's '100 days' – now happily coming to an end. Yet the idea of a succession of immediate, far-reaching decisions that would transform the direction of our economic activities follows inevitably from the belief in central planning. Clearly, to accuse 'blind market forces' of producing the wrong things and pursuing false priorities must imply that the critic knows what should be produced and what are the true priorities. Unless he knows, or honestly thinks he knows, the right answers, his criticisms are without visible foundation. And if he does know the right priorities, the sooner central planning is asserted to enforce them the quicker our economic ills will be cured. Indeed, why wait 100 days – or even 10?

The reason, of course, is that, despite years of talk about, for example, import saving, Mr Wilson does not know what we could produce more cheaply at home rather than buy from abroad. Indeed, if he had known all these years, he need not have waited to become Prime Minister to tell us. He could have set an example, advanced the public interest – and made (or should I say 'earned') a whacking profit – by getting into business (whether as economic adviser or entrepreneur) and increasing the production of cheap domestic substitutes for those machine tools or other foreign goods that were mistakenly being imported. If market forces are so blind, those with sight, or second sight, should be able wonderfully to lighten our darkness.

This simple example is doubly revealing. In the first place, it suggests that the assumption of superior knowledge, for example, about comparative costs, on which much of the argument for central planning rests, lacks empirical foundation. In the second place, it emphasises that if better or cheaper sources of home supply can be revealed, central direction would not be necessary to ensure that they were exploited. The publication of information could be expected to awaken users to the existence of cheaper sources of supply and stimulate domestic producers to cater for the resulting increase in home demand. Likewise, if the central planners can show that investment is inadequate to increase productivity, or how far business education would improve managerial efficiency, which new techniques would most reduce costs, or where more computers would more than earn their keep, it would seem that they have only to publicise the relevant data in order to get competitive firms to plan their own businesses on the most enlightened and efficient basis.

But all that this preliminary discussion amounts to is the self-evident proposition that there would be less misdirection of effort and resources if only we possessed fuller information about consumer preferences and the alternative means and costs of supplying them, which involves knowing more about the optimum combination of specific materials, manpower, machinery and marketing methods for producing all types of goods and services.

Perfect Knowledge Unattainable

As soon as we pose this proposition it becomes clear that complete information even of the recent past – let alone of the present or future – is unattainable. Even an expert under the most refined system of the division of labour cannot attain what might be called perfect knowledge – much less perfect foresight. It follows that all plans – private or public – which involve committing resources to specific uses, the outcome of which will be reliably known only afterwards, must involve the risk of error and loss. Thus the installation of a new machine depends on estimates of future demands for the output (volume and price) and of the future course of costs of inputs and of alternative methods of production. When we reflect how variously costs and prices may be influenced by technical, psychological, political, military, trading, population and other changes, we may find cause for wonder that we have survived, let alone enjoyed the most flourishing decade of economic progress this century, with so much reliance on 'blind market forces'.

The explanation is to be found partly in a neglected merit of the broad system of competitive markets which compensates for some of its more apparent shortcomings. Thus a large part of the success of a dynamic economy depends on making the best use of economic data about the alternative employment of scarce resources to produce goods and services efficiently in anticipation of the final demand of hundreds of millions of consumers in Britain and our export markets overseas. The question is not whether to employ planning, since without foresight and design in matching resources to requirements there must be total confusion and chaos. The intelligent question is whether economic planning is best performed by a single central authority or dispersed among many individuals and groups, including public and private authorities, within some general institutional framework that will dovetail together these separate but related plans.

How to Plan

Leaving aside the political dispute about individual freedom versus the concentration of power, the economic merits of these opposed systems would turn on which might be expected to make the fullest use of available knowledge. In the scientific area it may be thought easy to assemble the experts who can command the knowledge relevant for various economic policies, although even here there is the problem of choosing which experts to consult and which to disregard as nonconformists or cranks. But over the larger part of the economy knowledge is widely scattered among individuals with incomplete and often contradictory information about techniques, stocks, supplies, substitutes, market opportunities, special circumstances, local conditions, new facilities and individual skills. The question posed by Professor Hayek almost 20 years ago is:[5]

> Not how we can 'find' the people who know best, but rather what institutional arrangements are necessary in order that the unknown persons who have knowledge specially suited to a particular task are most likely to be attracted to that task.

Hayek's answer is worth pondering at a time when Mr George Brown, Mr Frank Cousins, Sir Robert Shone, Professor Stone and others are all bent on precisely the task of trying to 'find the people who know best', which Hayek rejects. His solution to the problem of securing the best use of knowledge is by competitive markets which leave the field open for anyone with a relevant contribution or a clue to missing information. Hayek regards markets as organisations for using and spreading information on which buyers and sellers can act so as between them to make the best use of economic resources. And competition further enables us to review the results and pass continuous judgement on all the participants. The contrasting, currently fashionable, approach is to try to cram all the relevant information necessary for central planning into

Table 1   Changes in labour force between 1954 and 1962

	% Increase or decrease
Total civil employment	+ 6
Engineering, electrical	+23
Paper, printing, publishing	+19
Vehicles	+12
Distribution	+12
Textiles	−18
Coalmining, quarrying	−18
Shipbuilding, marine engineering	−17
Agriculture, forestry, fishing	−13

the heads of a few experts, an exercise which will prove impossible even with the help of computers. Readers in doubt about the impossibility should re-read Mr Owen Hooker's article in the *FBI Review,* October 1964, particularly the significant singling out of 'lack of data' as the major weakness of Professor Stone's SAM (Social Accounting Matrix) model at Cambridge.

The critical importance of information arises mainly from the very fact of economic change. If techniques, population, demand stood still, economic activity would settle into a 'same again' pattern in which habit and custom took the place of decision and direction. An unfortunate consequence of the Keynesian revolution has been that economists have increasingly tended to play down or ignore continuous small changes which even in the not-very-long-run can add up to decisive redirection in methods and output. The fashionable concentration on macro-economics at the expense of rigorous microanalysis has led to a growing pre-occupation with statistical aggregates which display a deceptive stability and mask significant changes in their constituent parts. How else could the British economy in the past decade have come to be plausibly written off as 'stagnant' if we had noticed the remarkable advances in chemicals, fibres, building, electronics, cars and other consumer durables, and no doubt in many smaller categories, which were buried beneath the average $2\frac{1}{2}$ per cent annual increase in GNP? Table 1 summarises some of the remarkable changes in the broad groups of employment over as short a term as eight years.

Planning for Change

Who could have foreseen these changes? And who knows what effect changing techniques, productivity, markets will have on the labour force by 1970? Incidentally, if you dwell on these questions too long, you may begin to wonder how an incomes policy can be devised which would not frustrate those very changes in relative wages and profits which have helped to bring about this re-allocation of labour and other resources to exploit changing techniques, costs, demands and prices.

The dilemma about forecasts like Neddy's 4 per cent growth rate is not merely that most are quickly exploded, but that we can never be sure that they may not be proved unexpectedly right for the wrong reasons. There have certainly been some spectacular misforecasts like the groundnuts scheme, the adverse terms of trade argument, the fuel gap, the decline in population, the steel programme, early atomic energy calculations, the perpetual dollar shortage, all of which provided the basis for mistaken Government economic policies.[6] My favourite example of the difficulties that beset forecasters is drawn from the Ridley Committee on fuel and power resources. In 1951, acting on what it considered the most reliable technical and economic advice, it offered its 'best estimate of the pattern and scale of consumption' 10 years on.

The Committee was quite near the mark on the total fuel consumption by 1961. Its estimates for the individual industries, however, were wildly out: which did not help producers, who are not interested in the demand expressed as 'coal equivalent tons' but in the market for their particular fuel.

The relevance of all this for the choice between planning from the centre and planning through competitive markets suggests lessons for both Labour and Conservative economists. Both should see the advantage of policies that will improve the supply of information for public and private decision-takers. Thus, official statistics should be improved, speeded-up and published with fuller and franker acknowledgement of margins of error, omissions, and of qualitative variations which defy accurate measurement. At the same time, legal requirements for disclosure by public and private companies should be widened to include information on classified turnover, stocks, capital valuations, marketing expenditure and other business operations discussed by Mr Harold Rose in his celebrated Eaton Paper.[7]

In the light of Hayek's view of markets as a source of information, public policy should accept freer movements in relative prices (and profits) as an essential feature of a dynamic economy in which variations in costs direct resources from low-yield uses into openings where their contribution to consumer satisfaction will be higher. It is movements in prices which inform and help to co-ordinate the dispersed planning decisions of firms, public bodies and individuals. If the supply of tin is reduced, or demand for it increased (e.g. by substitution of tin for glass or cardboard), users do not need to be lectured about the reasons, nor exhorted to economise tin. Its price will rise to whatever extent is necessary to keep enough marginal buyers out of the market, and/or to release stocks to meet the swollen demand. Unfortunately, inflation often masks such changes in relative prices which should serve as altimeters or speedometers to help regulate the decisions of the scattered army of entrepreneurs, managers, traders, consumers whose individual plans must be brought into relationship within the total market of available resources.

I am not here concerned with the Government's rôle to balance out the economy by avoiding excessive demand or excessive unused capacity, beyond emphasising three shortcomings of Conservative monetary and fiscal management which look like being perpetuated under the new Government. First, public expenditure ought to be variable downwards in order to offset unforeseen increases in demands on resources arising from investment, foreign trade and even consumer spending which otherwise set up one-way pressures for inflation, balance-of-payments trouble and devaluation. Secondly, as Mr Christopher Dow has shown,[8] Government policy has more often than not upset the economy by errors of short-term forecasting which have led to the exaggeration first of the upswings and then of the checks on total demand. What a dynamic economy requires is an easier hand on the reins and more margins of safety in foreign reserves, capacity, employment, mobility, Government expenditure, to absorb short-term variations in demand for final output.

Burden of Change

Thirdly, by courting inflation that destroys all safety margins, the Government have constantly thrown the burden of adjustment on to the hard-pressed private sector (60 per cent only of the economy) by taxing companies, imposing purchase tax on selected products, varying hire purchase terms, first giving and then snatching back tax concessions on new investment, and alternating a cheap money policy with sudden lurches to 7 per cent. All these stop-gap policies are examples of Government-imposed disturbances on business information which make private *planning for profit* more difficult and expose public *planning by prophets* to the sort of disenchantment that Neddy has suddenly encountered from Mr Michael Shanks and other former disciples.

If a Labour Government think they know better than businessmen in one industry or another, it is preferable for them to take over a firm or establish a public enterprise as pace-setter in free competition for profit with other firms, rather than exhort, bribe or compel the whole industry to act on the central planner's information, which we have shown must be incomplete.

If the Conservatives want an intelligent alternative to the pretensions of central planning, they should reconsider the requirements of a competitive market economy, drawing on a distinguished line of scholars including Marshall and Keynes, and among whom Professors Lord Robbins, F.A Hayek, John Jewkes, B.S. Yamey, Colin Clark, Frank Paish, G.C. Allen and A.R. Prest are fortunately still very much alive.

If businessmen come to decide that, after all, they like central planning less than risk-taking private enterprise, they will have to stop looking for Government favours and look more to self-help. They can do this by avoiding rigid restrictive practices, welcoming fuller disclosure of business information, and tackling the risks of an uncertain future with the help of better market research and more flexible advertising and pricing policies. There is also scope for a variety of insurance hedging contracts, and other neglected devices that would reduce risks or transfer them to specialists in speculation. Such a reconstruction of competitive markets could bring better planning by reference to making profits (or minimising losses) than by reference to false prophets with their flawed crystal balls.

4   WHEN THE PRICE IS RIGHT[9]

Devaluation has forced the Government to admit the central importance of market pricing, even for a country's currency. Here is the case for pricing throughout the economy.

Suppose Mr Aubrey Jones, now awakening to the futility of periodic edicts on the price of bread, milk, detergents, haircuts and newspapers, stalked into the nearest supermarket and shuffled the price tags round in accord with his vision of 'the public interest'. It takes no economic genius to predict confusion, with queues to buy up the bargains and piles of over-priced goods left unsold.

Such a far-fetched experiment would at least have the merit of exposing in a single stride the distortion and ultimate disruption of economic activity towards which we are at present merely shuffling. If today the fortunes of coal, electricity, railways and even newspapers are heading for crises that politicians euphemistically call 'major adjustments', it is because for years their prices and costs have not been permitted to reflect changes in conditions of supply and demand.

Imagine how much bleaker the post-war years would have been if the 'planners' had stopped the prices of plastics, artificial fibres, antibiotics, chicken, ballpoints and detergents, washing machines and television sets from falling in relation to the prices of their old-fashioned substitutes.

Indispensable Guide

Short-sighted politicians might be excused for embracing the will-of-the-wisp of prices and incomes policy as a smokescreen for their failure to stop sowing the seeds of inflation, to weed-out restrictive practices, and to prune the sprawling public sector. More puzzling is the cavalier attitude of many professional economists towards the system of market pricing which Professor James Meade, writing as a 'liberal-socialist', once described as 'among the greatest social inventions of mankind'.

The paradox is that pricing is the pivot of economic analysis and action. It is to the economist what the slide-rule and scales are to the scientist or, more dynamically, what the instrument panel is to the test pilot. Who can say whether scarce resources are efficiently applied unless he can measure and compare their yields in alternative uses? Even in a not very competitive economy like Britain's, the catalogue of relative prices represented by rates of interest, profits, wages, provides an indispensable guide to getting existing savings, risk capital, labour, from less efficient to more efficient employments.

Our stubborn economic problems stem from the failure to understand and apply the logic of pricing as the regulator of supply and demand. Regional

Papers on markets and freedom

unemployment could be tackled by moving away from national wage rates so as to cheapen labour in depressed areas, as the Government's payroll subsidy has belatedly and indirectly acknowledged.

It is even possible that the worst of the brain drain could be avoided by raising the price for brains at this end. Most of the reasons given for emigration in the Jones Report – better prospects, facilities, conditions – are simply euphemisms for more money. But even if non-monetary attractions like sunshine and elbow-room accounted for the flow of British talent to the United States, it would not mean that financial recompense was ruled out. Indeed, the less we can do about the British weather, the more we should rely on the relative counter-attractions of higher income and lower taxes, about which we can do much.

Perhaps the most convincing demonstration of the pivotal importance of pricing is the mess we get into when prices are artificially reduced or eliminated altogether – as in the social services. Contrast the ample provision of what Mr Wilson used to deride as 'candy floss' with the inadequate supply of what all politicians like to describe as 'free' welfare.

We are not short of entertainments, or hi-fi, or garden furniture, or fashion wear, or (till the Government clamped down) of foreign holidays, or of any goods and services which are permitted to be bought and sold commercially at prices that cover their costs. In sharpest contrast, we are short of most 'public' goods and services. We always seem to need more doctors, teachers, hospitals, schools, subsidised council houses. What is missed by the economic Bourbons but as plain as a pikestaff to the market economist is that whenever valued goods or services are offered at zero price, demand will be inflated and supply attenuated.

Nor can the egalitarian console himself that if 'free' services lead to lower standards, at least all suffer equally. In practice, the most vicious kind of free-for-all flourishes beneath the surface of 'fair shares' in the Welfare State. Doing away with pricing does not dispose of scarcity: limited supplies still have to be rationed among competing customers by some device or other.

The Pick of the Draw

In state schooling, even under so-called 'comprehensive' equality, it is the parent who can afford to move to the right 'catchment area' whose children will get the pick of a very mixed bag. With subsidised council houses it is the luck of the draw, depending on local administrative rules and the possibility of getting round them. With expensive lifesaving equipment like the artificial kidney machine, the chance of a patient's survival may turn – as does much else – on the push or prominence of his relatives.

'Rationing by the purse' may sound a hard-headed doctrine, although it can be softened by putting more cash (or vouchers) in the lightest purses. But who would knowingly vote for what might be called 'rationing by the pat on the back' whereby those with the best contacts, the right accent, the tallest story, the biggest bribe (or smallest conscience), may get the lion's share of whatever 'free' goods and services are going? The fallacy of abandoning pricing is that the neediest may benefit least while the better-off or politically well-connected wrangle their way to the top. A lottery is always more capricious than an auction.

It was the widespread neglect of such economic analysis that prompted the Institute of Economic Affairs last year to launch an essay competition for young economists on 'the scope of pricing in maximising the efficiency of resources'. The essays of the winners and runners-up were published yesterday in a volume[10] that focuses attention on pricing as a weapon in our struggle against waste, inefficiency, rigidity, lethargy and other symptoms of the 'English disease'.

The significance of this collection of 14 essays is to show that pricing can help solve an infinite variety of problems, minor or major, ranging from refuse disposal, fire-protection, water supply, seaside amenities, and egg marketing, to the broad issues of central planning, taxation and agricultural policy.

Economic Realism

The essay by a Bradford University lecturer shows how the average cost of electricity might be reduced by charging higher rates at peak periods. Here is a nationalised industry with £4,000 million of precious capital, investing more than £700 million a year and earning a paltry net return of 5 per cent, compared with 14 per cent in private industry. By charging the same rate on a cold winter night as on midsummer eve (when costs are much lower) the industry has to install new capacity and keep high-cost old plant running in a desperate effort to avoid power cuts in periods of exceptional demand. The author's solution of seasonal variations in price would leave the consumer to decide whether to pay the high costs of supply at peak periods or to economise demand and enable the industry to reduce its costs.

It is precisely the neglect of such economic realism that has paved the way to devaluation and needs more urgently than ever to be put right.

The reader of this volume may think of other applications of pricing – in pay-television, public libraries, art galleries, opera, the post office, Civil Service salaries, and throughout the social services. What such fearless economic analysis demonstrates is that the neglect of pricing, particularly throughout the public sector, causes or aggravates more problems than politicians can ever hope to solve without its help. When Government is piling compulsion on cajolery in a vain effort to suppress the price system, it may seem perverse to emphasise its incomparable efficiency. Yet, as disillusioned economists in Eastern Europe have learned the hard way, so long as 'planning' tries to prevail against 'supply and demand' – that is, the wishes of people as suppliers and demanders – no battery of computers or coercion will prevent consequent confusion and even chaos.

5   GRAVE-DIGGERS OF PLANNING[11]

Disillusionment with Mr Wilson and all his works should cause no more than modified rapture for those who care most deeply about the health of a free society.

Massive as his guilt may be, we are inviting trouble in the future if we overlook the responsibility of so many others for the phoney policies which date back to 1961, although they have only now finally collapsed on our heads. The alarming lesson is that most politicians of all parties, the majority of business 'leaders' at the CBI, and the more articulate journalists, broadcasters, academic publicists, and opinion-formers only began to question the planning swindle after the entire house of cards fell about their credulous ears.

'We Told You So'

Indeed, among politicians, who but Enoch Powell and his friends are entitled to say, 'We told you so?'. In November 1965, eight months before the hasty interment of George Brown's and Mr Callaghan's 'vision for the future', the Conservative (and Liberal) 'leaders' in the Commons accepted without a division the resolution: 'That this House welcomes the National Plan'.

In his new book[12] Professor Jewkes has no difficulty in demonstrating the total failure of the NEDC plan which Macmillan launched with the confident aim of conjuring up a steady 4 per cent annual growth in output from 1961–66. Instead, in the five years growth ranged from under 1 per cent to over 5 per cent and averaged less than 3 per cent as in the bad old days of 'stop–go'. The errors in specific targets, like investment, exports, earnings, were even more laughably and perversely wide of the mark.

Before Conservative apologists wriggle with talk that Neddy at least did no harm, Professor Jewkes points out that it was misplaced belief in the 'plan' which darkened counsel and delayed remedial measures in the inflationary boom of 1964. Likewise, under the new Labour Government, obsession with the even more ambitious National Plan distracted attention away from the sombre realities of impending disaster and put policy (particularly on Government expenditure) into a straitjacket from which even Mr Jenkins showed himself last month still unable to escape.

If this book was simply a post-mortem with the aid of hindsight, the first 40 pages would provide a valuable summary of what went wrong in the 1960s. But it is very much more. For good measure the remaining 200 pages reproduce the greater part of a brilliant book *Ordeal by Planning,* which he first published in 1948 after top-level experience of planning in war.

Twenty years after first reading this exposé of the inevitable failure of such 'short-cuts' as central economic planning I am more than ever impressed by the quality of the author's analysis, his sure grasp of essentials, his wise acknowledgement of fallible human understanding, and his flowing clarity of exposition. Thus on the noble aspirations of (some) planners for a more humane, secure, scientific, just society, Jewkes pointed out that such legitimate hopes are in practice self-frustrating:

> For central planning ultimately turns every individual into a cipher and every economic decision into blind fumbling, destroys the incentives through which economic progress arises, renders the economic system as unstable as the whims of the few who ultimately control it and creates a system of wire-pulling and privileges in which economic justice ceases to have any meaning.

If planning has failed everywhere – and is being reversed even in Communist economies – why are so many 'sophisticated' people taken in? Professor Jewkes diagnosed – in 1948 – several sources of confusion in human weakness: 'The turbulent craving for a new order of things' (how's that for George Brown or Dr Balogh?); 'an itch for novelty' (the occupational hazard of journalists); 'a remarkably over-simplified conception of the task which lies before them' (Callaghan and Wilson); 'exaggeration of the benefits to be derived from mechanisation' (Wedgwood Benn, Wilson, and other 'technological' addicts); 'a strong predilection for tidiness in the economic system' (Aubrey Jones, Fred Catherwood, and the restless tribe of tinkerers).

Superficial Appeal of Planning

The superficial appeal of planning owes much to the greater intellectual effort required to grasp the more subtle, complex, wide, and long-range considerations in favour of a free economy, which the author illustrates vividly from his own capacious knowledge of the indispensable role of the entrepreneur and the practical working of the price system. Many who might resist the Utopian claims of planning fall victim to the more plausible argument that more of it is necessary in a mixed economy. Hence the 'economic appeasers' who pride themselves on having a 'balanced and judicial mind'.

> Yet no democratic community can exist save where its members understand the difference between having their hair cut short and having their scalps taken clean off, and recognise in the former the ever-growing dangers of the latter.

The central reason for rejecting economic planning is not because the planners are incompetent but because what they are attempting is impossible. To stand any chance of success a central economic plan would call for a degree of understanding we do not have about the precise ingredients of growth, complete knowledge of all available resources, absolute power to control and relate myriad components accordingly, supernatural powers to predict changes in techniques and consumer preference.

Politicians Decide

Even if the theory of central planning were less ramshackle, Jewkes reminds us that it is *politicians* who decide the plans in the light of ill-considered election commitments, and it is 'comically naïve' to expect Wilson, Jenkins, or even Heath to allow the economic or statistical experts to try to determine the planning of output or employment *objectively* – without calculating (however wrongly) the response of trade unions, farmers, MPs, marginal voters, the regions, and other lobbies. Hence the descent from the high theory of planning to the low-down.

No review can do justice to a book which packs into 240 pages more wisdom and constructive thought than could be gleaned from the mostly barren literature of planning during the 20 years the author bestrides with such easy mastery. And let the non-economist also buy or borrow from the nearest library a book which attacks the obsessive materialism of those who would have us devote all our waking lives to a vain effort to rescue their plan from its inevitable doom. The truth is that the planners are digging their own grave and this book shows how we can hasten the funeral and resume the neglected task of reconstructing the free economy on surer foundations.

6   ON HAYEK[13]

Had Hayek been an apostle of collectivism instead of its most lethal living opponent, his 70th birthday would have been the signal for the whole apparatus of press, radio and television to rejoice in the presence among us of a truly great thinker. The BBC would have vied with the *New Statesman* to mark 1969 not only as the 70th anniversary of Hayek's birth (in Vienna) but symbolically as the 25th of the publication of *The Road to Serfdom*. On the latter event, one can picture Robin Day, David Dimbleby and all the other up-to-the-minute men interviewing victims of collectivist oppression in Russia, China, Czechoslovakia, Cuba and some of the newer African countries to test Hayek's thesis that political control over the means of production, distribution and exchange inevitably extinguishes individual freedom in political no less than in economic affairs.

Contrast the audible silence which greeted Hayek's double anniversary with the tributes showered in their lifetime on such now largely forgotten socialist folk heroes as G.D.H. Cole, Hugh Dalton, Harold Laski and even R.H. Tawney. More specifically, contrast the slender basis of intellectually reputable writing that has made J.K. Galbraith into the undergraduate equivalent of a matineé idol and brought him an invitation to Trinity in the university of [Alfred] Marshall, [John Maynard] Keynes, [Arthur] Pigou and [Dennis] Robertson. The survival of belief in the free economy against such one-sided attention testifies to the power of ideas and to the practical failure of the opposing philosophy to supply a tolerable alternative.

Hayek's most exacting admirers may doubt whether *The Road to Serfdom* is his best claim to fame, but a re-reading will satisfy most sceptics that it combines more intellectual force, analytical subtlety and mature wisdom than all Galbraith's superficially more appealing works put together. Indeed, from a list of well over 100 essays in Hayek's repertoire, single efforts like 'The Meaning of Competition' or 'The Use of Knowledge in Society' throw more light on the rôle of the market mechanism than a bookshelf of more widely known and acclaimed volumes in the libraries of many university departments of social science.

If we can still rely on profound ideas having a larger (though later) impact on events than more shallow, showy 'new thinking', there need be no undue anxiety that the contemporary world appears largely to be ignoring Hayek's contribution to politics, economics and philosophy. But if his genius must await posthumous recognition by the many, it is a modest consolation that some of the few who have grasped his importance should meanwhile honour his 70th birthday by a volume of essays entitled *Roads to Freedom*.[14] None of Hayek's friends will be wholly satisfied that this *Festschrift* does full justice to the man it celebrates, despite characteristic contributions by [Karl] Popper, [Friedrich] Lutz, [Frank] Paish, [James] Buchanan, [Gottfried] Haberler, [Fritz] Machlup, [Peter] Bauer and half-a-dozen other champions of the free market economy. But none, even of his critics, can fail to be impressed by the evidence these 15 essays give of the many-sidedness of Hayek's contribution to theory on the trade cycle, money, interest rates, wages, pricing, planning and competition as well as to the practice of law, political institutions, the scientific method, history and even language in political thought.

7 LET US GIVE TWO CHEERS FOR CAPITALISM[15]

'. . . *even the remnant of capitalism in Britain – though it accounts for whatever success our economy still enjoys – is not safe from further erosion until we can instruct both its practitioners and its critics that competitive enterprise is superior . . .*'

If the issue turned on a purely materialist reckoning, the triumph of capitalism over socialism could hardly be in doubt. Even if we had forgotten the miracle of material progress achieved in the West by largely unguided private enterprise in the 19th century and earlier, the lesson has been hammered home in the post-war years by the contrast between the bustling creation of wealth in Germany, North America or Hongkong, and the drift of persistent poverty throughout India and most of Africa from Egypt to Northern Rhodesia despite the massive transfusion of 'aid'.

In Eastern Europe the poor performance of central planning has forced even Russian Communists to try to bring back the alien concepts of market pricing, enterprise and profitability.

The superiority of capitalism in making the best use of scarce resources is in principle not hard to understand. History is full of examples of countries richly endowed with natural resources, fertile land and favourable climate that have languished until the most vital resource of all, individual enterprise, is unleashed to co-operate in harvesting the latent wealth.

Circumstances of course, must be right. The most adventurous innovator will not invest effort and capital in projects yielding their return over many years, unless there is a framework of law and order which promises some security against force and fraud – whether from common thieves, less scrupulous competitors, corrupt officials or grasping governments.

Merits of Competition

Within such a setting, competition must be most effective because it allows better ideas to supersede prevailing ideas by giving them a chance to prove themselves – without seeking the approval of central planners who can never have a monopoly of wisdom to match their monopoly of power. It provides a trial-and-error system open to people with varying talents, knowledge, visions, techniques, effort and perseverance, all seeking ways of making scarce resources go furthest in meeting the demands on them.

Throughout the economy, in welfare, nationalised industries, taxation, land development, atomic energy, transport and broadcasting, public policy is diverted from its most efficient, creative course because of objections on allegedly moral grounds to competitive enterprise and market pricing. In each case, confusion between the motive and the outcome of human action leads to a mis-judgement of market-based policies.

Central to this widespread moral obfuscation is dislike of the appeal to self-interest which it is supposed private enterprise peculiarly exploits. After 25 years' study of the writing of the classical liberal economists from Adam Smith to Keynes, Hayek, Robbins and Milton Friedman, I believe this supposition is without theoretical or empirical foundation.

Particularly during the past decade since resuming regular churchgoing, I have questioned whether a belief in capitalism conflicts with the best in the Christian ethic. Why do I unhesitatingly prefer the capitalism expounded by Mr Enoch Powell and Sir Keith Joseph to the mixed (or mixed-up) economy of many Conservatives or the socialism of Mr Wilson and Bishop Trevor Huddleston?

At the outset it must be emphasised that so-called self-interest is not simply a result of original sin, but also of fallible knowledge and understanding which limits our comprehension to what best suits our family, friends, neighbourhood, and other specific causes we make our own. Insofar as fallen man generally prefers his own interest in this sense to that of others, the capitalist system, even as practised in the USA, has two decisive advantages over a socialist regime as practised in Russia.

In the first place, as Adam Smith emphasised nearly 200 years ago, competitive markets can harmonise private and social interest by harnessing to productive, creative tasks what he described as 'the uniform, constant and uninterrupted effort of every man to better his condition'. By leading individuals to apply their talents and property where they yield the highest wage, salary, rent, profit, the market system provides a systematic mechanism for getting immensely varied human material resources into employments where they contribute most to what Smith called 'opulence' or 'the wealth of nations'.

No Compulsion

Notice, by the way, that nobody is compelled to maximise his monetary return. Those who prefer leisure, contemplation, voluntary work, getting into the honours list, or other satisfactions can, under capitalism, turn aside from the 'rat race' and maximise whatever combination and forms of income and idleness suits their tastes. Furthermore, although most people will work harder for their families than for whatever passes in peacetime as 'the national interest', they can often best help their favourite good causes by maximising their monetary income so as to afford larger contributions to charities.

It may be more emotionally satisfying for a student to talk of going to Africa during the vacation to involve himself in 'community service' among the natives. But he will probably be highly incompetent at nursing the sick or instructing Africans in better crop and animal husbandry; whereas by staying at home he could easily earn £20 a week as a building labourer and send money to Africa which would do far more good. Into the bargain, he would save his fare which would alone be enough to keep an African family in luxury for a year or more.

Confronted with such realistic alternatives which the market system makes available, the preference of students – and other idealists – for so-called 'community service' is not more moral but merely a disguised form of self-interest or self-indulgence, and one which does less, if any, good to the intended beneficiaries.

The second enormous advantage of capitalism over socialism in dealing with the widespread phenomenon of self-interest is best grasped by dwelling on the following quotation from Keynes:

> [D]angerous human proclivities can be canalised into comparatively harmless channels by the existence of opportunities for money-making and private wealth, which, if they cannot be satisfied in this way, may find their outlet in cruelty, the reckless pursuit of personal power and authority.
>
> It is better that a man should tyrannise over his bank balance than over his fellow citizens . . . The task of transmuting human nature must not be confused with the task of managing it.

If self-interest – or what I prefer to call 'individual purpose'– is as strong, widespread and persistent as Adam Smith and Keynes believed and as idealistic socialists deplore, how can it be subdued?

Socialist Self-interest

So far from scorning an appeal to self-interest, from 1964 to 1970 socialist policies have exploited the honours system and extended patronage in the form of subsidies and well-paid prestigious public appointments to divert (or pervert) individual purposes wherever they have been inconvenient to public policy.

Royal Commissions and independent committees have been packed with partisan allies; permissions for firms to merge have been granted in return for undertakings to bolster the political purposes of Ministers; grants from public funds have been used to advance Labour's electoral prospects or to placate trade unions in industries like shipbuilding where restrictive practices have enriched sectional interests and brought firms to the verge of bankruptcy; and following the Budget in 1970 a wages scramble was connived at in order to win short-sighted votes in the June election.

Ministers who denounce private provision as introducing double standards into education or medical care themselves betray a far more culpable dual standard in public profession and personal conduct by patronising private schools and health insurance. Some of the most indignant critics of inequality look to spread a nation of council tenants whilst themselves living in fine style between two or three residences.

The Minister who singled out private employment agencies for attack as a threat to official labour exchanges was simultaneously negotiating with one of

tics. If, by some gamble against all the odds, this latest sample of Government by Chequers tea-party came off, it would prolong the distortion of relative wages and prices which already diverts too much of our resources into wasteful misemployments.

Above all, it would be a further retreat from the rule of law to the regulation of our affairs by medieval guilds and private cabals which impose their whims by devious pressures on free men guilty of no worse sin than conducting business in the light of their best judgements and according to the law of the land.

So long as they pay lip-service to norms, however, they should be ready this time to deal firmly with the inevitable abnorms which militant trade unionists (or political wreckers) will throw back at them.

Here, Conservatives could not do better than take their cue from a self-confessed liberal-socialist, Professor James Meade, who in his Wincott lecture last year proposed that unions striking for unacceptable demands should lose their accumulated rights for redundancy pay and have their supplementary benefits either financed by the union or in the form of a loan they would have to repay.

After that bright interval the bad news comes thick and fast. No incomes policy or curb on labour monopolies will touch inflation unless buttressed by a tight rein on the money supply.

It follows remorselessly that public expenditure must be cut back to reduce the budget deficit now financed more or less directly by the printing press.

There is no escape in trying to balance the books by raising taxation, which is already a major independent spur to inflation.

The mischief is revealed with the help of a few figures. A family with two children having no more than 20 debased pounds coming in each week now pays about £2 in taxes.

$$*\quad*\quad*$$

On Mr Heath's handout of £2, the breadwinner's tax rate is 35 per cent, so that take-home pay goes up much less than the apparent 10 per cent.

Indeed, for such a family to hold its own in face of a 10 per cent price rise, an increase in gross income of 14 per cent would be needed.

High taxes are thus an inbuilt inflator which can be pricked only by drastic cuts in public spending.

In gloomier moments I confess to seeing Britain becoming a kind of nature reserve for Europe in which are harmlessly preserved every variety of sacred cow, dying duck, nationalised dinosaur, trade union cart horse, and specially fattened underdogs, all jostling at the public feeding trough.

But before this animal farm attracts the rude attention of an Orwellian pig,

I fancy we will bestir ourselves and strive for the higher standards of living most of us plainly think worth earning – and even striking for.

Straining for good news, therefore, I interpret the evidence of so much wrong with the British economy as showing scope for just a little less nonsense in one or two directions to yield a galvanising effect.

It is remarkably encouraging news that we have survived thus far, despite the laceration of self-inflicted wounds.

*   *   *

If any forgivably sensitive souls fear we must fail to head off inflation because of the risk of higher unemployment, I conclude with more good news.

While the experts of the Department of Employment were busy cooking up press releases for trusting journalists to make headlines about 1,000,000 on the dole, an Institute of Economic Affairs report took the official statistics apart and found at least half this crude, alarmist total were either unemployable or busy moving between jobs, often cushioned by an untaxed benefit (plus tax repayment) higher than their previous (taxed) take-home pay.

No doubt any solution to inflation will add to the unemployment statistics, particularly if unions try to defy monetary discipline and follow the dockers, miners, printers, and Clydesiders in pricing more of their unfortunate members out of jobs.

But this increase would be the more short-lived if we copy the Swedish example of confining generous unemployment pay to people who retrain for new work. After inflation is mastered, we are left with the task of getting people now in protected, artificial employments to shift to new and expanding firms earning high profits.

9   WHO ARE THE GUILTY MEN?[17]

Suppose we take a break from the party political shadow-boxing that passes for a mature democracy in action and ask who, if anyone, is responsible for the latest economic assault perpetrated on the poor old pound – with at least 15 per cent inflation generally expected this year.

There would be a number of charges on the sheet but all are subordinate to what might be summarised as economic arson – the setting light to the powder trail of inflation. A full-scale court of inquiry would take time. Meanwhile, at the preliminary hearings any competent judge would dismiss from the case several popular suspects such as property speculators and foreigners, and put the trade union bosses on bail as accessories before or after the fact. On circumstantial evidence, the most likely-looking incendiaries to be hauled up for questioning would certainly be Mr Heath, his Chancellor Anthony Barber, and that unquenchable prophet of boom, Peter Walker.

There are now very few expert witnesses who would seriously challenge the empirical evidence Milton Friedman has assembled from many countries over long periods of history, irrespective of trade union power or government controls, that 'inflation is always and everywhere a monetary phenomenon in the sense that it is and can be produced only by a more rapid increase in the quantity of money than in output'.

After consulting his customary advisers Mr Heath might plead that in the past when money supply was momentarily cut back, prices went on rising; but his objection would be over-ruled by reference to any standard monetary text which emphasises under some such heading as 'lagged response' that the first impact of a change in the quantity of money is on the level of real output for up to nine months with the major effect on the rate of inflation taking nearer 18 to 24 months to work through the economy.

At this stage, the plight of the defendants would look distinctly shaky. After all, since 1972 the Chancellor allowed the money stock to increase by more than 20 per cent a year and yet was taken by surprise 18 months later when inflation started escalating beyond 10 per cent. Indeed, the three leading exponents of the gamble on growth can be shown by copious quotations to have gone on denying the danger signals up to December when the oil crisis gave them a temporary alibi for all that has followed.

'Classic Symptoms of Inflation'

By the autumn all the classic symptoms of inflation were plainly visible. Abroad, there was the sinking pound (which, please note, *raised* the sterling prices of imported raw materials, etc.) and the record balance-of-payments deficit (which, pray ponder, *moderated* the domestic inflation by exporting excess purchasing power to our overseas suppliers). At home, witness after witness called attention to spreading shortages, unfilled vacancies, lengthening delivery dates, quickening pace of price increases, and other familiar evidence of overheating.

Faced with the record, and remembering he is under oath, Mr Heath might go for a strong plea of mitigation. Had not his motive been of the purest? Faced with statistical unemployment approaching the million mark and anxious to dodge the old 'stop–go', he decided to 'reflate' the economy in the hope that increased output would match the massive injection of purchasing power which culminated in a 'borrowing requirement' (i.e. over-spending) of £4,000 million in the Budget a year ago. Even when businessmen complained of labour shortages, Mr Heath remained mesmerised by the macro-statistics of unemployment. Hence, his oft-repeated grouse that the grand strategy for perpetual growth was being sabotaged by feeble industrialists who failed to expand output, investment and employment to keep ahead of inflation.

The significance of this line of defence is that Mr Heath's misjudgement was shared by a large number of other accessories. For a start, Mr Wilson and his most vocal colleagues are immediately removed from the spectators' gallery into the dock. After exaggerating unemployment in 1972, they had welcomed the 'commitment to growth' as had a very long list of gullibles headed by Mr Campbell Adamson and the CBI, to say nothing of such other weather-vanes as Lord Vic Feather and the combined TUC, Sir Fred Catherwood and NEDC, the ever-expansionist NIESR, Andrew Shonfield, Roger Opie and endless participants in *The Money Programme* and similar TV phoney inquests. Little better can be said of most leader writers (including, alas, *The Economist),* Michael Stewart and other trendy authors of Penguin Specials, and similar hindsighted pundits now shaking their heads over the collapse of the umpteenth experiment in forced growth.

'Witnesses to Error'

Indeed, it is easier to single out the comparative handful of witnesses innocent of what Lord Robbins dignified as a 'crisis of intellectual error'. Among journalists, the most persistent warnings came from Graham Hutton, Paul Bareau, Samuel Brittan, Peter Jay (who wrote 'The boom that must go bust' last May), and Patrick Hutber, with *The Daily Telegraph,* the *Banker* and *The Spectator* keeping their heads. When one outstanding independent banker, Walter Salomon, repeated a year ago his urgent warnings against inflation as the 'arch-disintegrator of society', his book *One Man's View* was loftily ignored by *The Times* and *Financial Times.*

Among MPs the unwavering voice of Enoch Powell was echoed audibly only by Nicholas Ridley and a handful of Tories with some muted mutterings on the Labour benches. Among professional economists, a relatively small if growing number mostly associated with the Institute of Economic Affairs and the Economic Research Council have maintained a spirited campaign against monetary excesses, led by such outstanding champions as Alan Walters, Gordon Pepper and Harry Johnson.

When so few appear wholly exempt from blame and so many (including all three party leaders) seem still to need to learn the full error of their ways, the detached observer is bound to search deeper for the tainted source of 'intellectual error' which appears no less rampant among the Treasury knights than among the Oxbridge peers ([Thomas] Balogh and [Richard] Kahn).

The trail would lead us back to the followers of Keynes who taught that governments could always mop up unemployment by 'fine-tuning' the economy and failed to see that insofar as the unemployed are immobile, have the wrong skills, live in the wrong place, insist through monopoly trade unions on uneconomic wages, or are better-off 'resting' between jobs, then increased monetary demand will drive up prices more surely than it will draw idle resources into production.

'Confusers of Counsels'

Confusers of counsels include the whole tribe of so-called 'labour economists' led by Hugh Clegg who have mostly shrunk from exposing the rigidities and restrictions of trade unions or the mechanism by which monopoly wage bargaining can price workers and firms out of business – unless governments obligingly float them off on a tide of rising inflation. Their sins of omission were inflamed by leader writers who beat their breasts about 'a million on the dole' when the IEA's *How Much Unemployment?* would have shown Mr Heath that it was largely a phantom army which could not be conscripted by old-fashioned Keynesian-type monetary expansion.

With so many guilty men, a strong plea for mercy might temper the verdict on the Conservative inflationists to a suspended sentence. Next week I shall review some of the far-reaching changes necessary to put an end to inflation. And you, dear reader, will have to judge what relevance the three parties' policies have to this central issue for the stability of our economy and society.

10   WHO WILL SAVE US?[18]

For all who have grasped the fundamental monetary nature of inflation, the economic issue at this election is not the price of milk, mortgages or mouse-traps but the general, continuing and accelerating debasement in the value of the £ at home and abroad. That debasement has followed the record growth in the money supply of between 20 and 30 per cent a year since Mr Heath took charge in 1970.

What is it that tempts so many politicians to play with the fire of inflation? The plain answer is that monetary expansion appears to offer a soft option by which governments can dodge awkward choices between unemployment and alternative ways of improving the working of a free economy in the face of obstruction from trade unions.

At the heart of the economic problem is the inescapable condition of limited resources against which competing demands are exerted by the sectional interests of unions, farmers, firms, regions, government departments, for the rival claims of consumption, investment, exports, welfare. In an environment of stable money, the division of incomes (i.e. claims over resources) is settled in however rough and ready a way by changes in relative market prices.

The unwelcome consequence is that if the general price level is held stable by monetary restraint, some prices (including wages as the price of labour) will rise less than others and may not rise at all, or may even fall in declining trades. Changes in relative prices call for adjustments which are particularly disturbing in a pampered, rigid economy where immobile labour, restrictive practices, dying ducks, subsidised stay-putters, and what Professor W.H. Hutt calls the 'strike-threat system' impair the responsiveness of labour and capital to the very shifts in demand and supply on which progress depends.

How much easier – in the short run – for government to squirt money around the economy and foster the illusion that everyone can get more without anyone having to move or get less; that all workers irrespective of skills or location can enjoy full employment without moderating their wage demands; that all firms can be kept in business without earning their own keep; and that the party men can spend more without the voters spending less.

Alas, after a brief boom while stocks and idle capacity are used up, reality reasserts itself with a vengeance. Inflated demand sucks in more imports, frustrates exports, sinks the floating pound, drives domestic prices higher and – witness the miners – sharpens the very conflicts which it was the dream of expansionists to banish.

'A Paralysis of the Pricing System'

So far from solving the problem, reliance on incomes policy first diverts attention from the true cause of inflation while things get worse and then spreads a paralysis of the pricing system on which our eventual hope of an efficient adjustment mechanism – as well as our freedom – must rely. As Professor C.J. Grayson, head of the Price Commission under Nixon's Phase 2, recently warned businessmen (no less than labour leaders and politicians), we are simply 'building our own cages' and have no escape except to 'get back to the competitive market system'.

Because of the delayed-action effect of monetary expansion, we have yet to reap the harvest of past excess which indicates a fall in the value of money nearer 20 per cent in 1974 than the 10 per cent of the recent past. In that case, whatever Mr Heath cooks up with building societies, interest rates must go still higher if the saver is to be left with a margin above the fall in value of his money and the tax on 'unearned' income.

Clearly, the sooner we stop inflating the money supply the sooner the fever will subside. Faced with a devil's brew of escalating demand and declining real output, the urgent desideratum remains for a large reduction in the budget deficit. Since taxes, whether on goods or take-home-pay, already inflame the symptoms of inflation, the most effective way for government to live within its income without resort to the printing press is by cutting expenditure.

BOX 1 RALPH HARRIS'S NOTE FOR THE GUIDANCE OF UNHAPPY VOTERS

Confronted with the choice of voting for nondescript nominees of Labour or Conservative parties, you may not relish your handiwork being brandished like a political scalp by Mr Wilson or Mr Heath as a statistic in favour or against the miners, the Common Market, incomes policy, high taxation, socialism, or 'conservatism', or either of the party leaders.

If you, nevertheless, wish to vote rather than abstain or spoil your paper, you may mark your cross against the least objectionable candidate and add a message to let him know what you really think on this or that – or of him or his leader.

So long as the 'intention is clear', your ballot paper will be sorted out on the night among a pile of 'doubtfuls'. It will then be shown by the presiding officer to all the candidates who are invited to adjudicate whether 'the intention is clear'. So long as your cross is marked against one name, the candidate claiming your vote is obliged to read your message publicly. After this salutary process, the winner is likely to be less cavalier in boasting of a triumphant vote of confidence in his party's policy or his leader's wretched record.

Economies are anyway long overdue in such bloated spending as the capital projects of public authorities, the enfeebling subsidies to nationalised and private industry, the spawning bureaucracies, and the misplaced generosity of indiscriminate welfare in cash and kind. In a forthcoming book from Churchill Press ominously entitled *Must History Repeat Itself?*, Mr Antony Fisher concludes with a 10-year programme that could bring income tax down to 15 per cent, with no surtax, capital gains tax or VAT [value added tax].

Removing Strikers' Privileges

To ease the withdrawal symptoms from inflation and assist the processes of adjustment, the monopoly power of unions must be prevented from pushing wages so high that a large number of workers and firms are left stranded once the Chancellor refuses to float them off on a rising tide of monetary inflation. The present picketing by miners of docks and power stations, however apparently 'peaceful', points to the critical reform. Strikers should lose their privileged exemption from the ordinary law on conspiracy which now enables them collectively in furtherance of an industrial dispute to inflict damage in ways that would be illegal if done by other groups or by individuals acting alone.

I can hear a chorus from shrill treble to growling bass objecting that resolute action to clip public spending and curb labour monopolies is 'politically impossible' and I concede it is not on the horizon of the three party manifestoes. But 12 per cent inflation, a statutory incomes policy and a three-day week were not in Mr Heath's prospectus in 1970, any more than devaluation, prescription charges and 'In Place of Strife' featured in Mr Wilson's euphoric pledges of 1964.

To judge from the mostly business-as-usual electioneering we have been witnessing, it is impossible to see any early escape from our present 'cage' of unavailing and crippling controls under either Mr Heath or Mr Wilson. Things will have to get worse before minds are concentrated on the fundamental redirection of economic policy based on monetary and competitive disciplines.

If you take the view that the sooner the rude awakening comes the quicker the reconstruction will start, you might grit your teeth and vote Labour for an early convulsion. Likewise, if you think the Conservatives will relearn their lessons better in opposition, you can bite the bullet and let Labour ruin things for a while – if they started their taxation/nationalisation nonsense, it would last a matter of months, not years.

On a dispassionate review, the only ground for positively supporting Mr Heath is if you think him sufficiently practised at somersaulting to turn back on such indelibly *dirigiste* and damaging policies as pay and price incantations, Wedgwood-Walker industrial tinkering, Willie Whitewash's compromising, corporativist, consensus consultations with the weary worthies of the TUC, CBI, NEDO, NFU [National Farmer's Union], *et mon oncle EEC aussi.*

Of course, you should not be doctrinaire in voting against Conservatives. Indeed, there are some I would welcome the chance of supporting such as Boyson, Biffen, Body, Bell, Bruce-Gardyne, Du Cann, Deedes, Dykes, Eyres, Hall (Joan), Lamont, Lawson, Finsberg, Griffiths (Brian), Ridley, Moate, Marten, Thatcher, Proudfoot, Spicer (on approval), Benyon (the white hope of Huyton), and Howe (the last hope of salvation).

On Labour, etc. candidates it would be combining business with pleasure for me to vote for Jenkins (Roy), Prentice, Pardoe, Williams (Shirley), Walden, Maxwell, Fletcher, Houghton, Taverne, Foot (mouth and all), Grayson (Bristol SE) and Hargrave (Sidcup).

Who else then will save us? Our surest hope is that we will save ourselves as soon as we can be set free from the palsied, paralysing grip of the puny party pontiffs.

11   LIKE IT OR NOT, OUR SOCIETY IS BASED ON THE THEORY OF CAPITALISM[19]

'Do those most eagerly seeking to deprive others of "privileges" set an example by adopting a simple life-style or do they appear to thrive on the trappings of power?'

The health and vigour of a mature political democracy must depend on unhindered debate between opposing philosophies. This process is imperilled if the scales are tilted so far one way that it becomes difficult to win a hearing for the broad concept of liberal capitalism that has been sustained by some of the finest minds of this century: [John Maynard] Keynes, [Ludwig von] Mises, [Karl] Popper, [Lionel] Robbins, [F.A.] Hayek, [Milton] Friedman. . . .

Yet we are in danger of reaching a point where intellectual discourse is sterilised by populist slogans and scolding. Even leading 'capitalists' are infected with an enfeebling guilt complex that makes them almost willing accomplices in the destruction of free markets which (as Bernard Levin warned last month) are the foundation of other freedoms: the right to vote – or even to strike.

No attack on economic freedom has proved more corrosive than the spread of the notion that its material superiority is fatally flawed by its moral inferiority to a centrally directed, statist economy. Wilhelm Röpke, the Christian author of *The Humane Economy* and tenacious critic of national socialism, used to say that, even if capitalism were not the best engine of material welfare, it would still merit our highest allegiance as the most moral social order available to fallen man. So I agree with Raymond Fletcher that the grand debate should start from the ethical credentials of alternative economic arrangements.

Even individuals who strive after the highest standards of moral conduct are moved by a complex mixture of motives. Adam Smith, who wrote *The Theory of Moral Sentiments* before *The Wealth of Nations,* thought that the most pervasive driving force in economic life was 'the effort of every man to better his condition'. This concept explains the stricture that 'capitalism' panders to selfishness, when what is meant is that individuals will exert themselves most keenly to advance the welfare of family, friends, locality, clubs, church or any other cause about which they care.

Some may wish it otherwise; but 'Man is very far gone from original righteousness', as the Prayer Book reminds us and I suspect most Jews, Humanists and Don't Knows will recognise the self-serving weakness of their own nature.

Which social/economic system provides the most fitting environment for man *as he now is* to live out his daily life and labour? Which system will function tolerably despite human frailty and fallibility? Does the fallen nature of man best accord with an open order of dispersed initiative which creates cohesion and harmony by harnessing self-interest through a direct link between effort and reward to achieve voluntary co-operation in production and exchange? Or should we applaud the collectivist vision which repudiates self-interest and elevates social goals that can be procured at the cost of private choices only by increasingly coercive central commands.

Liberal Capitalism, Law and Philanthropy

Certainly, 'capitalism', like nature itself, favours the strong and fleet of foot, but the demonology of *laisser faire* has not stopped societies resting on economic freedom from using taxation to help the halt and lame. Liberal capitalism does not operate in a vacuum but within a framework of law, enriched in the West by philanthropy, voluntary societies, civic pride, individual example. . . . If – in Alfred Marshall's dichotomy – it appeals to the strongest motives, it leaves ample scope for the highest.

Yet, because what Samuel Brittan has called 'the corrected market economy' puts a high value on freedom for consumers and so for producers, it confines governmental coercion to specific *public goods* not amenable to competitive supply. National defence, internal law and order, standards of safety, honest weights and measures (including money) and government guarantee of basic needs – in cash or kind – go back beyond Beveridge or Lloyd George to the first Elizabethans.

In contrast, the approach favoured increasingly by all three parties since the war gives priority to collective consumption, uniformity, equality – even where human conditions differ. It extends the range of public goods by enforcing 'social objectives' in the production and distribution of an indefinitely extensible list of everyday personal goods and services. Economic freedom is consistent with prescribing a minimum standard of education, medical care, pensions, housing; collectivism drives on towards a monopoly of state provision outlawing private effort, preference and supply.

If human nature were immaculate, social goals would establish themselves more or less spontaneously. If we were not 'all socialists now' we would at least be fit to dwell in a collectivist paradise without the tensions, temptations and torments caused by frustrated private purpose. As it is, collectivism must apply increasing coercion to override individual striving and keep wayward man on the prescribed straight and narrow. That is why the further we depart from a recognisable 'capitalism', the faster we slide towards authoritarianism.

Morality and Choice

Moral growth for individuals springs from the exercise of choice. There is no moral merit in 'doing good' at gun-point. Merciless taxation – rising to 98 per cent on private income – blesses neither giver nor taker: it leaves the victim with the choice of acquiescing in legalised theft, fiddling his tax returns or fleeing while he may. Thus the denial of economic freedom induces schizophrenia or corrupts the governed. But does it foster virtue among the governors? If there are not enough saints to form a cabinet, let alone supply the armies to enforce its commands, how can we expect the politicians in charge to serve the 'public interest' instead of feathering their nests? Do those most eagerly seeking power to deprive others of 'privileges' set an example by adopting a simple life-style? Or do they appear to thrive on the trappings of power?

Consider how corruption has already tarnished the selfless ideals of those who would centralise power for noble ends. Observe how politicians who in theory most recoil from the sordid play of self-interest, in practice promote a daily, deafening appeal to covetousness. In my lifetime it has been politicians describing themselves as 'socialists' or 'progressive conservatives' who – with few honourable exceptions like Sir Stafford Cripps – have more often led the field in promising voters *self*-enrichment at the expense of landlords, profiteers, speculators or some other convenient – even non-existent – minority. Beneath the moral-political crusade invariably dwells a careful, corrupting calculation about the short-term material self-interest of at least a working majority of the electorate.

The 'unacceptable face' of human nature is far worse in government than in business where competition and law can set limits to the harm that bad men will do. So I conclude that the avoidable excesses of the profit (and wage) maximisation incentive under economic freedom are as nothing compared to the incurable moral hazards of the vote-maximisation appeal by which collectivists entice us to surrender power to them. And for what end? We have 'castrated capitalism' in return for [Arthur] Pigou's mess of political potage which now threatens both individual freedom and national solvency.

12   NEDDY FOR THE KNACKER'S YARD[20]

Ralph Harris finds the track record of the National Economic Development Council too harmful to justify running it again.

With the Government now talking about 'picking the winners' the question asks itself whether we should put any more of our money on Neddy in the economic recovery stakes. The National Economic Development Council, to give it its full dignity, is after all no promising yearling. It has been around a long time and the form book tells its own story.

Set up by Mr Selwyn Lloyd as Chancellor in 1961, the council was to provide a top level, semi-independent forum in which senior economic Ministers could consult with representatives of the CBI, TUC and nationalised industries. In euphoric phrases worthy of Mr Wilson, Neddy was to 'formulate broad national objectives' aimed at 'securing and controlling sustained expansion' by an approach which 'can be characterised as a changeover from the static to the dynamic which, because of its concern with growth, has added a time dimension to policy-making'. There were always plenty of words, but what of its works?

In the bad old days before Neddy tried to transform Britain's economy, the balance of payments generally ran a current surplus measured in hundreds of millions of pounds (compared with today's deficit in billions); unemployment ranged between 250,000 and 500,000 (now well over a million), national output rose annually between 2 and 3 per cent (at present falling); prices increased by 3 or 4 per cent a year (now 25 to 30 per cent).

Clearly, 14 years and two devaluations later, Neddy cannot be credited with having helped. But should we give the old nag another chance to prove its paces under ringmaster Denis Healey? Before putting what's left of our shirt on Neddy, we should pause to ask whether its past failures were due to bad luck or whether they follow from the nature of the beast.

'By Consensus Out of Frustration'

In the parlance of the turf, Neddy was sired by consensus out of frustration. In the 1950s Britain's economic performance lagged behind France and Germany, but every time Chancellors tried to 'go for growth' the rise in wages and prices pushed the balance of payments into deficit, brought the pound under pressure and provoked credit squeezes which prompted complaints about the 'go–stop' cycle. If only we could increase our growth rate, the circular argument ran, higher output would take care of everything: exports, investment, consumption, Government spending could all go merrily ahead without inflation.

It was to square this circle that Neddy launched into what was then all the rage in the form of French-style 'indicative planning'. In a highly impressive statistical report entitled 'Growth of the UK Economy to 1966' it argued that the growth in output could be lifted from its previous level of 2.7 to 4 per cent a year provided all concerned – Government, management, employees – put their shoulders to the national wheel.

Brave new words were endlessly coined to express the consensus. Neddy's planning was to be 'consultative', 'purposive', 'coherent' and 'comprehensive'. The Neddy Council smugly commended its programme as 'a new departure', while its first Director boasted of a 'major revolution in attitudes'.

Journalists took it all very seriously and outdid one another in rivalling *The Economist*'s 'Loud cheers for Ned'.

The dismal outcome hardly bears retelling. With Neddy's expert reassurance (in March 1964) that the balance of payment need not inhibit growth, Mr Reginald Maudling kept his foot on the accelerator. Yet before the end of 1964, it was the worsening balance-of-payments deficit that compelled the new Chancellor, Mr James Callaghan, to step on the brakes by raising Bank rate, squeezing credit and inaugurating the familiar 'stop' phase of the cycle. In vain the new Labour Government sought to escape from reality by launching George Brown's National Plan into orbit – complete with Neddy's 'Statement of Intent' to check inflationary wage claims – only to acknowledge failure with the July freeze of 1966.

The epitaph on Neddy's fine hopes was the devaluation of the pound in 1967. So far from being ineffective, Neddy did positive damage by encouraging dreams of easy expansion. Its legacy can be inflation, which has made necessary the most severe contraction yet, thereby adding record unemployment to our witch's brew of inflationary recession.

The Cloven Hoof

'No recriminations', said Mr Wilson from the cosy Neddy re-union at Chequers the other day as he and his colleagues sought to resurrect the corpse with novel incantations about 'common strategy', 'involvement', 'participation', 'turning point, 'rolling plans'. The music changes but the ballyhoo lingers on . . .

Is this 'new initiative' likely to prove any more successful? As Mr Wilson's old ally Aneurin Bevan used to say, why consult the crystal ball when you can look up the book?

The fatal fumblings of Neddy were not due to clumsy fingers but to its cloven hoof. However dressed up, the interventionist-planning approach is founded on a false diagnosis which leads unerringly to a wrong prescription. The essential *non sequitur* is that because competitive markets work imperfectly, politicised markets will work better.

Thus the latest talk from Neddy was all about 'identifying' particular 'sectors', 'sub-sectors', 'individual firms' for special support. But who will do it – and how? There was not a glimmer of the need for a general pervasive mechanism to enforce the efficient use of resources and keep all the multifarious parts of a complex economy working in step with the changing forces of supply and demand. Enoch Powell once likened competitive markets to computers which digest daily countless millions of facts, mostly unknown (and unknowable) to any central planners, and which emit price and profit signals for the guidance of consumers, producers, exporters, importers, savers, investors.

'Massive Incubus of Distortion'

Can it be imagined that a Neddy, ridden uneasily by TUC–CBI–Government, could ever tackle the real job of purging the mixed-up economy of the massive incubus of political distortion through taxation, price control, inflation, rent restriction, subsidies, nationalised monopolies, and all the rest? It was because the Neddy method relies on *ad hoc* intervention and endless exhortation that I charged it in the early days with substituting a hand-and-mouth-operated economy for the impersonal computer of competitive markets.

Rather than undo the mischief of past interferences, Neddy will be drawn on to add further absurdities in the hope of neutralising their worst effects. Instead of sweeping away price control which brings firms to the brink of bankruptcy, Neddy will rattle the begging bowl for Government relief – which might be forthcoming on condition that what's left of private industry does as it's told.

Whatever the last-ditch hopes of hard-pressed businessmen, I profoundly believe the CBI should take no further part in the charade. It after all shares enough blame for its part in Neddy's past failures. Let it, at least for a start, withdraw until the Government has struck from its wrists and feet the shackles of price control and excessive taxation both on its employees and on such profits as are left by inflation.

Perhaps it will take one more disastrous flutter before the Government and unions awaken to the plain truth that Neddy is the living embodiment of the mule, without pride of ancestry or hope of progeny. Until it is carted off to the knacker's yard, there is not much hope for revitalising Britain's over-burdened economy.

13 FREEDOM WITHOUT UNEMPLOYMENT [21]

Unemployment or inflation were once thought to be alternatives. Now they rise in harness. Ralph Harris, Director of the Institute of Economic Affairs, argues that monetary control must be combined with policies to prevent trade unions pricing members out of their jobs.

If politicians refuse to learn from economic analysis, they will be driven in the end to learn from the often costly errors of experience. I have frequently pointed out that the Heath Government could have avoided stoking up the biggest inflation in British history if leading Ministers had read Milton Friedman's Wincott Lecture delivered a few months after they took office in June 1970. Entitled 'The Counter-Revolution in Monetary Policy', the lecture drew on empirical studies of many countries over long periods of history to conclude: 'inflation is always and everywhere a monetary phenomenon in the sense that it is and can be produced only by a more rapid increase in the quantity of money than in output.'

How many billions of pounds of lost output and hundreds of thousands of unemployed might have been avoided if Chancellor Tony (now Lord) Barber and his Treasury advisers had grasped the point and refrained from the inflation of M3 in the early 1970s?

Painful Lessons

It was the painful lesson of experience – reinforced perhaps by the writings of his son-in-law Peter Jay – that prompted Prime Minister Callaghan to relearn the truth which he told the Labour Party Conference in October 1976 as follows:

> We used to think that you could spend your way out of a recession and increase employment by cutting taxes and boosting government spending. I tell you that that option no longer exists, and that insofar as it ever did exist, it only worked by injecting bigger doses of inflation into the economy followed by higher levels of unemployment as the next step. That is the history of the past twenty years.

The enormous cost we are now paying for the wrong-headed pursuit of full employment through monetary excess might yet prove a good bargain if we truly learn from this example of Tory/Labour/Treasury/NIESR/Bank of England/Cambridge folly.

Perhaps the first lesson is that the existence of a consensus is far from proving that the favoured idea is necessarily right. Indeed, when we recall all those panaceas backed by the post-war economic establishment – from NEDC and National Plan to EEC and incomes policy – it might seem sensible to start from the probability that anything about which there is agreement between the TUC, CBI, Treasury, NIESR Balogh–Kaldor axis must be wrong. Thus today we might be on guard that all would certainly agree that the nationalised industries are here to stay and the welfare state cannot be dismantled. Might they not be proved wrong again?

But returning to inflation; what are the lessons we could learn that would make the terrible experience worth having endured? The first I would express more precisely than Mr Callaghan along the following lines: when the 'full employment' target is set above the equilibrium level consistent with stable prices, the result is *unnecessarily high unemployment* as well as *mounting inflation*. The importance of my formulation is that it directs attention to the best method of tackling these two evils that were once thought alternatives and have become twin torments.

Unemployment

If we ask how we can raise the equilibrium level of employment without inflation, we are driven back to ask what determines the safe level of unemployment – what Friedman calls the 'natural rate'. The short answer is: anything that obstructs the occupational or geographical matching of unemployed people with unfilled vacancies. At once attention is redirected to impediments and frictions that have nothing to do with increased monetary demand. One obvious example is the immobility of labour induced by rent control and subsidised council houses. Another is the national uniformity of wages and salaries in both public and private sectors which prices labour out of jobs that could be made available in less favoured areas. Above all, the major imperfection in the labour market is revealed as the monopoly power of trade unions.

It is a matter of elementary economic analysis that even the most entrenched monopolist cannot dictate both the price of its product or service and the amount it can sell. If it pitches the price too high, less will be bought and some part of supply will be left unsold. Thus we can explain inflation as the result of the government's effort to restore the full employment of over-priced labour by stimulating monetary demand through the Keynesian mechanism of budget deficits. Once monopoly unions take account of the resulting inflation by pushing their wage demands still further ahead of the marginal (current) value of output, government can try to maintain their full employment target only through speeding up the monetary inflation. In effect, it reduces the value of the money in terms of which higher wages are paid.

New Policy

The importance of this diagnosis is that it points to a prescription quite different from – and almost the precise opposite to – the policies Mr Callaghan inherited from Harold Wilson. It is true that since 1974, Mr Healey has somewhat erratically tried to get hold of the money supply and moderate the rate of increase below the record levels permitted under Mr Heath. But as theory tells us, the inevitable transitional effect is an increase in unemployment as the government refuses to supply the additional monetary demand that would be necessary to bring over-priced labour back into employment.

But a Labour Government built up on the historic foundation of the trade union movement has found it impossible to admit it is the pressure of these very labour monopolies that has brought the equilibrium level of employment so far below the oft-proclaimed target of full employment. If Mr Callaghan acknowledged that simple analytical insight, he would logically have to concede that the only way to combine monetary stability with higher levels of employment is to curb the monopoly power of trade unions to impose wage increases that price their members out of jobs. The appropriate policies would then be seen as making unions compatible with competitive market wages by attacking such monopoly devices as closed shop, blacking, boycotting, oppressive picketing and the subsidisation of strikes through social security and tax repayments.

Weakness

Of course, the Government's policies have been in the diametrically opposite direction of still further entrenching the monopoly power of unions – and then begging their leaders not to throw their weight about. In short, instead of tackling the institutional and legal impediments to a more freely competitive market – which could reduce the friction of unemployment without resort to inflation – recent policies have reduced freedom and flexibility still further. Thus as a price for imposing stricter monetary policy to reduce inflation, the Government has conceded trade unions additional power to increase unemployment. And in the process it has, in the name of the social contract, imposed higher taxes and more punitive controls over prices and profits that severely threaten freedom and can only weaken the economy's recuperative ability to extend viable employment.

The dearly-bought lessons from Tory/Labour post-war economic mismanagement, therefore, run far wider than the obvious and accepted need for monetary prudence. The most generally applicable lesson is that major economic disorders flow from impediments to the operation of the competitive market. Those disorders will not be remedied but aggravated by adding further impediments to the freedom and responsibility of employers and employees to strike mutually beneficial bargains on payment and productivity as the foundation of a high and stable level of employment. This is the lesson that most Conservative spokesmen show little sign of having learned. Until they do, we shall continue to pay the price in higher unemployment and diminished freedom.

14   THE PROTECTION RACKETS[22]

Ralph Harris attacks a system which aids inefficient producers at the customers' expense.

Beware of economists. They are not always right. They often disagree with one another – and with themselves. All the more striking, therefore, is their consistent support over two centuries for the proposition that freedom of international trade advances the economic welfare of all participants.

The play of competitive markets is not like poker, where winners gain at the expense of losers. All trade is what the textbooks call 'a positive sum game' in which buyers and sellers join because *both* finish up better off than if they tried to be self-sufficient. The gain from trade in any particular case may be marginal, but the widening chain of domestic and international trade has transformed the efficiency with which every individual's labour or capital is applied.

Contrast the standard of living enjoyed in Britain or Hong Kong with the poverty of an isolated African or South American tribe. It is no exaggeration to say that all improvements in real income have followed the extension of trade from primitive barter between neighbouring families to the exchange of goods and services by individuals at opposite ends of the world.

Protectionism Damages Your Wealth

Protectionism, on the other hand, can seriously damage your wealth. The danger comes from the ease with which it can be dispensed for every economic malady under such reassuring labels as: employment tonic, foreign pest repellent, infant growth stimulant, geriatric reviver, strike soothing ointment, redundancy pain-killer pills and, of course, all-purpose tranquillisers. Once swallowed, increasing doses may become necessary.

The process that has already started, to fend off awkward adjustments in employment and investment, is in danger of being extended and perpetuated. The result would be that the body economic could no longer maintain present standards of living around the world, much less resume the improvement many have come to take for granted.

Such fears may seem remote. Yet in many countries nominally conservative, liberal or social-democrat governments are turning away from the post-war presumption in favour of free trade. Without the pretext of national defence or infant industries, they are improvising domestic subsidies and foreign quotas in such long-established industries as textiles, steel, motor cars. They have been increasingly led to protect particular incomes and maintain employment against disturbance due to market changes in supply and demand.

It is to this political search for security that we can trace the malignant infection of protectionism at home and abroad. The simple truth is that all economic progress depends on shifting capital and labour into new products, methods, locations. Every invention which ends up benefiting the consumer starts off by hurting the producers of whatever it supplants.

The strongest pressure on government is, therefore, to protect entrenched producers against the dispersed interest of consumers. Though some producers appear to benefit in the short run, everyone stands to lose in the end. The favoured gain not only at the expense of foreign competitors but also of domestic consumers and workers in exporting industries, or, in the case of subsidies, at the expense of the taxpayers.

What we are again witnessing is the age-old battle between the conflicting requirements of social security and economic progress. By intervening to protect particular incomes and employments, government frustrates the process of adaptation to change.

Political Intervention Disrupts Change

Politicians invariably excuse their interventions as 'temporary measures' to ease the path of change. More often the result is to replace prompt, gradual and continuing adjustment to market forces by delayed and discontinuous disruption through the contentious political process. The danger we see around the world is that by further weakening the incentives for producers to adjust, protectionism reinforces the already powerful anti-market forces making for rigidity, immobility, instability and economic stagnation. While it is always possible for a single country to benefit by checking imports that compete with domestic production, once other countries play this game it becomes self-defeating.

Protectionism is thus a costly form of economic warfare that impoverishes all and cannot be relied on to afford security. The solution is all-round economic disarmament, each country agreeing not to use economic weapons it does not relish having used against it. In 1947 the General Agreement on Tariffs and Trade was established to conduct and police such mutually beneficial agreements. GATT stood then as it stands today for the proposition that the national interest of all countries is served by an open international order of free trade based on clear rules that limit government meddling with the market.

It may be asked: if a government abides by GATT does it not lose part of its own sovereignty? The answer is that all governments do sacrifice some power – the anarchic power to hurt one another and damage themselves – but they also gain or regain an important source of power, the GATT-given power to resist the pressure of domestic vested interests and to transmit the discipline of competitive markets from international trade to national industry.

Reversing Decades of Protection

Britain's relative decline over the past century illustrates the folly of seeking security by shielding from change. Mrs Thatcher's task can be summed up as reversing decades of protectionism resulting from increased subsidies, state welfare, nationalisation, trade unionism and so-called 'employment protection'. With the best of intentions weak government had allowed the economy to become rigid and resistant to the adjustments now made irresistible by such changes as advanced technology, expensive oil and new competition from developing countries, especially the market oases of Asia, including Hong Kong and Japan.

Mrs Thatcher's central strategy is to replace past weakness by strong, unyielding government – starting with monetary discipline – and so to impose flexibility, mobility and adjustment on the previously cosseted managements and workers of British industry. If Mrs Thatcher can hold her course, we will see a more competitive Britain earning its own security without the need for protectionism in its various disguises.

The only lasting cure is the tonic of the free-market economy. Milton Friedman has suggested a text which every entrepreneur should hang over his desk: 'If I knew for a certainty that a man was coming to my house with the conscious design of doing me good, I should run for my life'. I will add my favourite text: 'No man's life, liberty or property are safe while the legislature is in session'.

And that goes, alas, even for the House of Lords.

15 WHAT ABOUT THE WORKERS?[23]

Ralph Harris examines the facts behind the three million unemployed and suggests a free market in jobs is their best hope.

Just as after 1945 there was too much optimism about full employment, there is now too much pessimism about unemployment. If economists had stuck to their last, as my old teacher Sir Dennis Robertson used to urge, they would always have insisted that the political slogan of full employment was a mirage. In a world of ceaseless change in techniques, demand and foreign trade, there is no way of guaranteeing old jobs in declining areas nor of shifting people instantly into new work developing elsewhere.

The traditional economists knew better when they distinguished such categories as frictional, structural and cyclical unemployment. The length of time people were out of work between jobs was then understood to depend on the occupational and geographical mobility of labour in adapting to new opportunities.

Among the worst obstacles have been council housing, which made people reluctant to move homes, and the antique system of trade union apprenticeships which prevented people acquiring new skills in mid-career.

To the unemployment inevitably arising from such inflexibility in the labour force, must be added the avoidable loss of jobs due to pushing wage costs above the value of output. Here trade union industrial and political power is the main culprit. This industrial power is deployed to impose restrictive practices that reduce output per man and simultaneously to extract unearned wage increases that raise unit costs.

Union political power has been exerted to saddle industry with welfare policies that now account for over a quarter of total labour costs. The resulting rise in British costs and prices has added to unemployment both by pricing our staple exports (e.g. ships) out of overseas markets and losing domestic trade (e.g. cars) to foreign imports.

No Penalty for Appeasement

A fair question is why British industry did not make a firmer stand against trade union restrictions and higher wages? The short answer is that as long as governments were committed to full employment the penalty for appeasement was not very pressing.

Until the 1970s, both Labour and Tory governments acted on simple-minded Keynesian lines to meet any threat of rising unemployment by increasing public spending or reducing taxes to stimulate demand so as to restore full employment.

So businessmen thought they had little to fear from yielding to trade union pressure. If they conceded excessive wages, the Chancellor would boost the general level of demand and they could hope to pass on higher costs in higher prices. Increasingly, the effect of increased spending was less and less to raise the demand for unemployed labour and more and more to finance the rise in costs and prices.

In the recent Hobart Paper[24] the authors Robert Miller and John Wood have a revealing table that shows the cost of accommodating union wage grab.

Thus in the four Macmillan years 1958–62 the effect of increasing total spending by 25 per cent was split roughly equally in raising output by 12.7 per cent and pushing prices up by 12.2 per cent. In the four Wilson–Callaghan years 1974–78 an increase in total spending of almost 100 per cent financed a derisory increase in output of 8 per cent and a rise in prices of over 90 per cent.

And let Mr Peter Shore take note, this massive increase in spending did not stop unemployment doubling from under 700,000 in 1974 to around 1,400,000 in 1978.

If rising inflation was bad for employment, the effect of slowing it down must make unemployment for a while even worse. Thus businessmen had got into the habit of allowing costs to rise in the expectation that the Government would provide the extra money to accommodate the resulting higher prices for their products.

The effect of Mrs Thatcher's refusal to finance increasing inflation is to return responsibility for employment to businessmen and their workers. Either they break the old habits and between them curb costs so as to survive as inflation comes down, or they price themselves out of markets at home and abroad, with predictable effects on bankruptcies and unemployment.

After decades of weak governments it was difficult in 1979 to believe that Mrs Thatcher's economic ministers would stand firm. Spurred on by [Hugh] Clegg, wages rose in the first year by between 20 per cent and 30 per cent. Since the Chancellor was not going to finance a similar escalation of inflation, only two outcomes were left. Either managements had to squeeze labour costs (which make up 90 per cent of total value added) to stay in business or they went to the wall.

Although both responses in the short run increased unemployment, wherever the efficiency road was taken it has led to often dramatic improvements in the competitiveness of British businesses.

The cost in lost jobs would have been less but for the appalling burden of local rates (60 per cent of which fall on business) and the unchecked price increases of nationalised industries which are sheltered from the discipline of competition.

The clear lesson of this Hobart Paper is that employment can be analysed in a market – like that for petrol or smoked salmon – where both supply and demand are influenced by price. Unfortunately, at the same time as demand for labour has been reduced by its high price, the supply has been discouraged by whittling away the incentive of many people to work for highly taxed wages rather than to settle for generous, untaxed social benefits.

Better Off On the Dole

Messrs Miller and Wood show that hundreds of thousands of family men are better off unemployed – even without taking account of the pickings available in what is variously called the informal, underground, hidden or black economy.

Grievous though high unemployment may be as the price of past folly by governments and trade unions, this Paper explains that the much-advertised three million are not to be thought of as an ever-lengthening queue of workless.

Even in 1980 there were over eight million changes of jobs, so that on average each month over 600,000 were taken into work. The trouble has been that a still larger number have lost their jobs. But that does not have to go on.

If we want the labour market to work better to raise demand for workers and encourage supply, the analysis points to a whole variety of measures that could help.

First, anything more Mr Norman Tebbit can do to weaken the obstructive power of trade unions will speed the return to realistic wages and working practices.

Second, the relative attractions of living on welfare would be reduced if the promised taxation of unemployment benefits was matched by lower taxes on earnings.

Third, Wages Councils and other protective measures that raise the cost of employing people, especially the young, should be abolished.

Abolish Rent Control for Mobility

Fourth, the abolition of rent control could bring a million or more empty houses onto the market to ease mobility of labour. And, of course, anything that improves the efficiency of nationalised industry would help by reducing prices and taxes.

Above all, it is no use looking to posturing politicians to tell us where future jobs will come from. If Mr Peter Shore had been told in 1950 that half a million workers were *permanently* to lose their jobs in agriculture, do you suppose he would have known that two million new jobs were going to be found in one single category of professional services?

If we remove present obstacles, I have no doubt the market will provide as many jobs as the producing population are willing to take – at prices the consuming population is prepared to pay.

16   DON'T JUST POLISH – ABOLISH[25]

Aside from its success against inflation, Mrs Thatcher's government has made disappointing progress in restoring vigour to the economy. A start has been made with denationalisation and trade union reform, but state spending has not been cut, local government is as big as ever and little has been done to free the labour market or to move welfare policy from universal provision to help for those in need.

I do not believe that, whatever the International Labour Organisation's objections, we could not get rid of wages councils, which set minimum rates for almost three million people, mostly in retailing – 60 per cent of the adult rate at 16, against 20 per cent in Switzerland – and which gravely damage youth employment prospects.

It seems strange that a government which professes to support a market economy should not have taken positive action against impediments that raise unit labour costs (employment protection, national insurance, trade union restrictive practices); that obstruct mobility (rent control, regional development, council house subsidies) or that reduce take-home pay (high taxes on low earnings) to little, if anything, above social benefits.

In most cases, the Government has not changed its policies. It has been diverted from its objectives by legislature and bureaucratic obstruction.

'An Insatiable Appetite for Legislation'

Modern government is appallingly complex and has an insatiable appetite for legislation. In a single recent year, 70 new Acts of Parliament and 2,000 'statutory instruments' were spewed over 6,000 printed pages. Here is a major source of power for civil servants who can blind even the brightest ministers with almost incomprehensible legalistic jargon in which they, as narrow specialists, are always more expert.

Suppose a company had to get approval for amending its articles of association every time it wanted to change a price, alter a product, withdraw a service, borrow money or make any one of hundreds of day-to-day adjustments to its operations. Imagine the staff it would need, the delay and distraction leading to virtual paralysis.

Yet we would all agree that bureaucrats cannot be allowed the range of discretion in dispensing state resources and authority that businessmen enjoy in balancing the interests of customers and shareholders. Because there is no government equivalent to the commercial price-profit system to keep civil servants in check, we have ceaseless legislative amendment and intolerable pressure on the parliamentary timetable to permit tardy adjustment to changing circumstances or a new government's policy.

These necessary restraints are so lethal to flexibility and change that government should be confined to the barest minimum of functions which it has to finance through taxation because a free market cannot provide them. The cumbersome processes of amendment and reforms should therefore take second place to outright repeal of unnecessary, obstructive statutes.

Like the Mikado's Lord High Executioner, the non-party repeal group in the House of Lords has 'a little list of society offenders that never would be missed'. In addition to the job-destroying wages councils, our targets include the restrictive Shops Act, the antique Truck Acts, the paternalistic licensing laws, such monopolies as the solicitors in conveyancing and opticians in selling spectacles, to say nothing of the Rent Acts that have shrunk the housing market and still impede the mobility of labour.

How to Reduce Taxation

We are left with the problem of reducing taxes as the golden route to reducing costs throughout the economy and sharpening incentives, especially for the lower paid to work rather than live off social benefits. To search out savings, we should examine every welfare and local government service now provided 'free' and ask why most people should not choose and pay through direct fees and insurance rather than indirectly through inflated taxes and rates. The way to help the poor is not to give everyone else free services but to top up low incomes and reduce everyone's taxes.

The aim should be to halve public expenditure and reduce total taxation to the safe limit of 25 per cent of national income. A subordinate aim is to restore politics to a part-time job suitable for gentlemen and lords, that is for unpaid amateurs who have to earn their living in the real world and pay their share of (lower) taxes like the rest of us.

17   WHERE AID IS SOWN, POVERTY AND DEBT ARE HARVESTED[26]

Ralph Harris argues that foreign aid hinders more than it helps.

It is hardly surprising that most people spontaneously support the idea of foreign aid. Who would not wish to help those starving figures from Africa, Asia and South America who periodically haunt our television screens? But emergency help for victims of drought or floods is quite distinct from annual subsidies to governments that are often directly responsible for the plight of their people.

Let us be clear. 'Foreign aid' has nothing to do with handing cash or food to individuals in need. It is a question-begging term to describe the continuing political transfer of funds between governments, originally intended to promote the long-term economic development of what used to be called 'backward countries'.

Despite having been tactfully rechristened Less Developed Countries, most of the recipients are still economically backward after 30 years of 'aid'. Their record mocks the earlier theory of 'take-off into self-sustaining growth'. The reality is that most 'aid' can be seen to have bolstered muddled/Marxist/ militarist régimes that have little to show except poverty and debt for past political gifts and soft loans.

This failure of 'aid' to yield lasting economic development should direct attention to the lonely critique deployed by the former London School of Economics professor P.T. (now Lord) Bauer, author of many scholarly studies grounded in first-hand knowledge of what used to be called, hopefully, the 'developing world'.

For all their apparent differences, most recipients of 'aid' suffer from a common handicap. It is not lack of natural resources, which many have in abundance and which are not necessary for economic progress, as demonstrated by the remarkable advance of Hong Kong, Taiwan and even Japan.

Delusion of Central Planning

The common handicap is self-inflicted. It is the once-fashionable delusion that central economic planning is the only way forward. The costs which this fallacy has visited on more than half the world's population are almost impossible to exaggerate.

Professor Lord Bauer never tires of reciting the multifarious ways in which such governments have retarded agriculture and distorted industrial development. We have seen them embark on extensive price control, suppression of private trade, restrictive licensing, indiscriminate nationalisation, the setting up of marketing monopolies, manipulation of exchange rates and the prohibition of holding stocks in the name of preventing 'hoarding'.

In a Lords debate on starvation in the Third World, I ventured to pose the question: Why is the weather always so much worse in socialist countries? I quoted evidence from an American symposium on 'The Distortion of Agricultural Incentives' that wherever prices are free to fluctuate, peasants respond to economic inducements by increasing output, just as traders shift stocks from areas of surplus to areas of shortage. If only governments would discharge their primary function of ensuring security for person and property, peasants and traders would automatically store food to provide against bad times.

In the absence of secure property rights over their land, peasants indulge in casual, nomadic cultivation which leads to over-cropping, over-grazing and the destruction of ground cover. The result has been to increase soil erosion and convert fertile land into desert. When the world was shocked by pictures of famine in Ethiopia, the Marxist government was pursuing a 'co-operative' policy of annual re-allocation of plots, which positively discouraged good husbandry. Why should itinerant farmers bother to fertilise the land, improve drainage or clear boulders?

Further south in Tanzania, President Nyerere was bathing in the flattery of western 'progressives' for his vision of African socialism, which herded millions into collective farms that converted an exportable surplus of food production into a chronic deficit.

If the primary failure has been to retard agricultural development, it has been reinforced by obstructing profitable industry. There has been widespread persecution of multinational companies which were a major instrument for spreading training, employment and prosperity. Yet throughout Africa (apart from the South) their operations have been fettered: managements compulsorily replaced by local staff, remittances of profit restricted, and assets often seized without adequate compensation.

'Aid' Encourages White Elephants

At the same time, 'aid' has enabled the recipient governments to embark on political prestige projects such as lavish building of capital cities, running subsidised airlines and 'investment' in every kind of industrial white elephant. Most shameless of all is the massive spending on armaments. An official West German source estimated that the Third World accounts for one-fifth of all arms spending. It hardly needs to be said that most of the weapons are for use by rulers against their own people or other Third World countries.

This list far from exhausts the catalogue of economic crimes by most recipients of 'aid'. Leave aside the corruption practised by many rulers and copied lower down. Consider the way ruling factions have persecuted rival tribes and immigrant minorities who are often among the most enterprising and productive people in countries desperately short of both qualities. A seminal insight of Lord Bauer is that 'aid' strengthens the power of recipient governments and so intensifies the politicisation of economic and social life. The individual's welfare, even survival, may depend on the whim of politicians or their *apparatchiks,* thereby raising the stakes in the struggle for power.

The resulting tensions periodically erupt into armed conflict. More generally and invisibly, the damage is done by diverting the energies and resources of the most able and ambitious individuals away from productive economic activity into personal fulfilment through politics.

Apart from a few successful projects – which could have attracted commercial investment – 'aid' has not generally helped. Worse, it has more often hindered by providing incompetent governments with a soft option that has enabled them to delay putting their economic houses in order. It has bred a surly spirit of dependency made worse by the piling up of debts they cannot pay. Just ponder. If past loans had been invested as risk capital the burden of failure would have fallen on foreign equity investors, not on governments with nothing to show for the money. Above all, commercial investment would have been more likely to create lasting wealth, employment and prosperity.

18   AN EASTER OFFERING TO THE BISHOPS[27]

Since confession is good for the soul, let me say straightaway that some practical manifestations of private enterprise strike me as unalluring. Forty years' study of economics have weaned me from Beveridge and Keynes to advocate competitive enterprise as the nearest we have to a panacea in this imperfect world. But I'm never surprised that this view is resisted by some of the nicest people – as well as some of the other sort.

While most company chairmen I have got to know would be equally at home in a university common room, or even on a church committee, a few leave a lot to be desired. Does that mark them out from others? What about top politicians, trade union leaders, academics, playwrights, broadcasters, who compete for our favour? Are they not a pretty mixed bag? Come to that, dear reader, what about you?

On Easter Sunday we might all, including our bishops, agree that we fall well short of the Christian ideal of selfless devotion to others. Oh yes, on our good days all but the worst are capable of rare feats of generosity or self-sacrifice. But the best of us can be horribly insensitive to the feelings and well-being even of those we like or love. (Here, all but the Perfect Ones can join in saying Amen!)

Old Adam

Such Easter reflections on human nature go to the heart of our choice between alternative economic and social systems. At its simplest the economic problem resolves itself into a continuous battle over the use of scarce human and material resources. More for one means less for another unless . . .? You've got it: unless human ingenuity goes on producing more for all by discovering new resources and increasing the efficiency with which they are used.

And how, pray, are we most likely to enlarge the supply of said scarce resources and economise in demand for them? By appealing to people as Perfect Ones who will always give of their best and never count the cost? Or by engaging their interests and making it worth their while to do their stuff by working, saving, investing, inventing and economising in competitive markets?

Adam Smith had no doubt about the answer. He is often mocked as the canny Scot who thought that inside every human being there was another Scotsman trying to get out.

Yet in his first treatise on *The Theory of Moral Sentiments*, he acknowledged the place of sympathy, fellow-feeling, benevolence and love in man's complex make-up. He warned, however, that such 'sublime' regard for others, 'can never be an excuse for his neglecting the more humble department . . . the care of his own happiness, of that of his family, his friends, his country'.

So before we can indulge our benevolent instincts, we need prudently to attend to our own affairs. Hence in his magnum opus entitled *An Enquiry into the Nature and Causes of the Wealth of Nations,* our Adam put his money on the 'uniform, constant and uninterrupted effort of every man to better his condition' as the most dependable engine of economic progress.

Shallow critics have denounced this mainspring of human striving in the market-place as narrow 'self-interest', or even 'greed' and 'grab'. But in Smith's vision the free market economy allows the widest play for us all to pursue our *self-chosen* purposes. We are all free to try fulfilling our ideals by working for others at a pittance. But we might agree that Ford, Nuffield, Sainsbury, Marks & Spencer have done most good by maximising their earnings so as to give more generously to good causes.

To avoid the parrot-cry of *laissez-faire*, I must add that a free economy requires an indispensable role for strong (not big) government. It calls for a legal framework that guarantees the security of person and property, partly by policing contracts and preventing force and fraud. It also requires some form of state (as well as charitable) provision of cash (and counsel) for individuals who are unable by their own efforts 'to better their condition'.

Consenting Adults

Hayek has claimed that the highest merit of the market economy is in checking the evil bad men can wreak in the centralised societies we see around the world. In the economic battle over scarce resources, competition within the law is a peaceful and productive way of resolving conflicts between individuals and interest groups. Buying and selling between consenting adults is most likely to confer what economists call gains from trade on both parties.

The chief danger, for both the economy and democracy, is of people ganging together to escape from the rigours of competition by seeking subsidies and protection from pliant politicians. We live increasingly in a world of pressure groups, from farmers, trade unions, the professions and other monopoly mongers, to the mixed bag of 'welfare' lobbies.

So let me ask each reader this Sunday: What's your particular racket? Why not repent of looking to government for special favours and settle for the market on the principle: Do competitively as you would be done by?

And if any bishop reads these words, I beg him understand that the market is morally neutral. It responds to higher demands as readily as to grosser appetites. His job is by preaching, prayer and example to help elevate vulgar preferences.

When bishops blame the market for every excess, they are no better than the fat man in the restaurant who blames his own obesity on the waiter.

19   £50,000,000,000 IS NOT ENOUGH?[28]

Alert readers will not have missed the recent contrast between this column's encouraging reflections on poverty and the earnest anxieties of my old friend Paul Barker about the losers from the Fowler reforms of social benefits.

I doubt whether anyone not paid to master the intricacies of income support (in place of supplementary benefits), family credits (in place of FIS [Family Income Supplement]), social fund (in place of single payments), housing benefits, and the rest can arrive at a confident verdict on how these changes will turn out.

Of course, we will hear more from the lobbies of losers (unemployed youths, better-off pensioners) than from the much larger number of gainers (disabled, single parents, low earner families, poorest pensioners).

Value for Money?

I certainly hold no brief for the details of the Fowler reforms, however well-intentioned their conception. They end marginal tax rates above 100 per cent on earnings, so that people are no longer worse off taking a job. But many will still face penal rates up to 95 per cent.

Let me repeat that there can be no tolerable solution to poverty and work incentives until the yoke of income tax is once and for all lifted from people on low incomes.

One proposition on which all might agree for a start is that the community should give highest priority – second only to wealth-creation – to helping those unable to help themselves. By that test this Government has failed, like its predecessors, to tackle the radical reshaping of spending, taxation, social and housing policies. That is one reason we get such poor value from spending the staggering sum approaching £50,000,000,000 on social benefits.

But who can name any major Government programme that gives us good value for money? Why is it that throughout my life state provision always appears to give so much less satisfaction than private suppliers?

Look around: Read the papers. Watch television. Where are the problems? Do we find housewives demonstrating against supermarkets, motorists besieging garages, handymen denouncing DIY centres, or paying-guests roughing-up hotel staff. Instead, the chief focus of discontent shifts back and forth between state schooling, council tower blocks, universities, local authority services, the NHS and now social benefits.

Why do so-called 'public' services, provided in the 'public interest' by 'public servants' at 'public' expense, so often fail to satisfy the poor old public? What is it about government that guarantees widespread dissatisfaction?

This is no party point. Bear in mind that throughout the post-war period something around half the national income has been spent, year in, year out, by both Labour and Conservative administrations. Recall all those confident election promises of remarkable solutions for every ill the flesh is heir to. With such a torrent of spending over four decades, should we not have swept away some of our problems?

Alas, there is no way we can ever get value for money from 'representative government' to compare with the value we get from self-government in the market-place.

It was Lionel Robbins who compared the competitive market to a perpetual referendum in which we all vote every day with our pennies and pounds. We choose between the widest conceivable range of goods and services supplied by myriad competing producers, each with a powerful incentive to meet our individual preferences and give value for money. However eccentric our tastes, there's likely to be a choice of suppliers.

In stark contrast, the political market offers us one vote between two or three brands every four or five years. Instead of item-by-item choice *à la carte*, each party manifesto offers a single *table d'hôte* menu on a take-it-or-leave-it basis. While competing market goods and services come in every shape and size marked with separate price tags, the rival packages of party policies are heavily wrapped in red or blue ribbons and are distinctly cagey on costs. (That's one reason people vote for more government than they really want to pay for.)

Respect for Minorities

Above all, the market-place caters for minority preferences in a way representative government can never match. Our ethnic minorities should be among the keenest champions of the market. They don't have to lobby or demonstrate to get what they want from competing suppliers. Indian shops and restaurants spring up, where Indian parents have no way of getting the schools they want for their children.

The enlargement throughout this century of the scale and scope of the state has led to the neglect by hard-pressed governments of their primary duties and the politicisation of more and more aspects of our lives. With the spread of politics we have seen the aggravation of conflict.

Take all the recent distasteful public debate about homosexuality in schools. Extreme bitterness is provoked by the use of state money to promote ideas which the majority does not like. If people must indulge their strange tastes, the general view would be that they should do so within the law, in private, and from private pockets.

In short, the market allows people to do their own thing at their own expense. By contrast, politicians before 1979 were always offering to do more things for us on the cheap. But as people tumble to the truth that political gifts come dear (and often shoddy) the revolt against bloated government will gather pace. Perhaps the Bishop of Durham should keep a few of his curses in reserve for use in those happier days.

20   STUDENT LOANS ARE BETTER THAN GRANTS[29]

Drawing on an insight of Adam Smith, I am tempted to unveil a variant of Hutber's Law ('improvement means deterioration') that might be called the Hutber–Harris Law. It would state, more cautiously, that political good intentions, especially in giving away money, tend to have disappointing, if not disastrous, consequences.

This law could be illustrated from a variety of social policies where more spending has simply bought more trouble. My chosen example to launch it is from the elevated world of universities.

Have you noticed the periodic turmoil ever since the well-intentioned expansion proposed by the Robbins Committee in 1963?

Judged by the £3.5 billion lavished on free tuition and student maintenance, unmatched in Europe and North America, you might expect that all would be very well thank you in the pampered groves of academe. But what do we find?

Free Port?

First take those grand swells of the Vice-Chancellor's Committee. They are up in arms against Kenneth Baker's great education reform bill.

They say he is going too far in controlling how they spend the massive grants to be disbursed by the University Funding Council (which replaces the UGC [University Grants Committee]). They fear a future government could impose conditions that would breach prized academic freedoms. It is a real danger. But shouldn't clever people like VCs understand there's no such thing as free port?

Then there is perennial student lobbying for higher maintenance grants, currently around £2,000 a year. Many get less under the parental means test and complain that their parents fail to make up the difference. It seems a fair complaint. Yet parents have a point against a second means test (on top of assessment for income tax) to finance 'children' up to the age of 25.

Nor are the staff exactly overflowing with gratitude for their comfortable jobs, long holidays, and life tenure (even for the most incompetent), crowned with indexed pensions. Yet when they are not demanding more salaries and perks, they are agitating for more 'research' funds and can turn nasty by denying the PM an honorary degree.

Then what about most taxpayers who never went to universities and earn much less than graduates? Where's the justice in making poorer people who start work at 16 or 18 pay higher taxes to finance more favoured or fortunate students in acquiring a passport to higher lifetime earnings.

If this catalogue of grievances were not enough to establish the Hutber–Harris Law, I have another objection that struck us both as among the founders of the independent University of Buckingham.

To avoid any suspicion of sour grapes, let me first report that since its formal opening in 1976, it has been plagued by none of the tears and tensions that have dogged the state universities. Instead, it has attracted a growing number of satisfied, mostly more mature, students by offering choices denied by the 'free' state sector. These include more broadly-based courses, an intensive two-year degree and more emphasis on personal tuition.

In short, Buckingham has been forced to compete for students by providing distinctive facilities that meet market demand for at least some students better than what's on offer without charge elsewhere.

Perhaps the least obvious objection to state-financed universities is not only that they lack the market incentive to cater efficiently for changing demand. Even worse, by the unfair competition of 'free' provision, they inhibit the vigorous growth of the more varied universities which have to charge students fees to cover tuition costs.

The overriding question is how many more Buckinghams, offering different options, might we have had if the state subsidy were paid direct to students who then paid it to the university of their choice?

It's a basic economic rule that if there are to be subsidies, they are best paid to consumers, not handed over to producers who are then free to please themselves rather than their non-paying customers.

Back to Independence

The second question is why don't we restore independence to all universities by moving to student loans which other countries, including socialist Sweden, find acceptable?

There is talk of a piffling Government scheme to lend students up to a total of £1,000 in return for a paltry cut of £100 a year in their maintenance grant. This feeble compromise would predictably stir the beneficiaries of higher learning into the higher decibels without giving them (or the rest of us) anything worth screaming (or cheering) about.

My proposal would be a loan scheme to cover maintenance generously up to £2,500 a year plus, say, a quarter of the tuition fees (ranging from £2,500 for arts at polytechnics to £8,000 for doctors and vets). Instead of Government capital, let banks put up the money and the Treasury provide a guarantee only in the last resort.

Students could then not only choose whether to study away from home, but could pick the course that offered the best value for money. Universities would compete to attract paying customers and receive the balance of three-quarters of fees for every student that chose them.

Sceptics might ponder this quotation: 'The whole system of student awards is thoroughly unfair . . . There is no point in tinkering: it should be swept away and replaced by a radical new approach in which student loans play a central part'. The author? Not Ghengis Tebbit, but that darling of the Left, Tessa (now Lady) Blackstone. We radicals are attracting some surprising allies.

21   A TRUCE BETWEEN THE GOODIES AND BADDIES[30]

I forget who said that when he heard politicians lay claim to 'compassion' he reached for his gun. In the mouths of party men, especially out of office, compassion usually amounts to the indiscriminate bidding for votes with other people's money.

Before the more biblical word 'charity' was driven out of fashion by the class warriors, we applauded *personal* giving of money or time to self-chosen good causes, with love and without self-advertisement. *Collective* compassion is a fraud because it always depends upon the coercion of taxation. What moral merit is there in making other people do good – if good it be – at gun-point?

The trouble with our modern 'do-gooders' is that they may mean well – apart from those party men who first and foremost are out to do well – but good intentions don't guarantee good results. There is so much evidence to the contrary that I hardly know where to begin.

Moral Outrage

My favourite example is rent control introduced back in 1915 to prevent land-lords exploiting possible war-time shortages by pushing up rents. What a perfectly splendid wheeze, say the 'do-gooders' in unison. Yet the malignant results of destroying the market for rented homes have been to imprison people in areas of high unemployment and condemn hundreds of thousands of others to homelessness, squalor, or bed and breakfast hostels.

Another example is foreign aid. What could be more 'compassionate' than for rich countries to send thousands of millions of pounds to governments of poor countries in Africa? It's not only bishops whose breasts are suffused with warm feelings by speeches calling for another billion or two of taxpayers' money on so good a cause.

Yet after decades of 'aid', good intentions have been mocked by wide-spread poverty, aggravated hunger, centralised power, civil unrest and the piling up of massive debts – which are then blamed on the creditors. If 'do-gooders' were paid by results, they would mostly be reduced to begging benefits for themselves.

Pray understand, my argument is not simply an economist's plea that government social policy is an inefficient way to improve the lot of the poorer people. It is not even that such well-intended collective action may do inci-dental harm. The case for the prosecution is that conventional 'do-gooders' often turn out, unwittingly, to be evil-doers on a rather grand scale.

Listening to the unending debates on the community charge, the NHS, the social security reforms, I believe the most urgent requirement for our democracy, no less than our economy, is to redress the balance of moral outrage which parodies serious debate as a battle between the goodies and the baddies.

Instead of joining in name-calling against the forces of darkness, I recommend a dose of dispassionate reflection. I start from a dictum of Gilbert Ponsonby, one of the noblest Christian economists I ever knew and an LSE man to boot. He used to say that our approach to social policy should be 'inspired by love, but guided by reason'. In short, good intentions are never enough. We must try to understand the often subtle linkages between cause and effect in economics, as in the natural sciences.

The worst failures in post-war social policy are the result of neglecting a central distinction economists make between the income effect and the incentive effect of all forms of subsidies. To help poor people, the government provides direct cash benefits or lower prices, which include lower rents and 'free' medical care. This has the intended, beneficial result of increasing their effective income so that they can consume more than they could pay for on their own.

At the same time, the subsidy or lower price operates as an unintended incentive to increase demand. A less obvious example from rent control is that protected tenants whose children have left home stay on in a larger house than they need, whilst growing families are doomed to live in a single room. With foreign aid, subsidies to poor countries increase the incentive for client governments to plead poverty.

Dependency Culture

With social benefits the incentive effects lead to even more perverse results. The more generously we raise unconditional benefits for the unemployed, the weaker the inducement for many recipients to work 40 hours a week for net take-home pay that is little, if any, above the value of benefits. Worst of all for my money is the multiplication of that new category of around a million 'single parent families', encouraged by the incentive of special benefits and priority housing.

The intention was no doubt generous, as with help for widows. Who can bear that illegitimate children or victims of broken marriages should suffer from the sins or failings of their parents? Yet immediate relief aimed at *existing* offspring cannot avoid creating a long-term incentive for *continued* irresponsible multiplication of children denied the blessings of family life. In effect, we offer prizes for behaviour most of us would not wish to encourage.

The logic of this neglected analysis is extremely uncomfortable for the majority on all sides of the present debate who care equally about true poverty. It is no good boasting compassion. The more generously we try to relieve hardship *for the able-bodied,* the more we tip the balance of incentives towards widening and deepening dependence on social benefits and against helping people wherever possible to help themselves.

We need a truce while we think how to do better in future. We are unlikely to silence party men seeking votes. But may we not expect more from bishops and others seeking the best long-term interests of their fellows?

22 NOW WHO'S BLOWING SMOKE IN YOUR EYES?[31]

The absurd case of the American tobacco company having to pay $400,000 damages to a husband because his wife allegedly smoked herself to death should not cause too much rejoicing even in the ranks of Tuscany.

It is not only as a life-long pipe-smoker that I judge the tobacco abolition-ists to be a more lethal threat to the sum of human welfare than the worst smoking can do to any of us. Like all single-issue pressure groups the anti-smoking lobby wildly exaggerates the benefits of its cause and ignores its costs. On tobacco there are several grounds for resisting the propaganda of Action on Smoking and Health (Ash).

First, we should be sceptical of all fashionable fads and fancies about what is good and bad for health. Milk was once so good for children that it was subsidised in schools – until we were warned against dairy produce as a cause of obesity. No less an authority than the government's Egg Marketing Board used to urge us to 'go to work on an egg' – until we learned that we might instead be heading for hospital. Am I now to sue my grocer for giving me too much cholesterol?

No doubt fruit and vegetables will continue to be judged good for most of us, though whether to the exclusion of meat and fish is less certain. But if you develop an allergy to bananas, should you have an action against your greengrocer?

More Doubts

The second doubt is about the 'proof' of a general link between smoking and cancer. The most impressive case for scepticism I have read is in a symposium on *Smoking and Society*.[32] It includes a review of the 'scientific' evidence by the internationally-famed pyschologist, Professor Hans Eysenck, with a list of references running to 17 pages.

He concludes that the conventional view is unproven and suggests as equally likely that people with a constitutional predisposition to such diseases as lung cancer and coronary heart disease may also have a predisposition to smoke. It seems we have to die of something.

The third doubt about the anti-smokers' case rests on an article in a medical journal which suggested that doctors who gave up the weed were more likely to fall victims to various stress diseases. Some even took to drugs and drinking. We all know of people who stop smoking and put on weight, with obvious costs to their health, to say nothing of their clothes bill.

Even more doubtful is the latest twist in the propaganda about the effect of my smoking on your health, so-called 'passive smoking'. In the symposium quoted above, an American Professor of Pharmacology, Dr Ariado, studies seven pages of 'scientific' references before concluding that the evidence does not support the charge.

But the case against the anti-smoking fanatics goes much wider than making propaganda on the basis of claims that are, in the words of the editor of *Smoking and Society,* 'either wrong, unproven, built upon faulty analysis, or pushed well beyond the point of common sense'.

The more weighty charge is that abolitionists are symptomatic of a naïve, paternalist, authoritarian view that increasingly threatens individual freedom and responsibility throughout Western society. The glory of a market economy is that it gives the widest scope for adults to lead their own lives and, ultimately, to choose the risks they will run.

Where would we be if we had to approve of other people's preferences – and they of ours? The freedom of every individual's choice should be upheld so long as it does not interfere with the exercise of like freedom by others. Purists might say their freedom to avoid contact with tobacco smoke is violated by my smoking. But what of my objection to their indulgence in damaging cosmetics, shocking garbs, frightening hair styles, distracting aftershave, dangerous sunbathing, risky barbecues, deafening pop music, to say nothing of such offensive habits as eating garlic, chewing gum, whistling, and for that matter laughing too loudly – to which I occasionally plead guilty?

The truth is that a free society depends absolutely on the widest degree of tolerance that our self-appointed guardians of taste would reserve only for themselves. Anti-smokers should beware of a pressure group to suppress other people's personal preferences, lest the same bullying technique is deployed against their minority obsessions like skiing, hunting, fishing, pot-holing, jogging, rugby, boxing, flying, horse racing or any activity that others may judge dangerous or undesirable.

Beware

But I have left to the last the most lethal danger which the American legal decision aims at the heart of a free society. Economists defend consumer sovereignty so long as goods and services are offered for sale on the basis of accurate descriptions, wherever appropriate, of their performance or ingredients. For the rest, the rule is *caveat emptor* or, for those of us who didn't go to Oxford, let the buyer beware.

The hidden peril of well-intentioned 'consumer protection' laws is that they lead innocent shoppers to lower their guard instead of keeping their wits about them in buying unproven or unbranded goods. Above all, they should be wary of high-pressure salesmanship. Free choice is a prized right which in turn demands that customers accept responsibility for their buying decisions.

The worst absurdity of the case against the American tobacco company is that its cigarettes carried a health warning. I'm offering a gift of cigarettes, tobacco or cigars for the best suggestion of a comparable warning to pin on these priggish enemies of consumer choice. My first shot is: 'Anti-smokers may damage their own freedom'.

23   THOUGHTS ON BUYING AN OLD SCHOOL TIE[33]

Considering that I left the Tottenham Grammar School in 1943, you may think it a bit late to have only now acquired an old school tie. But the circumstances are rather special.

Although my school dated back to Elizabeth I, if not to Edward VI, it was never as distinguished as such famous foundations as Birmingham and Manchester. Yet it provided generations of boys from poor or modest families in north London with a springboard into industry, the professions and, increasingly in my time, into universities.

I never got caught up with the Old Boys' Association, and feared the worst when it went comprehensive and was re-named Somerset School after our revered benefactress, Sarah, Duchess of Somerset.

Why then did I find myself back at the school last month, queuing-up to buy an old boy's tie? The occasion was a dinner to mark the closure of the school by Haringey council under Bernie Grant. The advertised reason was the continuing fall in numbers of children of school age.

Reasons of Sex

On closer inquiry I gather the number of children attending Tottenham and other Haringey schools has declined faster than elsewhere since Mr Grant and his friends took over. Could it be that Labour is bad for births or good for child mortality?

No, the explanation is that an increasing number of parents are smuggling their offspring across the borders to schools under less malignant régimes like Barnet and Enfield. But why close my old school which remains as strikingly handsome as the day I moved into it, newly-built, in 1940? Surely there are plenty of buildings more fit for demolition?

Maybe, but this school had a far worse defect in the jaundiced eyes of its political masters. As a boys' school, it defiled the pure doctrine of universal, undifferentiated, homogenised comprehensive education.

I found myself reflecting how differently this tale – and so much else – might have turned out had it not been for R.A. Butler. It was 'Rab', once my hero, who I now see fatally weakened the British educational system with his acclaimed 1944 Act which abolished fee-paying in state schools. According to left-wing humbug, those of us who got to grammar school as scholarship boys were psychologically scarred for life by being segregated as 'goats' from the fee-paying 'sheep'.

Of course, Butler and the other fashionable education dandies, including most Tories and the middle-class Labour intellectuals, were then public school men. Their fancy, fee-paying schools were left intact. It was only the peasants who could not be expected to pay towards the education of their children!

Yet suppose my old school had retained a fee-paying element? The Institute of Economic Affairs would not have had to launch the idea of an education voucher. With spreading post-war prosperity, more parents could have afforded full or partial fees, especially if the taxes they paid for 'free' education had been reduced. The scholarship element would have declined to the dwindling minority who could not afford to pay. Voters would have learned that a good education was worth buying before a holiday in foreign parts. And then . . . ? A number of advantages would have followed.

The present generation of children would have been rescued from the grip of the educational faddists. Parents could have voted between schools that were comprehensive, grammar, traditional, modern, single sex or mixed, just as they already vote between supermarkets, corner shops and delicatessens, simply by switching their spending power.

And as in other competitive markets, schools governors would have to cater directly for parental demand. There would be less talk about scruffy, incompetent teachers and more evidence of school uniforms and discipline. And my old school would now be closing down only if it had failed to justify the fees it was charging.

Indeed, if we are to judge by the products of today's flourishing public schools, many of whom are the offspring of self-sacrificing, state-educated parents, there would have been even greater prizes. Not only would there be less educational failure, but less truancy, hooliganism and political contention.

Fitted for Crime

Above all, I venture to assert that in a world where most parents had power to insist on value for the money they spent directly on their children's education, fewer school leavers at 16 or 18 would turn out fitted for little better than unemployment, soccer violence or crime.

Nationalised schools have failed us for the same mixture of reasons as council housing, the NHS and other state monopolies in transport, energy, shipbuilding and motor cars. All end up the playthings of party politics. All yield far too much sway to trade unions and other producer pressure groups. All lack the competitive life force that makes even humdrum managers more efficient. All turn out poor products. Yet all can nevertheless survive for ever on taxpayers' subsidies without heeding the wishes of taxpayers as parents, patients, tenants and customers.

A possible consolation is that the school foundation is likely to finish up with a site worth several million pounds which would be enough to restore the old Tottenham Grammar School with a mixture of fee-payers and scholarship boys. So can we turn the tables on the ghost of Butskellism, put our grand-children's names down for future places, and wave our old school ties at the impotent local miseducation authority?

Alas, the unenterprising foundation governors appear to have thrown in their lot with local councillors to use the money for the wider 'benefit' of polit-ically dominated 'education' in Haringey. Sarah, Duchess of Somerset, must be spinning in her grave.

24   SOCIALISM A MISTAKE – OFFICIAL[34]

Recent dazzling, crisp sunny Sundays in the run-up to Christmas should provoke greater awe at the infinite wonder of God's creation, of which it would be refreshing to hear more from the bishops!

But when did you last ponder the miracle of the economic order? How does it come about that millions of shopping baskets are daily filled with our distinctive choices from thousands of products grown, prepared, packed and transported by anonymous people from distant lands of which we know noth-ing?

In our working lives most of us contribute towards one link in the chain of invention, production, and distribution leading we often know not where. We are like puppets dancing on strings pulled by wholesalers, retailers and consumers scattered around the country, if not the world.

But why don't the strings get hopelessly tangled? How does it all fit together? Is anyone in charge? Could Bryan Gould's industrial strategy provide an adequate substitute?

The questions multiply. Can anyone know the full ramifications of what is glibly called the 'world economy'? Could the present system ever have been invented by a single mind, or be redesigned by a committee of Nobel laure-ates? Do we even understand how it came about?

'The Fatal Conceit'

Having devoted most of his 89 years and dozens of publications to puzzling over these questions, the greatest economic and political philosopher of this century, Friedrich Hayek, has now written what may prove his crowning work. It is a brilliant effort to illuminate such mysteries. His title, *The Fatal Conceit*, is a challenge to the ruling intellectual élites of rationalists, empiricists, positivists, utilitarians and other assorted collectivists who think they know it all. Lacking humility, they scorn the spontaneous evolution of what Hayek calls 'the extended order' in which – without human design or central coordination – we find:

> thousands of millions of people working in a constantly changing environment, providing means of subsistence for others who are mostly unknown to them, and at the same time finding satisfied their own expectations that they will themselves receive goods and services produced by equally unknown people.

The secret weapon that produces coherence from the apparent chaos of individual striving is, of course, our old friend the market. It appears a simple, even mundane, concept of people shopping around for everyday goods and services. But its ramifications are of wondrous import

It is markets that make possible an international division of labour which has mocked the Malthusian and Marxist fears of increasing poverty to enable multiplying millions to live at ever-rising standards of living.

It is markets that enable more of whatever people want to be extracted from available scarce resources. The central fact that makes markets more efficient than planning is that relevant knowledge about the possibilities of production, resources, wants, transport and all other variables is widely dispersed. It is certainly not 'given data' as economic theory supposes. Nor is it constant, but ceaselessly shifting with every change in invention, innovation, exploration, individual preferences.

The true miracle of the market is that it takes into account more information than could ever be assembled by the most competent team of central planners, let alone by Lady Blackstone's Institute of Public Policy Research!

'This Marvellous Market'

So what does this marvellous market do? It brings all the scattered, changing information into the reckoning and effortlessly computes and re-computes relative prices as signals which guide equally scattered entrepreneurs, managers, investors, borrowers, dealers and consumers how best to achieve their individual purposes.

If adaptation to changing circumstances is not perfect, a major reason is government intervention to fix prices, protect producers, subsidise declining industries and in a host of other ways to restrict competition and thereby obstruct its pathfinding rôle as the 'optimum discovery procedure'.

Superficial critics object to the idea of buying in the cheapest market and selling in the dearest. To the critics' cry of selfishness or profiteering we may observe that, so long as competition is not suppressed, the effort to maximise profits compels producers to offer customers better price, quality or service. In the market over the long run you have to do good to do well.

Perhaps the most absorbing revelations in Hayek's riveting book are the chapters exploring how the extended order depends on individual property, contract, trade, honesty, law, peaceful striving and saving; and how it evolved from narrow, self-contained, warring, communal, hunting groups in primitive times.

He shows how this evolution required our forebears to subdue the instincts of collectivist solidarity and altruism that were essential to small groups but would have frustrated the morals appropriate to an impersonal market order.

Primitive man sought the obvious visible targets of food and shelter. Today most of us can hardly grasp ultimate ends which our daily labour serves. But this is difficult stuff and must be read in the original by highbrows with the necessary combination of patience, perseverance and sufficient humility to suspend initial disbelief.

Challenging Conclusion

I return to the introductory chapter for Hayek's most challenging conclusion. It is headed: 'Was Socialism a Mistake?'. His answer is an unqualified 'yes' and I am now convinced that he is right. The charge against the collectivists of every stripe is that they are wrong about the *facts*.

Their argument is founded on the delusion that the strategic guidance system of market prices can be replaced by what they would call 'rational' commands by some super group of central planners. They believe they could assemble enough facts to redirect human efforts and to redesign the structure of incentives in conformity with some model of 'social justice'. In place of Adam Smith's 'invisible hand' of competitive markets, socialists would find themselves steering blind what I have called a hand and mouth-operated economy resting on coercion and exhortation.

Where has socialism ever worked to raise standards of living and civilisation? After high hopes, it has failed repeatedly in Russia, China, Poland, Yugoslavia, Vietnam, Tanzania and Nicaragua, despite help from the West in both copying and credits. Who can dismiss Hayek's magisterial verdict: 'To follow socialist morality would destroy much of present human kind and impoverish much of the rest'.

25   LET'S PRIVATISE STERLING NEXT?[35]

Despite the Conservatives' better record on inflation since 1979, renewed anxieties about rising prices pose a fundamental question which came to the fore in the 1970s when Labour presided over inflation rates of between 10 and 25 per cent.

The question is whether money is too important to be left to party politicians. Of course, all governments pay lip service to stable prices. But when faced with awkward choices of policy, can we really expect them to stick to the straight and narrow path of financial rectitude?

It was all so much easier in the days of the gold standard. Not only was the pound sterling tied to a specified weight of gold; the Bank of England was a private company not subservient to spendthrift politicians. True, it had an effective monopoly over the issue of notes, but any temptation to print too many was checked by its liability to give gold in exchange for unwanted currency.

The importance of this discipline was vividly demonstrated during the Napoleonic war when the government suspended convertibility and borrowed heavily from the Bank. Inevitably, the increased supply of paper money forced up prices and the mischief was not checked until gold payments were restored.

Glory of the Gold Standard

In its full glory the gold standard was a self-correcting market mechanism. If prices rose, and people feared for the future value of their savings, they could simply demand gold in exchange for their notes at a fixed rate. The consequent squeeze on the Bank's gold reserve compelled it to contract the supply of notes in circulation, which reduced prices and restored their value.

Since 1931 the pound has lost this anchorage in real value and in 1946 the Bank of England was nationalised. As a result, it is no longer scrupulous bankers but the government of the day that determines the quantity of cash and so the size of the inverted pyramid of bank money built up by traditional ratios on that cash base.

The baneful result of trusting politicians with our money is crudely exposed by a chart I have hanging in my office. It shows a rise in the average prices of standard commodities amounting to 30,000 per cent over the seven centuries from 1280 to 1980. Of this 300-fold debasement in our coinage, more than 95 per cent has occurred since the 1930s, and most of that since the last war!

Keynesian Age of Inflation

This great age of inflation has been blamed on the followers of Keynes who, after his death in 1946, went further than him in preaching the expansion of monetary demand as the magic path to perpetual full employment.

To politicians it sounded like a free lunch. They could pursue their favourite pastime of spending more money and have economic growth thrown in as a bonus. Alas, with the help of predatory trade unions, an increasing part of the additional demand was diverted from raising employment and output into boosting incomes and prices.

It was the achievement of Milton Friedman in the 1970s to remind us of the old quantity theory which warned earlier generations that if you increase spending faster than production you are most likely to buy more inflation. His solution seemed simplicity itself. If governments were limited to increasing the money supply by around 2 or 3 per cent a year, it would match the average rate of increased output and so keep prices stable.

But how could party politicians be held to such a strict monetary rule? A number of suggestions were forthcoming in the 1960s. One wicked idea was that Ministerial, Parliamentary and Treasury salaries should be inversely related to prices!

More seriously, Peter Jay suggested that the management of monetary policy should be taken away from such scalliwags and entrusted to a group of independent wise men appointed for long terms and paid well to maintain stable prices. Others went further in suggesting that the Bank of England should be denationalised to remove it from interference by short-sighted, opportunistic politicians.

'Entrenched Legal Limits'

Professor J.M. Buchanan, who recently won wider fame outside America as the leader of the 'public choice' school and a Nobel Laureate, so despairs of democratic governments resisting the temptation to inflate that he now recommends entrenched legal limits on the discretion of politicians to tamper with monetary policy. But what of countries that don't have written constitutions to check the power of temporary majorities?

It was left to the master of them all, F.A. Hayek, to go to the root of the trouble. In 1976, before 'privatisation' had been heard of, he published a Hobart Paper with the remarkable title: *Denationalisation of Money*. His analysis was original yet irresistible. Its essence was that the mismanagement of money is no more than a special case of the abuse of monopoly power. At once the solution suggested itself.

Thus by long usage, reinforced by laws on legal tender, modern governments can require citizens to accept and use the national unit of money, however variable its value. Accordingly, politicians have little incentive to persevere through thick and thin in maintaining honest money. But if people could choose between a number of currencies, the managers of each would have a powerful inducement to check over-issue and preserve its value.

New Monetary Units

The first steps for Hayek were the abolition of exchange control and legal tender laws so that Britons could choose to make contracts in Deutschemarks or Swiss francs, which have proved a better store of value than pounds sterling. It would also be open for banks to launch new monetary units and win customers by doing even better.

Not to be outdone, a young economist named Kevin Dowd has now trumped Hayek in the latest Hobart Paper, entitled *Private Money*. He would go all the way by abolishing the Bank of England and welcoming new brands of pounds tied to the value of specified commodities. It may all seem remote, but so was the abolition of exchange control recommended by yet another Hobart Paper in 1979.

So the Chancellor had better live up to his earlier promise of getting inflation down to zero. Otherwise, more of us will look for a better hole for our savings. But, please, no more talk about a single European currency run by a bunch of super-monopolists fighting over the money supply in a dozen different languages.

26   HIDING BEHIND MRS THATCHER'S SKIRT[36]

Since Mrs Thatcher let Jacques Delors's European cat out of the Brussels bag in her Bruges speech last September, debate on the transition from Common Market to Single Market has certainly warmed up. And the more the Bruges text is studied, the less it is seen to deserve the instant outrage of professional Euro-cheer leaders.

Sir John Hoskyns was not the first to comment on the sensitivity of many European spokesmen to any breath of criticism. It would be easy to say too many of them are making too good a living on the Brussels gravy train. But a kinder explanation was offered in the *New European* quarterly by Christopher Tugendhat whose *communautaire* credentials are not inferior to Ted Heath's. He reminds us that the Common Market was conceived after the war by leaders of countries that had been invaded and occupied, if not all defeated. No wonder that outside Britain the concepts of nationality and the nation state were widely discredited.

Hence the dream of federalism, which has survived even after memories of war faded and the nation state reasserted its claims as the primary focus for loyalty and obedience. Now will you insensitive British see why Mrs Thatcher can be pilloried as nationalistic, or at least insufficiently European? Tugendhat patiently explains that all governments believe in *Europe des Patries,* but 'the *federal dream* is still alive . . . and is held in respect by many who do not in practice subscribe to it. For that reason attacks upon it are widely and deeply resented'. Got it?

Earnest Eurocrats

When the British are most often accused of hypocrisy, it's a bit rich to be lectured by earnest Eurocrats for not joining in their silly make-believe about early progress towards political integration, if not a United States of Europe. Such political posturing is especially infuriating because it diverts attention from what Tugendhat agrees is 'the real question', namely, the extent and forms of government intervention within our national economics. This is the issue we should be studying and debating. Just because M Delors believes in more socialist policies than Mrs Thatcher, he can hardly claim to be more European – any more than socialist Neil Kinnock could claim to be more British than non-socialist David Owen.

Tugendhat's illuminating amateur psycho-analysis of our European friends provides a further explanation of why Mrs Thatcher appears more isolated than she really is. Thus there are plenty of French, German, Italian and other European political leaders who privately share her non-socialist views. But lacking her courage, they prefer to join in the well-established game described by a French observer as *se cacher derrière la jupe de Madame Thatcher.* They can hide behind her skirt and keep quiet, confident in the knowledge that in the last resort she will use the veto (wherever it is still effective) to prevent worker participation and all the other socialist mischief of M Delors's 'social dimension'.

What remains true is that the programme for removing obstacles to trade, investment and migration throughout the Community by 1992, does not require a common statute for companies, or the right of trade unionists to sit on their boards, or to enjoy equal access to social benefits, let alone uniform or minimum wages or conditions of work

What 1992 does require is the rooting out of all the remaining national restrictions on the freedom of entrepreneurs, employees and consumers to earn their living and spend their income on terms equally available to citizens in all member states.

Gains from Trade

The gains from free trade will be widely shared. Open access will enable all of us to enjoy what was once thought the enriching prerogative of the powerful, to buy in the cheapest market and sell our labour or output in the dearest. Of course, at the start, labour is cheaper in Spain, Portugal or Greece than in Germany, France, or Belgium; just as labour was once dirt cheap in Hong Kong, Singapore – and Japan! But for how long?

Economic theory and recent experience confirm that international trade operates to raise the standards of the poorer and less productive people and regions. In a free market cheap and abundant labour will attract employers, just as high wages elsewhere will attract employees from lower wage areas. Trade depends on geographical difference in costs and other circumstances and the resulting competition tends to equalise prices, incomes and opportunities.

The folly of the so-called 'social dimension' is that M Delors would like to *start* by equalising or 'harmonising' conditions between areas of high and low labour or tax costs to prevent 'social dumping'. Yet if Greek or Portuguese employers were saddled at once with paying higher wages and social benefits, the resulting unemployment would be used to justify increased regional subsidies.

In the latest CPS tract, *Europe 1992: The Good and the Bad,* John Redwood MP describes the result as a 'gigantic merry-go-round raising costs, raising taxes and raising subsidies throughout the Community'. As it is, he points out our bill from Brussels will more than double from under £1,000 million last year to close on £2,000 million this year.

Plenty of other voices are at last being raised against the already excessive power of the Commission. They include well-merited attacks on its protectionist proclivities from the Adam Smith Institute in *Bricks in the Wall* and from Professor Brian Hindley in *The World Economy* showing that anti-dumping duties are manipulated to block legitimate competition from lower cost Far Eastern producers – where wages, incidentally, have risen from the pre-war bowl of rice to approaching European levels. Even more fiercely, the radical No Turning Back Group of MPs are shortly weighing in with *Europe: Dream or Nightmare.*

The Promise of 1992

Yet all these critics strongly support the 1992 prospectus which does not include Jacques Delors's fevered socialist hopes for a *dirigiste* Europe. As explained in the recent classic IEA Paper by Professor Victoria Curzon Price,[37] 1992 simply promises the removal of impediments to the free movement of goods, services, people and money. Within a single market, differing national social policies, company structures and tax régimes can compete. In this way we will better learn what serves our changing need than by heeding the backward-looking, pre-Gorbachev nostalgia of Master Jacques.

Sir John Hoskyns may or may not be correct in his measured judgement that the Commission lacks the managerial competence to deliver 1992 on time. Certainly it is an ambitious programme with glittering prizes and prospects for all who count themselves European. In the hope that the dreamers and *dirigistes* will not desist, I hereby reveal the new slogan for our Bruges Group.

A boarding party is flying into Bruges next Friday to join other European allies in opening up a second front against M Delors. On our banner will fly the simple advice *1992 First*. If only he were a fellow cockney, I'd add: 'Come orf it Jack!'.

27 AFTER TEN YEARS HER WORK IS NOT YET COMPLETE[38]

The reasons for Margaret Thatcher's towering ascendancy – spreading far beyond Britain, as I have discovered in recent visits to Australia, New Zealand, the United States and Russia – will be debated well beyond the 1990s. Her lasting impact on policy around the world is unlikely to be disputed, especially if we take seriously the deathbed conversion of the British Labour Party and the East European ex-Marxists to 'market socialism'.

At every stage, Mrs Thatcher was assailed for wanton confrontation, even conscious cruelty. Every day her resolution was tested. Her unique, indispensable contribution has been the combination of calm, consistent clarity of thought with a personal moral courage that has not been matched by a British politician since Churchill as war-time leader.

The puzzle remains, from where did her transformation of political thinking and policy come? Keynes argued in 1936 that radical changes in the political agenda, such as he was seeking to achieve, stemmed from intellectual influences. He claimed, hopefully, that 'the world is ruled by little else [than] the ideas of economists and political philosophers'. I doubt if Mrs Thatcher would think of herself as an intellectual, though like her political mentor Keith (now Lord) Joseph she enjoys the company of intellectuals, and has even been seen to fall silent in the company of Milton Friedman or Friedrich Hayek. Certainly, a new idea has never entered her head, not in the seminal sense implied by Keynes.

'Thatcherism'

'Thatcherism' is no novel, far less alien, creed. Its central belief in the general benevolence of free market forces operating in a framework of strong but limited government is little more than a return to the broadly shared assumptions of Liberal and Tory leaders during Britain's last great eruption of economic change in the 19th century. If Mrs Thatcher owes a large debt to ideas, they were not her own. Her initial contribution was to be receptive to the seminal, scholarly thinking stemming from Adam Smith and David Hume, as refined in our own times by such Nobel Laureates as Friedrich Hayek, Milton Friedman, George Stigler and James Buchanan.

If the importance of competitive markets, consumer choice, incentives, property rights, stable money and the rest, had been understood for a century or two, wherein lies the lady's claim to fame? As the historians ponder this central riddle, they might start with A.V. Dicey's *Law and Public Opinion in England*. In 1905 he reviewed the progress of legislation since 1800 as a background to what he called 'the growth of collectivism' after 1870. The story was one of multiplying laws, each capable of justification to remedy immediate grievances, but enacted without deep thought about their cumulative, long-term effects. The ruling assumption was 'a belief in the benefit of governmental guidance or interference, even when it greatly limits the sphere of individual choice or liberty'.

'The Mounting Collectivist Consensus'

There followed seven decades of what I call the mounting collectivist–Keynesian–Beveridge–welfare consensus. Encouraged by mobilisation for two world wars and sped-up by Labour governments, policy was guided by the paternalistic, basically anti-democratic sentiment that every economic or social imperfection of a free society justified new laws that diminished the individual action and aggrandised the state. But the philosophers of the market economy predicted that government failure would prove more crippling than market failure.

Politicians not only lack the knowledge to control an increasingly complex, changing economy; their policies are distorted by special interest groups, like trade unions, farmers, welfare and other lobbies. Worst of all, their *ad hoc* interventions wreak havoc in the market-place with disruptive strikes, distortionary inflation, demoralising unemployment, debilitating taxes and the dubious black economy.

The question being asked in the 1970s was whether Britain was any longer governable by the weakened authority of parliamentary democracy. After the debacle of Ted Heath's U-turn, it was Mrs Thatcher's good luck to have her turn at reversing the tables in 1979 when Labour was caught out treating deep-seated union ills with the political poultice of a 'social contract'. After 1979 Mrs Thatcher simply went ahead and governed.

The consensus lauded by the great and the good can now be seen to have been no more than civilised but cowardly appeasement.

'Pricking the Bubble'

All other post-war prime ministers had shrunk back in fear of powerful unions in alliance with the dominant collectivist sentiment that Fabian and Marxist intellectuals have been puffing up over almost a century. Mrs Thatcher alone took courage to prick the bubble.

Her work is far from complete. Ten years is not sufficient to reverse a century of relative decline. When the time comes, her successor will need, first, similar courage to resist the re-grouping of remnants of the old consensus; and second, the same commitment to enlarge individual choice against the Hobson's choice of ever-growing government.

I do not know Michael Heseltine personally, but I'm still looking for evidence that his splendid self-confidence conceals a little modesty about the ability of politicians, here or in Europe, to solve all our problems.

28   HIGH PRICE OF A SOCIAL MARKET[39]

A trendy new label disguises the sacrifice of more and more of our incomes, writes Ralph Harris.

What are we to make of the recent discovery, by Mr Norman Lamont and Mr Christopher Patten, of the 'social market' as the Conservative watchword for the 1990s and beyond? First, it should be pointed out that the two politicians are not two of a kind. Their past attitudes suggest that Mr Lamont attaches more importance to the market half of the phrase and Mr Patten to the social. Mr Patten's contribution came in a contrived address to the leftish Policy Studies Institute, whose acolytes lap up such a think-piece like the Anglican Synod swallowing yet another revised services sheet.

But was it simply a PR gloss by a hard-pressed party chairman to divert attention from deepening economic gloom? Or was it another semantic effort to distance the Tories from their deposed leader – who kept them in power for more than a decade? Or might it portend a shift towards the middle ground where Neil Kinnock has been driven by the very success of the Thatcherite market economy?

Since Mr Patten is a leader of the wet tendency and currently drafting the next election manifesto, we must try to take his words seriously. So let us ask what exactly is meant by the 'social market economy'.

The most precise answer I can offer is either absolutely nothing – or almost anything. If Mrs Thatcher and her supporters believe in the unadorned 'market economy', does that mean it is unsocial – or antisocial? Are we to understand that Hume, Smith, Robbins, Jewkes, Hayek, Friedman and other sophisticated champions of the market were engaged in some plot against society?

Free Markets Are Social Markets

If you wish to be analytical, the reality is that the competitive market is necessarily a *social* instrument. It is nothing less than a network of local, national and international links that enable people to trade together freely for their mutual benefit, as workers, consumers, producers, dealers, savers, borrowers, investors.

It is the spread of this market that has so wondrously widened prosperity and extended freedom of choice throughout the West. Because it developed spontaneously (in Hayek's words 'the result of human action but not of human design'), is it to be stigmatised as unsocial?

The market could be regarded as 'social' in another sense. Thus it operates within a developing framework of laws, customs, and standards which extend from approved weights and measures to help in cash and kind for those who cannot help themselves. Its supporters differ on the scope for reforming the legal framework. But for true market men the test is to avoid sapping its efficiency in maximising valued output or its flexibility in adapting to ceaseless changes in resources, technology, competition and consumer preferences.

For all the 19th-century jibes against the phantom of *laissez faire,* there is no such animal as a free market operating in a vacuum of state inaction. If we stick to precise language, then full-blooded socialists aside, we all accept some measure of a mixed economy. But as with whisky and soda, everything turns on the mixture.

In his crowning work, *The Fatal Conceit*, Hayek quotes Confucius: 'When words lose their meaning, people will lose their liberty.' On this text he hangs a warning against the misuse of the words 'social' and 'society' which too easily imply a common pursuit of shared objectives wholly hostile to individual freedom. He cites the *Fontana Dictionary of Modern Thought* with 35 uses of 'social' which come, he thinks appropriately, after the entry for 'soap opera'!

Weasel Word

Hayek scorns 'social' as a weasel word, which empties the noun it qualifies of all meaning, just as a weasel is said to empty the contents of an egg without leaving a trace. He adds that it is 'a semantic fraud from the same stable as "People's Democracy".'

Mr Patten and others have been known to take refuge behind the German adoption of 'social market' to describe their successful post-war economy. Hayek who knew Ludwig Erhard as a professor, not a politician, quotes him as saying that the market economy did not have to be *made* social since it was already so by its very nature. In any event, the German miracle after 1948 owed everything to curbing the state, unleashing market forces, and learning from past suffering to avoid the plague of inflation.

Should we then dismiss this latest talk about the 'social market' as no more than a verbal flourish or a harmless misunderstanding? I find no grounds for such comfort. Mr Patten's speech went on to hint that his ambition is to lavish more resources on yet another bid to rescue failing state social services from public obloquy. He wants to make them so good that people no longer think it worth paying for private education or medical care. Not much hope, or danger, of that.

But let me ask bluntly in his own terms, why it is more 'social' to go to a state school (as I did) rather than to Eton, or to use an NHS bed rather than subscribing privately (as I do) for a Bupa nursing home? If Mr Patten wants more state (nationalised) welfare, with all the attendant waste and damage to the market, why not say so openly and argue his case on costs, rather than hide behind obfuscations about the 'social market'?

His fuzzy approach was well exposed by Professor Robert Skidelsky, who as Keynes's official biographer understands economics and wrote an impressive tract on *The Social Market Economy* for David Owen's old SDP [Social Democratic Party] group. His central principle is that 'we turn to the market as first resort and the government as last resort . . . our first instinct is to use the market, not to override it'. His own commitment to the market led him to conclude from endemic congestion in the public sector that rationing by price is both feasible *and necessary* in such services as roads *and hospitals*. He emphasises that without direct payment there is no accountability. No 'social market' nonsense here.

Political Cost of 'Social Market'

I would go further in challenging Mr Patten's version of the 'social market'. His wing of the post-Thatcher Conservative Party have always wanted a larger role for government. Their inspiration is not so much social as self. Thus they are self-conscious intellectuals of the self-confident, not to say self-righteous, school who do not easily defer to ordinary people's preferences expressed through the market. They put more spending before tax cuts, especially if superficial pollsters say there are votes in it. They prefer politicisation to privatisation.

Above all, these new missionaries of the so-called 'social market' have not reckoned on the cost of whetting appetites for more state spending in the run-up to an election. Once politicians relax their guard, there are a thousand lobbies each with plausible claims for a few more millions, or tens of millions.

Even Mrs Thatcher's determination could not hold the line against mounting government spending, which by 1990 was running above 45 per cent of the nation's income. What will satisfy these closet collectivists – 50 or 60 or

70 per cent? Thus does talk of 'social market' raise the spectre of socialist market – just when a growing army of young Thatcherite economists in the East are looking to us for inspiration.

29   CAN BRITAIN SURVIVE WITHOUT SIGNING?[40]

Yes. If John Major can summon up the courage of his own convictions, he will pack some throat lozenges and earplugs but no pen or chequebook when he leaves on Monday for Maastricht. There's more talking than listening for him to do but absolutely no need to sign anything, least of all damaging and expensive commitments.

The Prime Minister neither wants nor needs anything from Maastricht – except, alas, the fig-leaf of an agreement. There is no question of Britain leaving the EC. The question always was how little must we give away this time round, in return for what? For nothing more than a good press in the run-up to the General Election?

But the price we would pay for signing – and therefore *what we stand to gain by not signing* – is much more than the concessions already yielded up, with more to come at the summit in return for dropping that F-word.

First, most of the provisions on political and monetary union would weaken the competitive efficiency of the Single Market and, secondly, would strengthen the remorseless federal, centralising tendencies. Thirdly, even if we keep our opt-out clause and let the rest go ahead with EMU, monetary union would still cost us a pile of Ecus towards the subsidies demanded by Spain and others to offset the damage to their less-developed economies.

Fourthly, the imposition of still more complex conditions of membership would make it more difficult for the liberated countries of Eastern Europe to join up. Finally, if we boldly play our precious veto, we would be keeping our shield against being outvoted again.

Such an outcome would in no way affect our continued participation in the Single Market. In his Commons speech the Prime Minister acknowledged that the 'positive advantages' we gained from Europe all came from participating in 'the world's largest single market'.

By not being stampeded into signing up for political and monetary union, Britain, along with the other 11, remains bound by the existing treaties. We lose none of the present advantages of free movement in goods, services, capital and people promised for 31 December 1992.

And if the others go ahead with political and monetary experiments outside the present treaties and institutions of the basic European Economic Community, they would end up burdening their own economies and handing a welcome competitive advantage for British exports in Europe.

30   A GLITTERING PRIZE IN MAASTRICHT'S MUD[41]

European integration can be achieved without the folly of federalism.

Ever since Margaret Thatcher spoke at Bruges of the danger of a European superstate, I have been trying to work out who really wants to speed up political union rather than consolidating the more widely supported common market – which is what Edward Heath sold us 20 years ago.

It is easy to see why Jacques Delors and his fellow commissioners should wish to enlarge still further their powers and prominence. Not only are they mostly former politicians with a fatal itch to do good, but several have ambitions to be called home to higher things. As for the bureaucrats under them, they are sufficiently human to favour enlarging their empires.

But why do national leaders want to cede further power into these grasping hands in Brussels? There is no mystery about Spain and the other mendicant nations whose support has been purchased by promises of subsidies from the new 'cohesion fund'. But what about countries that will pay the higher bills?

Two Europes

In his recent paper, *A Tale of Two Europes,* Lord Beloff recalls the laudable post-war aim of the Treaty of Rome, to construct a Franco-German axis around which there could be integration of the continental states 'whose confidence in their own institutions had been destroyed'. Alas, they also shared many inward-looking, cultural, *dirigiste,* and legal traditions that remain wholly different from, even hostile to, Britain's international, liberal, Anglo-Saxon roots.

Why then should British leaders tag along – apart of course from John Major and the dwindling band of sycophants who regard Maastricht as Mr Major's personal triumph? Above all, how can this statist progression be supported by Tories, least of all the numerous erstwhile allies of Mrs Thatcher? Part of the answer is that severe whipping dragooned many doubters into the Aye lobby. But what of Geoffrey Howe, David Howell and others who share my understanding and enthusiasm for a liberal market economy?

One clue may be a speech by Geoffrey Howe as Foreign Secretary in 1989 when he described Europe as 'the necessary vehicle, the central fulcrum, the basic lever for Britain to exercise the influence it wishes to exercise in the world'. Such Foreign Office games-playing does not take into account the real world and is doomed to exacerbate national rivalries. Above all, it underestimates the glittering prize of true European integration, without Maastricht, through completing the single market in a liberal framework.

One of Adam Smith's insights was that if all barriers to free trade were ended '*the different states into which a great continent was divided would so far resemble the different provinces of a great empire*'. In short, a genuine common market based on mutual recognition is a benign method of integration; an invisible empire which is the best antidote to the recurrence of war. It was specifically to speed the removal of tariffs, subsidies and other distortions to competition that Mrs Thatcher assented to the Single European Act in 1986. Alas, by ending the national veto, this crucial federalising measure opened the door wider to the subordination of British law to edicts from Brussels, and the imperialism of the European Court in Luxembourg.

Costly Standards of the Superstatists

Ever since, the superstatists have exploited majority voting to impose ruinously costly standards that are not only unnecessary but diametrically opposed to competing jurisdictions implicit in free trade. Where trade depends on differences in national, regional and local production costs, the corporatist pressure from Brussels is for harmonisation and standardisation to suit established interests. M Delors recently gave the game away by calling for 'a global social charter' to stop competition from the East. This is not a level playing field. It is the ultimate in flat earth economics.

Forget the nonsense about the British sausage, French cheeses, the straight cucumber. Even without Maastricht, remote Eurocrats are forever pushing to impose the 48-hour week, discourage part-time working, ban schoolboy newspaper rounds, censor tobacco advertising, push equal pay to absurd limits, harmonise taxes and more mischief besides. What is all this to do with them, or with the single market? How long before nothing is left for us to decide for ourselves? Poor Mr Major takes refuge in talk about enlarging membership, but how will the less productive economies of Eastern Europe jump these hurdles, which are in truth designed to keep them out?

The case against Maastricht is that it mightily accelerates this intrusive process. It enlarges the so-called 'competence' of the Commission. It extends majority voting in 100 directions. It augments various slush funds and increases taxation. It inflates costs, reduces flexibility and brings fortress Europe nearer. Above all, the obsession with an irreversible monetary union threatens to reduce economic self-government to empty ceremonial. It is a distraction and a detraction from the single market.

'Centralising Logic'

It is simply adding insult to injury for whipped friends of Maastricht to boast of the insertion of 'subsidiarity' and the removal of 'federal' when actions and analysis tell so eloquently of the centralising logic of European political union. By now the emollient Mr Major should have discovered that appeasement – as in 1938 – buys only temporary respite from pressure. Already we read another federal ambush is being prepared when the Belgians take over the presidency next month.

Constitutional scruples aside, the real case for a referendum is that it would buttress the government for the continuing struggle, which I fear would be all the more acrimonious if the sovereign people misguidedly voted Yes.

NOTES

1. *Yesterday, Today and Tomorrow*, March/April 1975.
2. British Institute of Management, 1965.
3. 'The Meaning of Competition', in *Individualism and Economic Order*, London: Routledge, 1949.
4. *British Industry*, 22 January 1965.
5. 'The Meaning of Competition', op. cit.
6. A sobering account of some recent forecasting efforts will be found in C. Pratten, 'The Best-Laid Plans . . .', *Lloyd's Bank Review*, July 1964.
7. *Disclosure in Company Accounts*, London: Institute of Economic Affairs, revised edition, February 1965.
8. *Management of the British Economy 1945–1960*. Cambridge: Cambridge University Press, 1964.
9. *The Daily Telegraph*, 21 November 1967.
10. *Essays in the Theory and Practice of Pricing*, Institute of Economic Affairs, 1967, 25s.
11. *The Glasgow Herald*, 8 February 1968.
12. John Jewkes, *The New Ordeal by Planning*, is published today (London: Macmillan 1968, 42s).
13. Extracts from *Swinton Journal*, Spring 1970.
14. Edited by Erich Streissler, London: Routledge & Kegan Paul, 1969, price £4.
15. *The Sunday Telegraph,* 13 September 1970.
16. *The Glasgow Herald*, 9 October 1972.
17. *The Spectator*, 23 February 1974.
18. *The Spectator*, 2 March 1974.
19. *The Times*, 4 December 1974.
20. *The Daily Telegraph*, 17 November 1975.
21. *Crossbow*, Summer 1977.
22. *The Daily Telegraph,* 23 November 1981.
23. *The Daily Telegraph*, 17 March 1982.
24. *What Price Unemployment?*, IEA, price £1.80.
25. *The Times*, 24 August 1983.
26. *The Independent*, 1 October 1987.
27. *The Sunday Telegraph*, 3 April 1988.
28. *The Sunday Telegraph*, 10 April 1988.
29. *The Sunday Telegraph*, 24 April 1988.
30. *The Sunday Telegraph*, 8 May 1988.
31. *The Sunday Telegraph*, 19 June 1988.
32. Lexington, MA: Lexington Books, 1986.
33. *The Sunday Telegraph*, 3 July 1988.
34. *The Sunday Telegraph*, 20 November 1988.
35. *The Sunday Telegraph*, 4 December 1988.

36. *The Sunday Telegraph*, 16 April 1989.
37. *1992: Europe's Last Chance? From Common Market to Single Market*, 19th Wincott Memorial Lecture, IEA Occasional Paper 81, London: Institute of Economic Affairs, December 1988.
38. *The Independent*, 31 March 1990.
39. *The Sunday Telegraph*, 17 February 1991.
40. *The Sunday Telegraph*, 8 December 1991.
41. *The Times*, 7 June 1993.

PART III

House of Lords speeches

No Minister! (Early House of Lords speeches, 1981–1984)*

ACKNOWLEDGEMENTS

I am glad of this opportunity to express the debt I owe my colleague Arthur Seldon and the hundreds of IEA authors whom he assembled and on whose publications I have drawn, largely without acknowledgement, in my writings and speeches for more than a quarter of a century.

I would also like to pay public tribute to the *Hansard* reporters who regularly produce such an accurate record of often imperfectly delivered effusions. Such minimum changes as have been made in this compilation are confined to clarifying the original verbal exposition, modifying inelegancies that jar in written form, and eliminating the elaborate forms of address and references to other speakers which help to civilise debate in the House of Lords.

27 January 1985   RALPH HARRIS

PREFACE

The Occasional Papers were designed as a series to accommodate texts of the spoken or written word originally addressed to specialist audiences but of wider interest to a larger assembly of readers. The first Occasional Paper was Professor George Stigler's *The Intellectuals and the Market Place* in 1963. Since then 70 have been published.

Number 71 by Lord Harris could be entitled *Legislators and the Market Place*. Professor Stigler analysed the intellectuals' misunderstanding, distrust and antipathy to the market. Lord Harris's speeches to the peers in Parliament are essays in explanation and advocacy that similarly indicate the misunderstanding, distrust and antipathy of peers ranging from seasoned Conservative, Labour and, alas, Liberal politicians to uninstructed bishops. Recent creations provide welcome allies for his campaign of enlightenment.

*   A radical challenge on economic and social policies from speeches in the House of Lords. IEA Occasional Paper 71, 1985.

The task of introducing and appraising this text after a quarter of a century of close partnership with the author is the task that would have faced Gilbert had he been asked to assess Sullivan (or vice-versa). These speeches form a fourth phase in Lord Harris's saga of education: from lecturing to students at the University of St Andrews, to informing readers of *The Glasgow Herald,* to enlightening IEA readers in our early collaborations on advertising, hire purchase and welfare and his later Papers, and now to entreating, admonishing and trying to persuade a mixed bag of mostly older men and women: heirs or recipients of peerages and bishops. His fourth phase has not, I imagine, been the easiest or most rewarding, for the standard of economic literacy in the Lords does not seem high, even among those who have exercised power in positions of state, and who now stand in judgement on those who follow them, even where in their time they did harm by misdirected policies. There are honourable, if rare, exceptions.

The substance of the 15 speeches between April 1981 and May 1984 assembled here display Lord Harris's gifts, which would have singled him out for distinction whatever work chance had led him to do. I think of him as a football centre-forward deftly picking up passes, thinking fast on his feet, outwitting the opposing fullbacks by clever dribbling, and distracting goalkeepers with jokes while shooting straight into the goal. The material is well-researched, tolerant in general tone, shot with gentle irony, and mostly temperate in language except when exceptional obtuseness provokes a flash of anger. From the cross-benches he is disappointed or impatient with the Government or Conservative peers (he speaks of 'Tory rustics and romantics' who oppose economies in government spending and reduced taxation), saddened by the clerical sophists who confuse motives with results, all the more because of his practising Christianity, and aroused by symptom-swatting Liberal simplicities and Labour fallacies, although I detect a shadow of hopeful sympathy with the Social Democrats, or rather with what they may one day do.

The edited speeches comprise instructive, entertaining and spirited reading for commoners, from students to entrepreneurs, as well as for peers. They show economics to be far from the dismal science. The 'national economic assessment' urged by Labour is dismissed as 'a pow-wow with the highwayman'. The National Plan 'mocked nature by passing from teething troubles in 1965 to death rattles in 1966 without the customary interval of hopeful life'.

The theme throughout is the consequences of abandoning classical economic liberalism and the urgency of applying its principles to policy in our day. The specific is that Britain's post-war discontents arise not from the use of the market but from its neglect in almost every part of the economy from the labour market, housing and coalmining to the sale of spectacles and public-house licensing. It should now comfort him that, whether the Lords are heeding him so far or not, the more able and perspicacious intellectuals of the ambiguously described 'Left' are revising their prejudices against the market and re-examining the reasons for its efficacy and increasing popularity that lie at the heart of the teachings of the no less ambiguously described 'new Right'. Although he finds the Government, which is at least trying, less culpable than the Opposition, which blindly ignores evidence of failure by the state, his philosophic position is liberal rather than conservative. A lordly Minister observed after a Harris speech: 'There is something about the *pur sang* of classical liberalism – very unlike the present incumbents – which is not my idea of conservatism but very much classical market liberalism'. The Harris speeches distil the essence of classical English (and Scottish) political economy which puts the general interest before special interests. Indeed, Lord Harris seems to have become the most consistent exponent of the general interest against some other peers who speak as 'experts' but for special interests – from mining to council housing and from opticians to (other) trade unionists; even the interests of the underdog – or the apparent underdog – from the unemployed to the disabled, are not always discussed by their lordships with requisite regard for the general interest

Some liberal economists may differ from several of his judgements. The speeches nominate trade unions and management as the main culprits who have applied or tolerated restrictive practices in industry as the root cause of British economic decline. It could be argued that trade unions have introduced restrictive practices because the law gave them the power to enforce them and government thoughtlessly equipped them with complaisant employers in public service monopolies that could pass on the resulting costs to defenceless taxpayers, especially in an inflationary environment. And managers tolerated restrictive practices because the economy was not sufficiently competitive to prevent them from passing the costs on to defenceless consumers. In both cases the ultimate culprit was government.

Not the least fruitful aspect of these speeches is their indications of the potential for influencing the upper chamber of the British Parliament by converting it from error. In his short five years Lord Harris has formed the view that the British economy requires not piecemeal reform but root-and-branch repeal of laws that have been outdated by technical advance but continue to hobble adaptation to change in supply and demand. To this end he has formed a non-party Repeal Group. Although repeal would presumably scare and alienate the peers even more than reform, his repealers have had some success, as in the argument on shop closing hours and on the opticians' monopoly. But so far the political and bureaucratic interests inside government and the sectional interests in industry have prevailed against liberalisation in housing rents, minimum wages, licensing laws, coalmining and elsewhere for which he pleads eloquently. Marx, who emphasised the force of interests, has proved more prophetic than Keynes, who emphasised the influence of ideas.

Moreover, the political process in the British Parliament makes it necessary, or at least desirable, to disarm criticism by ritual genuflections that never question the motives of opponents: 'I do not doubt for one moment that many of the early pioneers and the modern inheritors of the trade union mantle were, and are, inspired by lofty idealism'. 'Many' is an ambiguous word which conveys an impression of general public-spiritedness among British trade union leaders. The economics of public choice discounts differences in motives between people in bureaucratic institutions, whether governmental or private, and people in the market. Lord Harris quotes a Conservative Minister as saying: 'I rather like spending other people's money; it is one of the most enjoyable functions of a Minister's life'. His sad reaction is: 'I have come to accept that there is not much prospect of getting politicians to treat the taxpayer's money with the most especial respect it should deserve'.

On the whole, standards in the market are loftier than in bureaucracies because rogue elephants are discovered sooner through the sifting system of competition. In any event, people do good not because their motives are noble but because they are apt to go broke if they do not. Here, as elsewhere, Adam Smith the philosopher whom Lord Harris likes to quote saw more truth than Tawney or Titmuss or Tory patriarchs.

Yet, as Professor T.W. Hutchison has urged, John Stuart Mill was more prescient than both Marx and Keynes when he observed that ideas had to wait for 'circumstances' to 'conspire' in their favour. Lord Harris has had five years of economic proselytising. The Conservatives and perhaps the Social Democrats are listening; Labour and the Liberals mostly seem deaf; and the bishops are the most compassionately reactionary of all, with a culpable disdain for the opportunity costs of playing God with other people's money. But Lord Harris is still young, as peers go, with at least two decades of reasoning and admonishing and exhorting to come in his 80s and into the 21st century. He deserves conspiring circumstance to come to his rescue sooner rather than later. Perhaps a monthly seminar in a Lords committee room on the elements of supply and demand, opportunity costs, elasticity, the difference between impact and incidence, the importance of price- as well as income-effects, and, not least, the economics of government and bureaucracy might help to save him time listening to sometimes over-simplified solutions to every 'problem'.

The Minister who distanced himself from Lord Harris's 'classical market liberalism' added that it had been 'an invaluable injection into the thinking of this Government and our national life '. With rare exceptions, such as the late Lord Robbins, Lord Harris has been almost a lone wolf as an economic liberal in the Lords. He now has the prospect of reinforcement, not least by Professor Lord Bauer of Cambridge and the LSE, and he may receive aid from Lord Bruce-Gardyne, a Whig rather than a Tory, the non-economist Liberal Lord

Grimond, who understands the market better than most British politicians in any Party, and the cross-bench trade unionist Lord Chapple, who once said, with a customary shaft of insight, 'In the end, it's the market or machine guns'.

If the Government is in earnest about deregulating an over-regulated economy, it could do worse (hardly better) than begin with the agenda of the Repeal Group which – in addition to wages councils, rent control, Shops Acts, licensing laws, and the Truck Acts – includes employment protection, equal opportunities, social benefits for strikers and the NCB monopoly of working British coal resources. Many items have not yet reached its list. There is no lack of tasks for the avid dismantlers of the modern mercantilism.

In the meantime, these speeches provide all who feel strongly enough about economic liberalism – a growing congregation extending to hitherto sceptics as well as true believers – with model texts on how to embark on the task of persuading reluctant transgressors.

January 1985 ARTHUR SELDON

THE AUTHOR

Ralph Harris was born in 1924 and educated at Tottenham Grammar School and Queens' College, Cambridge. He was Lecturer in Political Economy at St Andrews University, 1949–56, and has been General Director of the Institute of Economic Affairs since 1957. He wrote (with Arthur Seldon) *Hire Purchase in a Free Society, Advertising in a Free Society, Choice in Welfare*, etc., for the IEA. His essay, 'In Place of Incomes Policy', was published in *Catch '76 . . .?* (Occasional Paper 'Special' (No. 47), 1976). His most recent works, written with Arthur Seldon, are *Pricing or Taxing?* (Hobart Paper No. 71, 1976), *Not from Benevolence . . .* (Hobart Paperback No. 10, 1977), and *Over-ruled on Welfare* (Hobart Paperback No. 13, 1979); he contributed the Epilogue, 'Can Confrontation be Avoided?' to *The Coming Confrontation* (Hobart Paperback No. 12, 1978); and his most recent IEA titles are *The End of Government . . .?* (Occasional Paper No. 58, 1980), and (with Arthur Seldon) *Shoppers' Choice* (Occasional Paper No. 68, 1983).

He is a Trustee of the Wincott Foundation and a member of the Political Economy Club, former President of the Mont Pèlerin Society, and a Council Member of the University of Buckingham.

Ralph Harris was created a Life Peer in July 1979 as Lord Harris of High Cross.

Part I   Unions and Unemployment

1.   A welcome for the Tebbit Bill

Debate on the Second Reading of the 1982 Employment Bill

In its press advertising campaign against the Employment Bill, the TUC said that Mr Tebbit is 'trying to crush trade unions'. Like Lord Marsh, I can think of some trade union leaders who could do with a bit of crushing. But I want to explain why I think the TUC claim is so misguided by reference to German unions which have achieved so much more for their members without the privileges demanded with menaces by the TUC and their dwindling friends.

If this Bill were passed unchanged, British trade union leaders would still enjoy massive powers not available to their German counterparts. The proof is set forth in the Green Paper on immunities.[1] Thus in Germany the closed shop is illegal and membership of the 17 industrial unions ranges from above 90 per cent down to 10 per cent. Collective agreements are binding and trade unions can be sued like other responsible bodies for breach of contract. The rules of all but one of the 17 German unions require a 75 per cent vote in a secret ballot to approve industrial action. Finally, German public servants have no right to strike, and indeed for all unions political strikes and political affiliations are forbidden.

I believe the contrast with Germany is instructive because, since the beginning of this century, average British wages have fallen from almost double the German level to nearer half today. My argument is that the chief cause of our long relative economic decline has been the unique power of British trade unions to restrict flexibility and efficiency, to obstruct or sterilise investment, to discourage management in all its endeavours and so to retard economic progress. It is legendary that professional economists have wide disagreements. But I believe that most will accept that a necessary, if not a sufficient, condition for economic progress must be the continuous adaptation of working methods to match ceaseless changes in techniques, products, competition, comparative costs and consumer demand.

To go back to the TUC commercial last week, I thought its most inventive claim was that trade unions 'stand for the future'. Trade unions stand for the future like the Argentine junta stands for sweetness and light. It would be a closer approximation to the truth to say that British trade unions include the most backward-looking, nostalgic and reactionary bodies since the Society for the Preservation of Rural England.

It is sometimes thought that such museum pieces as the ASLEF [Associated Society of Locomotive Engineers and Firemen] train drivers, the printers, the dockers, the TV crews and even the miners are passing aberrations, and that they are exceptional in their obstruction to efficiency. But a truer observation, in my view, would be that British trade unions have historically too often stood for restrictionism. Their over-bearing legal powers have first magnified and then institutionalised the natural human resistance to change, which is one of the most common barriers to economic progress.

Examples of Luddism   For historical evidence, I will offer two episodes in the long catalogue of Luddism. The first goes back to 1897 when the new model trade union, the Amalgamated Society of Engineers, went on strike over the manning of machines – how many men to a machine was the issue. My witness is the Cambridge Professor of Economics, Alfred Marshall, who was known to be a warmer friend of trade unions and of the co-operative movement than he ever would have been of the employers. Not wishing to take sides publicly against the union, he poured out his frustrations in a private letter to the Master of Balliol, which included the following sentence: 'If the men should win and I were an engineering employer, I would sell my works for anything I could get and emigrate to America'. He went on in a later letter to refer to trade union restrictions in the bricklayers' union; and on locomotives he noted: 'Three Glasgow men needed to do the work of one American'.

Marshall did not by any means exempt complacent management from his strictures, but he saw the strongest threat to what he called 'national well-being' as 'the dominance in some unions of the desire to "make work" and an increase in their power to do so'. That was before 1906, when the Liberal Government was pressurised into conceding these large immunities in the teeth of strong opposition from Asquith and his legal colleagues in that Cabinet.

My second example of the arch conservatism of trade unions is drawn from the war. After 1939 it was discovered very quickly that the munitions industries could not work with the customary restrictions on entry, manning and demarcation. It was also found that for many jobs girls could be trained in a few months to replace time-served craftsmen who had been called-up. The official war history rather delicately describes this episode and mentions how even Ernie Bevin, formerly a trade union secretary and now war-time Minister of Labour, was unable to get agreement to what was called 'dilution' from his trade union colleagues without a cast-iron guarantee to revert to the *status quo ante* the moment the war was over. So it came about that, in 1942, Parliament turned aside from more pressing business to pass a full-blown statute, the Restoration of Pre-War Trade Practices Act. Its explicit purpose was to ensure that the efficient methods devised to win the war should not be available in helping to win the peace.

I do not doubt for one moment that many of the early pioneers and the modern inheritors of the trade union mantle were, and are, inspired by lofty idealism and voluntary action. It seems to me that the real error of many of their more political colleagues has been to seek higher wages through monopoly pressure and restrictionism, rather than through efficiency and expansion in marketable output. Their astonishing, if unintended, achievement has been simultaneously to depress British standards of living while inflating money wages and costs so as to cause an alternation between faster inflation and rising unemployment.

It has taken the deepest post-war recession to enable managements in the private sector to win support from their employees, often over the heads of the trade union leaders, for the shedding of decades of slack working habits. It seems to me that this beneficial process would be assisted and extended into the public sector if this Bill went further in relieving trade union leaders of their self-destructive weaponry.

2.   Labour costs versus jobs

Debate on the Queen's Speech, following the 1983 General Election

It is a new experience for me to follow Lord Kaldor, with whom I have had some disagreements in the past. But on this occasion I think it might be best to respect the informal economists' protection society by not immediately following his speculations on Saatchi and Saatchi, George Orwell and sundry other matters, which I found difficult to follow. Rather, I would start by congratulating Lord Bauer on what I thought was a notable maiden contribution to our discussion. I thought his cogent criticism of the welfare state for robbing individuals of responsibility was by no means lacking in true concern and compassion, which is often interpreted in a different way by the Labour side of this House.

In a rather different mood, I enjoyed the typically combative performance of Lord Bruce of Donnington. When I am listening to him I always think that he is somebody I should like to have with me in a tight corner. But until he faces the right way I have decided that it would be better to keep out of tight corners. I can agree with him from the cross-benches on one matter: that the Queen's Speech is sadly lacking on the major issue of unemployment. Even if we allow, as I would, that the official statistics include a good deal of voluntary unemployment – as well as ignoring the black market – the lack of job prospects remains a dark shadow, especially over the lives of young people. But on this occasion Lord Bruce turned aside to offer some interesting reflections on past Tory failures. Some of his criticisms of the exchange rate might be seen with hindsight to have some justice, but he overlooked telling us what proposals he had in mind to support his amendment calling for relevant measures to reduce unemployment.

In anticipation of this coy modesty, I have turned again, for what the Labour Party called 'New Hope', to their election manifesto. There we find two main lines of action against unemployment. The first is the promise of what they call 'a massive programme for expansion', with increased public spending on investment, social services and most other things they can think of. This is the plausible Keynesian panacea, of which we got a whiff from Lord Kaldor. It is the doctrine that I dutifully imbibed with my beer at Cambridge after the war and went on for some years trying very hard to believe.

The alluring theory was that increased monetary demand would draw idle resources into employment. Alas! Repeated experience showed that once the trade union highwaymen got wind of this extra money on the road, they perfected their 'stand and deliver' act, whereby the larger part of the extra money got diverted into higher wages. It is to this spectacular wages snatch over the 1960s and 1970s that I trace our record of accelerating inflation and rising unemployment. Indeed, the Labour Party manifesto actually acknowledged this very danger. It sought to fend off the risk of inflation with all that stuff about 'a national economic assessment' – that is to say, a pow-wow with the highwaymen – which was code language among the faithful for another incomes policy.

Like a fifth or sixth marriage, it represents the triumph of hope over experience. The last time Mr Healey walked up the aisle with the TUC it was in the name of the 'social contract'. The outcome was that, between 1974 and 1979, total national spending increased by 130 per cent over five years. But of that massive spending spree, less than 10 percentage points went to raise output, while 110 percentage points went to boost prices. The modest rise in output was not enough to stop unemployment more than doubling under Labour – from below 600,000 to approaching 1½ million.

If we turn to the Conservative Government, we find that the last Chancellor did not reduce demand but only the rate at which it increased. Thus, from 1979 to 1982, total spending still rose by 45 per cent over the three years. The result was that prices increased by 50 per cent and output fell by around 4 per cent, with unemployment again doubling – from 1½ million to 3 million.

From all this I deduce, by logic which I have not time fully to elaborate, that the Government's target for monetary growth of 7 to 11 per cent this year is perfectly consistent with declining inflation and increased output only so long as the additional spending is not absorbed by higher costs.

Causes of unemployment We are therefore brought back to confront the central importance of labour costs as a cause not only of inflation but also of unemployment. I have some hope for at least silent agreement from the Labour benches because their manifesto promised further measures against unemployment, which rather gave away the whole trade union game. Thus, in addition to expanding demand, Labour promised a second line of action in the form of what it specifically called 'employment subsidies'. These were to be given to firms which avoided redundancies or created new jobs. But why subsidise wages if they are not already too high? Here was a frank admission that labour costs are above the market value of labour's contribution to output and are therefore at least one cause of unemployment.

This truth is illuminated by OECD [Organisation for Economic Co-operation and Development] figures which show that by 1981 labour costs in Britain had grown to absorb over 80 per cent of GNP, compared with around 70 per cent in France, Germany and Japan. Precisely the same trend is revealed by other indications of declining long-run profitability in British industry. Thus, if we exclude North Sea oil, we find that the average real rate of return on capital in Britain fell from above 10 per cent in the 1960s to 5 per cent in 1979 and 2 or 3 per cent more recently. We really cannot escape the conclusion that a major domestic cause of avoidably high unemployment is the rise in labour costs per unit of output and the resulting decline in profitability. Such a shift in rewards must reduce the incentive to employ more people. At the same time, it reduces the funds available for investment which would create jobs directly in new buildings and plant, or indirectly by improving efficiency and sales in competition with foreign suppliers.

We all say, and endlessly repeat, that we deplore the economic and social consequences of unemployment. But suppose we cared above all else for bringing lasting jobs to those who are genuinely seeking work, would we really go into the Lobbies again to preserve the Wages Councils which we know, at the margin, price young people out of the market? Suppose we cared less for maintaining outdated political prejudices, might we not think of new ways to encourage employment, mobility, investment and, if I dare say it, entrepreneurship? What about such measures as repealing stamp duties, reducing the tax on capital transfers and stock options, or encouraging portable pensions? Not least, what about ending the taxation of low incomes, which now reduces take-home pay to little, if anything, above the value of social benefits?

As a gesture, for my part I would overcome my deep doubts and distrust about further government intervention and even agree to some new programme of public spending, if only it could be shown not to make things worse by raising taxes and other costs elsewhere so as to damage existing employment.

My concluding thought is that an agenda for radical reform to reduce unemployment would range far wider than the measures outlined in the Queen's Speech. Certainly, it would include action on nationalised industries, trade unions and local authority spending – for the reasons so splendidly developed by Lord Boyd-Carpenter and Lord Marsh. But it would extend to long-overdue measures to reduce government spending and taxes – especially for misdirected welfare – which was so powerfully exposed by Lord Bauer from the Government benches.

3. When Len Murray was almost right

Debate on a motion by Lord Wilson of Rievaulx (formerly Mr Harold Wilson) calling attention to high unemployment

I listened with close attention to the speech of Lord Wilson of Rievaulx and thought I detected just a note of conflict between the fun he made of the low level of the exchange rate and the approach of his former economic adviser, Lord Kaldor, who made rather heavier work of the earlier rise in the exchange rate. But I do not doubt for a moment that Lord Wilson would be equal to providing a perfectly convincing reconciliation of this apparent disharmony.

I want briefly to join issue from the cross-benches with three claims that are most commonly heard from Labour speakers. The first concerns the magnitude of unemployment; the second is its true nature and cause; and the third, following Lord Thorneycroft is what might be called non-solutions.

First, on magnitude, the challenge that confronts us is stern enough without rejoicing in exaggerated talk about 4 million, $4^{1}/_{2}$ million or 5 million unemployed. Even the official figure, which is stuck around 3 million, conceals to some degree the active nature of the labour market, with a turnover every year of some 7 million changes of jobs. It also magnifies the jobless total, at least to the extent of the black economy, which some estimates have pitched as high as 1.4 million people. We may deplore the extent to which otherwise law-abiding citizens feel themselves driven into the underground economy, but it is instructive to ponder for one moment the reason. There cannot be much doubt that it is because the black economy comes closest to the free market, which was mocked by Lady Seear, where the cost of employing somebody is not inflated by taxes, closed shops, restrictive practices, employment protection, equal opportunities, equal pay and all the rest.

This modest insight emphasises that the demand for labour depends chiefly upon its price. It seems to me not to require a grasp of higher economic theory to know that, other things being equal, the higher the cost of employing someone, the fewer will be the number of people likely to be employed. Otherwise, why has everyone joined in condemning the National Insurance Surcharge as a tax on jobs? Why did Labour's 1983 General Election manifesto call quite explicitly for employment subsidies, unless it was thought that the cost of employing people stood too high for their own good?

I have today a more telling witness to this truth in Mr Len Murray who, at a special conference in February to discuss the reduction of the working week, explicitly warned: 'There is a trade-off here. It is a trade-off between incomes and jobs'.

Even in this burst of candour the General Secretary of the TUC was not exactly accurate. Except in the black economy, the trade-off is not between incomes and jobs but between total labour cost and jobs. That is a very important distinction. The cost of employing a worker in the regular economy is not equal to the worker's take-home pay – as in the black economy – but nearer twice as much. The reason is that the employer faces, on top of wages, an on-cost of 30 or 40 per cent for National Insurance, pensions, employment protection, health and safety, and all the rest. On the other hand, the worker receives his wages only after deductions which can also amount, similarly, to 30 or 40 per cent of the wage paid by his employer. Governments have created a kind of topsy-turvy world which perversely combines high labour costs to employers with take-home pay often not much above social security benefits.

I am therefore led to take issue with those critics who blame unemployment and every other ill to which the economy is heir on the cruel operation of unchecked market forces unleashed by higher capitalism. Our famous mixed economy is well on the way to being a halfway house to full-blown collectivism. Even the present administration is spending more than half the national income and is employing nearly one-third of the entire labour force. In addition, it intervenes extensively throughout the whole economy with a confused mixture of subsidies and taxes – to say nothing of controls over all rents and the pay of more than 10 per cent of the labour force locked into Wages Councils. The resulting mess of political potage is not only an over-governed society but an inflexible, sclerotic economy that is slow to adjust output and jobs to new opportunities.

An end to phoney full employment   I come to my third issue of whether still more government is the cure or the chief cause of our economic malady. If we look back 20 years to the days when Lord Wilson was cheerfully lighting his pipe by the white heat of a technological revolution, we might recall all the well-intentioned but ill-fated policies to protect jobs and pick winners. Out of natural delicacy I will refrain from dwelling on the National Plan, which mocked nature by passing from teething troubles in 1965 to death rattles in 1966 without the customary interval of hopeful life. But what about all the nonsense of regional policy, indiscriminate subsidies, selective employment tax, bale-outs by courtesy of the Industrial Reorganisation Corporation or the National Enterprise Board when the embrace of the state was often the prelude to the kiss of death? Those were the years when foreign observers diagnosed the 'British disease' and when more homespun talk against 'de-industrialisation' did not prevent jobs in manufacturing falling from 8.5 million in 1966 to little more than 7 million in 1979.

Looking forward in this debate, I hope Labour speakers will agree that there is not much scope here for self-righteous indignation over what is in my view the present unnecessarily high level of unemployment inflicted unintentionally by governments. In retrospect we can see that the seeds of our present troubles were sown in the years of phoney full employment without full efficiency. They were the years when trade unions insisted on two men doing the job of one man; when employers acquiesced in over-manning and opted for a quiet life even though their profits were declining; when governments of both Parties accommodated ever-rising costs by inflationary finance. Yet through those years – in the 1960s and 1970s – the trend towards rising unemployment was still visible. Throughout those dream decades of relative economic decline, what was most lacking was any effective penalty for the economic failure of unions and managements to put their ramshackle house in some kind of order.

It seems to me little surprise that the present Government is not basking in universal acclaim. It has been the first government since the war to make a start with restoring discipline, by phasing out the soft – and, I may say, 'wet' – option of cost-plus inflation. We should not wish it to contract out of the continuing struggle for higher employment through increased efficiency by returning to the discredited expedient of still higher government spending suggested by other speakers.

As we see from the National Union of Mineworkers, the National Union of Railwaymen, the National Union of Teachers and others, irresponsible union leaders are still lying in wait – ready to hi-jack any increase in monetary demand for unearned wage increases rather than for increased production or investment. If we wish to make room for more employment, the rough rule of thumb is that wages and salaries should increase by *less* than the rise in prices, except where employers have difficulty recruiting sufficient labour. That is what happens in many of the countries with which our industries and products have to compete. I say again to the Government that wage restraint along these lines would be far easier if they would reapply their minds to ways of reducing government expenditure so as to make possible a continuing prospect of reduced taxes on low incomes.

Postscript by Lord Gowrie, answering for the Government: *I was absolutely fascinated by that part of the debate when Lord Bottomley spoke and then Lord Harris of High Cross. There is simply no meeting of minds whatsoever. If Lord Bottomley reads the speech of Lord Harris, he will learn something – I would say to his advantage. If Lord Harris reads the speech of Lord Bottomley, he will see just how far he has still got to go in this economy in order* *to get people round to slightly nearer his point of view. When I listen to Lord Harris of High Cross, I always feel like a rather over-weight, middle-aged man – which is not, perhaps, too inaccurate a description – in the company of a seasoned jogger. There is something about the* pur sang *of classic liberalism – very unlike the present incumbents – which is not my idea of conservatism but very much classic market liberalism . . . which has been an invaluable injection into the thinking of this Government and our national life. . . .*

4. The British disease

Debate on a motion by Lord Cledwyn of Penrhos calling attention to the need to stimulate industrial growth

I hope it might be of service if I try to fill in something of the missing background of post-war economic difficulties, going back well before 1979, if we are to make any kind of judgement on recent developments. For example, have any of us forgotten all the endless agonising in the 1960s and 1970s over the British disease? Does Lord Cledwyn not recall all the talk of the economic league tables which showed our progressive decline from among the leaders to a straggling laggard in real income per head of developed nations?

I doubt if anyone in the House so easily remembers the post-war Anglo-American Council of Productivity which brought together the TUC and the Federation of British Industries in a rare search for ways of achieving greater efficiency. In 1953 it published a report with the hopeful title, *We Too Can Prosper,* which makes instructive reading some 30 years later. The author, Mr Graham Hutton, is a lifelong friend of mine and I recently read again with special care that he attributed the better performance of United States industry chiefly to their more intensive use of modern machines through the greater flexibility and mobility of labour. In contrast, Mr Hutton referred to the strong Luddite tradition of British trade unions which, allied to weak management, had given rise to what he then explicitly called 'concealed unemployment'. In my view, it has been, above all, the failure of managements to tackle restrictive practices in industry that explains Britain's long relative economic decline.

Of course, politicians have made endless speeches about productivity. The Conservative Party invented the National Economic Development Council, and the Labour Party conjured up national plans without number – and largely without effect. Both parties multiplied subsidies; at one time for capital investment, and then for the employment of labour. But I would argue that no sustained progress was made until after 1979.

If we go back to 1964, an American consultant, William Allen, hit the headlines in *The Sunday Times* with an article asking: 'Is Britain a half-time country, getting half pay for half work under half-hearted management?'. His bleak answer gave countless examples from many differing industries where it took two or three British workers to produce as much as one in other countries, often with similar plant.

Two years after William Allen's article there was a debate in the House of Lords (May 1966) when Lord Byers from the Liberal benches opened a discussion on the need to increase efficiency. In that debate he estimated that between 10 and 20 per cent of the working population was under-employed. In the same debate, Lord Shawcross claimed that there was 'concealed under-employment of at least 2 million men and women', and he went on to argue that they would be available in expansionary times for redeployment in other industries and services.

If all this is even approximately true of that period, we are bound to ask why managements and unions failed to grasp the nettle of slack working habits. It is a non-political revelation that these restrictive practices were deeply embedded in industry and indeed go back more than half a century to the birth of British trade unionism. When we look even in recent years to examples in printing, docks, railways, shipbuilding, most recently in the car industry, we find that where managements do tackle restrictive practices or overmanning they are in for costly battles which, in some cases, can set a term to the existence of their companies.

Soft option of inflation   Against the confrontation that would have been involved to tackle these problems, it was so much easier for the CBI and the TUC to get together at their cosy meetings and to press government to stimulate demand for inefficient labour in the sacred name of Keynesian full employment policies. That is the nub of my criticism of that period. I believe it has been the major cause of Britain's record inflation, and I think it is also the explanation of Britain's poor record of growth and the consequent industrial decline.

The lesson ignored by today's self-styled 'reflationists' is that monetary expansion – though again and again intended as a stimulant to employment and growth – simply acted as a sedative that sapped the will to tackle the root causes of our poor industrial performance. Even worse, these political pep pills became addictive, so that increasing doses yielded a diminishing effect on employment and output, with worsening side-effects on inflation. As Hayek has pointed out, more and more jobs became dependent not only on the continuation of inflation but on its acceleration. That helps to explain why the Labour Government's success after 1974 in getting inflation down pushed unemployment up – under a Labour Government – very close to $1^1/_2$ million.

It is true that the real wages of British workers rose more slowly than elsewhere, but they still rose faster than flagging output. Positive proof, from a great many conflicting statistics, is shown by the decline in the real rate of return on capital from an average of 10 per cent in the 1960s to below 5 per cent in 1979, which was an ill omen of higher unemployment still to come.

The crime with which this Government is charged is simply that it has refused to accommodate the higher inflation that would have been necessary to keep workers in over-priced jobs. The Government is not guilty of reducing or deflating demand, but only of allowing it to grow more slowly to bring inflation down from above 20 per cent to below 5 per cent. In the process, the concealed unemployment of the 1950s and 1960s has come out into the open and onto the register. I agree that it is nothing less than tragedy that this long overdue corrective for the enfeebling British disease coincided with a record world recession on top of a structural shift of industry into new products and new sources of supply for older products.

I conclude with the thought that there is a silver lining to the heavy clouds of unemployment. It is that in many sectors of industry there has been a dramatic rise in productivity since management and trade unions found they could not take the soft option of inflating their costs and prices. As I have said before, Mrs Thatcher is like the wife who has hidden the gin – and that is not popular, especially among old soaks who are by no means confined to the Labour benches. I believe it gives us the best chance since the war to expand our production and employment as the world recovers from a recession, which has been little more than a return to earth after the prolonged illusory joy-ride of international monetary inflation.

PART II   Cases for Repeal

5.   Towards limited government

Debate on a motion by Lord Renton calling attention to the volume of legislation and the desirability of repealing outdated or unnecessary statutes

Perhaps I should start, almost as a maiden speaker, by asking for the indulgence of other speakers who bring such legal distinction to our discussion of the quantity and quality of legislation. As a mere economist, my approach will be somewhat more down-to-earth – although others may wish to describe it rather differently. As Lord Elwyn-Jones partly implied, much of the indiscriminate multiplication of statutes has aimed to improve our economic and social welfare, yet it has conspicuously failed to usher in the promised millennium.

In economics we have a serviceable law of diminishing marginal utility. It is the neglected foundation of much economic analysis and tells us that increasing supplies tends to decrease the additional value or satisfaction we derive from any line of consumption. So it has proved with legislation; the growing volume has led to diminishing utility. There is no dispute among us about the long-run tendency for the quantity of legislation to increase. With 3,100 general public Acts in force, plus 13,000 general statutory instruments, it is surely not inappropriate to talk of an over-governed nation sinking in a morass of regulation and control – much of it wholly incomprehensible to the layman and apparently even to Lord Denning.[2]

I am not a wild anarchist. I regard law as the indispensable buttress of all our prized freedoms, but we can have too much even of so good a thing. We have carried the necessary ordinances to the point of inordinacy. It is an example of the same undisciplined tendency to excess which Sir William Rees-Mogg has blamed for monetary inflation. For me the lesson is that we urgently need to restore limits to both the activity and ambitions of modern government.

I believe the best guide for the reforming efforts of lawyers, economists and others may be found in the seminal trilogy by Professor Hayek entitled *Law, Legislation and Liberty.* Even if time allowed, I am not qualified to do justice to Professor Hayek's grand thesis. But I found helpful his distinction between law, as the evolution of general rules of just conduct, and legislation, as the often arbitrary commands of governments vested with temporary authority to impose their will or even their whims. Thus legislation is often linked only rhetorically with any universal, permanent principles of justice, of equity, or indeed of law itself in its original meaning.

Special-interest groups Hayek is not the only economic philosopher to diagnose legislative incontinence as the occupational hazard of politicians in a democracy. The economic analysis of politics starts from the commonplace observation that politicians are not wholly disinterested in gaining votes. Of course they have long-term ideals, and I understand that some even have principles. But such intellectual baggage tends to get mislaid or left behind in their natural haste to win a majority. The simplest way to amass votes at one time was for politicians to buy them. But since open corruption was made illegal – and was anyway expensive – the next best thing was to buy votes with promissory notes, politely referred to as election pledges.

Instead of bidding for individual votes, parties have come to seek wholesale support from large or powerful groups such as trade unionists, farmers, old-age pensioners, tenants, owner–occupiers, and other significant minorities. The method is to pass laws conferring privileges or immunities on sufficient special-interest groups to build up a winning coalition of votes.

One reason why politicians are vulnerable to pressure from lobbies of sectional interests is that democratic governments are thought to be omnipo-

tent. They have unlimited powers to pass laws to remedy every passing griev-
ance, real or imagined. As we now see, when the ruling party withholds its
favours, an irresponsible Opposition stands ready to promise to oblige after the
next election. Thus, unlimited government has unchained insupportable
demands from the populace and has brought nominally all-powerful government to the brink of impotence.

By a different route from that taken by Lord Hailsham in his remarkable
Dimbleby Lecture, I have come to follow Professor Hayek in favouring a written constitution. Its aim would be to entrench limited government – perhaps
even by specifying limits on the discretion of politicians to spend, to tax, to
expropriate, and maybe even to discriminate in favour of sectional interests.

All that is for discussion and for the future. Meanwhile, I should like from
the cross-benches to commend the efforts of the non-party Repeal Group,
which encouraged Lord Renton to bring this debate before us. The Repeal
Group offers a modest prospect of relief from excessive legislation by seeking
the outright repeal of unnecessary or restrictive statutes. As Lord Renton has
said, we have made a start with Lady Trumpington's Bill to end the Shops
Acts. After the Recess, there will be a chance to debate the Second Readings
of the Rent (Abolition of Control) Bill introduced by Lord Vaizey, and the
Truck Acts (Repeal) Bill, which I introduced recently. Like Ko-Ko in *The
Mikado,* we 'have a list of society offenders that never would be missed', and
we would welcome suggestions for statutes to be added to our worthy candidates for repeal.

6. Statutory minimum wages

*Debate on the Second Reading of the Wages Councils (Abolition) Bill
moved by the late Lord Spens*

I congratulate Lord Spens for his perseverance in moving from asking polite
questions about Wages Councils to proposing their outright abolition. In this
he has the support of the informal group known as the Repeal Group, whose
efforts I referred to when Lady Trumpington moved her Bill to repeal the
Shops Acts in February. I am delighted to follow Lord Roberthall and hope to
demonstrate that economists are not obliged to disagree. I urge him to keep on
raising his voice in the Alliance, because he may help to lead the Lady Seear
back into the paths of true liberalism.

The case for this Bill is a good deal stronger than that for the Shops Bill, to
which we recently gave an unopposed Second Reading. Wages Councils had
their origins in 1909, when four Trade Boards were set up to fix minimum
wages in the sweated trades of tailoring, lace-, box- and chain-making. The
Act was extended in 1918, and the Boards were renamed Wages Councils in

1945. Since 1938 the tally of workers covered has increased from $1\frac{1}{2}$ million to $2\frac{3}{4}$ million.

A number of speakers have raised the question that what was fitting in 1909 – when workers lacked the bargaining power that comes from education, from knowledge, from employment exchanges, from easier mobility and from generous social benefits – bears no relation whatsoever to the conditions of the 1980s. Lady Seear might ponder the transformation in conditions of domestic servants before telling us these stories about the likelihood of workers being greatly exploited in the absence of minimum wages.

It seems to me that what started as benevolent welfare policy has come to exert a malevolent economic effect. It has done so at a time when low pay has much less to do with poverty because the low-paid are preponderantly young people or women who live in households with two or more earners. What is worse, from prescribing bare minimum wages which the least efficient employer was compelled to pay, Wages Councils have come to set what they regard as 'reasonable' wages, especially for young people, at levels that even the most profitable firms find it difficult to improve upon.

The report *Priced Out* by the National Federation of Self-Employed and Small Businesses shows that during the 1970s the dubious 'independents' and employers' representatives on these Councils did not prevent the more single-minded trade union representatives from pushing up wages much faster than inflation. The figures show that over this decade the six largest Councils increased adult wages 4-fold and juvenile wages $4\frac{1}{2}$ fold, compared with a 3-fold rise in prices. At the same time, in retailing the age at which the adult wage was paid has been lowered from 21 to 19. So that whereas, 10 years ago, a school-leaver would start at a little over half the adult wage, he must now be paid 60 per cent, and by the age of 18 he must be paid 85 per cent of the wage of an adult with perhaps a lifetime of working experience.

The Wages Orders issued by the Councils are often of the most baffling complexity. They deal with holidays, hours, regions, meal and rest breaks and unsocial hours, and they prescribe different rates of pay at varying times. An LSE study in 1980 identified in one Wages Council that 166 minimum rates were prescribed. The personnel director of a leading retail chain has told me that he could not be sure of understanding the annual changes even when he had expert legal advice at his elbow. Nor are wage costs the end of the matter. At least 30 per cent must be added for national insurance and other employment expenses, without allowing for what are called compliance costs and for such benefits in kind as staff buying discounts and meals, which are totally ignored by the jolly quango men on these Wages Councils.

Effect on employment   There can be no doubt that the escalation of total wage costs has reduced employment opportunities. The foundation of all economic analysis is nothing more arcane than that prices affect quantities. If wages are increased, other things being equal, the demand for workers will be reduced at the margin. All the empirical evidence on the operation of minimum wages, particularly in the United States over a very long period, shows that they cause unemployment especially among the most vulnerable. Two leading black American economists, Professors Thomas Sowell and Walter Williams, have recently shown that when the cost of employing people is artificially raised under the Federal minimum wage law, the resulting unemployment is concentrated on the young, unskilled, inexperienced, female and, even more severely, on the ethnic minorities.

Nowhere – except perhaps in rent control – has well-intentioned policy produced more perversely damaging results than in raising wages without regard for market realities. Thus in Britain the pace has been set by the Low Pay Unit, which would today be more accurately branded the 'No Pay Unit'. Why could they not learn from the evil experience of South Africa, where minimum wages were deliberately supported by white trade unionists to reduce the job opportunities of unskilled black workers by pricing them out of the labour market?

It is no use opponents of this Bill taking refuge behind their undoubted good intentions. In economics – as in much well-meant private conduct – good intentions are no guarantee of good results. In Britain the bleak road to high unemployment has been paved with good intentions. Indeed, all our most grievous economic and social disorders have been caused not by malevolent design but by the amiable confusions of mis-named 'do-gooders', who undoubtedly meant well but who have inadvertently caused much of the havoc that we see around us.

I hope we shall avoid verbal competition in compassion. There is no important difference between us in all parts of the House on the principle of a minimum income. But whether that is provided through supplementary benefits or, as I would prefer, through a reverse income tax, it is the province of social policy and should not be attempted by manipulating prices, such as wages, rents or interest rates, which must lead to costly distortions throughout the economy. Whatever the sceptics may say, we know that wages can be too high for the good of employment. That is why Labour and Conservative governments have been driven to multiply job subsidies – especially for the young – simply to undo the damage of trade union wage-push. It is also why some workers have voluntarily settled for wage standstills or even for wage reductions to save jobs – an option that is rendered illegal by the Government's stubborn enforcement of the Act which we are now seeking to repeal.

I urge all who care more for reducing unemployment than for preserving their emotional purity to join in supporting this Bill, if necessary through the Lobby.[3]

7. The opticians' monopoly

Debate on the Second Reading of the Opticians Act 1958
(Amendment) Bill moved by Lord Rugby

I congratulate Lord Rugby on his persistence and perseverance over a number of years in opposing the opticians' monopoly in selling reading glasses. The Repeal Group has encouraged him to bring this Bill forward and I personally hope that he is ready to carry the issue to a Division if that looks like being necessary to jolt the Government into taking some action in place of their repeated words of concern.

Others have exposed the questionable, if not false, medical arguments that buttress the present scheme which requires 7 million people buying glasses each year to shop at a registered optician for what are grandly called their 'optical appliances'. I want to develop a more general argument. The essence of my complaint against Section 21 of the 1958 Opticians Act is that it confuses the roles of the professional and the tradesman in a single person and gives that person power to raise his income by keeping up the price of what he sells.

The consequent abuse of collusion among opticians was predicted over 200 years ago by Adam Smith in *The Wealth of Nations* from which I will offer one of my favourite quotations: 'People of the same trade seldom meet together even for merriment and diversion, but the conversation ends in a conspiracy against the public, or in some contrivance to raise prices'. In this, a profession is not wholly different from a trade union which naturally endeavours to raise the income of its members by restricting competition from alternative suppliers who could do the job equally well. Lord Richardson[4] took the view that anyone concerned with the profession of medicine or its ancillary activities is somehow above concern for his income. I beg leave to doubt that – and I could bring many friends from the medical profession, at any rate in private, to my side against him.

No-one denies that opticians perform valuable services and that may include diagnosing eye diseases which call for treatment. For this purpose opticians receive due training, as do electricians. But we are not required to hire an electrician when we want to change a light bulb or to mend a fuse. Yet most people who, as Lord Rugby said, wear glasses for simple magnification are now legally compelled to go through a full medical examination each time they want stronger spectacles and are then compelled to buy those spectacles from a registered optician. It was likened by Lord Winstanley,[5] in an earlier contribution, to requiring a medical examination before allowing anyone to buy a walking stick. He did not add that it would also be like giving doctors a monopoly of selling walking sticks, which we may be sure would then come in more ornate varieties at suitably fancy prices.

If we turn to another useful profession, it is true that regular dental examination can spot tooth decay. But we would not think of making everyone buying a toothbrush go to the dentist and buy their toothbrush only after submitting to a full inspection of teeth. Periodic check-ups with dentists or with opticians are a matter of prudence. May I suggest to Lord Hunter[6] that the proper role of compulsion in optics is in school examination of eyes, especially for squints which I gather are best corrected at an early age.

Special pleading   Despite what we have heard, it remains true that among the fears that are played upon by the apologists for the opticians' cartel is the old wives' tale that wearing the wrong glasses can damage your eyes. We are now told that it can no more damage your eyes than listening to pop music might damage your ears. I think the House ought to recognise that the opticians' union is running one of the most blatant, government-protected closed shops. Of course, it dresses up its special pleading in a professional white coat. The game was rather given away in an earlier code of practice by the now-defunct British Optical Association, which regretted that for over 300 years opticians had practised in shop premises and went on to urge them to get away from the shop atmosphere and above all advised: 'No prices should be exhibited, otherwise the optician can hardly escape from the accusation that he is a salesman rather than a professional man'.

Difficult though it may be for some of the earlier speakers to accept, I believe that there is no hard and fast dividing line between a profession and skilled trade – except perhaps the accent of the practitioners. There is certainly no justification for questioning the restrictive practices of ASLEF and SOGAT [Society of Graphical and Allied Trades] whilst viewing the professional restrictive practices that we are here concerned with through the rose-tinted spectacles conveniently provided free by the Association of Optical Practitioners. I would venture to say that anyone who cannot see through this optical illusion needs more than his eyes examined. Accordingly, I commend this Bill[7] and would leave with you the magisterial words of a leading article in *The British Medical Journal* of 13 December 1980:

> Deletion of the monopoly clause from the Act . . . will be hotly contested by opticians. Yet what harm would result? As in other countries where there are no statutory restrictions, the mass of the public would continue to have their eyes tested by opticians or eye doctors, and the simple purchase of glasses over the counter would be confined to the normal-sighted over-50s who simply need reading help.

8. No truck with cash

Debate on the Second Reading of the Truck Acts (Repeal) Bill moved by
Lord Harris of High Cross

In bringing this Bill before you from the cross-benches, I have been encouraged by the non-party Repeal Group. It has three purposes: first, by the simple device of repeal to slim the statute book which has become grossly inflated until, like a fat man, we can no longer see where we are putting our feet. Secondly, we wish to reinforce Her Majesty's Government on the urgent need to set limits to endless talk and to speed action. Our third substantive aim is to remove an obsolete barrier to spreading payment of wages by a variety of more modern, economic and safe methods than carting £1,000 million of notes and coin around the country every pay-day.

The origins of the Truck Acts take us back to a vanished world peopled by such ghosts as the 'bagmen', 'petty foggers', 'butties' and other middlemen who paid workers in goods or in 'tommy tickets' that could be exchanged only at the company store or 'truck shop' which belonged to their employer. 'Truck' apparently comes from the French word, '*troc*', meaning barter, and it sometimes served a useful purpose in earlier centuries when people lived and worked in remote districts away from towns or markets. But it was open to the obvious abuse of any monopoly and became the target of public policy as early as 1411 when a local ordinance required Colchester weavers to be paid in gold and silver rather than in merchandise or victuals.

The Truck Acts (Repeal) Bill would decently bury the carcases of five outdated laws. The 1831 Act in its time replaced no fewer than 19 statutes by a wide prohibition against contracts for artificers' wages being specified in other than 'current coin of the realm'. Its 27 clauses applied to a dozen specified trades and excluded agriculture and domestic service. The 1887 Truck Amendment Act extended protection to all manual workers covered by the Employer and Workmen Act of 1875. The 1896 Act strengthened protection against deductions from wages. In 1940 a further Act was necessary to protect employers against some of the resulting anomalies – for example, where meals were served at work. Finally, the 1960 Payment of Wages Act permitted payment in postal orders, money orders, cheques or direct bank credit in place of cash. But it allowed these alternatives to cash subject to three conditions: first, that the employee agrees in writing to forgo cash; secondly, that he can withdraw that agreement at four weeks' notice; and thirdly, that the employer provides a full statement of gross wages and deductions.

Reflecting on the amendment in the name of Lord Rochester, I imagine that at some Liberal seminar on the theme of 'Forward from 1831' my legal outline might be puffed up to sound a progressive and satisfying development. The reality is less flattering to our Parliamentary forbears. As was made clear by the American scholar Professor George W. Hilton in his standard work entitled *The Truck System*,[8] most of these laws were out of date before they were enacted. Thus the practice of truck has been extinct for more than a century and the only patchy remnants of any value in this legal rag-bag relate to deductions from wages.

It is central to my case that deductions from wages could be far better dealt with under the quite separate Contract of Employment Act of 1963 and the Employment Protection (Consolidation) Act of 1978. In the contemporary world of written contracts of employment, it should be straightforward to protect everyone, not only manual workers, against unauthorised deductions by extending the right of appeal to industrial tribunals. In this way we can satisfy what matters in our obligations under the International Labour Organisation and the European Social Charter.

Central fallacy The Truck Acts are not merely an historical curiosity and therefore apparently beloved by the Liberal Party as the museum for lost causes. The law as it now stands has become a positive nuisance. It is like the decayed remnants of some long-dead corpse that has been resurrected to serve a purpose wholly different from its original intention. As a non-lawyer, I hope to make clear what is the central fallacy in the modern interpretation of the Truck Acts and the resulting error, as I see it, that was embodied in the Payment of Wages Act 1960.

The plain purpose of the historical campaign against truck was to ensure that workers were not paid in goods. The aim was never to guarantee that they were paid in some specified form of money. Indeed, the 1831 Act said that the contract was to be made in cash. Of course, in the 19th century coins were the standard medium of exchange, just as today cheques, bank cards, Giro, and direct debit are the predominant means of payment. Even so, Section 8 of the 1831 Act provided that workers *could* be paid by a cheque drawn on the Bank of England or on any other note-issuing bank within 15 miles of their place of work.

This neglected provision completely explodes the case of those TUC Luddites who now want to go on discussing and negotiating for ever to delay action on the switch from cash to credit transfer. The key safeguard of the 1831 Act and subsequent Acts was not cash in the form of coins, but generalised purchasing power in place of payment in unwanted goods. It was only the accident of the 1844 monopoly of the Bank of England over the issuing of notes that invalidated Section 8 and made the Payment of Wages Act 1960 necessary. Yet this latest Act now works to slow down the development of those very modern means of payment through the banks that were its original justification.

The chief obstacle to progress in various forms of credit transfer is the unjustified requirement that, not only must every worker give written permission to be paid by cheque, but that he can at any time change his mind and at four weeks' notice insist on cash. Thus, we find that a complex system of law evolved over 400 years to prevent a forgotten abuse can, 150 years later, be brandished to obstruct developments beneficial to workers no less than to the economy and to society.

Is it any wonder that we lag so far behind America and Europe, with 13 million British earners still paid by the week and over 10 million paid in dangerous, clumsy and inefficient cash? The Central Policy Review Staff in 1981 doubted whether the Truck Acts were high on the list of obstacles to further progress. With rather more direct knowledge, employers have called for repeal of the Truck Acts as a barrier to modern methods of payment. Among the leading supporters of this Bill I am pleased to cite the Confederation of British Industry, the National Federation of Building Trades Employers, the Engineering Employers Federation, and the Federation of Civil Engineering Contractors. No less impressive, the Institute of Personnel Management has supported repeal of the Truck Acts as an overdue step towards obliterating the increasingly meaningless distinction between wages and salaries, as between workers and staff.

More than 20 years ago the Karmel Committee[9] urged repeal. Since then the banks have improved their services, including more flexible opening hours and wider access to cash dispensers. Further developments are already on the way. I believe that few initiatives would give stronger encouragement to the rapid extension of an efficient, modern banking network serving the entire population than the repeal of these backward-looking statutes. I beg to move that the Bill be now read a second time.

Postscript: Reply to the Debate: I should like to thank all the speakers who have taken part in this admirable, brief debate. I do not think a good case has been made out for the amendment,[10] and I do not think the Lord Rochester gave any reference to the merits of the present truck legislation. Nothing I have heard suggests the least difficulty about giving the Bill a Second Reading and continuing at Committee stage the discussions about the single issue of deductions. In view of the Minister's most amiable advice on these matters, and also in view of his splendid attack on the pretext of the Liberal amendment, I want to offer him a warning, if it is not impertinent. My warning is that he may find his advisers are making rather heavy weather of the international conventions and charters. Having poured over these stupefyingly mundane documents in recent weeks, I find them to be mountains of bureaucratic pomposity, signifying very little indeed.

For example, let us come to the ILO [International Labour Organisation] Convention No. 95, the date of which is 1949. We discover that its key article (Article 8) is partly reproduced as Article 4, Section 5, of the European Social Charter, about which we heard a good deal from the Minister. Both these remarkable documents that we are in danger of violating say nothing more than that deductions from wages shall be permitted only to the extent allowed by national laws, regulations, collective agreements or arbitration awards. If I may say so, it is difficult to see how such solemn trivia could be taken seriously by anyone who is not paid a fat fee to keep a straight face when they read it. In Britain, we already have written agreements of terms of employment, and we have put on employers the duty to itemise deductions from wages. We have appeals to industrial tribunals for unnotified deductions, and we have civil remedies before the county court. If more is necessary, it should not be difficult to graft it on to the Employment Protection (Consolidation) Act, so long as that inflated statute survives.

Bureaucratic bluff   Certainly a coherent solution to these problems cannot be cobbled together from the scraps of Truck Acts concerned with quite different, and now wholly extinct, practices. These Acts will have to be abolished – there is no question of that. They will have to be repealed and obliterated before there can be new reconstruction. So why not call the bureaucratic bluff and repeal these old Acts? In the alarming jargon of international bureaucracy, I would urge the Government to 'denounce' the ILO Convention No. 95 and, for all I know, Conventions 1 to 94 at the same time in order to save postage. If we do inadvertently put the Government off-side in terms of international obligations, we should simply be generating more pressure to get on-side again, with up-to-date and relevant legislation.

Of course the Minister's advisers and the international bureaucrats have a great interest in mystifying us all and alarming us if we appear to be wanting to take what seem to be quite sensible steps. As Lord Orr-Ewing and Lord Selkirk said so forcefully, 20 years after the Karmel Committee urged repeal, the Liberal amendment seeks further to prolong delays. I have noticed before this tendency on the Liberal benches to shield behind caution and compromise as a pretext for indecision and inactivity. If we are serious in wanting progress, there are few better ways of encouraging the Government than by resisting this amendment and giving the Bill a Second Reading.

It is to the credit of a Conservative Government that on truck, as on other issues, it shows signs of awakening to the advantages of radical change. It is notable from the speeches we have had that the case for radical action came from the Conservative benches and the case for dragging our feet from Liberal and Labour speakers.

We are still paying a high price for our tardiness in adapting to new needs and new opportunities. I suggest that our attitude to this Bill and to this amendment should be taken as a measure of our readiness to turn our backs on nostalgia for the past and to rise to the challenge of still glittering prospects for economic and social progress. Unless Lord Rochester is so gracious and well-advised as to withdraw, I urge all those who do not owe him some loyalty to vote[11] against his equivocating amendment.

9. Closing time

Debate on a Question by the late Lord Spens asking whether
the Government will introduce flexible opening hours for
public houses in England and Wales on the Scottish model

I congratulate Lord Spens in promoting a sober and interesting debate on the merits of more flexible opening hours. He has received support from the informal Repeal Group, which seeks to challenge outdated laws that restrict the freedom of adult citizens to live their own lives without hurting the like freedom of their neighbours. One test of whether legislation is outdated is to ask: If this law did not exist, would it be necessary to invent it? I believe the present licensing laws impose objectionable fetters on millions of people that are not justified by any overriding imperatives of public policy.

Since some time ago the Tory Party appeared to cause confusion in the public mind between the peerage and what became known as the 'beerage', I think we should all declare an interest, or lack of interest, in this particular form of consumption. From the published figures I find I am well below the average annual consumption of 200 pints of beer per head of the population, although in wine I am safely between the annual average of 170 pints in France, and the 14 pints in the United Kingdom. Although I have never regularly taken advantage of the varied facilities of the 76,000 public houses and licensed hotels in the United Kingdom, I have to admit that on rare occasions I have been known to curse mildly because I could not find a single pub open at a time when it would have been convenient on a journey, on holiday or to celebrate a family or friendly reunion. I commend to your Lordships the thought of how much worse it must be for the millions of our fellow men who through work, or from choice, do not live their waking lives from approximately dawn until after dusk.

We have heard that the present licensing laws were introduced under emergency powers in the First World War, just as Tudor monarchs once clamped down on ale houses to encourage archery. I have no doubt that the stipulated 9 or $9^1/_2$ hours of opening time between 11 a.m. and 10.30 p.m. or 11 p.m. generally suit the average convenience of the population. But the question I want to ask is why averages come into it? The average man does not play golf or visit Covent Garden or even indulge in hunting, shooting and fishing. It does not follow that strictly minority activities should be regulated by reference to average tastes or majority prejudices.

In one of the appendices to the excellent Erroll Report[12] there is a summary of an official survey into public attitudes towards licensing laws. It shows that about half of the random sample in 1970 favoured keeping opening hours as they were, and as they still are. But the other half was divided between a larger

fraction favouring later closing and a smaller fraction preferring earlier closing. For a liberal democrat the only logical deduction from such a conflict of
views is that the more flexible the hours of opening the larger the number of
people who would get what they want.

Choice and variety for minorities   It is only in politics that we think it right
for majorities constantly to impose their will on minorities. In the
market-place, of which I am known to be an admirer, it is minorities that rule
the roost all the time. Except for monopoly services such as the letter post,
telephones, gas or electricity, almost everything we buy and where we choose
to buy it reflects our individual preferences. In the cars we drive, in the clothes
we wear, in the food we eat, we are all minorities. We would be voted down if
we had to carry a democratic majority with us on every line of consumption.

I do not deny that all freedom is capable of abuse. We should, every one of
us, be concerned that there are approaching 50,000 cases of drunken driving,
but that remains a minute fraction of the $2^{1}/_{2}$ million serious offences recorded
by the police in a recent year. Although no more than 0.004 per cent of men
are treated for alcoholism, we all know of others who are at risk. But the Erroll
Report confirms our everyday observation that there is no simple correlation
between excessive consumption and the number of hours that pubs are open,
especially when drink can be so easily obtained for consumption at home. This
lesson has not been disproved by experience in Scotland since the law was
liberalised in 1976 and is upheld by evidence from places as far apart as
Sweden and Australia, where severe restrictions on hours have not checked
abuse. Nothing in the interesting sociological speculations of Lord Minto
linked more flexible hours with proven excess. In the end he seemed to me to
fall back into agnosticism.

I believe that we cannot make people better by legislation. That is the task
for teaching, preaching, personal example and, in the last resort, enforceable
laws against anti-social behaviour. It is clearly not a sin to drop in at the local.
Indeed, no less an authority than the Director of the Christian Economic and
Social Foundation, the Reverend George Brake, recently urged the need to
preserve the place of the pub, which he thought 'the most favourable
controlled environment for the consumption of alcohol'. He added: 'the
well-managed public house provides a convenient controlled environment for
drinking and is to be preferred to the uncontrolled situations in which drinking takes place at the present time'.

If the licensing laws were abolished, as I would wish, no pub would be
required to open for more hours. Some pubs in some areas would no doubt
preserve the present arrangements, while others elsewhere on some days or at
some times of the year would open longer and later. The Erroll Report quotes
the licensing authorities in London as granting 64,000 extensions in 1970,

while a sample of 29 petty sessional divisions gave 28,000 exemption orders for an average of between an hour and an hour and a half of extra opening. No wonder the witnesses petitioning the Erroll Committee in favour of almost completely relaxing the law included the Metropolitan Commissioner of Police, as well as tourist boards and various catering and hotel organisations. There were of course then, as there will be again, familiar lobbies in favour of tighter controls. The question is: Who will speak for the millions of unorganised consumers?

I would argue that, whether any one of us would personally wish to take advantage of more flexible hours, we should not stand in the way of removing restrictions upon others with different preferences. Opening hours are no more a matter for majorities to override minorities than the times at which cinemas, restaurants or shops ply their trade between willing buyers and willing sellers. The contract that is implicit in a free society is that, even where our emotions are involved, we respect the choices, even the whims, of our fellow men as a condition for having our own differing tastes and values tolerated by others. If we admit that all freedoms are subject to abuse, we must acknowledge the need for penalties where excess may harm others. But such possibilities do not in my view justify the condescending paternalism, however well-intentioned, that tries to impose a selective morality by the crude, insensitive steamroller of statutory prohibition.

10. Rent control

Debates on two motions by the late Lord Vaizey calling attention to the problems of housing, and moving the Second Reading of his Rent (Abolition of Control) Bill

I would add my voice to that of Lord Robbins[13] and say I can think of no issue in political economy on which professional economists of widely differing tendencies are in more substantial agreement than on the unholy mess successive governments have made of the housing market. It is surely worth pondering that, despite the spending of mounting billions of pounds over half a century by governments of both Parties, housing has become a growing cause of human misery. I would go so far from the cross-benches as to argue that the so-called 'housing shortage' is largely the creation of politicians by their destruction and demolition of the market for rented accommodation.

It becomes a little easier almost week by week to assert the economist's basic proposition that prices do affect supply and demand. As we see with the EEC's Common Agricultural Policy, an artificially high price will increase supply and reduce demand, thereby creating an embarrassing surplus of farm products. In precisely the same way, rent control, by holding the price below the market level, will increase demand for accommodation, reduce the supply, and create the infamous housing shortage. I am afraid the real handicap from which the occupants of the Labour benches suffer is that this kind of logic is simultaneously irresistible and unacceptable.

As others have said, rent control was introduced in 1915 as an emergency wartime measure. As a self-confessed market economist I have no difficulty in defending that kind of intervention. Indeed, as Lord Robbins has taught in his writings over many years, price control – and even rationing – are appropriate to a condition of siege, for one simple reason. Whereas a rise in price can generally be relied upon in an open market to call forth an increased supply that helps to redress the shortage, no such corrective is possible in the abnormal circumstances of war.

The trouble is that, instead of ending rent control with the end of the emergency that was its justification, successive governments have found it electorally profitable in the short run – which is the only run they know – to extend control and even to grant life tenancy into the second generation. As Lord Robbins has said, the ill-effects of drying up the supply were not immediately visible, simply because houses last a long time before they need replacing. But under rent control they just do not get replaced.

It is no wonder that politicians really thought that at last they had stumbled on a free lunch. They could indulge their favourite passion for doing good, or at least for feeling good, and at the same time serve their own electoral interest by collecting millions of grateful votes for keeping rents down. The cost was obligingly paid for by the landlords, who had conveniently little political weight.

We have heard about the injustices between prosperous tenants and often poorer landlords, and also between favoured tenants in controlled property and their unlucky neighbours forced into lengthening queues for council houses or into uncontrolled houses at inflated rents. The lesson of every country that has resorted to rent control has been that market forces are not so easily cheated. As the Francis Report[14] conceded back in 1971, the combination of low rents and security of tenure ensured that no new family houses were built for letting. Even worse, by holding rents below the rising cost of maintenance and repair, especially in an age of inflation, political expediency has caused the decay and rapid decline in the number of houses under control. The statistics are remarkable. From a peak of $8\frac{1}{2}$ million after the Second World War, the number of private tenancies fell to $4\frac{1}{2}$ million in 1960 and to $2\frac{3}{4}$ million today.

The Bishop of Southwark spoke about the sorry sight of decay in New York. But New York is a classic case of the devastation created by rent control. It was indeed the universal phenomenon of devastation by rent control that produced a verdict from a Swedish professor, Assar Lindbeck of sufficiently good Social Democratic credentials to appeal to Lord Roberthall. In his book

The Political Economy of the New Left he wrote as follows: 'In many cases rent control appears to be the most efficient technique presently known to destroy a city – except for bombing'.

It is a by-product of this destructive policy that has caused governments to mount the treadmill of building houses to let at subsidised rents, in a vain effort to make good the shortage contrived by their own past follies. Others have spoken of the ill-effects on the mobility of labour, and I would underline an observation by Lord Vaizey[15] that rent control has forced many people into the market for buying a home when they would much prefer the convenience and flexibility of renting in a free market.

Direct help for the poor The pretext for all of this costly and damaging policy has always been that poor families cannot afford market rents. But this is no new discovery. Poor families cannot afford sufficient food or sufficient clothing. It has been increasingly accepted, over a very long period, that the appropriate solution to this social problem of poverty is to top up their incomes in some way, not to fake the price system with all the consequent distortions of supply, demand, and consumer choice.

There is not time to go into alternative policies. My preference would be that of Lord Vaizey along the lines of straightforward repeal. We should sweep away the damaging rent controls as well as the wasteful, indiscriminate subsidies. We should address ourselves to people in need by introducing some coherent system of personal and portable housing allowances that would not be tied to staying-put in the same home. In my view, we should also phase out mortgage tax relief in return for progressive cuts in the rates of income tax.

In the past the partial and piecemeal efforts of Conservative governments to tackle these problems have been frustrated by what Lady Birk acknowledged was the 'threat' that the next Labour government would repeal any sensible measure in this field. I hope the remaining occupants on the dwindling Labour benches will forgive me for speaking frankly, but the emotional muddle of the last Labour Cabinet was revealed by a chastened Joel Barnett[16] in his remarkable recent memoir, *Inside the Treasury*,[17] which I commend to them. He wrote as follows: 'Talk of increasing council house rents and it was as if you were planning to snatch children from their mothers or put them to work down a mine'.

I sympathise with Mr Barnett because I know what it is like to be made to feel that kind of guilt. But to conclude on a more positive note, we should not allow that kind of mentality to obscure the merits of radical reform to remedy a housing problem that has been caused by an unholy mixture of misplaced benevolence, intellectual confusion and electoral opportunism.

10A. Rent control, again

I congratulate Lord Vaizey on bringing forward this Private Member's Bill to repeal the Rent Acts. His initiative has been encouraged by the non-party Repeal Group, following the debate which he opened in June last year. In that debate, all 11 speakers were in perfect agreement about the widespread human misery inflicted, especially on young people, by the difficulty or impossibility of finding a place to rent. Even more remarkable, four of the half-dozen professional economists in this House, speaking variously from the Conservative, Social Democrat and cross-benches, were found in rare unison emphasising that the major cause of the housing tragedy was rent control.

In the earlier debate, a notable contribution was made by my friend Lord Robbins from these cross-benches. Since he is tragically laid low by a most grievous stroke, I should like to quote three sentences from his speech.

> Rent control is essentially the fixing of maximum rents below the level which would prevail in a free market. Thus it affords an incentive to an excess of demand and a disincentive to spontaneous response of supply. This has occurred whenever and wherever it has been introduced.

In a single sentence, it is a self-evident truism from elementary economic analysis that, in peace or war, in North or South, in houses or in ham sandwiches, if the price is held below the market-clearing level, the resulting excess of demand over supply will create a shortage. This prediction from basic theory is amply borne out by all the evidence.

More than 10 years ago the Institute of Economic Affairs, with which I must declare some connection, published a study entitled *Verdict on Rent Control*.[18] It assembled researches by leading international economists, including three Nobel Laureates, on countries as varied as Austria, France, Sweden, the United States and Britain. The introduction was written by a foremost British authority, the late Professor Fred Pennance, who entitled his essay 'Fifty Years, Five Countries. One Lesson'. The lesson was that rent control had done more harm than good by

> perpetuating shortages, encouraging immobility, swamping consumer preferences, fostering dilapidation of the housing stocks and eroding production incentives, distorting land-use patterns and the allocation of scarce resources.

In every case studied, rent control was introduced as an emergency response to the disruption caused by war – after 1914 in Britain, Austria and France, and after 1940 in Sweden and the United States. Where control had been abolished, as in Sweden and most of the United States outside New York, the housing shortage had miraculously vanished. But wherever control has been perpetuated it has intensified the plight of people seeking even a temporary roof over their heads. For example, writing of rent control in Paris after 1945, the formidable, internationally famous philosopher Bertrand de Jouvenel concluded: 'It is self-perpetuating and culminates in both the physical ruin of housing and the legal dispossession of the owners. The havoc wrought here is not the work of the enemy but of our own measures'.

Evidence of dilapidation   In the debate last year, the Bishop of Southwark gave a rather depressing glimpse of what might politely be called the ineffable innocence of Church thinking on these worldy matters. He reported his shock at seeing the urban devastation in New York, which he implied was due to inadequate public spending. In truth, that devastation is directly due to the usual ravages of rent control. My authority is a Professor Peter Salins of the New York University Department of Urban Affairs. In 1980 he published a book called *The Ecology of Housing Destruction*, with a more revealing sub-title, 'The Economic Effects of Public Intervention in the Housing Market'. He showed that public spending of more than $10,000 million has not prevented the appalling deterioration and continuing destruction of the New York housing stock at the rate of 200,000 apartments every decade. In addition to reducing maintenance and construction, he showed that artificially depressed rents have increased demand and encouraged small families to occupy large premises. Professor Salins calls for the abolition of rent control and all its associated complexity of regulations. His conclusion on New York is, I believe, equally applicable to London and is as follows:

> There have been so many unsuccessful twists and turns along the path of well-intentioned tinkering that perhaps it is time to test the possibility that the generally reasonable incentives and disincentives of an unconstrained market might do a better job of allocating and conserving the housing stock.

I draw precisely the same moral from the First Report of the House of Commons Environment Committee, which was published last year. Paragraphs 100 and 101 confirm that a major cause of the decline of the rented sector, from 7 million in 1945 to below 2 million today, was rent control and lifetime security of tenure. The impossibility of gaining repossession appears even more oppressive for small landlords than the derisory gross return of 2 or 3 per cent on their capital. Evidence was given that, in the decade since 1970, what are fraudulently called 'fair rents' doubled, while prices trebled and earnings quadrupled.

Baroness Birk: *I think Lord Harris must agree that the whole situation in New York is entirely different from that in London. In New York you have apartments with very high rents. Has he seen some of the properties that people are renting at the lower end of the scale? I imagine that he is talking* *about property around Manhattan and that sort of area. Certainly nowhere in his quotations from the report of the Environment Committee does it state that a repeal of the rent control Acts would improve or increase the quantity of rented housing. In fact, when the Committee discuss it they point out what has happened and also what would happen if this was reversed – that it would not make the situation better, but in fact would make it worse.*

Lord Harris: The whole of Professor Salins's report on New York concentrates on places like the Bronx. He is concerned with the poor end of the market in New York and not with Manhattan.

In the House of Commons Committee report, to which I have referred, paragraph 101 says that

> Most witnesses argued that a revival of supply in the [rented] sector would require the removal or reduction of rent and security controls, together with a growth of confidence that future changes in legislation and government policy would not reimpose tighter controls.

Baroness Birk: *Would he mind reading the following sentence?*

Lord Harris: Not at all. It reads: 'However, many felt that even this could not succeed and removal of controls would simply exacerbate housing stress without achieving acceptable housing conditions for those in the sector'.

Baroness Birk: *Thank you.*

Lord Harris: But they say that the *majority* of witnesses gave the earlier view, and the witnesses included Shelter, the Small Landlords Association, Professor Donnison, Brighton Borough Council, the City of Manchester Council, Chestertons, and the Paddington Federation of Tenants and Residents Associations. I am establishing that no clear-cut view is handed down from the House of Commons report. It is all open for argument, and we propose to continue that argument.

From the evidence in that report I was surprised to discover that those who derive much satisfaction from baiting the landlords and working up prejudice in this matter, argue that rents may be held low but the owners would gain from increased property values over a period of years. Yet in practice it is elsewhere acknowledged that a house with a sitting tenant might be lucky to fetch 20 per cent of its market value with vacant possession. The whole point is that it is just such grotesquely falsified values which provide less scrupulous owners with a strong temptation to neglect repairs and get sitting tenants out.

Leaving aside the immorality of rent control, which I think should trouble its defenders rather more, the down-to-earth economic question is whether repeal would bring more lettings onto the market at rents people can afford. I believe that clear evidence is provided by the orchestrated complaints about 'loopholes', which take the form of holiday homes, company lettings, licences and shared occupancy in place of full tenancies. The success of these escape clauses in my view provides proof beyond any doubt whatever that, where the legalised theft of the Rent Acts can be avoided, new accommodation is forthcoming to relieve the distress of homelessness.

The best way to end the 'loopholes' is simply to repeal these obstructive statutes by supporting Lord Vaizey's Bill in the Lobby.[19] The way to help the poor is not to control rents any more than it is to control the price of food or clothing. To distort the price system obstructs supply and demand, as we see to our cost in a quite different connection with the Common Agricultural Policy.

Social versus economic policy   In conclusion, I would emphasise that poverty is the proper province of social policy and is best tackled by topping-up low incomes in some form. It should not be confused with general economic policy nor with policy on particular prices. Alas! It has to be said that for decades the Labour Party has won votes by confounding these wholly distinct issues to the detriment of both economic and social progress. It has further obstructed reform by reckless threats to restore or even to extend rent control, as we have been reminded that Mr Crosland did – to his eternal shame – in 1974 by destroying the market for rented furnished premises. I take some encouragement that, now the Labour Party looks like being reduced to talking to itself, a special responsibility shifts to the Social Democrats as the alternative government of the future. It only needs David Owen and the eagerly awaited Lord Grimond to teach the Liberals some economic sense for the repeal of rent control to open up the way for long-term reconstruction of the much-needed market in rented accommodation.

11.   The coal monopoly

Debate on a motion by Lord Ezra calling for a
long-term energy strategy

We must all have been impressed by the wide-ranging opening speech by Lord Ezra. As with other orations from the Liberal benches, I found myself wondering what link it had with the fundamental principles of liberal philosophy. I shall try to remedy this deficiency by warning against pinning too-high hopes on a long-term energy strategy. He displayed a wide knowledge gained from a lifetime of some 35 years in the coal industry. I hope, however, he will bear in mind that a lot of knowledge can be a dangerous thing, unless informed by constant humility about the changing variables which can never be known in advance.

The complaint might be made that we have suffered by not having a long-term energy strategy over recent decades. Yet the question I want to pose is: Who could have foreseen the dramatic transformation of supply and demand in the United Kingdom and indeed in the world energy market? In 1960 coal represented almost 100 per cent of British fuel production and we relied for some 30 per cent of our consumption on imported oil. By 1973, despite the eruption of natural gas, we relied on imports for one-half of our then substantially increased consumption. When we come to 1982 we find that, with North Sea oil in full spate, we produced a surplus of fuel to export while coal accounted for no more than one-third of our total production. Could any long-term fuel strategy have predicted such far-reaching changes?

If we have survived without too much difficulty, it is thanks chiefly to the adaptation of production and consumption to price adjustments in the market – a market, I may say, made more imperfect by government obstructions and intervention. Allowing for the long time-lags for producers and consumers to adjust their supply and demand from one fuel to another, is it not astonishing that we have avoided disaster without Lord Ezra's strategy? Indeed, at intervals since 1973, the only disruption has been caused or threatened by the coal industry which, as I shall try to argue, has suffered from the handicap of a long-term plan.

The folly of the *Plan for Coal* as with all similar political aspirations, is that it was an example of physical planning without too much regard for changing prices. I recall a speaker in our recent debate on unemployment urging government planning on the analogy of private enterprise companies which, as we all know, may plan for five or 10 years ahead. But competitive planning by separate companies is quite a different matter from centralised government planning. No company pretends to plan for the whole industry, and it certainly does not inscribe its targets on tablets of stone.

All business planning is tentative and conditional upon changes in the market-place. Each firm estimates the future market and its likely share, but then stands ready to adapt to unexpected changes. Competition provides a perpetual feedback of movements in relative prices reflecting substitution of new sources of supply. If things turn out worse than expected, enterprising businessmen are ready to lower their prices to sell their current production, and to cut back their plans for the future.

National or corporatist planning stands in the sharpest contrast. For a start, it will always include a large dash of political expediency. Its targets will often smack more of hopes than of practical realities. Secondly, government plans are cast in terms of physical quantities that extrapolate forward from past experience in a way which has been compared with trying to steer a boat by looking backwards at the wake. Thirdly, once government has set its seal on a plan, it takes on a life of its own and becomes highly rigid. It is then likely to be persisted in long after the assumptions on which it was based have been falsified by changing circumstances. Above all, official plans or strategies give hostages to fortune. They raise expectations among favoured interests and so provide a breeding ground for bitterness when the expectations are not fulfilled.

The need for competition So we come to the *Plan for Coal*. By far the best obituary was written by Professor Colin Robinson and his colleague, Eileen Marshall, in their evidence to the recent Select Committee on European Coal Policy. They pointed out that the past decade 'should have provided a favourable environment for the British coal industry'. In 1973 the Arab oil cartel handed coal a massive competitive advantage. So the plan in 1974 projected an optimistic target, centred on production of 135 million tonnes for 1985 and based on a government commitment to a large-scale investment programme. Success of this plan depended upon a 4 per cent annual increase in average output per man to be achieved in part by closing down high-cost pits and opening up new, lower-cost capacity.

Despite Mr Scargill's Marxist–Leninist mathematics, the investment of £7,000 million is the only part of the plan to have been fulfilled. Output per man, assisted by the bonus scheme and the 1979 tax cuts, has increased by an annual average of nearer 1 per cent than the promised 4 per cent, largely because the closure of high-cost pits lagged behind the programme until Sir Norman Siddall's surgery last year.

Behind Mr Scargill's inflammatory and ideological rhetoric lies the damning truth that British deep-mined coal, at a cost averaging £46 a tonne after subsidies, costs twice or three times as much as the best achieved in the United States or Australia. But the paradox is that, by protecting British coal against imports and by raising subsidies, governments have weakened the very competitive pressures that would have made for more efficiency. They have thereby enabled the National Union of Mineworkers to keep pushing average costs up much faster than the cost-of-living index. In short, the *Plan for Coal* inflated the monopoly power of Mr Scargill and of his predecessor to obstruct adaptation to market changes, to milk the taxpayer, and to impose higher prices on consumers – including housewives, industry and the captive Central Electricity Generating Board.

I believe that our best strategy is to get markets to operate more freely and more flexibly. As the National Coal Board's outstanding marketing director, Malcolm Edwards, never tires of repeating, the best way to check imports, to stop more nuclear power stations and to speed conversion from oil in industry and electricity generating, is to produce a dependable supply of British coal at

£30 to £35 a tonne. That simply means a lot less coal produced at £50 to £80 a tonne, which now requires the public to pour in capital and current subsidies which are equivalent to approaching £150 a week for every miner in the industry.

I share the view expressed by other speakers that there is great hope for the future of British coal. But it is a hope that can be fulfilled only if the price of coal is made competitive and customers can rely on an uninterrupted supply, without the costly insurance policy of massive stocks or keeping alternative generating capacity in reserve. There is no future for British coal under Mr Scargill's political programme of high costs and unreliable delivery.

For the good of coal miners and their customers, our strategy should be to break up the present politicised monopoly, phase out the subsidies, and find ways of giving workers a personal equity in the success of their own efforts. As a first step towards such a competitive strategy, I want to offer the Minister a simple proposal. It is that the Government should repeal Section l(1)(a) of the 1946 Nationalisation Act which gave the National Coal Board the exclusive power to work all new discoveries of coal found in Great Britain. I believe we would soon find that there is nothing like competition, even the threat of competition, to galvanise a monopoly into greater efficiency.

Part III   Markets, Taxation and Equality

12.   Up with the market

Debate on a motion by Lord Beswick calling attention to the effects of over-reliance on market forces

I should like to try to explain in very general terms why I consider that Her Majesty's Government are so far from deserving the well-worn strictures as a band of extremists hellbent on turning the clock back to the heyday of 19th-century liberalism. I believe that these charges show the danger of politicians being misled by their own rhetoric, and sometimes by the rather robust rhetoric we have from some members of the Government.

Over many years we have heard a popular fiction, especially dear to Liberals and Social Democrats, that since the war public policy has oscillated between the opposing poles of two distinctive ideologies. From where I sit on the cross-benches, it seems nearer the truth that, in the balance between market and government, the pendulum that we used to hear about has increasingly been replaced by the ratchet.

Since 1945 – I would argue in many respects since 1906 – party politics has seen a cumulative, if you will, a progressive, shift away from the dispersed initiative of ordinary people in the competitive market and towards increasingly centralised direction, bureaucratic control and pervasive state power. To my imagination politicians often seem like mediaeval knights, with multiplying bands of retainers, all clad in such a weight of armour as to be deprived of the flexibility necessary for effective action. Thus in office they appear to wield great power, and yet so often in practice have proved impotent to achieve their most basic aims.

I think it right that this House should pay attention to the wisdom of the past. I therefore bring you some words written more than 200 years ago by Adam Smith, when he warned politicians against excessive intervention, in attempting which he said: 'they must always be exposed to innumerable delusions, and for the proper performance of which no human wisdom or knowledge could ever be sufficient'.

On this issue of the general superiority of the market it is not sufficiently understood that Keynes was more frequently in some agreement with his classical forebears. Significantly for this debate, in 1926 he wrote an essay, entitled 'The End of Laissez-faire', in which he stated: 'Capitalism, wisely managed, can probably be made more efficient for attaining economic ends than any alternative yet in sight'.

That was in 1926. Lest it be thought that his *General Theory* changed all that, I should like to quote from his best-known work in 1936, when he wrote:

> The advantage to efficiency of the decentralisation of decisions and of individual responsibility is even greater perhaps than the 19th century supposed; and the reaction against the appeal to self-interest may have gone too far.

If that were true almost 50 years ago, how much further have we now strayed down the wrong road? So I would ask: Where is the excessive reliance on market forces that haunts the Labour benches? Take the labour market. It is perfectly true that the ending of prices and incomes policy has permitted much more flexibility for managements and men to adapt to changing economic realities. But there remains a fearful incubus of trade union monopoly power and legal privileges, added to what now appears the hollow mockery of 'employment protection' laws, wages councils, rent controls, and, above all, the confused and conflicting operation of high taxes, social benefits and all kinds of subsidies that make it profitable for thousands of people to choose unemployment rather than work.

Public versus private sector   On top of all that, approaching a third of the entire labour force is locked up in the public sector, mostly cushioned from the invigoration of market forces, and the results for over-manning and inefficiency are increasingly visible and indeed widely acknowledged. Before the eruption of Mr Wedgwood Benn, the Labour Party saw itself essentially as a moderate movement. Yet by 1979 it had brought about far more extensive nationalisation in Britain than in such model social democracies as Sweden or West Germany.

The essence of a market economy is not simply the private ownership of industry, as some of its defenders imagine. The essence of a market economy is that production is guided by competition between alternative suppliers to serve the changing demands of consumers at home or abroad. The really fatal flaw of nationalised industry is that governments, for political expediency, seek to shield it from competition, knowing that the domestic consumers or taxpayers can always be made to pay, no matter how high costs may rise.

The contrast between public and private industry stands out more starkly today than ever before. At a time when private industry has been compelled by hated market forces to transform productivity, we see a lagging performance in many of the nationalised monopolies: I would say in railways, coal, and postal services – and I am not enamoured of gas and electricity. An instructive contrast is that where even a nationalised industry is faced by market forces in the form of foreign competition – as in steel, motor cars, or shipbuilding – determined management has been able to achieve some of the glittering prizes being won by private industry.

I readily agree with the critics here and elsewhere who say that market forces do not operate with anything approaching perfection. But I would strongly argue that the well-intended effort to remove every blemish has invariably led to a far worse situation. In a fastidious endeavour to cure a skin rash we have spread a bubonic plague of bureaucratic regulation into every crevice of the economy. One result is a standard tax rate, including national insurance, of 40 to 50 per cent on wages as low as one-third of average earnings. A quite different kind of outcome, which we shall witness in this debate, is the politicisation of every aspect of economic affairs, with increasing contention and bitterness which in the world outside has led to a declining respect for politicians and indeed for the law. It is true that the market economy requires a framework of law for its operation, but that is a far cry from the present legal straitjacket into which it is clamped in so many respects.

I therefore conclude by saying that if the Social Democrats really want to break the mould they might start ostentatiously by burying the old consensus that has got us into so much difficulty. They might then join the intellectual vanguard of economists and others, including many disillusioned socialists, who are endeavouring to redefine a new public philosophy of limited but effective government that works with the grain of market forces. 'Market forces' are the only way of describing ordinary men and women as consumers and producers, co-operating in competition to their mutual benefit. When members are not in this House to tell us about the cold and crude concept of the market, they go about their business as part of these market forces outside.

I conclude by urging the Government to continue moving more decisively towards the market, which is not only most fully consistent with individual freedom and responsibility but, as a direct consequence, offers the best spring-board to lasting economic recovery.

13. Down with taxes

Debate on a motion by Lord Boyd-Carpenter calling for urgent liberation of resources for the creation of wealth and the reduction of high taxation

The motion in the name of Lord Boyd-Carpenter exactly reflects my own impatience with the failure of the Government to push on more rapidly in reducing the burden of taxation which has grown remorselessly throughout the whole of this century. If we look back to 1900 we find that government took 15 per cent of the national income. By 1938 it took 30 per cent of the national income, by 1960 40 per cent and, through the 1970s, around 50 per cent. I checked back with the Blue Book for 1982 which showed that total state spending was then £128,000 million out of a net national income of £240,000 million. Those two figures tell us that central and local government and their various offshoots laid claim to 53 per cent of all the income earned by the exertions and enterprise of this nation.

In a prudent world this mounting public spending has to be financed from rates and a whole variety of taxes, or it has to be borrowed from current savers and eventually repaid by future taxpayers. It must be obvious, even to such overflowingly generous and well-intentioned people as Lord Beswick, that there is some limit to the amount of tax that governments can take without doing more harm than good. This is a matter of judgement. Unlike Lord Barnett, I judge that we have already gone beyond the bounds of prudence.

I would assert that, above a modest level, all taxes damage our economic performance in a variety of ways. Most people, despite what Lord Beswick has said, do not positively rejoice in paying higher taxes. There is no such thing as a free tax. We all know that, as local authority rates have rocketed, firms have been forced out of socialist city centres and sometimes, too often, have been forced out of business.

Lord Beswick: *I did not talk about rejoicing in paying higher taxes. I rejoiced that we had a system which could give the surgical treatment which a poor man needed. Does not the speaker also rejoice in that; and, if he does rejoice, does he not accept that it follows that we must pay taxes?*

Lord Harris: Lord Beswick implied that people should take pleasure in paying taxes because it led to some good things of which they approved. I approve of some things the Government does, but I thoroughly disapprove of many other things where I can see that my money is wasted. So I cannot take pleasure in the total burden of tax that falls upon me. My argument is that income tax and national insurance contributions raise costs, depress efficiency, distort effort, make British products less competitive than foreign competition and so destroy jobs.

I was not impressed by the complacent comparison of Lord Barnett with European tax levels – and for a number of reasons. In the first place, the structure of our own income tax is more onerous, especially on lower and higher incomes. Secondly, European earnings over the post-war years have risen a good deal faster than those in Britain; so that, despite rising taxes, take-home pay has also risen faster. Furthermore, Britain suffers from larger handicaps than France, Germany or even Sweden, especially in our troublesome trade unions and in the more extensive nationalisation. Therefore, we need all the additional help that we can get from lower taxes.

It is a fallacy to suppose that taxes do not matter because only some people are affected by their disincentive impact. Lord Barnett conceded that some people are so discouraged; the only dispute is how widely that particularly damaging effect runs. I wholly agree with Lord Barnett in his attack on taxes on lower income. Before the war working-class families like my own parents never paid taxes unless incomes rose to something like two or three times average earnings. Today income tax starts for many at levels nearer one-third of average earnings, and even below the entitlement to supplementary benefit. It is no wonder that we hear of the unemployment trap and the poverty trap where people are discouraged from taking a job which would leave them worse off, after loss of tax and benefits, than if they stayed on social security. As Lord Barnett acknowledged quite explicitly, we are literally taxing people into poverty and unemployment as well as taxing other people into the black market or the underground economy.

Spending other people's money   Another count against this great tax snatch is that, by knocking-off almost 40 per cent from take-home pay, workers are encouraged to try to pass the buck to their employers by demanding wage and salary increases which firms cannot afford. The buck eventually has to stop somewhere, and it tends to stop on the backs of the creators of wealth. It is indisputable that all taxes are a negative transfer of goods and services away from individuals and towards government. The trouble is that higher taxes must, however, marginally, reduce the flow of wealth which alone enables us to pay increasing taxes in the future.

A further disadvantage of high public spending which has not been touched upon is that no government can give as good value for our money as we get when we spend it for ourselves and our families. The men in Whitehall cannot know and cannot really even care about individual preferences which differ very widely. They are inevitably inclined to spend other people's money just as though it was other people's money. A Minister in this House for whom I have a great deal of admiration was nevertheless reported in *Hansard* as saying: 'I rather like spending other people's money; it is one of the most enjoyable functions of a Minister's life'.

At that time I was deeply shocked. That was four years ago. Now I am a hundred years older and wiser and sadder; and I have come to accept that there is not much prospect of getting politicians to treat the taxpayer's money with the most especial respect it should deserve.

Even if Ministers were recruited exclusively from the legendary one-armed Aberdonians with sewn-up pockets, I would argue that it is impossible for public services to be as cost-conscious as private suppliers who have to compete to win customers. Even in this recession, we have seen that managements in local government, in education, and in health services have faced none of the market disciplines which have compelled private enterprise to improve efficiency by cutting out waste, ending slack working habits, and reducing manpower often by 10, 20 or 30 per cent, without in many cases reducing output or capacity. The additional difficulty which has been touched upon is that state services and nationalised industries breed over-powerful trade unions that have fought, often without scruple, to retain every over-manned post and preserve every demarcation and restrictive practice. I heard Lord Ezra say that the National Coal Board has won Queen's Awards for some of its technical triumphs; but it would win no taxpayers' or customers' awards for its efficiency or its return on capital over a period of years.

The trouble fundamentally is that, wherever any activity is plugged into government, all the pressures are for more spending. Lord Barnett would agree, I know, with this proposition in the light of his own excellent post-mortem on the years 1974 to 1979 when he was Labour's Chief Secretary of the Treasury. His remarkably readable requiem, entitled *Inside the Treasury*, is full of instructive revelations which I never cease to advertise. If his sales are doing well it is partly due to my advocacy. Early in his book he lamented: 'The days had long since passed when I naively thought it would be easy to persuade my colleagues that two plus two really did make four'. A little later he said: 'So many of my colleagues wanted to have their cake and eat it; even the most intelligent of them wanted both tax cuts and public expenditure increases'.

I think his Labour colleagues are not so different from many Ministers on the other side of the House. But I think I can say with some confidence that at least the present Government has not been guilty of that degree of folly. I have no doubt that the Chancellor would like to get spending and taxes down, even if Mr Peter Walker and other Tory rustics and romantics are not entirely in agreement. I would therefore urge Mr Nigel Lawson to persevere, and I offer this concluding thought: no single boon would do more for growth and employment prospects than a large and continuing reduction in the burden of taxation on workers, savers and investors. It is they – millions of ordinary and extraordinary people, not governments of any party – who are the true source of Britain's wealth and future prosperity.

14. Goodbye to equality

Debate on a motion by Lord Longford calling for greater equality

I do not know Lord Longford enough to judge whether his amiable qualities include absent-mindedness. But I have a special reason for hoping that he forgets to withdraw his 'motion for papers' at the end of this debate.[20] I have been wondering what papers we could recommend to advance his education – not more Blue Books, not more Fabian tracts or official reports, of which he may have swallowed too many. What other papers would cheer him and help persuade him that his plea for 'greater equality' has already gone a long way towards being fulfilled in our lifetime by the remarkable operations of private enterprise in competitive markets? My choice of papers to put this debate into perspective would be the social commentaries embodied in bound volumes, not of *Hansard,* but of such journals as *Homes and Gardens, Good Housekeeping, Woman's Weekly,* and all those contemporary magazines on holidays, motoring, eating out, foreign travel and other growing national pastimes.

Who now remembers the working-class world in which at least some of us were brought up? Who remembers the world of fly-papers, of gas coppers and black-leaded grates, of mangles and meat safes, of boiled milk in the summer and acres of lino – or should I say linoleum? Such domestic horrors have now been banished by aerosols, detergents, washing-machines, heaters of all kinds, fitted kitchens, refrigerators, deep freezes and wall-to-wall carpeting. Critics can dwell on sad exceptions, but the lives of most ordinary people have been transformed in two generations. I am arguing – and I think it a fair point from the cross-benches – that none of this practical progress owes very much at all to politicians and governments.

The larger part of government social spending consists in taking money from the majority of people and returning it to much the same people in cash and kind – minus heavy freight charges in both directions. While the forebears of many members here were calling for the 'elevation of the masses', the practical process of improvement was being advanced by businessmen, galvanised by unequal incentives in the market, to find better ways of serving their consumers and, at the same time, offering more rewarding employment. The whole history of liberal capitalism is one of extending the luxuries of a privileged minority ever wider to become the everyday conveniences, even necessities, of growing majorities. The tragedy of the last 100 years is that the market worked so well that we took it for granted and began to make its operations more difficult.

It has been said that in confronting social policy we should be 'inspired by love but guided by reason'. My reasoning tells me that many noble intentions aired in debates such as this are likely to finish up doing more harm than good. Our concern should not be with the distracting and destructive phantom of equality. It should be with a realistic discussion of how we can revive our economy so as to afford a more humane minimum standard for those who cannot maintain themselves in the market. We would all agree that no-one should be allowed to fall below what we judge an acceptable poverty level. But I want to ask why today's conception of a minimum standard is so much above what I will call the 'skimmed-milk standard' that was applied by Booth and Rowntree in their poverty surveys 100 years ago? The improvement owes far less to the second-hand generosity of politicians, doling out other people's money, than to the application of capital and labour in multiplying marketable output.

More discriminating welfare benefits It is clear that 'greater equality' has a powerful emotional and even aesthetic appeal for its advocates. But its danger lies in the conflict with the indispensable requirement of incentives for a free and efficient society. My argument in a nutshell is that the disincentive cost of the British welfare state has now become the major obstacle to spreading prosperity through the more effective operation of vigorous competitive enterprise. I agree with the tendency of much of the remarks of Lord Young of Dartington. I express them in this way: our mistake in social policy has been that instead of concentrating help selectively on those in need – for example, as he said, by a reverse income tax – British policy has indulged the essentially collectivist folly of universal free services and benefits which are both inefficient to the recipient and inordinately expensive to the taxpayer as provider. That is why we now have at the same time excessive taxation going hand in hand with inadequate help for some categories of special need.

The burden of indiscriminate benefits is damaging in a host of ways. I shall mention briefly four. First, high taxes necessarily inflate labour costs, at the same time as they deflate the incentives to effort and enterprise. Secondly, the availability of universal services puts a premium on sloth and safety-first. Thirdly, the spreading burden of taxes down the income scale impoverishes millions of families who thereby become dependent upon multiplying state subsidies. And finally – for the moment – the narrowing or non-existent gap between taxed income from work and untaxed social benefits must increase voluntary unemployment and so reduce real output.

Sceptics will find much more interesting evidence than provided in the Diamond Reports[21] in a recent compilation by Ralph Howell, MP, entitled *Why Work?* Why indeed, when taxation on a family of a man, wife and two children starts at a wage of £41 a week compared with tax-free supplementary benefits on offer at £66 a week? Why work indeed, when the head of that family would need to earn £115 a week to be better off than collecting unemployment benefit plus tax refunds? Why work indeed, when the same breadwinner in a family of four earning £105 a week comes out of the tax-benefit mangle only £11 better off than if he earned £35 a week? Greater equality? No – not unless we want, in Churchill's phrase, 'equal sharing of miseries' rather than 'unequal sharing of blessings'.

I conclude that, instead of sliding with Lord Longford down the slippery slope of equality, we should urgently seek to reduce the half of national income now spent by government, to cut taxes and to widen differences of income from both work and investment. We should in my view pursue a deliberate policy of differential incentives in the long-run interests not least of the poor and the handicapped. If we really want to encourage employment and enliven our economy, we need above all to free this economy from decades of self-inflicted political mutilation.

NOTES

1. *The Consultative Document on Trade Union Immunities*, Cmnd. 8128, HMSO, January 1981.
2. Earlier in the debate Lord Denning, for 20 years (1962–82) Master of Rolls, had condemned 'our statutes [as] still appalling in their complexity', and referred to Section 17 of the Employment Act 1980 as 'the most tortuous section I have ever read. It defies understanding'.
3. As a result of Labour and Liberal opposition and Conservative abstentions, the Bill was defeated by 42 votes to 25.
4. A former President of the General Medical Council on the cross-benches.
5. A practising GP on the Liberal benches.
6. A former Professor of Pharmacology on the cross-benches.
7. Lord Rugby withdrew his Bill, but the opticians' monopoly was repealed by the Health and Social Security Act 1984.
8. Published by Heffer, Cambridge, 1960.
9. *Report of the Committee on the Truck Acts*, HMSO, 1961.
10. Lord Rochester as Liberal spokesman moved an amendment to delay the Second Reading until further consultations were completed.
11. On a Division, the amendment was lost and the Second Reading passed by 39 votes to 36. The Government subsequently agreed to denounce the ILO Convention in preparation for repealing the Truck Acts.
12. *Report of the Departmental Committee on Liquor Licensing*, Cmnd. 5154, HMSO, December 1972.
13. Until the illness leading to his death in 1984, Lord Robbins attended the House regularly as a cross-bencher and was a powerful voice in favour of economic liberalism.
14. *Rent Acts: Report of the Committee*, Cmnd. 4609, HMSO, 1971.

15. The untimely death of Lord Vaizey in 1984 at the age of 54 removed an outstanding liberal economist from the Conservative benches.
16. Since 1983 Lord Barnett.
17. Andre Deutsch, London, 1982.
18. IEA Readings in Political Economy No. 7, 1972.
19. The debate on the Second Reading was adjourned and no vote was taken.
20. Debates are staged in the House of Lords in the form of a motion 'calling for Papers' on the chosen topic. The mover concludes the debate by withdrawing his request for papers.
21. *Royal Commission on the Distribution of Income and Wealth* (Chairman: Lord Diamond): Report No. 6: *Lower Incomes*, Cmnd. 7175, HMSO. May 1978, Ch. 4.

House of Lords speeches, 1984–2004

WHERE ARE THE NEW JOBS COMING FROM?

13 November 1984

My Lords, I find much to applaud in the gracious Speech – the harmless circuses as well as the bread of life, which was touched upon by the noble Earl, Lord Stockton, in his delightful and uplifting maiden speech. If I join my old friend, the noble Lord, Lord Alport, in lamenting, though from a rather different standpoint, the lack of radical policies to tackle unemployment, I do not of course doubt that Her Majesty's Government are deeply concerned about this grave problem. At least in this House we can agree that the issue dividing the two sides is one not of motives but of methods. Put simply, the critics think that the remedy for unemployment is always to increase public spending, measured in nominal pounds, while the Government believe (as the noble Lord, Lord Bauer, explained lucidly) that the planned increase by the Government in the money supply is already sufficient to create more real demand for labour if we hold down costs and improve incentives for more efficient production.

Quite apart from the differences in temperament mentioned by the noble Earl, Lord Stockton, it is natural, in my view, that the parties in opposition would always take more risks in expanding demand and have their fun mocking monetary policy as being either mean or meaningless. But, from the vantage point of the Cross-Benches, it carries more weight, as the noble Earl, Lord Gowrie, said, that throughout Europe, governments – whether run by Social Democrats, Christian Socialists, coalitions or in France by, nominally, Socialists – all end up deploying prudent monetary management to check inflation. For all the most amiable rhetoric of the noble Lord, Lord Barnett, the last Labour Government, when it came to the pinch, were not bad monetarists, especially after 1975, with the nudge and guidance of the International Monetary Fund, despite unemployment rising remorselessly towards one and a half million in 1979.

It is also natural that unemployed politicians in opposition can always afford to be more supremely confident that increased spending will create jobs, whereas experience in office teaches again and again that unchecked spending creates inflation. We have all learned the lesson that by distorting and discouraging investment, inflation in turn destroys future employment.

The question which keeps asking itself is: where are the new jobs coming from? In a paper with that very title for the National Economic Development Council last November, the TUC admitted, in what I can only describe as a rare lapse of candour, that nobody really knows. Indeed, it took refuge in history, as the following remarkable, if somewhat opaque, passage will show. I quote from the TUC document of 24th November 1983:

> Two centuries ago, the overwhelming majority of the working population was employed on the land. If, during one of the periodic crises of recession and unemployment in that period the question of where new jobs were coming from had been raised, it would have been impossible to envisage that the answer lay in a rapid upheaval characterised by a massive move of population from the land to the cities and a rapid restructuring of economic activity from agriculture to manufacturing.

That paragraph may not exactly be a literary gem, but it is struggling to convey what I believe to be a seminal historical insight. The TUC are saying that no-one could have foreseen the transformation of the first industrial revolution but that, on the day, it turned out all right for employment. A moment's reflection will explain why the trade union leaders were unable to draw the correct and hopeful lesson from this shrewd observation.

Can anybody imagine that the industrial revolution could have worked its wonders of increasing jobs and raising standards of living fourfold in a century if the dear old TUC had been around at the time to stop it? How could Lancashire cotton have circled the world if some rustic Arthur Scargill had been able to preserve in perpetuity the handloom weavers? Would the new factories, railways and docks have sprung up if fancy apprenticeships, closed shops, demarcation and other restrictive practices had been allowed to stand in the way? Could jobs have been found for the multiplying children of our Victorian forebears, if minimum wage laws had said that they must be paid a half, or more, of adult rates? Would even the devoted working class readers of Samuel Smiles' *Self-Help* have sought out new jobs, if high taxes had cut their take-home pay to within a few pennies or shillings of social benefits?

The questions ducked by the TUC are without end. Anyway, how could the new works have been developed if planning laws had frozen development and imposed delays of years between the conception and completion of new buildings? And how could workers have moved to new jobs if rent control had destroyed houses to let? If only the TUC had persevered with their history lessons they would have learned that the way forward for the first industrial revolution was prepared in the early years of the 19th century by a liberalising programme of monetary reconstruction, free trade and the radical reform of such obstacles to economic advance as taxation, trade unions and the old Poor Law.

I would argue on the Government's behalf that since 1979 a nominally Conservative administration has shown a more truly liberalising intent than any British administration for 100 years. It has been the first to begin to reverse almost a century of progressive collectivism which has weakened the vigour and flexibility of this economy. The trouble is that there is still a long way to go if we want production and employment to adapt to changing markets, new methods and novel ways of living, to which the noble Earl, Lord Stockton, lifted up our eyes.

It seems to me that the best pragmatic test of economic policy for employment, as Samuel Brittan never tires of teaching us and as the noble Lord, Lord Barnett, almost conceded, is its effect on labour costs per unit of output. Total demand is increasing sufficiently to raise real production and to employ more people, so long as the extra spending is not absorbed in higher costs and faster inflation. The reduction of labour and other costs should, in my view, become a crusade to release more purchasing power to spend on new production. Wherever overmanning is tolerated under the pressure of trade unions in the public services, wages should be allowed to fall. Where the market value of a worker's output rises, as at Jaguars, then wages can safely rise – and rise quite steeply – so long as management is left with enough profit to maintain and extend the capital equipment without which there can be no lasting jobs.

I believe quite passionately that the tragedy for Her Majesty's Government is that they are confronted and partly hypnotised by a nostalgic, backward-looking Labour and trade union movement which professes overriding concern about reducing unemployment yet which in practice always shrinks from helping to sweep away policies, practices and institutions that restrict progress to the desired end. If wages and salaries are to be more flexible, we should not only abolish wages councils and weaken the wrecking power of union Luddites. In the end we shall have drastically to reform and prune the monstrous tax benefit jungle. The most urgent requirement is to restore incentives not only for able-bodied men to seek work, but for efficient employers to offer more people the boon of a job at wages which can be afforded by performance in a competitive market.

REFORMING THE LICENSING LAWS

7 April 1986

My Lords, I congratulate the noble Viscount, Lord Montgomery, on his persistence in pressing Her Majesty's Government to reform the licensing laws in England and Wales in the light of experience in Scotland. I am sure that he would join in tribute to our late friend Lord Spens, who showed himself well ahead of his time in raising a Motion in almost identical terms three years ago. I have thought very hard about this in the meantime and I can think of only one serious ground for not welcoming an early Bill to permit freer opening of public houses in England and Wales. There cannot any longer be the fear of awful consequences from alcoholic excess which Scotland has now proved to be without foundation. For my money, the worst aspect of early reform would be the prospect of a repetition of all those speeches we heard from the temporal and spiritual opposition when we had the Shops Bill before the House.

If the Government heed the noble Baroness, Lady Macleod, and take courage to trust the people with freedom in this matter, I have no doubt that we can expect the right reverend Prelates to wax indignant, if they have any wax or indignation left, about the end of Sunday as we know it – in which case I hope that in large numbers deaf ears will be turned to that argument, as happened with the Shops Bill.

It seems to me that the issue of freedom is the same in both cases as, indeed, would be the likely outcome. If pubs and shops were equally free to open for the convenience of their customers, we know from Scottish experience in both cases that not all the outlets would equally avail themselves of the opportunity. We know that in some areas, on some days, at some times of the year, some shops and some pubs would find it worth opening to cater for their own clientele. We know that the public have differing patterns of working and differing styles of recreation. And we know that for holidays, locals and tourists from home and abroad choose differing patterns of going out, eating out and drinking out. There is enormous scope for expanding the service sector to provide more facilities and employment in serving both drinks and also, as the noble Baroness has said, meals and other refreshments.

There is no longer any objective, logical justification for imposing these restrictive and uniform prohibitions on opening times for pubs, any more than for shops, cinemas, restaurants, hotels or clubs. Why should not willing buyers and willing sellers be permitted the freedom to trade when it suits them? If the law of nuisance is insufficient to prevent damage to third parties, by all means let the law be strengthened on the general principle that the polluter should be made to pay any costs he imposes on others.

The only conscientious ground for hesitation about applying the liberal rule of *laissez-faire* to the sale of alcoholic refreshment has been that a minority will harm themselves and harm others. There is a danger that this incantation can become the refuge not only of killjoys and paternalists but even of tyrants. All freedom carries costs and dangers: consider motoring, air traffic, point-to-point racing, eating, dieting, smoking and, I would add, even stopping smoking. All are manifestations of free choice and all bring risks of suffering, handicap and possibly premature death.

I personally have no more reason than the next man to be complacent about alcoholic excess. Like others, I have friends or relatives who are or have been in danger from the affliction of alcoholism. But the joyful news is that experience in Scotland confirms the judgment of the Erroll Report that there is no correlation between the misuse of alcohol and the hours at which pubs open and close. Indeed, as the noble Baroness, Lady Sharples, has said, so long as pubs are licensed, landlords have a very powerful incentive indeed to check drunkenness. And, as the noble Lord, Lord Molloy, has said, the worst manifestations of the abuse of alcohol occur well away from pubs, in private homes and elsewhere.

Lest I am thought complacent, I would draw the attention of remaining sceptics to a very thorough assessment of the Scottish evidence in the *British Medical Journal* of 4th January this year. There were two authors, a Dr Plant of the Alcohol Research Group and a Mr Duffy, a statistician with the Medical Research Council. I should like to put on record their summary of the findings in their own words. They said:

> The study showed no appreciable effect on the level of alcohol related morbidity and mortality, though some improvements were noted in relation to the rates of convictions for drunkenness. The changes introduced since 1976 appeared to be popular and there was widespread perception that public drunkenness had become less commonplace.

If your Lordships read the detail of the article in the *British Medical Journal,* you will see that it shows that although mortality and hospital admissions from alcohol remain higher in Scotland than in England and Wales, the previously rising trend shows a more marked relative improvement in Scotland since longer opening was permitted after 1976. The report also shows that for both public order offences of drunkenness and drink-driving there has been a relative improvement in Scotland, especially compared with the rising trend of convictions for drinking and driving in England and Wales since 1977.

The noble Viscount, Lord Montgomery, quoted the report of the Office of Population Censuses and Surveys. For me, the most impressive single finding appears in table 4.3 on page 13, which shows a marked fall in the average number of drinks consumed per hour. It lends credence to the view quoted from a licensee at the very end of the report, on page 42: 'To me, the Scotsman at one time drank against the clock. It's a better way now; no screaming for drinks in the last hour; a much more civilised way of drinking. Scotsmen used to go out to get drunk, but that's changed now – like the English they go out for a drink'.

As a mere Sassenach, who spent seven years in those rougher parts in the days of the bogus *bona fide* traveller who invented journeys to get a wee dram in Scotland, I may say I rejoice in this transformation since I left those parts. The quicker the Government can bring the boon of reform to the English, the sooner we can further civilise our own pattern of drinking.

THE EFFECTS OF RENT CONTROL

28 January 1987

Lord Harris of High Cross rose to call attention to the effects of rent control on unemployment and homelessness; and to move for Papers.

The noble Lord said: My Lords, I beg leave to move the Motion standing in my name on the Order Paper. I should like to start by saying that I am grateful to my noble friends for allocating their second Cross-Bench debate to a discussion of what I regard as the evils of rent control. I must emphasise that this does not imply any concerted view on these Benches, though I shall be looking for a certain amount of support from behind me. I think it is appropriate that those of us who enjoy the comparative safety of the Cross-Benches should give a lead in raising an issue that is still unfortunately regarded as a political hot potato.

On broad issues of economic analysis and development I have before ventured the view that this House is not sufficiently backward-looking. If we are concerned with conditions favourable to economic advance we might learn lessons from the past, when Britain was in the van of progress rather than jostling in the rear. Accordingly, for encouragement and perverse inspiration I sometimes turn to the pages of Cole and Postgate's history book entitled *The Common People: 1746 to 1938*. I hope that that will inspire some confidence on the Labour Benches.

The authors of course provide a strictly socialist interpretation of the transformation which we loosely call the Industrial Revolution and which shows no sign, even today, of slackening. If I were asked what was the characteristic most essential for changes that were to liberate the common people from centuries of grinding poverty, I might as a first approximation offer a single word – mobility. Certainly without occupational and geographical mobility in human resources the new mechanical contrivances could not have yielded their full fruit.

Industrially, before the transformation, Cole and Postgate say: 'England was still hollow – a circumference of activity surrounding a central area which lived largely by self-subsistent agriculture'. The density of the population was then dictated largely by the location of the woollen industry and access to seaborne trade. In 1750, outside London only Bristol and perhaps Norwich might rank in population as major towns well ahead of Manchester, Liverpool, Birmingham and the rest. Indeed, on Cole and Postgate's showing Norfolk was exceeded in population only by Middlesex, Yorkshire and Devonshire. The growth of new industry and of employment therefore depended not only on the multiplication of population but on its migration from farming to industry, from countryside to the towns, and from the South and the East to the North and the West.

My entire case in this debate is that the past transformation of wealth and standards of living would have been totally frustrated if some well-meaning 18th century crackpot had hit on the disastrous notion of controlling rents, let alone obstructing new building in deference to town and country planning regulations. Today we are faced with the urgency of a shift, not so much from agriculture to industry but from old industry to new industry and from the traditional localised manufacture of goods to the more widely dispersed provision of services – not perhaps from the South and East to the North and the West but more likely the other way.

Once again I believe mobility of labour is required to adapt to new and emerging opportunities, yet movement is severely restricted by a host of policies, including uniform national wage rates and planning restrictions. However, prominent among the obstacles to mobility is the distortion and destruction of a flexible housing market to accommodate the changing and diverse needs of our enlarged population.

There can surely be less dispute today that rent control has been the chief source of the mischief that now afflicts hundreds of thousands of homeless and others who are frozen in unemployment by the inability to move to where jobs that they could do are going begging. It was, after all, the original impact of rent control in 1915 that caused the shortage of homes which appeared to justify the building of millions of council houses. It was subsidised council house rents that then became a further brake on people moving home. Moreover, it was the discouragement of house building for rent, reinforced by tax incentives, that led millions more to become owner–occupiers rather than enjoying the flexibility, convenience and choice of remaining tenants at least for some part of their family and working lives.

It is true that professional economists are known to disagree on many issues of policy, although I notice a widening measure of support for market propositions even in recent Fabian tracts, in the speeches of Mr Roy Hattersley and in the less sensational pages of recent copies of the *New Statesman*. But I think I can say – as I heard the noble Lord, Lord Robbins, say in this House – that there are few questions on which economists are more unanimous than the evil effects of rent control. As so often is the case, social and economic objectives are in total conflict. After all, rent control is only the application of price control to housing. All price control has what economists call an income effect and also an incentive effect. The income effect refers to the socially desirable result of raising the real income of the consumer or tenant by keeping the price or rent lower than it would otherwise be.

However, the lower price or rent simultaneously and inevitably has an incentive effect which is economically undesirable. For example, a married couple whose children have left home have less incentive to economise in accommodation by moving to a smaller house or flat so long as they have security of tenure at a controlled rent; and so we can predict that rent control will increase the demand for accommodation.

More seriously, at the same time the incentive effect on the landlord of a lower rent operates to reduce the supply of rented accommodation. This may come about by waiting for a protected tenant to die or offering him a cash inducement to quit so that the house can be taken out of renting and sold for the market price to an owner–occupier. Reduced supply has also come about by the decay of property on which the controlled rent, particularly in the days of high inflation, afforded the landlord an income wholly insufficient to cover the cost of repair and maintenance of the property. Even when the rent is closer to the market price, security of tenure imposes a cost on the landlord.

It follows that rent control, introduced for wholly benevolent and social reasons, inevitably has had malignant economic consequences. By increasing demand and reducing supply the politicians have themselves created the famous housing shortage. They have then exploited the resultant distress to indulge in such further mischief as the indiscriminate subsidy of council housing, the costly inducement of owner-occupation for people who would prefer the option of renting and the politically profitable confiscation by leasehold enfranchisement. All these expediencies would become unnecessary if party men would separate the social from the economic aspects of policy by allowing housing to reflect market prices and rents while topping up low incomes to enable the poor to pay.

It must be said from these Benches that all parties have contributed over seven decades to the unholy muddle and mischief which is dignified by the name of housing policy. It gives me no satisfaction to say that the Labour Party has come to play the most obstructive part by meeting every call for reform with the threat to restore full control if it is ever again in government. It thereby frightens off new building and renovation to rent by investors who think the political risk is a possibility, however remote. I look forward to hearing the noble Lord, Lord Winstanley, since if only the Social Democrats and even the Liberals would take courage to support this Government as a start in freeing new lettings from rent control, the Labour Party's electoral bluff would be called and its palsied veto on progress would go the way of Clause 4.

The Labour Party attempted to discredit the last effort on relaxation by a Conservative Government by blaming them for Rachmanism. I have spent a great deal of time rummaging through old newspaper clippings in order to establish an accurate view of that matter. I offer two clippings. One is from *The Observer,* which in July 1963, at the time of that controversy, said: 'For the Rachmans of this world, rent restrictions and controls – the solution advocated by the Labour Party – are not so much an obstacle as an opportunity'.

I then turned to my favourite journal, *The Economist,* and I offer your Lordships a quotation from 27th July 1963: 'Where the solution cannot lie is in Mr. Wilson's repeated promise that a Labour government would restore and re-expand rent controls'. It continues: 'the re-extension of rent control would extend the area in which Rachmanism would again thrive'. The gap between the controlled depressed rent and the market value of the premises without control provides the temptation even today for harsh or unscrupulous landlords to attempt to resort to efforts of eviction, against which, I am glad to say, the law is fairly strongly established.

I do not attach great weight to such precise statistics as 100,000 homeless, 1 million crude surplus of empty dwellings and perhaps 300,000 job vacancies in areas where housing is not available. But I have no doubt that a major reduction in homelessness and unemployment will be longer delayed unless we tackle the rigidity of rent control to encourage the provision of homes where people want to work and live.

So long as control in its present form survives, the form of rented accommodation most convenient to young people, to itinerant individual workers and to mobile families will continue its tragic decline. The Government would then be drawn still deeper into the swamp, with mounting costs in council house-building that might hardly dent the housing lists and would certainly not cater for the short-term needs of people moving in search of work.

Meanwhile, the very success of the Government's policy in selling off 1 million council houses has further reduced the total supply of rented accommodation from 44 per cent in 1980 to 39 per cent of the present housing stock, compared with well above 70 per cent in 1950 and, in many European countries, typically 45 or 60 per cent of all houses rented through the private sector.

I salute the courage of the present Minister, Mr John Patten, in opening up the debate on the issue, and I look forward to hearing what measures the Government have in mind for the next session, which may turn out to be their next term of office.

DENATIONALISATION AND COMPETITION

25 November 1987

My Lords, I join in congratulating the noble Lord, Lord Ezra, on what I regard as his boldness in bringing this Motion before us. After all, the fact that his formidable talents, devoted over a lifetime to the National Coal Board, did not produce a more fruitful outcome is, in my view, the most plain indictment of the failure of the Morrisonian model of nationalisation.

In readiness for the rather gloomy reflections of the noble Lord, Lord Basnett, I go back to my earliest Questions for Written Answer which I put down when I first came here as an innocent and happier recruit to your

Lordship's House. In October 1980 I asked politely the amounts of taxpayers' money sunk into the nationalised industries since 1945. From the detailed Answer of the noble Lord, Lord Cockfield – those were the days – I can summarise the tally as follows. In the 20 years 1960 to 1980 more than £25,000 million was lavished in grants and in write-offs of capital and revenue deficits, in which the Coal Board was second only to British Steel. We must bear in mind the change in prices since 1978–79 and ponder that we are talking about something like £50,000 million at today's values.

It was the objective of the earlier pioneers of nationalisation to overthrow capitalist production for profit. How well they have succeeded. Was it their intention to enthrone losses as a way of life for a large part of British industry? We might blame the failure on the exploitation of monopoly power by the unequal forces of aggressive trade unionism and appeasing management. The symptoms. we recall, were over-manning, industrial unrest, weak incentives to efficiency, misdirection of capital and recurrent deficits. But in fairness I believe that we should dig deeper.

We find that the underlying sources of most mischief stems from the truism that public ownership unavoidably means political control. So-called public ownership in the so-called public interest was in my view always a fraudulent prospectus. It was never the public but the politicians who ruled the roost and still rule the roost in coal, steel, railways and electricity. I was not surprised that the recent arbitrary and in my view unjustified hoist in electricity prices was denounced by Labour spokesmen as being politically motivated. They should know. For years in power they and in their turn Conservative Ministers regularly played the party game in the same way. For years the investment programmes and pricing policies of the commanding heights of the British economy were the periodical playthings of Chancellors pursuing short-term electoral calculations rather than long-term economic objectives.

Elementary economic theory – as I hope the noble Lord, Lord Peston, will agree – offers strong arguments why public utilities should be vested in the control of government. But in the light of mature practical politics, I believe that there are still stronger arguments why the control of production should be put beyond the reach of politicians. Nationalisation was another example of putting the cat in charge of the cream jug but it turns out not to have been in the best interests even of the cat.

The worst error of nationalisation was therefore that it united economic monopoly in the same hands as political power. Friedman has long taught that where monopoly is inevitable the choice is between three evils: you can have private monopoly, public monopoly or regulation. We have tried public monopoly and found it sadly wanting. Now in British Telecom and most culpably in British Gas, the Government have fallen for a private national monopoly moderated by a severe regime of regulation. In Professor Carsberg they have found a remarkable regulator, who sees his job as simulating the pressures of a competitive market. If it will not damage the professor to say so, I know him and like him well and I have the highest regard for his qualities of both intellect and courage, which he will need. However, I do not think he would mind my saying that I have an even higher respect for the impersonal forces of a competitive market wherever it can be activated. The more competition we can mobilise, the more we can rely on general laws and the less on complex regulation which must test the power even of Professor Carsberg.

Thus I come from a different route to support the noble Lord, Lord Ezra, in his call for more competition in future acts of denationalisation. In electricity and water where competition in local distribution is ruled out, we must still endeavour to break up the monopoly of supply. I was disappointed that the noble Lord did not give a lead in calling for the denationalisation of coal, which was left to the noble Lord, Lord Bruce-Gardyne. The National Coal Board, after all, was always the most contrived and artificial of all monopolies, where competition could and still can bring the largest gains to consumers, employees, taxpayers and overburdened politicians.

That case was powerfully argued in a CPS paper by Professor Colin Robinson and Allen Sykes, a formidable academic and a long-experienced practical businessman. They have both now produced an even more remarkable paper which is entitled *Current Choices*. In this paper they discuss six options of which only two would offer the benefits of genuine competition in both generation and regional distribution. Their conclusion, with which I fully agree, is that all the monopoly expedients would be worse than leaving things exactly as they are, because if we left them exactly as they are at least it would leave open the competitive option for the future.

What I should like to say with some impudence from the Cross-Benches is that I, and I believe some others, expect rather more from the present Secretary of State than from his predecessor. But he has been served notice by many speakers that if he thinks of any repetition of monopoly-mongering on the model of British Gas he will not only bring his party's nationalisation programme into difficulty; he will bring it into final disrepute.

THE BEAUTIFUL SIMPLICITY OF REPEAL

31 January 1990

My Lords, I am delighted to follow my old friend the noble Lord, Lord Grimond, and I specially commend the Social and Liberal Democrats for fielding a second speaker, the noble Earl, Lord Russell, whom I always enjoy hearing. I can say with total honesty that I agree with all three speakers and shall largely go over the same ground, perhaps carrying their criticisms a little further.

I thank my noble and learned friend Lord Simon of Glaisdale not only for raising this neglected question but also for expressing it so briefly: to ask whether the Government, 'will reduce the quantity and improve the quality of legislation'. He could teach the parliamentary draftsmen a thing or two about concision.

This recalls a debate in December 1982 on a three-pronged Motion by the noble Lord, Lord Renton, calling attention to the volume of legislation, to the desirability of some repeal, and to the same need to improve the quality of legislation. At that time the number of public general Acts in force was above 3,000, with 13,000 statutory instruments. As we have heard, after 10 years of Tory administrations solemnly pledged to reducing the burden of government, we have seen no relief from this cascade of legislation. Every year the statute book becomes more bloated.

As an earlier convert than Mr Gorbachev to the self-correcting possibilities of a competitive market economy, I acknowledge an indispensable role for a strong legal framework. We need laws to define property rights, to enforce contracts, to maintain competition and to support people who are unable to take care of themselves in the market place. But the first indispensable condition for a free society is a rule of law that is understandable, predictable and stable, and all three desiderata are mocked by continued legislative incontinence. The pressure on parliamentary draftsmen aggravates their apparently natural tendency towards prolixity and undue complexity. The multiplication and constant amendment of statutes bring the aims of simplicity, certainty and stability into contempt.

As an economist, I would add that this hyperactivity of our legislators imposes massive costs not only in devising and enforcing so many laws but in the uncounted charges for compliance by the victims. It seems to me that we have at once trivialised the majestic business of lawmaking and magnified the burden of administration in our over-governed economy. As others have said, it is especially disappointing that there has been no perceptible improvement since the notable report of the 1975 Renton Committee on ways of 'achieving greater simplicity and clarity in statute law'.

As a layman I would normally hesitate to voice doubts about the clarity of so many Bills that come before this House. I am, however, emboldened by Appendix B of the Renton Report which illustrates the mumbo-jumbo that passes for the law of the land. It offers eight densely packed pages listing extracts from important statutes, with detailed and devastating comments by leading legal luminaries who frequently confess total incomprehension of their meaning.

On page 28 of the Renton Report, the committee offers a classic example

from the National Insurance Act 1946, brought to its attention by none other
than my noble and learned friend Lord Simon. It reads:

> For the purpose of this part of the schedule a person over pensionable age, not being
> an insured person, shall be treated as an employed person if he would be an insured
> person were he under pensionable age and would be an employed person were he
> an insured person.

As the report observes, if eminent judges find the law difficult to grasp, 'how
can the layman be expected to fare?'. The report added: 'The Statute Book
might sometimes as well be written in a foreign language for all the help the
citizen may expect to obtain as to his rights and duties under the law'.

In the 1982 debate I ventured to refer to the seminal trilogy of Professor
Hayek published in the 1970s as *Law, Legislation and Liberty*. At the centre is
this Nobel Laureate's distinction between law, as the evolution of general rules
of just conduct, and legislation as the often arbitrary edicts of governments
vested with transient authority to impose their will or even their whims with
the full force of civil or criminal sanctions.

From Chapter IX of the Renton Report I gather that Hayek's approach is
closer to the European tradition of legislating principles of wide application
and practising restraint in the proliferation of detailed rules, with large gains
in simplicity and clarity. I was certainly struck with the force of the Renton
Committee's recommendation in favour of this less detailed style, leaving
judges to give effect to such principles in the light of well-established prece-
dents.

In conclusion, I have two further helpful suggestions. The first is to
commend the beautiful simplicity of repeal as a partial remedy for what might
be called indiscriminate legislative pollution. We must of course be more
selective than recent legislators. Indeed the non-party repeal group some years
ago set a good example with a one-clause Private Member's Bill which helped
to prod Her Majesty's Government to repeal a mouldering pile of obsolete and
obstructive statutes on truck so as to enable wages to be paid more safely and
economically by cheque and credit transfer.

Strong candidates for similar summary treatment, in my view, might be the
Trade Disputes Act 1906, the ragbag of Acts specifying when shops may open
and what goods and services they may sell, and large chunks of the proliferat-
ing laws on planning, equal opportunities and race relations, where broad principles might suffice to guide judges in deciding the equity of conflicting
claims.

My second suggestion offered for further reflection is that we could
dispense with many complex statutes specifying exactly how government
should provide national and local services if we relied instead on simple laws

that laid a general duty on Ministers and statutory authorities and left them free to put provision out to competitive tender and to contract with specialist suppliers. There is mounting evidence that in this way local government services can be more adequately and economically provided, with additional gains in transparency and accountability. A further bonus would be a long overdue step towards the objective of my noble and learned friend of reducing the quantity and improving the quality of legislation.

MAASTRICHT AND THE MADNESS OF BRUSSELS

18 December 1991

My Lords, I regret to say that nothing I have heard in the three eloquent opening speeches alters my Cross Bench view that it is easier to vote against the amendments than to support the Government's claim to have secured all their negotiating objectives.

I ungrudgingly congratulate the Prime Minister on a doughty fight for damage limitation in the teeth of a threatened mugging, if not a gang rape. However, even without seeing the final details, it is quite clear that further damage has been suffered from both the political and monetary treaties.

I shall stick to the monetary principles which I best understand. I do not want to dwell on the folly of monetary union, which, in company with other leading students, I regard as unnecessary, undesirable, uncertain of outcome and unlikely to be established. The latest verdict delivered by Harvard professor Martin Feldstein, President of the National Bureau of Economic Research, was that: 'An artificially contrived European Monetary Union would almost certainly increase the average level of unemployment over time'.

Turning to the revised treaty on political union, it is plain that most extensions of what is called the Commission's competence – which I prefer to call the Commission's incompetence – fly in the face of the economic requirements of a single market. Free trade calls for the elimination of subsidies and the removal of restrictions, not the imposition of fresh regulations disguised as harmonisation or, most deviously, as the 'social dimension'. My overriding concern continues to be that extensive politicisation will weaken the single market, which for me is the jewel in the European crown. The Social Charter may have been fought off for the moment but it will return again and again to haunt us.

I believe that the Prime Minister deserves special congratulations for withstanding a good deal of bullying and bluster from Monsieur Delors and Herr Kohl. Like union-programmed parrots, they keep repeating a wholly bogus claim. They say that, since the single market gives capitalists the benefit of increased efficiency, it is only fair to give employees the protection of the Social Charter. There is nothing in that. How can producers alone be said to benefit from the enlarged market when keener competition will compel them to minimise costs and prices or go out of business? The logic of free trade is not to make life easier for producers, whether capitalists or workers. Rather, free trade compels producers to serve the wider interest of consumers. And who are the consumers that benefit? Why, none other than the great body of workers and their families. I am tempted to add, 'QED'.

The second argument for the Social Charter is that minimum wages and uniform conditions of work are necessary for what is called a 'level playing field'. There is nothing in it. The big idea is to prevent what union spokesmen call 'social dumping', which simply means competition from lower cost production.

Any analysis of international trade must start from differences in comparative costs of production between countries in differing locations, with differing natural or acquired endowments, and at differing stages of development. Wherever labour is abundant in relation to capital or raw materials, it will command a lower wage. The boon of a dynamic free market is that it progressively increases demand for cheap labour, thereby reducing its comparative abundance and raising its market price.

Nor can all that be dismissed as mere theory or, worse still, shopkeeper economics. History confirms the benevolence of competition in action. I recall trade union leaders in my youth denouncing 'unfair' competition from Hong Kong and Japanese workers who were said to be paid in handfuls of rice. The predictable socialist clamour was for protection to prevent low-wage foreign labour from undercutting our civilised standards. As your Lordships may have noticed, without any nonsense about social charters but through the magic of imperfect international trade, wages and working conditions in Hong Kong, Japan and other Asian oases of private enterprise have now caught up or over-taken those in many European countries.

That experience leads on to the third spurious argument for a European Social Charter. It is surely transparent special pleading for trade union leaders and their Labour apologists to claim that if Germany can prosper so wondrously with high social protection, it cannot be bad for the rest of us. There is nothing in that. It is a vulgar error much practised by a reincarnated Monsieur Kinnock in another place. It puts the cart of bigger benefits before the workhorse of higher production. By an extension of such logic, sufficient cosseting of African labourers would enable them all to drive around in Daimlers.

Even today's occupants of the Liberal Democrat Benches might agree that the marvellous spread of prosperity since the war has come from opening up national markets to the competition of international trade and investment. Why have China, India, Africa, the former USSR and much of South America lagged behind? They lagged behind largely because their myopic leaders pursued short-term, national protectionism inspired by the same narrow, collectivist cult that now obsesses the ruling political elite in Europe.

In conclusion, we should ponder deeply what kind of madness impels people in Brussels who prattle earnestly in nine languages about subsidiarity, even to contemplate keeping our morning paperboys tucked up in bed at the edict of the Brussels bureaucrats. How can politicians, who choose to work 12 hours a day, six or seven days a week, have the gall to try enforcing on their constituents a maximum 48-hour week? I am prompted to say that it would be much better for the rest of us if politicians throughout Europe were restricted to a 48-hour month. Is it not a precious part of the free society that all of us should choose for ourselves the mix of income and leisure that we prefer?

Whatever our doubts on the Maastricht compromise, let us at least vote down these shady amendments by Europhiliacs who would barter even more of our precious personal freedoms for a place at the Napoleonic court of that dreadful, dreaming, dotty Jacques Delors.

SNARES AND DELUSIONS OF SOCIALISM

19 May 1993

My Lords, I also congratulate the noble Lord, Lord Bruce of Donington, on his unusually restrained and statesmanlike opening to the debate, which I fear I cannot hope to emulate. He certainly produced a Motion that we can all accept, even those of us on the Cross-Benches. After all, he does not state in the Motion that he 'recommends' but only that he 'calls attention' to the case. He calls attention to 'the case' for his panacea, not to 'a strong' or an 'irresistible' case.

If he had dared to use the words 'urge the case' in the Motion, he would have had to move for rather more than Papers. I would have thought it prudent at least to move for help or to move, like the noble Lord, Lord Healey, in 1975, for an early invitation to the IMF [International Monetary Fund]. We should be grateful to the noble Lord because he has raised an intriguing question which no one, apart from Fidel Castro and some ageing Chinese communists, has mentioned recently.

Growing up as a young man in High Cross, Tottenham, I was not unmoved by the strength of the emotional case for socialism. I was never at all troubled by what is called inequality. I have resolved that the reason is that I could look around me and see within the working classes wide inequalities. I could detect that those frequently sprang from differential habits, training, perseverance and even sobriety – what economists call differential contributions to the national product justifying differing rewards.

However, like most people I was then and am still moved by poverty. I once tried unsuccessfully to persuade Lady Gaitskell that my heart was in the right place, which was left of centre. The trouble was that, having gone to Cambridge just before the Keynesian iron curtain came down, I had the idea that on important matters my head might frequently overrule my heart. On poverty both head and heart cry out for a better way than the present all-party socialist method of indiscriminate subsidies to ensure a decent minimum for people who cannot help themselves in my own preferred market economy.

I look forward to hearing the noble Lord, Lord Plant, but unfortunately there is no time to do justice to the great philosophical issues. With due apologies for appearing dogmatic, I offer my view, for what it is worth, that both in theory and especially in practice the apparent delights of socialism – which Lord Robbins used to call the 'mystic joys of tribal unity' – are but a snare and a delusion.

I shall not rehearse the superior case for the market on grounds of incentives to efficiency, technical progress and wealth creation to resolve problems of poverty, and so on. Instead, I shall reject socialism in four minutes flat by reference to the single issue of individual liberty.

I found it interesting that one of the great advocates of socialism, Professor Richard Titmuss, always cast his mind back to the example of the war and urged that we should wear the socialist badge as 'a badge of citizenship'. Even liberals as far gone as myself accept that some form of socialism is indispensable in a state of siege. Indeed, in wartime socialism is inescapable. It does not function very well, but it cannot be avoided. However, it involves – as Professor Titmuss seemed to be unaware – severe suppression of individual freedom of movement, of spending, of consumption, choice of job and the rest.

Briefly recalling another socialist saint – Aneurin Bevan – I would point out that socialism is concerned not only with deciding priorities but above all with imposing priorities. The dilemma is this. First, the waging of war offers a single overriding criterion by reference to which priorities can be set. Secondly, war brings a shared sense of danger which makes central enforcement more tolerable. Except to serious social engineers, neither of those two crucial simplicities applies in the diverse world of a free society in time of peace.

Despite all equivocations, democratic socialism means a continuing, progressive extension of coercive government far beyond the necessary role of supplying what economists debate as public goods. Democratic socialism means the pervasive spread of politicisation to more and more aspects of our daily lives. I recall a book by a former Labour Minister, now I believe sheltering somewhere in this place, entitled *Politics is for People*. To that I say

'Bah!' and 'Humbug!'. Normal people have been fed up with politics and politicians for years. My colleague Arthur Seldon quipped that a truer title would have been: 'Politics is for political people'.

Politicians are, of course, personally often very nice. We would all agree that they are even better when they reach the eminence of the Back-Benches in this House. Mixed up with vanity, histrionics, zest for power or the illusion of power, they mostly have good intentions. Socialism is the means of converting those golden intentions into dross. We have seen that the progressive aggrandisement of the state has been a total failure. The further it has been pushed in Eastern Europe and throughout Africa the greater the failure and the less individual liberty there is left.

Nevertheless, I am grateful to the noble Lord, Lord Bruce, for drawing our attention to the case for democratic socialism. He appears in rude health, but I suggest that he should take up a less strenuous and taxing hobby than advocating socialism. I suggest that instead of withdrawing his call for Papers he asks for a copy of Adam Smith's *Wealth of Nations*.

MAASTRICHT: A LEAP TOWARDS FEDERALISM

7 June 1993

My Lords, much as I respect the noble Lord, Lord Jenkins of Hillhead, and much as I have admired my old friend the noble and learned Lord, Lord Howe, as the best non-resigning Chancellor since the war, I heavily discount their judgment on Maastricht for reasons to which I shall turn in a moment.

We all agree, from our different standpoints, that there has been a good deal of confusion over Maastricht. The latest sample of deception or, to be more kind, self-deception, is a somewhat contradictory circular from the CBI which was distributed among your Lordships on a strictly selective basis – presumably to those thought to be the most gullible. At first sight it seemed to be on the side of the angels. Thus it offers, 'A Europe of independent nation states'. It goes on to abominate Brussels for 'pettifogging regulations', 'arrogance', 'dirigiste philosophy', 'Napoleonic edicts' and 'protectionism'. Indeed, the author mocked Brussels as, 'ideally liking to organise European industry as well as they have organised European agriculture'.

I turn to my reasons for discounting the judgment of the noble and learned Lord, Lord Howe, and the noble Lord, Lord Jenkins. It is that from their lofty European perches they have totally failed at any time to sound warnings to Brussels against the excesses that the CBI mentioned. They have left it to my old friend, the noble Baroness, Lady Thatcher, to incur the odium of saying what the CBI and others have not dared to say.

The CBI criticisms sound like a promising preface to my more extensive charge sheet against the European virus of Delorean delirium. We must ask how the CBI reconcile such a damning indictment with support for the Maastricht Treaty on European Union. By the old trick of the sly *non sequitur,* all that Brussels mischief, they plead, 'is no reason to abandon the Single Market as the so-called Euro-sceptics would wish'.

The formidable coalition against Maastricht no doubt includes a minority who are unenthusiastic about the market. But I must repeat the pronouncements of others and tell them and the CBI that if we take courage to block the treaty, as the French nearly did in the referendum that they were privileged to have, the European Economic Community would still stand as the guardian of the single market. Indeed, as an economist my decisive reason for opposing Maastricht is that it is not merely a distraction from completing the market; it is in head-on conflict with that great project.

If professional economists are agreed on anything it is that free trade is the nearest we have to a panacea for poverty, not only in Europe but throughout the world. However, many speakers have argued that economics is not enough and that a political dimension is necessary. They persist in asking the vulgar question, 'What is the alternative?'. I am pleased to say that the noble Lord, Lord Cockfield, who was one of the principal authors of the 1992 project, gave us the answer. He said that he would have preferred us to complete the economic agenda and leave the political agenda to a later generation. That was his preference and it shall be my policy from this moment forth.

Free trade is much more than the high road to economic efficiency and national prosperity. In the wider tradition of political economy it offers our best prospect of peace and guarantee of liberty. Of course, the central objective of the founding fathers in Europe was political: so to unite the warring nations as to make impossible a repetition of the European civil wars of 1870, 1914 and 1939. But their chosen chief method was economic. It was to supplant the national socialism of the Kaiser and Hitler by the liberalism of Adam Smith and Cobden. In place of protectionism and autarchy, which Smith denounced as mercantilism, the founders sought integration into a single market through the removal of tariff and non-tariff barriers to free movement of goods, services and capital. The common market was a peace treaty based on economic disarmament which rendered impossible the building up of war-like industry.

I may be forgiven for once again quoting the neglected wisdom of Adam Smith. In the great work, *The Wealth of Nations,* he said, 'Were all nations to follow the liberal system of free exportation and free importation, the different states into which a great continent was divided would so far resemble the different provinces of a great empire'. In short, he was saying that interdependence through trade is a means of spontaneous unification; if you will, a form of natural federalism or, as the absent noble Lord, Lord Joseph, would prefer, confederalism.

It was on that precise analysis that the Treaty of Rome promised the best of both worlds – the economic and the political. Under free trade we would enjoy full economic integration as though part of a single empire. At the same time we would preserve the advantages of political decentralisation under otherwise independent governments. In short, we do not need political union, much less Delors's new European empire. Through free trade we could have the invisible empire of Adam Smith. A large bonus is that trade unites people where politics divides them.

Inevitably, so long as each member of the EEC could veto agreements, progress in the removal of barriers was slow and invariably blocked by vested national interests. It was to overcome such obstruction that the noble Baroness, Lady Thatcher, assented to the Single European Act in 1986 which extended majority voting. The lawyers sold the Single European Act as a necessary but limited concession of sovereignty for the specific purpose of completing the market by the end of 1992.

It was the unprincipled exploitation of that measure by the Commission, for purposes far removed from the single market, that first alerted me to worse dangers ahead. In the name of harmonisation, health and welfare, environment, social policy and other innocent-sounding purposes, majority voting has been perverted to overrule national self-government in the interest of creeping federalism, to which the CBI object but which Maastricht would accelerate to a gallop.

We have seen the pressure to impose the 48-hour week, the threat to ban newspaper delivery boys, the imposition of TV quotas, censorship of cigarette advertising, equalisation of taxes and unrelenting pressure for minimum wages, uniform conditions of work and other nonsense. It displays an abysmal failure to understand that free trade essentially depends on differing costs and circumstances – what economists call comparative advantages. As the contrasting fortunes of Hong Kong and Africa so vividly demonstrate, trade not aid is the way to economic progress. The level playing field of M. Delors is the crudest example of flat earth economics.

The case against Maastricht is that it would carry this Euro-phoria further and wider. Majority voting would be extended – and no doubt again manipulated – to include economic policy guidelines, commercial policy, consumer protection, common standards on road, rail, telecommunications, and much else. Increased taxation and spending on a cohesion fund is presented as uplifting poorer members but in practice aims to ingratiate them to M. Delors and his apparatchiks. Above all, enforcement of convergence under Stage 2 of monetary union – plus unceasing pressure to railroad us into Stage 3 – threatens to reduce Britain's economic self-government to what the noble Lord, Lord Tebbit, once called the power of a rate-capped local authority.

Labour may say that government from Brussels could not be worse than the regime we have suffered lately under Mr Major. But Liberals might dimly recall the cautionary adage that self-government is preferable to good government. And Tories might share my doubts whether M. Mitterrand, Herr Kohl and other spent European forces would really provide good government.

After the soft shoe shuffle of the Single European Act, Maastricht threatens a leap towards full federalism with one money, one chancellor and, in the end, one economic policy. As the noble Lord, Lord Carrington, and others have hinted, it is in fact even more out of touch with European sentiment today than when the Euro-elite dreamed it up two or three years ago. It is not wanted and I have absolutely no doubt whatever that it will not work. But in the process of over-toppling, it would almost certainly stop progress towards completing the market and bring present gains into jeopardy.

My Lords, for what purpose? Is it to appease the most extreme federalists in France, Belgium, Germany, Italy and Spain – all with their own differing national anxieties, ailments and appetites to be relieved or gratified by ever more centralisation, subsidies, harmonisation and disguised protectionism? I was alarmed when the noble and learned Lord, Lord Howe, warned us against strong expressions of the kind I am now uttering because it might 'try the patience of our European partners'. I shall try their patience again. Or are we to be mesmerised and intimidated by slogans? Must we keep on the Euro-express despite the fact that it is speeding towards the buffers? Must we be at the heart of Europe at any price, as though you would help people struggling in quicksands by jumping into the middle? Or is Britain's best contribution once again to stand her ground, and with wise counsel on completing the single market, seek to save our European friends from this collectivist folly?

MONETARY UNION IS A SPOOF

23 June 1993

It is always helpful to have such magisterial pronouncements from the noble Lord, Lord Cockfield, whose experience and knowledge of these matters command attention. However, his words do not carry us much further.

I am interested in Amendment No. 17 which the noble Lord, Lord Tebbit, suggested was a probing amendment. There have been some observations from rival economists and other parties and it is difficult to know where to begin. With regard to the matter which the noble Lord, Lord Cockfield, has just mentioned, with a sleight of hand that reminds me of my early interest in conjuring, he says: 'Of course, this is not carrying us any further forward. It is dotting 'i's and crossing 't's because it is in the Stuttgart agreement that we should work towards monetary and political union. The previous documents have implied continued progress towards that end'.

I recall at Second Reading an impressive speech by the noble Lord, Lord Carrington, who took my breath away by commending the treaty on the basis that it probably would not happen; circumstances have changed; this is a whole world away from 1989–90, and so we must not worry too much. I believe that this is one of the great difficulties with which we wrestle. It divides good men on opposite sides of the argument. There is a complete evasiveness, slipperiness and I would even say slyness, in some sense, in presenting broad statements to which everyone can agree about political union, incorporating them in declarations and so on, and saying that we have no details; and then coming back later with the details. So we find that we have a *fait accompli*. We now have a full-blown detailed monetary union proposal.

Despite what the noble Lord, Lord Desai, said, I honestly believe that the monetary union is a spoof. I truly believe that. Moreover, I believe that it is on the same level as the proposition put forward by George Bernard Shaw to invent a new language like Esperanto. One can argue along the lines of 'Wouldn't it be nice to have a new language? Let's invent a new language. We can all speak it to one another and it will overcome so many difficulties'.

We say here that we need a new currency. If we had one single currency for the area which was a stable currency and everyone joined it, would it not be helpful in promoting trade and maintaining stability? That begs all the questions. You cannot just create a currency in that way. The noble Lord mentioned the gold standard. That emerged. It was part of what Hayek would refer to as 'spontaneous evolution'. The Tory Party used to believe in spontaneous evolution. It now believes in planning, constructionism and detailed intervention in the economy – all that in the wake of Citizen Delors. I am being very correct now. We are citizens and, if we are to be citizens of Europe, we are entitled to speak frankly to one another.

We admire the stability of the deutschmark and acknowledge that it is due to the Bundesbank which has a degree of independence, though it is not totally independent, in operating a stable monetary policy. The conundrum with which I am faced is that first of all there is no guarantee whatever that the future ecu will be as stable as the deutschmark has been. Indeed part of the argument in France and Italy is that the deutschmark has been run too severely and with too little regard to unemployment and other considerations apart from price stability. The implication is that when we all share in running the currency, we shall be able to abate the obsession with price stability. I do not at all accept the blind faith of the noble Lord, Lord Ezra, that if we are to have new money, somehow it will emerge and will produce that stability.

I put this proposition to the Committee. If European countries pursue stable monetary policies on the model of Germany, an ERM [Exchange Rate

Mechanism] or an EMU [European Monetary Union] would not be needed. If stable monetary policies are not pursued, an ERM or an EMU will not work. There is no way round that. To maintain stability you must have regard to monetary and fiscal policy. It could be done outside the ERM.

As many noble Lords were at the uplifting memorial service to the late Lord Ridley, I looked up his last words in this House which were in February, on a Motion moved by the noble Lord, Lord Pearson. Those last words, which had a ring of defiance, were: 'Surely it is time to recognise that it is the single market which matters and that the single currency does not'. [*Official Report*, 17/2/93; col. 1177.] Nick, as we all called him, was not a fool. There is no inconsistency in that proposition. In a single market you can have free trade between areas without any monetary connections whatever. The North Atlantic Free Trade Area has not anticipated changing from floating currencies between America, Canada and Mexico.

I have two main anxieties to which I want the Government to attend. It may be tempting for the noble Lord, Lord Desai, to say that people who oppose monetary union are closet devaluationists; they want to keep taking the soft option and do not want the discipline of fixed exchange rates. I am saying that if you have a monetary policy, you can do it yourself. You do not need a piece of steel inserted into your backbone, which will have other painful consequences.

The point is that economists have been debating for the past 20 or 30 years – we must not enter into an economist's argument – the optimum currency unit. They have been debating what circumstances would enable various countries to join into a single monetary unit. To go back to our own experience, throughout the whole of this century we have had a single currency in the United Kingdom. One result was that monetary policies that were appropriate to the South of England left Scotland, parts of the North-East, the North-West and the Midlands behind and we had to have a development policy. The development policy was in some way to accommodate different regions to the discipline of the single currency that involved them in economic distress.

Areas are dependent upon different sorts of industry. They have different structures and there are immobilities. An alternative to a single money between England, Scotland and Wales would be to have three currencies. We did not have three currencies but we introduced a payroll tax to try to reduce labour costs in some areas because the national wage level bore harshly upon those areas with declining industries.

The 12 economies have wholly different structures with wholly different levels of development. They are progressing, in economic terms, at different rates and are affected quite differently by external shocks – for instance, oil or a new imposition from outside. Several Members of the Committee talked of convergence over two or three years. But over a period of 10 or 20 years, and a cycle or two, one has quite different circumstances. Therefore, to incorporate monetary union into the treaty is bad for Europe. If we believe that it is bad for us, why do we allow it to go forward under the treaty and the institutions of Europe and try to say that we are opting out? That is my question. If it is bad for us, is it good for Europe?

My second question is perhaps more manageable. It arises from a legal document by someone with the same name as the noble Lord, Lord Howe, but who, in my view, holds rather better, more congenial opinions. Martin Howe wrote a paper, *Monetary policy after Maastricht: How much independence will Britain possess?*. To sum it up he says that even without our opt-out we are still caught up in Stages 1 and 2. We are caught up by the general expression of support for monetary union, going back to the earlier documents and proclamations. He says that there is a possibility that we will find ourselves brought up before the European Court of Justice.

Martin Howe is a lawyer. He is not as distinguished as the noble Lord, Lord Howe. However, he is a barrister and specialised in this kind of issue. In his paper he said that the European Court could find that we were failing to fulfil our obligations to bring our economy into convergence in readiness to join the ERM, although we are not going on further into the EMU. He said,

> that the ECJ would find that a policy of indefinitely remaining outside the ERM on the part of the UK is a clear breach of the Treaty. First, in such circumstances, the United Kingdom would be avowedly pursuing an exchange rate policy based on its own national interest rather than treating it as a matter of 'common interest' as required by Article 109m. Secondly, the UK would be failing to adopt a 'multiannual programme' intended to ensure 'economic and monetary convergence': moving towards and when possible adopting a fixed ERM parity is one element of 'convergence' since it forms one of the convergence criteria set out in Article 109j(1).
>
> Thirdly, and most fundamentally, the whole structure of Stages 1 and 2 monetary union presupposes that member states are striving towards achievement of the convergence criteria, including more tightly aligned parities. Although the UK has opted out of the prime objective of 'irrevocably fixed' parities in Article 3a(2), it has not opted out of the lesser objective of exchange rate convergence. It is an important aspect of the single market as envisaged by the Treaty that there should be currency stability as far as possible across the whole market, and that the UK's conduct would be considered by the ECJ as imperilling the attainment of that central Treaty objective.

Perhaps the Minister could say what view he takes. Was the opt-out to avoid trouble now at the risk of piling it up for the future? Was it to be agreeable, to be *communautaire*? Was it to obtain the opt-out and then shield behind it? Have we thought out what may lie ahead if we sign the treaty with those clauses included and then find ourselves faced with the European Court of Justice? How seriously does the Minister entertain that possibility?

SMOKING BANS AND FREEDOM

1 December 1993

My Lords, after the devastating indictment of the Government by my old friend, the noble Lord, Lord Aldington, on the Tory Benches, there really is no necessity for further contributions to this debate on the Question. But since when has necessity been a pretext for speeches in this House? I do not want to make heavy weather of this matter, but I have a number of interests to declare. I am a pipe smoker of long standing, though less so than the 60 years of the noble Lord, Lord Aldington, by a decade or so. I am a train traveller – if it cannot be absolutely avoided. I am chairman of FOREST, which is the Freedom Organisation for the Right to Enjoy Smoking Tobacco. It does not promote smoking; it defends the right for citizens to enjoy a pipe or cigarettes.

I have been a strong and lifelong supporter of individual freedom. For me the hallmark of a free society is that it permits adult citizens the widest conceivable choice attainable without significantly subtracting from the like freedom of others. The key is that we do not simply uphold popular freedoms. Indeed the acid test of a democratic temper is to defend other people's choices of which we actively disapprove; that is to say, tolerance. That is not particularly virtuous because the unwritten contract of a free society is a tolerance of other people's strange preferences for such things as male cosmetics, foxhunting, jogging, eating fish and chips or black pudding, in exchange for their tolerance of our eccentricities.

Democracy does not mean permitting freedoms practised by 51 per cent of the population. A civilised society is marked by respect – if possible, courteous and good natured – for minority tastes and activities of which we may actively disapprove. Whatever its demerits, the great merit of the competitive market is that it caters sensitively for individuals and consumer idiosyncrasies. Even small minorities favouring fancy waistcoats, pink socks or other familiar Front Bench government styles can have their particular tastes served in a free market. Majority agreement is not required. There is a tendency for small minorities to have their way. Because in nationalised industries that kind of preference is not possible, all the nationalising Acts made provision for consumer representatives to have their voice heard on consultative committees.

The chairman of the British Railways Board, defending the ban, wrote a letter to say that BR liaise carefully with statutorily constituted representatives of transport users, and so forth. There has been much talk of getting approval in that way. This morning I ventured to 'phone the Transport Users Consultative Committee for Southern England and spoke to the acting Secretary, Mr Edwards. He told me that on 8th December last year the committee received an announcement from British Rail to the effect that all smoking carriages were being withdrawn from Kent and East Sussex. Shortly thereafter the committee was told that smoking facilities had been withdrawn elsewhere on the SouthEast network.

There was no question of consultation. There was absolutely no effort to ascertain the views of the consultative committee, much less to take notice of the views of the consumers themselves. As the noble Lord, Lord Aldington, said, the survey that British Rail conducted last year, in the autumn of 1992, showed that 61 per cent of passengers on non-banned stations thought that the provision for smoking should either be kept the same or increased.

I turn to British Rail's own charter, which is a rather less pretentious document than the Government's to which I shall come in a moment. British Rail say that it undertakes to: 'ask your views and publish the results'. They asked views through the survey but they did not publish the results. There had to be a Question in this House from the noble Lord, Lord Aldington, before British Rail agreed to put a copy of the findings in the Library. Of course the charter does not say, 'We will take notice of your views'. It says, 'We will ask your views and publish the results if compelled to do so; but we will not necessarily feel obliged to proceed any further'.

That is all small beer. We come to this great document that I hold in my trembling hand the – *Citizen's Charter* – and see what the Government have to say to give comfort to smokers and others. It says,

> The Citizen's Charter applies to all public services. These include government departments and agencies, nationalised industries,

and so forth. The key principles will include,

> Evidence that the views of those who use the services have been taken into account in setting standards.

It goes on to say,

> The task is an ambitious one. We are determined to make it happen as quickly as possible . . . We will be taking immediate steps to encourage all public services to adopt Charter principles and to apply them to their own operations.

We move on to transport where it has a section acknowledging that,

> British Rail's performance too often falls short of what the public has a right to expect.

It says we expect,

> simple and effective complaints procedures; a straightforward system of redress in cases where the level of service is unacceptable . . . BR will seek to make its service to the public friendlier and more personal.

We have heard that before. We move on to the penultimate section and I shall not bother your Lordships beyond that. The heading is 'Prisons'. It states,

> All citizens are entitled to consideration, including those who offend against the law. The Mission Statement of the Prison Service undertakes to look after all prisoners with humanity.

The deduction I draw from this document is that it is not so much that smokers are second-class citizens. So far as the charter is concerned, smokers on trains are non-citizens.

SUNDAY TRADING AND COMPETITIVE MARKETS

8 March 1994

My Lords, I am delighted with the prospect that this may prove to be the final joust before we pull down the shutters altogether on this long-running shops saga. I am sorry that the noble Baroness, Lady Jay, is not in her place. I particularly wanted to pay her a tribute for her role in bringing about this happy development, though I am not sure whether her function was in the nature of maternity or midwifery.

For my money, the true mother – indeed I would almost say grandmother – of this great breakthrough since 1950 was the noble Baroness, Lady Trumpington. After all, it was her modest Motion in 1981 on the need to amend the Shops Act that initiated me into the mysteries of the schedules with their forbidden fruit. It was the reception in your Lordships' House that emboldened her, with the support of the Repeal Group, to produce a Private Member's repeal Bill. I brought it here today to display it in all its simplicity – a one-page, two-clause Bill which passed through this House on a free vote in all its stages in April 1982. The Chief Whip, the Lord Chancellor, the Leader of the House and all kinds of other Tory swells trooped through the Lobby of their own accord to support repeal.

Though the repeal was not pursued at that time, it was that event which led to the setting up of the Auld Committee in 1983–84, which recommended outright repeal with protection for existing employees who did not wish to become entangled in Sunday working. Following that report the Government courageously brought forth their own Bill for deregulation with protection for existing staff, which passed through this House in all its stages with minor amendment, despite spirited opposition by the Bishops' Bench and the noble Lord, Lord Graham of Edmonton. But it was overturned in the Commons on Second Reading in April 1986.

We now have the great British compromise, which I regard as splitting the difference between good sense and nonsense. I regard the compromise as being unnecessary because today, with some slight exaggeration, everybody admits the anomalies; everybody acknowledges the impossibility of enforcement, and everybody has witnessed the wide consumer demand for family shopping on a Sunday. Today even USDAW [Union of Shop, Distributive and Allied Workers] is prepared to admit the truth, which it previously denied, that a return to the 1950 Act would severely reduce jobs.

What is the reason for this fantastic conversion in the past five or 10 years? Obviously the reason is good empiricism; it is the experience that we have had with the virtual abandonment of enforcement over recent years. We have found that *de facto* deregulation is acceptable. We have found that freedom actually works. Yet in place of the straightforward, one page, two clause Bill of the noble Baroness, Lady Trumpington, we now have 20 tortuous pages of tortured lawyers' English. I thought of the old couplet:

O what a tangled web we weave,
When first we practise to deceive.

When we read through the Bill we find three pages on the meaning and treatment of large shops. We find three more pages of supplementary provisions, including forced entry by inspectors, and all the rest of it. We then find two pages on the certification of members of the Jewish religion. We have a page on the loading and unloading of vehicles. Then, I am afraid, we have eight pages of what I regard as verbiage on the protection of shopworkers who do not wish to work on Sunday. Does anyone suppose that shopworkers or independent retailers would really understand all of that detail? It is a tangled web, but where is the deception? The deception is that all the parliamentary draftsman's gobbledegook is really necessary, when we actually know people are queuing up to work on Sundays and forced working on Sundays is an extremely rare event that has caused very little outcry or difficulty.

I agree with the noble Lord, Lord Elton, that the assurances advertised in the *Sunday Shopper* which the SHRC distributed do not amount to very much. They talk of an 'historic agreement' with the union. They say that employers undertake to continue current premium rates. They say that they: 'will only deviate if there is a significant change in the circumstances in which retail work is rewarded'. They continue: 'Employers recognise that a premium will be required to attract sufficiently high quality employees'.

Why then all this fuss? What we are seeing is that the market will itself make reasonable provision. The employers have put their name to an agreement which is governed by their ability to employ and to pay premium rates. They acknowledge that if circumstances were to change to make that difficult the matter would have to be looked at again.

We must acknowledge that it is inevitably the needs of a competitive market that will ultimately determine both the amount of employment and the premium rates that might be paid. We should not shrink from the notion of the market deciding, because the market is people. It is those people whom the noble Baroness, Lady O'Cathain, tries to avoid on a Sunday if they have children. She goes elsewhere. Market forces are us going to shops and our friends, neighbours or relatives serving behind the counter at the same time.

I really am distressed that we should run to a 20-page statute with all this fine-sounding, empty nonsense about employee protection. I am not a lawyer, and that is a handicap in some respects, although when I asked two solicitors to explain some part of the schedules that I did not understand, they both withdrew and said that it was not their special subject. I did not try offering them a fee because I did not any longer have confidence in their answers. For my money, as a non-lawyer, I regard the whole of this as bringing the majesty of law into something approaching contempt. Law is defiled and belittled by this kind of free-range writing and scribbling on every feature of shopping that occurs to the parliamentary draftsman's mind.

What is it all for? It is to regulate the right of ordinary people to go about on a Sunday of their choice to buy things from people who wish to sell things to them. There are two quite distinct issues that divide the openers from the closers. The first is the fundamental economic question which I phrase as being the choice between progress or security. It is whether we put flexibility before fixity; whether we put dynamism before stagnation; whether we put the future before the past; whether in fact we support the liberalism of a Conservative Government rather than the conservatism of the Labour and Bishops' Benches. The second question is a political question: whether we trust the people as free-choosing, responsible agents.

In my view the casual coercion still scattered throughout the Bill would be justified only to prevent a major national public evil. The Scottish experience reveals that there is no such justification, and therefore I look forward to joining the noble Lord, Lord McIntosh, and others, with whom I have not normally been seen in the Lobby, in supporting the total deregulation option and, as a fallback, the Government's half-way measure which I still think is a courageous effort by the present Government.

THE CORPORATIST TRADITION IN EUROPE

8 March 1995

My Lords, I fear that I am rather ill-prepared to stem the tide of so far mostly uncritical Euro-enthusiasm. I am bolstered by the fact that further down the list of speakers there will be support coming to my help. We have missed the contribution of the noble Lord, Lord Tebbit.

I say that I am unprepared because I learnt of this debate only this morning. I have just returned from Italy where, some will be shocked to hear, at the invitation of the British Council I have taken part in a debate with an Italian, Professor Comba of Turin, on the issue of free trade and economic co-operation. I hardly dare hope that the remarks I draw from my paper will be as well received here. I was totally astonished. Older people in Italy drawn from the Oxford and Cambridge Society, among other exemplary bodies, acknowledged that Italian enthusiasm for Brussels had hitherto been due to total disillusion with their own political and economic muddles. They said that anything would be better than Rome. Older people in Italy regretted that younger Italians did not share that view. They were much closer to the Thatcher view. They described it as the Berlusconi and Antonio Martino view of the last government.

I was shocked to hear the noble Lord, Lord Thomas, speak about a 'simple customs union' as though it were to be despised as a marginal addition to economic policy. On my argument the Treaty of Rome is based on the central idea of promoting the lasting peace of which we have heard, by replacing economic nationalism with a framework for a competitive common market. That was a central notion of the Treaty of Rome. I shall not provoke hostility by developing the theme that follows from that beyond saying that the case to economists was that in place of protectionism and autarky, which caused so much trouble before the war and which Adam Smith had denounced as mercantilism, the founders of the EC [European Community] principally backed the notion of integration through economic trade and investment by removing tariffs and non-tariff barriers to the free movement of goods, services, capital and people.

When apologetic British spokesmen say that we are isolated or marginalised in Europe and the noble Lord, Lord Ezra, says that if we had been in it earlier we would apparently have refashioned the entire operation to our taste, they ignore the totally different tradition in political economy and economic philosophy on the Continent of Europe from that prevailing in this country. Classical liberalism never won the intellectual ascendancy on the Continent that it achieved in Britain during the 19th century. Apart from a few isolated economists such as Einaudi, Rueff, Erhard, Röpke and a few others, the prevailing philosophy owes much more to the intellectual tradition of Catholic social doctrine. That is closely linked with corporatism, which is a somewhat elusive concept. I argue that corporatism is redolent of the seven Cs, beginning with consensus and conformity, going on to co-operation and centralism, and then collectivism, carve-up and not forgetting corruption, and all the time increasing coercion. That is the corporatist tradition.

The impact of the Catholic social doctrine on the Continent has been reinforced by the way in which proportional representation has led to fragmentation of government support. It has enfeebled governments – and Italy is a classic case – where party *apparatchiks* become very powerful; there is a premium on coalition, compromise and backstage deals between political elites disregarding entirely public opinion and always favouring a consensus which has little merit necessarily to the balance of argument in the case.

In 1971, before the referendum, the Institute of Economic Affairs, in which I must declare an interest, having run it for some 30 years, produced a classic paper with a most important title, *Rome or Brussels?*. It posed a real choice between the liberalism that was inherent in the Treaty of Rome and the burgeoning bureaucracy that was already visible in 1971 in Brussels. Since the 1980s, it has daily become more clear that the bureaucrats of Brussels have triumphed altogether over the Rome liberalisation.

This week, the same institute (without my wise guidance) produced a further paper, which I am allowed to advertise, called *The Centralisation of Western Europe* – not by what the noble Lord, Lord Gilmour, would call a 'Euro-hater' or a 'Euro-hooligan' but by one of the leading German economists, Professor Roland Vaubel. I advise your Lordships to watch Vaubel as a likely entrant in the next 10 or 15 years for a Nobel prize. Vaubel shows that instead of encouraging trade, integration, closer relationships and interrelationships through trade based on mutual recognition, whereby the products and standards that are acceptable within any member country can be exported freely throughout the whole Common Market, the Commission and its *apparatchiks* have exploited the plausible pretext of 'harmonisation' and 'level playing field' to set about flattening and homogenising the very differences in costs and qualities on which a large part of free trade fundamentally depends.

Helped by the Single European Act, which had the aim of completing the market by 1992 – it is still, alas, incomplete – we had the great development of qualified majority voting which was necessary in place of the old veto. However, as a result – an unintended result – there has been a tidal wave of Brussels legislation. According to Vaubel, at the last count there were 24,000 regulations and 1,700 directives. He argues that despite recent talk of 'subsidiarity', they are growing at the rate of 1,500 regulations and 120 directives per year.

What emerges from Vaubel's study, which is a very close and intricate economic analysis of the whole operation, is that there has been a tremendous development of lobbying. He reveals that there are now 3,000 lobby organisations and 10,000 lobbyists in Brussels. He quotes the calculation that 70 per cent of Community legislation and subsidies is concerned with special interest groups, including the common agricultural policy. He explains that lobbyists find it easier to tackle the bureaucrats who enjoy enlarging their bureaux and who are not subject to the same restraint of democratic control as politicians, who can often tell a lobbyist on the make.

The noble Lord, Lord Gilmour, asked what was objectionable about the Social Charter. I probably have the time to answer that question for him. It is perfectly clear that when you introduce free trade in a Europe that has had a history of Colbert restrictionism over the decades you will have a varying impact on different parts of the market. Some countries will fare worse than others and their interests will be badly affected. The only solution to that is to develop a flexible labour market. That is a phrase that the Liberals find rather distasteful, but a flexible labour market has enabled the great countries of the Far East, such as Hong Kong, to adapt to changing opportunities and to shift resources, such as labour and capital, into industries where the prospects are better. Instead of that, the EEC backs the Social Charter. You even hear nominal Liberals like the noble Lord, Lord Ezra, asking what is wrong with it and saying that we should get in there.

For the information of the noble Lord, Lord Gilmour, among the aims of the Social Charter is the imposition of uniform requirements on all aspects of working conditions, including redundancy, maternity leave, pensions, social benefits, hours of work – and ultimately a European minimum wage. The protectionist intent of all that – not protecting standards, but protecting economies against the impact of change and trade from abroad – became clear in 1993 when M. Jacques Delors – happily departed to, I hope, more agreeable activities – launched the bizarre idea of incorporating into the GATT [General Agreement on Tariffs and Trade] negotiations a 'global Social Charter'. The idea was to prevent European standards of living being undermined by what he called 'social dumping' from low-wage Asian competitors. He had not looked closely enough to find that the effect of trade is always to tend to equalise standards of wages upwards, so that in Hong Kong we have seen people who were paid a handful of rice in my youth now enjoying wages and benefits that are at least on a par with the English standards.

Since the noble Lord, Lord Tebbit, has allowed us a little extra time, I must, I am afraid, deal with the question of nationalism, which is constantly being put forward. My argument in conclusion is that for Britain to play its most helpful role in Europe, it must stand by its guns and develop its different vision of Europe. That is a perfectly honourable position, as opposed to being in the middle with constant compromises being struck against the development of the free movement of goods and services and all the rest of it. There is nothing despicable about nationalism. It does not mean narrow chauvinism and the 'trappings of sovereignty'.

*   *   *

Adam Smith, David Hume and those other great men saw international free trade as a way in which independent nation states could co-operate together, pooling such sovereignty as was necessary to remove barriers, but not getting drawn into deep political involvement and engagement with other countries.

RESTRICTIONS ON MEDIA OWNERSHIP

13 February 1996

Lord Harris of High Cross moved Amendment No. 156DA: Page 89, line 19, at beginning insert ('Subject to sub-paragraph (4) below').

The noble Lord said: I propose, with the Committee's indulgence, to speak also to Amendment No. 156GD which is grouped with Amendment No. 156DA. Amendment No. 156GD seeks to insert the following new subsection:

> Sub-paragraphs (1) to (3) shall not apply to prevent any newspaper proprietor controlling a body corporate which holds any licence unless a reference of that newspaper proprietor's control of that licence holder has been made under paragraph 9 below and the Monopolies and Mergers Commission has found that that control operates or may be expected to operate against the public interest.

Some of this argument repeats what we have discussed on previous issues. I was rather disappointed by the Minister's bearing this afternoon. I hope that he will not be off colour for too long. I remind him that in last Thursday's debate – at cols 349 to 350 of *Hansard* – he described his standpoint as deregulatory. There was a splendid purple passage where he urged the importance of stability and consistency in regulation, not least to encourage continued investment. We are expecting billions of pounds to be shovelled into this fast moving industry. We are confronted with a cable, satellite and digital revolution. The Minister talks of stability; but this is a second effort in barely five years of Parliament to regulate such a rapidly changing industry. I look at this complex and, for me, largely incomprehensible Bill and I cannot help wondering what would have happened to the first Industrial Revolution if well-meaning politicians had spun and respun a comparable web of restriction around developments in textiles, coal mining, iron and steel, shipbuilding, canals, railways, roadways and the rest of it.

This group of amendments seeks to remove another 20 per cent arbitrary restriction – this time not as regards the circulation of newspapers but the ownership by a newspaper of a satellite; namely, BSkyB. It is part of the deregulatory feature of this Bill that it would now allow satellite and cable companies to control Channel 3 and Channel 5 licences, which in turn are free to move into satellite broadcasting, as the Minister has explained. That gives a welcome green light to cross-media or cross-sectoral growth so that companies can take advantage of internal and external economies in developing a structure which we cannot at the moment even begin to predict. Yet once again BSkyB is cast as the Cinderella at the feast. It is to be excluded from the general rejoicing. In Schedule 2, in the provisions relating to restrictions on proprietors of newspapers, a new formula is conjured up which deliberately excludes BSkyB from that otherwise welcome liberalising process.

Under that formula a satellite company can control a commercial terrestrial television company, but it may not do so if it is more than 20 per cent owned by a newspaper company with more than 20 per cent of the total national newspaper circulation. It could do so if it was owned by a duff company which does not have a large circulation. News International, alas since taking over the ailing *Sun* and the threatened *Times*, has built up their circulations. News International is guilty of building up a total diversified newspaper circulation in excess of 20 per cent of the national circulation. That is naughty. The mathematical application of the rule concerning 20 per cent control and more than 20 per cent of newspaper circulation succeeds in singling out Sky for punishment.

I argue that both of the 20 per cent rules collapse on close examination. News International owns more than 20 per cent of Sky. Indeed, it owns 40 per cent. However, that 40 per cent does not give News International a controlling interest. There are two reasons for that, which the Minister can verify. First, Stock Exchange rules require that a company is capable of operating independently of any shareholder owning 30 per cent or more of the voting rights. Secondly, the board of BSkyB numbers 18 directors, of whom only five are News International appointees. Therefore, the 20 per cent control by News International is a phantom. It is frightening Ministers needlessly when there are many other things for them to be frightened of.

In the same way the 20 per cent control of national newspaper circulation has already been exposed to a good deal of criticism by the Committee, in particular by the noble Lords, Lord Thomson of Monifieth, Lord Desai and Lord Donoughue. We are not faced with News International as a unique mixed media giant. Together with Carlton, Granada, Pearson, the *Daily Mail,* or the proposed United News/MAI merger, it is one of a number of strong, powerful, mixed-media companies. The Mirror Group has other titles. It is naughty that its circulation is now 22 per cent or 23 per cent of total circulation, but it is allowed to have part of Scottish Television, a bit of cable channel and to become involved in satellite television if that takes its fancy.

I return to the study which I mentioned earlier, towards which I believe the noble Lord, Lord Desai, as a fellow professional economist, will be more sympathetic. The survey, by Arthur Andersen, sought to measure the influence of companies on public opinion. Instead of trying to compare the BBC's 40 per cent share of television viewing and *The Sun*'s 40 per cent of newspaper readership, it drew on a whole range of sources relating to viewing and readership. It assessed the degree of concentration of attention by calculating for each of the media companies – Carlton, Granada and so on – the total amount of time that viewers, listeners and readers devoted respectively to its television programmes, radio broadcasts and newspapers.

Towering above all other influential forces in our society was the BBC. Of audience attention and the time people devoted to these activities, 44 per cent was controlled by the fearsome BBC. Second was Carlton, that monstrous mixed-media corporation, with 6.9 per cent of audience attention. Channel 4, another public interest company, had 6.2 per cent. Poor News International, with its newspapers and television stations, was sixth with a paltry 3.4 per cent of audience attention. That is a degree of influence which has Ministers and former Ministers cowering in their tents for fear of the takeover of opinion by those powerful companies.

The success of News International in building up newspapers that attract growing readership, and launching, with enormous courage, risk and enterprise, the satellite television stations, has been turned against their creator by excluding it from more than a 20 per cent share of Channel 3 or Channel 5 licences. Why should Sky's success be curbed simply because a minority shareholder also owns and runs a successful newspaper? I hesitate to say in front of the noble Baroness, Lady Dean, that it is a company which has contributed much to the multiplication of channels, including newspaper facilities. It is treated less favourably, even in my opinion grossly unfairly, in regard to terrestrial television. Channel 3 and Channel 5 companies can exploit BSkyB's pioneering enterprise by entering satellite broadcasting but BSkyB is not free to become involved in terrestrial television.

If we recall that the pretext for all that discrimination is to guard against undue influence, we need to remind ourselves that consumer protection and positive programme requirements are already in operation and are designed to protect the public against undue influence. The argument behind the amendments is that there is no need for that discrimination in the form of the 20 per cent restrictions. The amendments seek to bring broadcasting more fully within the general framework of monopoly law and practice on which we rely elsewhere to maintain the vigour of competition. I beg to move.

TAX, BENEFITS AND THE FAMILY

27 March 1996

My Lords, I am grateful to the noble Lord, Lord Skidelsky, for introducing this Motion and I have learnt much from the other speeches made so far. I have one quibble with the Motion. It refers to, 'the effectiveness of the current tax and benefit system in supporting the family structure'. I should refer to the 'ineffectiveness'. There is no dispute about that. I understand that the noble Lord, apart from natural courtesy and gentleness, has to be better behaved on the Tory Benches than I can allow myself to be from the Cross Benches.

In the short time available to me I do not wish to qualify all I have to say. I wish to declare some missionary truths as they have struck me not only recently but in watching the developing situation of the welfare state since I taught this subject back in the Scottish university of St Andrews 40 years ago. Then there were high hopes in the wake of Beveridge that we could solve all the pre-war problems of want, hunger, idleness and so forth. With social benefits now roaring towards £100 billion, those high hopes of post-war reformers have been totally shattered. Multiplying benefits have not only failed to usher in the millennium or satisfy the general social aspirations; they have had unmistakeably a perverse effect: they have aggravated the problem by attracting ever more claimants.

This perversity of outcome is no accident. Indeed, market economists used to distinguish between what they called the income effect and the price effect of a subsidy. Thus when the Government offer cash or free services to help particular groups of people judged to be deserving, the direct, immediate and intended effect is to raise the real incomes of the recipients. Alas, inevitably, at the same time the indirect longer term unintended effect is to offer an inducement for other people to put themselves in the position of beneficiaries enjoying these new subsidies. If sceptics doubt that, the noble Lord, Lord Skidelsky, might confirm from his great knowledge that such a sensitive observer as Lord Keynes acknowledged that even the inadequate and derisory dole of the 1930s had some effect in diminishing the incentive to work. In a radio discussion reproduced in the *Listener* in 1930 Keynes, talking to Lord Stamp, acknowledges that, 'the existence of the dole undoubtedly diminishes the pressure on the individual man to accept a rate of wages or a kind of employment which is not just what he wants or what he is used to'. These effects at the margin of decision, of people going for jobs or not going for jobs, switch people into totally the wrong direction and those marginal changes build up to massive redirections in lifestyles and employment.

In economic terms, if you offer a higher price for the unemployed, you will get a larger amount of unemployment. That is what Keynes taught. He called it voluntary unemployment. He did not wish to stand in judgment. That was just an effect that these subsidies had. If you offer a higher price for single parent families, you will get more single parent families. That is a matter of ordinary common sense. I do not regard the cost of £9.4 billion a year as the major cost to our society of this development. I regard the main cost to our society as the effect on children. The noble Baroness, Lady Young, has told us about presenting young children, the victims of this system, with the prospect on average of much worse life chances in employment and education and of future delinquency and so on. It is on the children that the handicaps are visited.

A number of speakers have quoted from a study, *Farewell to the Family?* by Patricia Morgan of the Institute of Economic Affairs. Some statistics have already been deployed so I shall add just two or three others from this splendid volume, priced £9 while stocks last. Of all families with dependent children, lone mothers and fathers, excluding widows, increased two-and-a-half fold, from 7 per cent in 1971 to 18 per cent in 1991; while the proportion of the total population living in single parent families increased fourfold, from 2.5 per cent in 1961 to 10 per cent in 1991.

The noble Lord, Lord Skidelsky, said that single parent families also suffer disproportionately from poverty. According to Patricia Morgan, that is not exactly the position. In the bottom decile of income distribution in 1991, pensioners accounted for 11 per cent, single and married persons without children accounted for 30 per cent and single parent families with children accounted for only 11 per cent. Couples with children – theirs is the burden and the handicap – accounted for 49 per cent.

*   *   *

There is not sufficient time to deploy one of the major forces that operates here, as in so many other sectors of our economic and social policy. Professors Tullock and Buchanan in America developed a marvellous analysis of what they call 'public choice' or the economic analysis of politics, in which they show the way in which our famed democracy can be so easily corrupted by the influence of pressure groups. They show how single-issue lobbies have a disproportionate weight in influencing government because they are concentrating single-mindedly their effort on particular demands that they wish to have satisfied. Against that concerted, orchestrated and persistent pressure, there is no counter-pressure from the general body of taxpayers and citizens who are in the end going to pay the price, so one has all the time pressure towards expanding government in the benefits that explicitly suit minorities.

In the long run there is no solution unless we restore the public philosophy of limited government and a presumption against the automatic enlargement of government to meet every problem. Buchanan and Tullock in America have shown how that presumption would have to be entrenched in some kind of constitutional deal to stop politicians constantly yielding to the temptation to buy votes by offering taxpayers' money to these persistent pressure groups.

I turn briefly to remedies. I make no apology for saying that we should shift the tax/benefit bias back at least to neutrality, if not in favour of married couples with families. It is wholly preposterous that my preferred family choice and that of many other noble Lords who have spoken so eloquently is handicapped and disadvantaged through the tax system. In the earlier debate the noble Lord, Lord Cockfield, urged that we should reduce income tax and the loopholes and, I am adding, raise the starting point to allow gross income to be reflected in higher take-home pay. Another figure from Patricia Morgan shows that in 1950 a married man with a wife and two children had to earn average manual earnings before starting to pay income tax. Today, tax begins to be deducted from earnings at one-third of average manual earnings.

If there were time I would argue that even the restoration of child adoption would make some contribution to rescuing children from some of the disadvantages which they suffer in these families. We should tackle the entitlement mentality that has grown. I recall my noble friend Lord Jakobovits, when we were debating the Family Law Bill, arguing that in Jewish families divorce was less common, although all the social pressures were the same as on the rest of the community, but he said that the stigma prevented Jewish families yielding to that pressure. Stigma is only the other side of pride in independence. That becomes caricatured as a stigma if we prefer independence to dependency on government.

The last refuge of a noble mind is to propose a Royal Commission. I very much supported the noble Baroness, Lady Thatcher, in her time in office, turning her face against Royal Commissions. They have been too easily resorted to by government for passing the buck to others. But I urge that we have a Royal Commission on the subject of the respective roles of the state and voluntary agencies in the future of the family. One of the most neglected publications in my lifetime has been Lord Beveridge's third volume on voluntary action. The other two volumes were on social insurance and full employment. The right reverend Prelate said that if we could stress the role that the Church and other voluntary organisations could play in helping to redress the position of the family, that would be a great advantage.

THE MINIMUM WAGE: AN ANTI-MARKET WHEEZE

23 March 1998

My Lords, I am not sure whether I should apologise for taking part in this debate as a former practitioner of the dismal science of economics. Next to the offer of a free drink, the mere mention of a minimum wage is best calculated to get most economists to their feet with their mouths open. It is a subject that disproves the old quip that if you ask half-a-dozen economists a question, you get six different answers – or seven if Lord Keynes was among them. In contrast, it requires no homework, no new research, no statistical models, no consulting – not even a fee – for most independent economists to agree *nem. con.* that a minimum wage is likely to be damaging and could be disastrous.

Of all the anti-market wheezes that I have come across, the idea of enforcing by statute a single, national minimum wage seems to me the most damaging in prospect. That is for several reasons. First, it seems superficially a painless way, as we have heard, to prevent the 'exploitation' of the weakest members of industrial society. Secondly, it can therefore be wrapped up in the rhetoric of fairness and so harness the moral passion of laymen, as the noble Lord, Lord Clinton-Davis, attempted. Thirdly, for politicians, less concerned with morality and guided by the vote motive, it serves wonderfully to promote short-term party popularity. At the outset it is an absolute winner. It is unstoppable. Apart from the Conservative Party, its only opponents are stony-hearted economists who, we all know, are lackeys of high capitalism.

Even if I could forthwith proceed to demonstrate the disastrous effects of a minimum wage on production costs and employment, I fear that the moral and political bandwagon could not now be halted. But, alas, I admit that I cannot demonstrate any such thing. I cannot prove the case against this massive, mammoth, monstrous Bill for the simple reason that I do not know what I am talking about. None of us knows what we are talking about. The Minister does not know what he is talking about. Not even the normally omniscient professor the noble Lord, Lord Peston, if he were here, would know what he was talking about. That is because we do not yet know the level at which the minimum wage will be set. I shall return to that challenge in a moment.

Any of us can conceive of a minimum wage low enough to do no harm, but then it would also do little good. We also understand that if the minimum is set above what economists call the 'market clearing wage', it will certainly hurt those it was meant to benefit. Thanks partly to the Institute of Economic Affairs, with which I have had some forty years' association, there is today a more general acceptance of what the late Lord Robbins used to call the 'invincible platitudes' of liberal market economics. It is a central precept of textbook analysis that a rise in price will reduce demand. Of course, in the lecture room, that missionary truth is hedged around with cautious qualification. Thus, the rise in price will only 'tend' to reduce demand and therefore to create unemployment, and it will do so only if 'all other things remain equal'. If I had the time I could tell the House of circumstances in which a minimum wage could possibly improve employment, but that is a textbook or examination exception such as one sets to catch out undergraduates.

The trouble is that there is not just one labour market. There are distinct labour markets in different regions, different industries and different skills. Although a single uniform minimum wage will have no ill effects for skilled workers in flourishing firms in the South East, it could do much damage at a number of other margins. It will bear most harshly on the least effective worker, in the least productive firms and in the less favoured regions.

A consistent lesson I recall from almost all of the empirical studies in the United States is that when the minimum was increased – usually around election time – the main victims of the resulting unemployment were the most vulnerable workers. They were typified by being unskilled, inexperienced, young, black and invariably women. It may not sound quite nice, but it follows that the one advantage which the least attractive, least employable people have in a competitive market is the freedom to offer their relatively unwanted services at a lower wage. At least they get their foot on the ladder. I wish that Milton Friedman were present to give his performance of thanking the almighty for the sweatshops on the east coast of America in the last century which enabled his immigrant parents to get a toe-hold on that great continent.

If we turn to the Bill, we find 50 pages of, for me, impenetrable legal mumbo-jumbo, with seven clauses giving wide powers of further regulation. There is no fear of unemployment, at least for lawyers. The prospect opens up of a new era of litigation by disaffected employees that will dwarf unfair dismissal cases. It should prove what I believe is called 'a nice little earner' in retirement for the noble Lord, Lord Wedderburn, and the noble Lord, Lord McCarthy, who do not appear at the moment to be present among us.

The concept of a minimum wage sounds simple enough, but we must bear in mind that the rewards of a job include what economists call the 'net advantages of employment'. Let us consider the impossibility of evaluating payment by commission, discounts, and benefits in kind, including convenience, regularity and flexibility of work. Mention has been made of McDonald's. It may once have paid lowish wages but, in my view, it has done more than many government schemes to initiate and train generations of young people for regular work and so improve their future employability. For my money, it merits the accolade 'McJobs' and it may now easily be in a position to cope with the minimum wage, but the same minimum will handicap smaller businesses in labour-intensive industries and prevent them growing into the McDonald's of the future.

I now come to the real heart of all this – I wish that there were time to go into it all. Let us turn to the Explanatory and Financial Memorandum and to the section headed 'Financial effects of the Bill. We read: 'the net effect is likely to be relatively small,' but we should note the preceding proviso, which states 'assuming the National Minimum Wage is set at a sensible level, with employment and the productive potential of the economy unchanged'. I need hardly say that if it is not set at a sensible level – that is, at a low level – the knock-on effects in the name of preserving differentials – whatever the noble Lord, Lord Clinton-Davis said – and the resulting unemployment will cost the Treasury many billions of pounds in wages and benefits.

Will the Minister take a moment at the end of the debate to confide in us his present judgement of a 'sensible' minimum wage? He must have given this a great deal of thought. Indeed, he is paid to do just that. It would be helpful if he could tell us so that at later stages we can have some idea of whether it is to be £3.50 or £4-something. It would be useful to have that knowledge.

Noble Lords will be pleased to hear that I shall trouble them no further by participating at later stages – because this is a totally misconceived Bill which, by massive amendment, could be made only slightly less bad. The whole gamble was, of course, intended as a flower arrangement, a bouquet, to appease Old Labour. I fear that it may prove to be a wreath of nettles.

NEWSPAPER PRICE COMPETITION

20 October 1998

My Lords, I accept the proposition of the noble Lord, Lord McNally, that newspapers are different. Indeed, newspapers are already constrained under the Broadcasting Act and by the merger provisions of the Fair Trading Act. As the Minister will no doubt tell us at greater length, the noble Lord's purpose is to graft on to a general competition Bill a most specific clause discriminating further against newspapers with the unconcealed objective of regulating the commercial policy of one newspaper.

As one of the independent national directors of Times Newspapers in the House, I believe that it may help the subsequent debate to set the context. History tells us that *The Times* has lost money throughout most of this century, despite successive changes of ownership from Northcliffe to Astor and to Thomson. When the Government accepted News International's last ditch rescue attempt in 1981, Rupert Murdoch followed the agreement with the noble Lord, Lord Thomson, in accepting six independent directors – I am one of them – with the responsibility of ensuring that the proprietor should not have influence over the editor or editorial policy.

Throughout the 1980s, severe losses continued and mounted despite several changes of editor, approved by the independent directors. The circulation of *The Times* fell to one-third of that of *The Daily Telegraph* which retained the dominant market position it had in turn acquired in the 1930s through the practice of old-fashioned price competition.

The aim of price cutting was not to destroy *The Independent*, nor even *The Daily Telegraph*. It was to escape from chronic loss-making and to endeavour to increase circulation, which is essential if advertising revenues are to be increased. Advertising revenues form the major part of the income of all the broadsheet newspapers. By any standard, that strategy has proved remarkably successful. The circulation has doubled, and advertising revenue roughly likewise. The total market for broadsheet papers has been enlarged; the size of papers has increased; and the average price has reduced.

Other papers naturally did not like price competition. As Corporal Jones used to say of the enemy's response to bayonets, 'They don't like it up them'. Nevertheless, *The Guardian* managed to retain its circulation and, with some less publicised price cutting, *The Daily Telegraph* has also managed to remain within the one million total circulation.

The noble Lord, Lord McNally, referred to Report stage at which he said that he had one intention and one only: 'to promote the framework of fair and transparent competition in our newspaper industry, with the intention of sustaining diversity, quality and choice'. [*Official Report*, 9/2/98; col. 913.] That sounds all very well, but it does not explain, let alone excuse, the noble Lord's vendetta against what was a deeply considered and widely researched policy by the executive and non-executive directors of Times Newspapers who carry the responsibility for its fortunes.

The noble Lord emphasises his good intentions. That is not enough. We know the road to hell is paved by little else. I wish to put a few fairly simply practical questions which are left unresolved. What constitutes fair and transparent competition? Does open price cutting have any part to play? If so, how much? If not, how could we prevent well established newspapers from colluding to raise their price, as they did comfortably enough in the 1980s? And how could a new entrant break into the market if it cannot deploy deep price cutting without the noble Lord's permission?

Closer to home, how can a declining newspaper attempt to revive its flagging fortunes if it is forbidden to deploy effective price competition? Price is not everything – that is a mistake which, to some extent, the noble Lord makes – but how important is price compared with the quality of the newspaper in building up circulation? If a declining paper such as *The Times* attempts a major reconstruction and relaunch, is there a better way of getting new readers to sample it than by dramatic price cutting? Those are not hypothetical questions. They are the do-or-die issues which came to a head shortly after I joined the board of Times Newspapers in 1988. When the circulation of *The Times* fell below that of *The Guardian* in 1992 or 1993, that may have been the galvanising element to radical reform.

No one supposed that cutting price would guarantee increased circulation – the key to higher advertising revenue. Many a hopeful entrepreneur has embarked on price cutting only to find that it is a spectacular way of throwing ever larger sums into a black hole. The perennial challenge for serious newspapers remains: what is the optimum blend of quality, quantity and price in a newspaper? We are not talking about baked beans, but about sophisticated products. So who is the best judge of the right mixture? Is it the scattered army of readers, faced with a wider choice in Britain than elsewhere in the world, or the noble Lord, Lord McNally, or even the Office of Fair Trading?

At Report stage, the noble Lord, Lord Peston, from his rather lofty professorial perch, airily countered my economic logic with his customary dismissive wave, although without anything remotely resembling coherent argument. Accordingly, I am setting a more scholarly example by avoiding dogmatic assertion. On this occasion I have relied on posing questions, although the answers may seem self-evident. One thing should be clear even for unworldly professors. It is that lasting success in competitive markets for complex products, such as newspapers undoubtedly are, could never be secured by price-cutting alone, however deep the proprietor's pockets.

Among other questions that remain I might ask: is a competitive dynamic market feasible in newspapers, or any other product, if no participant is to risk getting hurt? Why should one participant, say *The Independent,* be shielded from the decline brought about, to a degree, by its own editorial and management failures? If such a paper is truly vital to some people's conception of democracy as we know it, why should not readers or backers be prepared to pay enough to save it? Has the noble Lord thought of putting *The Independent* on the protected list, or perhaps launching a flag day?

I come to the most awkward question of all on the noble Lord's amendment. How can *The Times* be charged with exploiting a dominant position in the broadsheet market when it was struggling against terminal decline in the early 1990s? In the earlier debate, the noble Lord, Lord Borrie, whom I see in his place, put his finger on the nub of popular concern when he said: 'News International holds a substantial degree of market power . . . and is able, for long periods, to cross-subsidise its loss-making newspaper sales from its highly profitable operations in satellite television'. [*Official Report,* 9/2/98; cols 915-6.]

That seemed quite powerful, but the noble Lord's finger pointed in several wrong directions at the same time. First, News International does not run Times Newspapers which is a wholly owned subsidiary, but operates as an independent, free-standing company, also running *The Sunday Times* and the three supplements. Secondly, the price cutting has been financed entirely within Times Newspapers' own budget, with never a penny piece from satellite television. Thirdly, the only cross-subsidy comes from the highly profitable *Sunday Times,* just as in the *Telegraph* stable *The Daily Telegraph* subsidises the less profitable *Sunday Telegraph.*

All this talk about predatory pricing is an excitable distraction. Serious, destructive predatory pricing is an extremely rare phenomenon, as shown by two classic texts: McGee on the celebrated Standard Oil case in the *Journal of Law and Economics,* and Koller's Empirical Study on Anti-Trust in the *Law and Economics Review.* My experts tell me that the worst recent example of predatory pricing was the collusion of other airlines, backed by government, to drive the challenger Freddie Laker out of the market.

What we have here is a good old-fashioned circulation war, such as helped to test and shape the present newspaper industry. If price competition is forbidden, will the noble Lord try to curb competition through bigger papers, give-away offers, lotteries, travel vouchers and all the other special deals? All such promotions are quasi or substitute price cuts, offering more without extra charge.

It seems characteristic of the Liberal Democrats to prefer a namby-pamby world of harmless, ineffective competition where no one must win lest their friends get hurt. The crowning facts are fourfold. First, *The Times* has been a loss-maker for most of the century. Secondly, Rupert Murdoch was allowed to take over the ailing paper in 1981 because he could carry current losses, though hardly increasing cumulative losses forever. Thirdly, he has found a strategy to put *The Times* on the high road towards self-sustaining profitability. Fourthly, his critics are outraged by his success.

My concluding question is: why should we let the Liberal Democrats, and sundry other malcontents, vent their pique against *The Times* by smuggling through this wholly unnecessary amendment?

REFORM OF THE HOUSE OF LORDS

23 February 1999

My Lords, my own considered view on the White Paper was well anticipated by the courteous dismissal of my noble friend Lord Chalfont. Like the noble Baroness, Lady Hooper, during my 20 years' membership of your Lordships' House, I, too, have tried to respect the established convention by sticking to economic affairs, in which I might claim some professional competence. But I have most assiduously followed *Hansard,* and particularly Select Committee reports, on a very much wider range of topics. I have been repeatedly impressed – even astonished – by the remarkable, consistently high contribution of working Peers, not least the hereditaries, performed without publicity and without payment.

The problem remains: what exactly have the Lords done wrong? What have we done wrong, especially when compared with the misdeeds of another place? I join others in saying that, if reform is required, a good start could be made along the passage by culling about half of the teeming total of 659 paid and whipped MPs.

Now that I have retired, I can whisper that economic problems are often much exaggerated, especially by economists. As we saw after 1979, a free economy has almost spontaneous powers of recovery so long as politicians do not muck it up. But the constitutional upheaval that is now threatened is altogether more serious. No one can foretell the results of disrupting the delicate balance of a sophisticated political system. And no one can doubt that Britain's envied stability – unique in Europe since 1688 – owes everything to the evolving checks and balances of the British constitution, with this historic House somewhere near the centre.

Like the noble Earl, Lord Sandwich, as a devoted Savoyard I often take refuge from present troubles in the wisdom and wit of W.S. Gilbert. I never did agree with the Earl of MountArarat in *Iolanthe,* who said that: 'If there is an institution in Great Britain which is not susceptible of any improvement at all, it is the House of Peers'. That cannot be true because it was written before 1958, when we had the leavening of life Peers here.

But Gilbert got it exactly right about the Commons when he put into the mouth of Private Willis the following words:

When in that House MPs divide
If they've a brain and cerebellum too,
They've got to leave that brain outside,
And vote just as their leaders tell 'em to.

It is in that fact that the critical superiority of this House lies.

As the noble Lords, Lord Eden and Lord Trefgarne, and others, have wondered, how can any process of popular election or appointment guarantee such independence? It is not only independence, but independence buttressed by the confidence which comes either from heredity or from wide experience, variously in law, economics, banking, business, technology, medicine, the arts, the countryside, charitable activities, voluntary action, the trade unions, the armed forces, education, public administration, foreign affairs, Europe and much more – including what the noble Lord, Lord Richard, once called the rough old trade of party politics.

I regret very much that the noble Baroness, Lady Jay, shows so little respect for this unique assembly – so rich in talents and characters, not least on the Labour Benches. If this House ceases to exist, it could certainly never be reinvented. Yet it is to be casually dismantled and a successor House conjured up just like that. Here we see old Labour reverting to its primitive shibboleth that a new institution is always better than an old one. We should beware of the same empty slogans – modern, progressive, democratic, comprehensive – that we heard in the 1960s and 1970s when old Labour destroyed proven grammar schools and undermined state education in the space of a single generation.

The country is endlessly told that there are 750 wicked hereditary Peers. Yet only 300 are Tories. Two hundred are independents and most of the rest never attend. Is it not sensible that the role of a checking and revising Chamber, acting on the periodic excesses of raw 'democracy', is best performed by more mature senators of a traditional, even conservative inclination? We have learned to defer, mostly gracefully, to the tyranny of the manifesto. Yet new Labour, in 1997, was supported by only 31 per cent of the electorate – and most of its footling pledges would separately command even fewer votes. It is time that we pricked the absurdly inflated pretensions of so-called 'representative democracy', with its focus groups, single-issue lobbies and media management.

So where is the popular mandate? Where is the public clamour for abolition? Despite all the manipulation of opinion, the latest ICM poll in December confirmed a rump of around 25 per cent of the population as abolitionists, leaving the vast majority of 75 per cent divided between keeping the *status quo* permanently or allowing hereditaries to stay until their long-term future has been decided.

Let me briefly touch upon the approach of the two Houses on three recent issues. I need hardly mention the shabby question of the closed list for the European elections, a system which, in the 1930s, might have excluded Churchill from Parliament at the behest of the Tory toffs of the time and which was steamrollered through against our principled objections. Second, on fees for Scottish universities, we had an absurdly Scots-dominated administration overruling us to favour Scottish and continental students against those from England, Wales and Ulster. My third example is more down to earth. On the repeal of restrictions on Sunday shopping, this House led the way with a Private Member's Bill by the then obscure, independent, Conservative Back Bencher, the noble Baroness, Lady Trumpington. Yet when a Bill to repeal the Shops Act was first moved in the other place, it was voted down on Second Reading in craven response to lobbying by USDAW and other vulgar pressure groups from which this splendidly undemocratic House was and remains gloriously immune.

I fear that the Royal Commission is not constituted to resist the trendy clamour by the political élite for a fudged compromise. I despair of the studied absence on that commission of a single hereditary Peer; I resent that absence. I worry a little at the chairman's reputation as a fixer. I recall A.P. Herbert – a splendidly independent university MP, before Labour abolished such valuable anomalies. In an IEA Hobart Paper back in 1960, APH warned against the temptation for Royal Commissions to fall for what he called, 'the nonsense of unanimity'.

Dare we hope that at least one of the members of the Royal Commission will read these debates and stick out for a continued, major, independent element of heredity in the House, a practice not unknown in religion, nor in trade unions, nor in most other aspects of real life? I earnestly urge commissioners to ponder deeply that fruitful debate would be better stimulated by a report which acknowledged a robust clash of principles rather than contrived consensus and conformity born of expediency and compromise.

AN INDEPENDENT TAXATION POLICY COMMITTEE

14 March 2001

My Lords, I very much enjoyed the contrasting opening speeches from the three main parties. I especially enjoyed the sparkling performance of the noble Baroness, Lady Hogg. I wish she had more time to tell us the extent to which this almost comically Scottish-dominated government favours the Scottish electorate. I thought that required further examination.

My view runs rather more radical than to that of the Front Benches. I come not only to bury Gordon Brown but also to highly praise him. From the vantage point of the IEA back in 1957, it was not only on taxation that the record of both governing parties inspired little confidence. As the noble Lord, Lord Barnett, may remember, those were the days of monopoly trade unions, protected state industries, incomes policies, central planning, multiplying subsidies, universal welfare, budget deficits and, of course, the consequent inflation.

The earliest brief stand against ever rising government spending was in 1958 when the then Chancellor, Peter Thorneycroft, with his Treasury colleagues, Enoch Powell and Nigel Birch, resigned over a mere £50 million. Today that would be equivalent to £1 billion. That was 'super Mac's little local difficulty', if I remember correctly.

If the Thatcher Government's demolition of union monopoly released new Labour from the TUC's inflationary grip, it was the 1979 Budget of the noble and learned Lord, Lord Howe of Aberavon, which put tax-cutting high on the political agenda. With his first Budget he reduced personal taxes.

Yet although Gordon Brown has not followed that example, nevertheless, with two cautions, I would give him high praise – higher praise than most post-war Chancellors, save possibly the noble and learned Lord, Lord Howe, whose Budget was particularly important.

My first caution is that the full credit does not properly belong to Mr Brown and his advisers alone, since – as other noble Lords have said – he has built on the unacknowledged Tory legacy of stability bequeathed by his predecessors, the noble Lord, Lord Lamont, and Kenneth Clarke.

My second caution is that Gordon Brown's outstanding inflation record over, so far, four years, has been achieved only by abdicating control of monetary policy to the Bank of England. Since I was among the first in this House warmly to applaud that bold departure, I might be permitted to remind the House of a certain irony. When the first majority Labour Government under Mr Attlee came into power in 1945, they could not wait to nationalise the Bank of England. That was among the first steps that they took. Here we are 50 years on when new Labour has, in effect, privatised the Bank of England; restoring that key power to Threadneedle Street.

My reason for wishing to bury the Chancellor – as well as to praise him – is that he looks to be in serious danger of fulfilling the political adage that all success tends to end up in failure. To explain that danger it is necessary to ask why Gordon Brown's Monetary Policy Committee was what the noble Lord, Lord Healey, would have called 'a jolly wheeze'. It is generally agreed that, since Keynes, successive Chancellors, irrespective of party, have been under incessant pressure to cure recessions or win elections by stimulating the economy with lower interest rates or taxes. The logic taught by Milton Friedman was that expansionary monetary or fiscal policies were like drink, with the good effects coming first to be followed by a nasty hangover some time later.

The value of the Monetary Policy Committee is simply that it removes the bottle from the reach of chronic tipplers. In short, it depoliticises monetary management. But on Friedman's logic, the removal of one weapon from the Chancellor's political armoury exposes the tax system all the more to manipulation for party advantage. Unfortunately, Mr Brown has shown himself no less inclined than the worst of his predecessors to yield to the temptation to fiddle with taxes. Here we have a born interventionist and social engineer, with a missionary – even Messianic – zeal to cure the ills of the world, with his hand not only on the tiller, but in the till.

To return to Friedman, increased government spending, like inflation is politically popular in the short run. But gradually, cumulatively, it raises costs, blunts incentive and, above all, it discourages everyday economy. Not even an Aberdonian spends other people's money as cautiously as he spends his own. And Mr Brown does not even come from Aberdeen. Indeed, he comes from nearer Glasgow where I am told they all have holes in their pocket.

Part of the technique of Mr Brown has been so to complicate the tax system, with perpetual, fiddling changes, that only experts can work out exactly what he has been up to. Accordingly, like others, I rely on the Institute for Fiscal Studies – many years ago, the noble Lord, Lord Taverne, played an important part in its development – to tell us that the Chancellor has raised taxes altogether by £24 billion to bring the total above £380 billion a year. As a proportion of national income, that represents an increase of 2.5 per cent to 40 per cent next year. That is different from some other figures, but I stick with the IFS calculations.

The lesson I would draw from the Chancellor's mixed record is that he is no more to be trusted with unchecked discretion over taxes than his predecessors could be trusted with control over interest rates. My proposals for reform are therefore twofold. First, as I have long argued, the Monetary Policy Committee should now be instructed to lower its average annual target for inflation from the present 2.5 per cent. That would still be sufficient to reduce the value of money by more than 80 per cent over the average expectation of life today – from £1 to 20p over some 80 years. As the present inflation rate is nearer 2 per cent, a reasonable programme would be to shave the target down by perhaps 0.5 per cent every four years to give us the boon of stable money and lower interest rates in 10 or 15 years.

My second reform would be to depoliticise the tax system by creating an independent taxation policy committee alongside the Monetary Policy Committee. Its task would be to review the Chancellor's Budget proposals, in advance of them being delivered to Parliament, against a target of reducing the total burden of taxes from 40 per cent of GNP to Colin Clark's safe figure of 25 per cent of GNP over a similar period of, say, 15 years.

Once launched, the expectation of stable money and lower taxes would bring earlier promise of unheralded prosperity, individual responsibility and consumer freedom to choose more leisure and that gracious living for which many new Labour and other Members of the House provide such an enviable example.

THE NHS: THE 'ENVY OF THE WORLD'

27 June 2001

My Lords, I was very much cheered up at the outset of this afternoon's debate to hear from the engaging maiden speech of the noble Lord, Lord Rooker, that the Government occasionally check out whether earlier Acts of Parliament have had the desired effects. I thought that comparing the unchecked flood of legislation year in year out with the, should I say, 'patchy performance' must be a rather disillusioning task, although I would very much like to offer my services in the assessment of some parts of legislation.

I shall take up where my former student at St Andrew's, the noble Lord, Lord Forsyth, left off. His clarity, candour and courage were all that I might have anticipated. I shall try to do justice to the theme, although perhaps at somewhat shorter length.

I personally was very disappointed with the grand debate on the NHS during the election campaign. For me, as I watched the television story unfold, it seemed like a twist on the old story of the emperor who had no clothes with a difference. While the three party leaders invited us constantly to admire the fine raiment of this institution, the nurses, the GPs, the consultants and many patients simultaneously blurted out that in practice much of it is in tatters.

I gave up collecting cuttings, but one single month's supply on the health service included the following headlines: 'NHS catastrophe in Kent hospitals', 'Ministers try to head off NHS mutiny', 'Hospital waiting lists rise', 'Hospitals move waiting list goalposts', 'Milburn abandons waiting list targets', 'Labour at war with BBC over NHS exposé', 'GPs threaten to quit over workload', 'Consultants may split with NHS', and 'Nurse's leader condemns third world health service'. That is not Tory Party propaganda.

It is not easy, even from the Cross Benches, to launch into a full-hearted denunciation of the concept of the National Health Service. I have long thought that the whole of the argument about it being the envy of the world, although nowhere in the world endeavours to copy it, was a spoof, if not a fraud. Of course, many families and individuals pay heartfelt tribute to the personal debt they owe to the National Health Service. But what has mostly saved lives, cured ills and eased pains is the miracle advances in drug therapy by profit-making multi-national companies, about which we heard from the noble Lord, Lord Fitt, and the developments in diagnostic and surgical practices through competitive innovation by dedicated professionals. The unique contribution of politicians of all parties over the past half century has been to hold back progress by confining investment in the health service to finance that could be raised through taxation, thereby suppressing choice, prolonging illness and even allowing premature deaths.

This harsh verdict is not based on hindsight. As the founding General Director at the Institute of Economic Affairs, I am proud to quote from one of our very earliest Hobart Papers, published in 1961. It was written by a young, physically handicapped, though intellectually gifted, lecturer at Keele named Dr Dennis Lees, who later became professor at Nottingham University. The text merits extensive quotation. I shall content myself with a single paragraph. The paper is entitled *Health Through Choice,* but it is now, alas, out of print. He said:

> The fundamental weaknesses of the NHS are the dominance of political decisions, the absence of built-in forces making for improvement and the removal of the test of the market. These defects bring dangers for the quality of medical care that cannot be removed without far-reaching reform.

He went on to make some tentative, hesitant proposals for improvement. I shall not go into those in detail. He said:

> My verdict would be that a monolithic structure financed by taxation is ill-suited to
> a service in which the personal element is so strong, in which rapid advances in
> knowledge require flexibility and freedom to experiment, and for which consumer
> demand can be expected to increase with growing prosperity.

His recommendations included diminishing the role of political decisions and enlarging consumer choice by moving away from taxation and free services towards private insurance and fees, but always allowing generous direct assistance for those who cannot maintain themselves.

Instead of arguing their case, the defenders of the NHS have gone on claiming the moral superiority of a system that attaches more importance to services being described as 'free' than to the fact that the services are not actually available. That moral smokescreen has for too long paralysed fruitful debate on alternatives to the elephantine, politically mismanaged and manipulated monopoly of the NHS. The growth in the private health sector is itself a measure of the failure of the NHS, since millions elect to pay twice over – once in taxes for the service they do not use and again for insurance out of their taxed income.

The easiest way to dispose of this kind of criticism is to dismiss it as the ravings of a right-wing lackey of capitalism in its advanced stages. That strikes the right intellectual note for some of the participants. But that will no longer do. All of those unpriced expectations are now coming home to roost and for reasons quietly anticipated by some socialists of unquestioned credentials.

I have long treasured a second IEA paper entitled *Paying for the Social Services*. It was written in 1968 by Douglas Houghton, who became a Labour Peer and will be remembered in this House as a wise old bird with the courage of his convictions. In that paper, written more than 30 years ago, there appears the following luminous passage:

> What is in doubt is whether we in Britain will ever give medicine the priority given
> to it in some other countries (and America is only one example) so long as it is
> financed almost wholly out of taxation.

It continues:

> While people would be willing to pay for better services for themselves, they may
> not be willing to pay more in taxes as a kind of insurance premium which may bear
> no relation to the services actually received.

That is my second witness. But, my Lords, I have further delights for you.

Lest those be thought the musings of a maverick, I shall now quote one of the great intellectual pillars of Harold Wilson's Labour Party, Mr Richard Crossman. In the introduction to his now long-forgotten panacea of *National Superannuation* in 1969, he wrote: 'People are prepared to subscribe more in a contribution for their own personal or family security than they ever would be willing to pay in taxation devoted to a wider variety of different purposes'. Contrast that clear insight with that of the Labour chairman of the parliamentary Health Select Committee, talking in 1999 of the private sector in language as crude as his intellectual processes. He said: 'I hate the bastards and you can quote me'.

Last year, the Minister himself, Mr Milburn, was quoted in the *Hospital Doctor* as describing private practice by consultants as, 'one of the 7 deadly sins'.

The logical consequence of the all-party collusion on a tax-financed National Health Service, in contrast with superior European systems, has been to prevent medical care becoming one of the major growth sectors of the economy to match homes, holidays, entertainment and sport, which competitive markets have transformed with rising standards of living. In welfare, the choice is not public versus private but monopoly versus competition. Competition alone can harness private health insurance, mutual aid, direct payment, vouchers, savings, family support, voluntary institutions, philanthropy and all the resources of civil society, with generous state aid for the declining minority unable to help themselves.

It was political monopoly that abolished matrons, introduced mixed-sex wards, manipulated waiting lists and surgical priorities and issued orders to clean up hospitals in areas to which the public had access. A monolithic state monopoly can never cater sensitively for differing and developing personal preferences. I describe it as essentially a Napoleonic, even totalitarian concept best confined to the Armed Forces, the police, the fire service and street lighting, where choice between competing suppliers is less feasible.

Dare I add, after the outbursts which have come from the Liberal Democrat Back Benches, that state dictation is especially inappropriate from a party that now attracts fewer supporters than there are adult smokers?

A EUROPEAN CONSTITUTION: THE AGGRANDISEMENT OF BRUSSELS

9 September 2003

My Lords, I believe there will be universal agreement that we have enjoyed a remarkable feast of oratory and the deployment of exceptionally wide knowledge and practical experience of the European Union. Nevertheless, wide differences still remain and some of us have to play our part in maintaining the argument. We have had a good deal of repetition but, from my point of view, not enough repetition. We have had some conscientious doubts from the

Eurosceptics and the endless easy, rather smooth reassurances from those whom I call the Euro-phorics.

We need to be rather wary of reassurances. We have been fed for some 30 years on a diet of reassurances, from a long line of Ministers and even Prime Ministers. It is not only the early reassurance of Prime Minister Heath about the limits of the Common Market which proved rather fraudulent. What about the repeated promises of successive governments, Labour and Conservative, to defend the British veto? What was all that talk from Prime Minister Major about subsidiarity? What confidence can we now have in the present Cabinet when the Minister in charge of the negotiations dismisses the whole operation as mere tidying up and unimportant?

Mr Blair has made a great deal of his victory in getting the word 'federal' removed. To remove 'federal' from this constitutional rigmarole is one thing; the trouble is that it would take nothing short of brain surgery to remove 'federal' from the aims and aspirations of the French, German and Benelux ruling élites.

The draft treaty is full of extensions of what its francophone authors call 'competences' which, in plain English, means 'powers'. 'Competence' implies the ability to deliver, whereas the Commission has proved incompetent to provide the first requirement of honest, uncorrupt administration. The prospect of enlargement of its powers over national governments is defended indignantly by reference to the increased numbers of members of the European Union. Would it not be more logical to offset an increase in numbers by a diminution in powers and, in this way, to prune much of the superfluous activities that we detect and have talked about? The truth is that the Brussels *fonctionnaires* have a truly Napoleonic appetite for power, as flaunted by the grand, superior former President of France, who would put our own George Nathaniel Curzon in the shade.

Why should Britain not turn away from this endless game of compromise and backstage deals by cynical powerbrokers? Why not set an example in candour? Why not admit that we have fundamentally different approaches in Europe? Ours is governed by both our economic outlook and our political background, and we should not apologise because our island history, our international stance and our national character are in sharp contrast to some of those that we detect on the Continent.

My own ideal of good neighbourly relations with Europe was exactly caught by Churchill in 1953, when he declared: 'We are with Europe, but not of it. We are linked, but not comprised. We are associated, but not absorbed'. So far from being a 'little Englander', this incomparable world leader constantly preached the virtues of free trade as not only promoting prosperity but as bringing nations together in peaceful intercourse.

Rather than rely, as I usually do, on Adam Smith, I shall offer a brief extract from Churchill's speech, way back in 1905. I have cribbed it from the quite outstanding biography of Winston Churchill by the late Lord Jenkins of Hillhead. I quote Churchill:

> The dangers which threaten the tranquillity of the modern world come not from those powers that have become interdependent upon others, interwoven by commerce with other States . . .

He went on:

> We do not want to see the British Empire degenerate into a sullen confederacy, walled off like a medieval town.

That brought to my mind the anxieties that some of us have long expressed about the danger of the European Union moving towards a fortress Europe, to look America in the face, but to enjoy a continuing relative economic decline. The proposed constitution, undoubtedly – we have all more or less agreed – marks a huge step away from any coherent concept of a vigorous straight-forward free trade area. Britain's best response would now be to negotiate joining the rest of the world outside this restrictive, rather self-obsessed bloc.

Short of regaining our full freedom in one bound, what can Her Majesty's Government now do by way of damage limitation? I have a number of help-ful suggestions. The first would be to follow up a proposal I first heard from the noble Lord, Lord Cockfield, in an earlier debate, which was that the CAP [Common Agricultural Policy] should be repatriated. Repatriation of the CAP is a splendid wheeze. It would free Britain, first, to lift trade barriers that, as the noble Lord, Lord Judd, has told us, impoverish poor overseas farmers; secondly, it would save a large part of the present budget, as the noble Earl, Lord Ferrers, mentioned; thirdly, it would scrap a large part – perhaps the larger part – of the 100,000 rules and regulations in the ragbag known as the *acquis communautaire*; and, finally, it would disengage us from an odious corruption which still disfigures the common agricultural policy.

A second modification would be to insist on the restoration of our opt-out from the Social Chapter, which is already burdening our own economy with costs that have visibly borne down the German and French producers and helped to inflict unemployment of above 10 per cent.

A third requirement is now, I hope, generally accepted and will be surely implemented by the Government, which is to remove the European Charter of Fundamental Rights, for the devastating reasons, I thought, which were given earlier today by the noble and learned Lord, Lord Howe.

A final reflection is that unless the Government curb the aggrandisement of the over-stretched Brussels Commission, the demand for a referendum will clearly become irresistible. The reasons are robustly set forth in the current issue of the *European Journal* by the distinguished historian, the noble Lord, Lord Blake, whose absence from this debate through immobility and not, I should explain, through incapacity, will be widely regretted.

'Unique' is no doubt an overused adjective in these excitable days, but one totally unique feature of the threatened new constitution is that when the final text comes before this House, we will be denied the customary right to debate its contents with a view to amendment and improvement. If we look at the agenda for the week, we see that on Friday we have before us the Second Readings of four Bills of varying significance. All of them may be transformed or rejected outright at your Lordships' pleasure. I ask the Minister: how can the country be expected to understand that, in these great matters before us, when Brussels proposes, this House, this Parliament, this nation, is impotent to dispose?

REGULATION MANIA

25 February 2004

My Lords, from the Cross Benches I should like to congratulate my old friend the noble Lord, Lord Vinson, on the Tory side on his splendid opening speech. I also congratulate the noble Lord, Lord Haskel, as the only occupant and spokesman on the Labour Benches.

The phenomenon of regulation is nothing new. The 19th century saw the introduction of extensive regulation in factories, banking, weights and measures, sale of goods, the adulteration of food, private contracts and much more. What is new is the scale of unchecked and indiscriminate regulation to restrict competition. It is yet another example of my favourite word these days, which is 'inordinacy'. That term suggests the temptation to take everything to excess.

An example that today would be widely accepted but which was much contested a few years ago is that of the Shops Acts. Here was a complex rigmarole of regulations on hours and days, opening and closing times and so forth. The intentions were benevolent in that they sought to prevent the exploitation of shop workers, but the consequences were wholly baneful. They froze competition and delayed the revolution in retailing which has extended choice not only to shoppers but, no less, to shop workers themselves.

A regulatory framework is necessary, but it must not swamp competition. Regulation is inevitably restrictive and unproductive. In contrast, competition is progressive, enterprising and dynamic. It is said that the trouble with competition is that it is not perfect according to textbook theory. However, it is one thing to provide guidelines, but quite another matter to bury competition beneath extensive uniform standards. I searched for a homely analogy and found that of the motorist. He will accept the *Highway Code,* speed limits, even congestion charges and perhaps the occasional speed camera, but he will not accept the Minister getting into the driving seat.

Why has regulation mania grown like Topsy over recent years, especially in the labour market? According to a recent Hobart Paper on employment tribunals by Professor Shackleton, the direct administrative costs total around £1 billion per year. However, the total cost of our compensation culture dwarfs that sum. Various estimates range from £5 billion according to the British Chambers of Commerce, £6 billion according to the Institute of Directors and an impressive £10 billion according to the Institute of Actuaries, including a steep rise in premiums for employers' liability insurance. My first question to the Minister is this: what is his best estimate of the cost of regulations in the labour market?

My second question is this: who pays the cost? Economic analysis shows that firms faced with a new levy or tax seek to shift the cost forward to customers in higher prices or backward to workers in reduced employment. If competition makes it impossible to escape the cost, it falls on profits, which means that investors will put up less capital for future expansion. Which of those damaging effects does the Minister prefer? Does he prefer higher prices to cover the cost, does he prefer lower employment, or does he prefer contracting businesses? Or does he prefer to dwell in Tommy Cooper's make-believe world where costs simply vanish – just like that?

There are several reasons why this costly mountain of regulation has grown. One is that regulations are cheap for governments because they do not have to meet the costs of compliance. Another reason is that while the apparent benefits of regulation are concentrated and highly visible, the costs are widely dispersed, delayed and obscure. Thus in the short run, trade unions stand to gain from regulation favourable to their members. It pays them to invest heavily in organising and lobbying for government favours without concern for the long-run damage, even to their own members. Since governments do not pay the bill, weak Ministers have no incentive to resist the constant pressure for more regulation. In any case, Ministers crave popularity.

The wider, deeper and longer-term unintended consequence is that costly job protection may end up costing jobs. If a restricted, rigid labour market prevents firms responding flexibly to the constant challenges of change in a global economy, British firms will lose out further to foreign competition. Thanks to radical liberalisation by the Tories after 1979, we forged ahead of France and Germany. Today their highly regulated economies have condemned them to massive unemployment and stagnation. Yet our head-in-the-clouds Prime Minister boasts of a campaign to liberalise restrictive economies in Europe while his colleagues yield to every pressure to restrict and rigidify the labour market at home.

The reckless increase in British regulation is encouraged, even incited, by the various commissions on equal pay, minimum wages, conditions at work and various forms of discrimination – real or imagined – relating to race, sex or age. Applications to tribunals more than doubled from 38,000 in 1985 to 80,000 in 1997, and rose again to 130,000 by 2002. This explosion of grievances is encouraged by absurdly inflated and well-publicised jackpot awards to lucky winners.

The full costs and consequences of regulation extend far beyond higher prices, lower employment and reduced investment. Most hidden of all costs are the daily frustration, hassle and distraction of complying with ever-increasing regulations and their frequent changes. Do Ministers simply not care that this inordinate legislative activism has already driven many small, defenceless businesses to the wall? Our complacent Chancellor may shrug off such warnings with the constant refrain, 'Behold! The economy is doing fine'. I believe that he once studied economics, so I shall remind him of an old Liberal adage: what gives regulation the illusion of working are the freedoms that regulation has not yet destroyed. A strong economy can bear much mischief, but this progressive process renders effort and enterprise ever weaker and less able to bear the increasing burdens.

PART IV

Selected obituaries

The Times

20 October 2006

FREE-MARKET THINKER WHO SERVED AS DIRECTOR OF THE INSTITUTE OF ECONOMIC AFFAIRS FOR THREE DECADES

For three decades at the epicentre of free-market thinking, Ralph Harris was decisive in converting the British political consensus back to liberal economics. He did this chiefly by informing – and often inspiring – an ideological underpinning for Margaret Thatcher and Sir Keith Joseph as they remodelled the Conservative Party after 1975.

Supplying the motivating energy (as its general director, 1957–87) behind the Institute of Economic Affairs (IEA), the most enduring and intellectually substantial of the think-tanks made famous by the Thatcher phenomenon, Harris had exhibited great character in maintaining his viewpoint while government by dirigisme dominated political fashion.

At the root of his thinking lay an abhorrence of the 'vain ambition' of economic planning – 1940s controls really did entail, he recalled, that 'the practical world was a kind of serfdom. You did as you were told'.

But his methods of changing matters were sophisticated. As far as the IEA was concerned, he was opposed to orthodox political involvement. Think-tanks should aim to change opinion, but remain uncontaminated by baser activity. He argued the point with inimitable style: 'Keep clear of politics. Politics is bad for you. It leads to compromise and deals and confusion and vote-getting and lying and cheating and all these, in the end'.

Thus protected, the IEA retained an invaluable aura of scholarship.

When appointed a life peer in 1979, Harris joined the crossbenches. A pipe-smoking devotee who carried spares in his pockets and extolled the joys of conjuring, he was a generous, energetic and charming man, with a seemingly irreverent but well-executed turn of phrase.

Even his hero, Friedrich Hayek, was fair game for deconstruction. Given the great ideologue's thoughtfulness, said Harris, 'I can't imagine, if I may say so, Hayek running a picnic'.

But behind the exquisite charm and premier skills as generous host and renowned after-dinner speaker lay a formidable intellectual sharpness – and an ardour that remained fiery despite the passing decades.

Once elevated to the peerage, his speeches achieved a following in the Lords which helped to crowd the chamber as if he were, in the words of one friend, 'the opposite of the dinner gong'.

His contact with the higher echelons of British politics had in essence begun in 1964, when he was visited by Keith Joseph. The IEA had already published an impressive array of tightly argued, mainly microeconomic studies of health, education and housing policy.

Joseph told Harris he had heard of his work – and ideas. Pleased to see the former minister making 'endless notes' Harris recalled giving him papers predicting that the NHS 'would never succeed as a monopoly, politicised institution'. Joseph left with ample reading material, and became a lifelong supporter.

Ten years later Joseph returned. The 1970 Heath Government had reversed its policies in 1971–72, had been humiliated by economic crisis, and had lost its majority.

Hearing that leading Tories on the Right were planning a think-tank that would exceed the IEA in political participation, Harris was enthusiastic for the new project. He added for Joseph's benefit 'I've even got a name for you: "the Centre for Alternative Policies – CAP".'

With characteristic generosity, he gave the new body – which became the Centre for Policy Studies – substantial assistance. True to his beliefs, he also noted that competition would enhance, not impede, the IEA's position.

After Thatcher won office in 1979 the overall influence of the IEA could be seen across the Government's innovations, most of all in counter-inflation policies to guarantee stable business conditions. Later it provided impetus for privatisation – and, through Harris's inspiration of the No Turning Back group, kept the Thatcherite policy flame burning.

In 1987 Thatcher used the opportunity of an IEA anniversary dinner to pay tribute to Harris's work, saying: 'What we have achieved could never have been done without the leadership of the IEA'.

Ralph Harris was born in 1924. He attended Tottenham Grammar School and he remained proud of his roots, noting that coming from a working-class family in Tottenham 'was my greatest shield, because people couldn't say, "Oh, you public school boys, you rich characters, you privileged people".'

After the war he took a first in economics at Queens' College, Cambridge, and from 1949 he lectured in political economy at the University of St Andrews.

As a young man he was conspicuous for his energy, intelligence – and crucially, his sense of humour. He was someone who clearly had passions about things, notably politics. He had become an active Conservative, standing twice without success at parliamentary elections in Kirkcaldy in 1951 and Edinburgh Central in 1955. He then became a leader-writer on the *Glasgow Herald*.

His chance to make his political mark came when Antony Fisher, a businessman and former fighter pilot, was inspired by Hayek's *Road to Serfdom* to create the Institute of Economic Affairs. Harris, in harness with Arthur Seldon (obituary, October 13, 2005), became its first general director.

The IEA, in Hayek's phrase, presented 'an intellectual case amongst intellectuals' – meaning teachers, students, academics and opinion-forming journalists – for free-market ideas.

Harris later denied that the IEA had been intended to change society, insisting: 'We would have thought that a little pretentious'. He and his small band of colleagues were 'lads of thirty' wishing to 'put a firework down and see what happens. We were out to have a little fun.

'We started in 1957 and genuinely told each other each week that we were now going straight and that you don't put your trust in principalities and power and politics and parties and all these frail characters. It was a marvellous period. We had no allies anywhere'.

But given the effectiveness of Harris's charisma and energy, that situation did not last long. Soon an eclectic mix, including 'a dozen or more really powerful academics', had gathered, giving the IEA vital credibility. The institute, said Harris, was 'driven not by Conservative-type leaders, but from a liberal, awkward squad'.

Nonetheless, some leading Conservatives did align themselves with it, including Enoch Powell, who wrote an early pamphlet, *Saving in a Free Society*.

After retiring as general director, Harris retained a measure of political involvement. As chairman of the Eurosceptic Bruges Group he found himself suddenly having to parry a storm created by the group's young secretary, Patrick Robertson. He also had to take steps to prevent the IEA shedding its free-market loyalties in an attempt to remain in step with John Major's premiership.

His loyalty to old friends was emphasised when he helped to assemble a fighting fund to assist Neil Hamilton in his libel battle against Mohamed Al Fayed. Harris had found it shocking that legal aid was unavailable, and had set about remedying the situation.

But Hamilton's defeat pushed the former minister towards bankruptcy – and placed Harris, then 75, under an obligation to name the leading donors to the fund. From his own funds he had contributed less than £5,000, freeing him of liability – but this good fortune did not apply to more significant donors.

Briefly he resisted, protesting that it would be grotesque to betray the confidences in which money had been given. As for possibly disobeying the court, he reflected: 'If it was a question of a week in jail for contempt of court then I suppose I'd have to do it. But I have a wife and lots of grandchildren and I can't disappear for too long'.

Still conspicuously sprightly, Harris also chaired the pro-smoking lobby group Forest. He relished opposing the 'authoritarian itch' of anti-smokers asserting 'with so many hazards to strike us down, how will the medics know which did us in when the time comes?'.

Pursuing into old age a robust raft of favourite causes, he also took on several board-room roles, including serving as an independent national director of Times Newspapers Holdings (1988–2001).

Harris published a great many papers and books, a fair proportion with deliberately provocative titles, not least his 1971 volume, *Down with the Poor*.

Ralph Harris was made a life peer by Thatcher in 1979. From the Upper House he observed her premiership at comparatively close hand. He confirmed the extraordinary emotions she incited. 'I see chaps in the House of Lords whom I know, who were contemporaries of mine at university. They won't talk to me and I'm not even Thatcher. I didn't like Harold Wilson as Prime Minister, but I never felt the hatred and animus towards him that they have towards her. Itching to kill'.

But Harris had always relished life and good company too much to let political boundaries affect his friendships, which were legion, and as many confirmed, often heartfelt.

He married Jose Pauline Jeffery in 1949. They had two sons, who predeceased them, and one daughter.

The Daily Telegraph

20 October 2006

GENERAL DIRECTOR OF THE INSTITUTE OF ECONOMIC AFFAIRS, WHICH PROVIDED THATCHERISM WITH ITS INTELLECTUAL FOUNDATION

The Lord Harris of High Cross, who died yesterday aged 81, was, with Arthur Seldon, one of the founders of the Institute of Economic Affairs, and perhaps the most successful polemicist of the second half of the 20th century, retrieving and advancing free-market ideas which were initially deeply out of favour and providing the intellectual basis for Margaret Thatcher's reforms of the 1980s.

In fact, though Ralph Harris was the first life peer appointed under the Thatcher government, and declared his admiration for her, he hotly denied being a Thatcherite. 'But I count it fortunate for Britain . . . that she was something of an "IEA-ite",' he wrote. He took his place on the crossbenches, to the approval of his intellectual mentor, Friedrich von Hayek. He decided, too, against obtaining a coat of arms because heraldry could not represent Adam Smith's 'invisible hand'.

But the IEA's success in persuading the Conservatives under Margaret Thatcher of the rightness of their cause did much to restore public faith in the party after the disastrous leadership of Ted Heath while the industrial unrest and rampant inflation of the 1970s provided a strong indication that Harris and his colleagues might not after all, be wrong in warning of the dangers of state ownership.

'A lot of our thinking was deliberately intended to affront [the establishment] and to wake them up', Harris conceded. The IEA had been set up as an educational charity by a Sussex farming entrepreneur named Antony Fisher from the profits of the Buxted Chicken company, and had been inspired by Hayek's *Road to Serfdom* which Fisher had read in condensed form in the *Reader's Digest*.

From the beginning, it made no attempt to put forward proposals which had been devised according to what was 'politically possible', but attempted to convince intellectuals and journalists of the case for the market, reasoning that politicians would follow.

The Tories' landslide victory in 1979 brought to the fore many of the policies for which Harris and the IEA had been arguing since the 1950s. Privatisation and cuts in income tax, which had been dismissed as mad by *bien pensant* opinion when Harris and Seldon began to publish, became popular and successful planks of government policy.

Ralph Harris was born on December 10 1924, and brought up in north London in humble circumstances of which he was extremely proud. He was educated at Tottenham Grammar School, and from there won an exhibition to Queens' College, Cambridge, from which he graduated with a First in Economics.

After coming down from Cambridge, Harris was appointed lecturer in Political Economy at St Andrews University. and during his time there stood for Parliament twice – at Kirkcaldy (as a Liberal Unionist) in 1951, and four years later in Edinburgh Central as a Conservative.

In 1956 he was appointed a leader-writer on the *Glasgow Herald*, a stint which was to stand him in good stead in his later work. He was a prolific contributor to newspapers for the rest of his life, providing both pieces for the comment and business pages and writing letters advocating his chief interests: lower taxation, less regulation, the dangers of the EU and smokers' rights. He became, in 1988, a director of Times Newspapers Holdings, a post he held until 2001, but – as he acknowledged in a letter defending Rupert Murdoch's launch of a price war – he was a longstanding reader of, and writer for *The Daily Telegraph*.

Harris had met Fisher in 1949 at East Grinstead, and in 1956 they met to discuss the founding of the IEA. The following year, Harris began as general director. At first, the Institute had no money (and, of course, its principles always forbade it to apply for any government grant). 'Butskellism' was at its height – although Harris, who wrote, in 1956, a biography of 'Rab' Butler, believed him innocent of the 'crimes' committed in his name – and Harris and the Institute were looked upon as cranks. Its annual income in April 1958 was £3,000.

But while Arthur Seldon, who had by then joined, took on the bulk of the IEA's editing responsibilities, stripping complicated economic papers of scholarly jargon and making them accessible to the general reader, Harris began to generate income, cultivating sympathetic businessmen and individuals. Since he was naturally charming and extremely skilled and engaging as a speaker, he proved to be very good at this, and after several financial crises during the 1960s, managed to establish the IEA on a stable financial footing.

Harris was also tireless in spreading the gospel at meetings at universities and in other forums and, in later years, at lunches at the IEA's eventual head-quarters in Lord North Street. A stream of publications began with the series *. . . in a Free Society*. The first, in 1957, was *Pensions in a Free Society*, and it was followed by similar publications about hire purchase and advertising. In 1959 the Hobart Papers were founded, a series which has now run to well over 100 titles, and published the works of men such as Hayek and Sir Alan Walters, Mrs Thatcher's chief economic adviser.

In the 1960s Harris wrote on public libraries (1962) and choice in welfare (1963 and 1965); in the 1970s he became even more productive. The charac-teristically direct *Down with the Poor* and *Crisis '75* were among several books, and in 1977, he and Seldon produced – in only six weeks – *Not from Benevolence* to mark the 20th anniversary of the IEA. The bluntness of the titles was typical of Harris's approach – a popular toast at the institute's Hobart lunches was 'Down with the public interest!'.

But Harris was as hard at work outside the IEA. He had become secretary of the Mont Pèlerin Society, a group of free market economists, in 1967, and organised the Adam Smith Double Centenary meeting at St Andrews in 1976. In 1969, he and Seldon had led a call for an independent university, which led directly to the foundation in 1976 of the University of Buckingham, on the council of which Harris served from 1980 until 1995.

He was also a moving spirit in the Wincott Foundation, which hosted lectures given by the likes of Milton Friedman, and was instrumental in the establishment of the Social Affairs Unit in 1980. In addition, from 2000, he was chairman of Civitas, the think-tank which developed from the IEA's Health and Welfare Unit.

Harris also devoted much of his energy to warning of the dangers of a European superstate and served as chairman of the Bruges Group – which had been named after Mrs Thatcher's sceptical speech about the EU – from 1989 to 1991.

Though scornful of the idea of economics as a mysterious art, Harris believed that intellectuals were enormously influential, and he worked to ensure that their influence was to the good. Considering himself a 'radical reactionary', he upheld the moral and political straightforwardness advocated by Adam Smith and attempted to reverse almost a century of unprincipled and unsustainable growth in government.

He certainly held no brief for the Conservative Party when he felt it was ignoring the principles of the IEA. In 1995, the darkest days of the Major government, he wrote: 'For the past five years we have suffered under a nominally Conservative government which has lacked any consistent sense of direction on central issues of policy. At home, its worst failure has been in not sticking to its pledges to contain public expenditure and reduce taxa-tion.

'In Europe, its only consistency has been in putting short-term party expediency before principle, seen most vividly in facing both ways on the single currency'. Harris's other great campaign was for the rights of smokers.

He was chairman of and the prime mover in Forest (the Freedom Organisation for the Right to Enjoy Smoking Tobacco), and a member of the Lords and Commons Pipesmokers Club. He was seldom seen without a pipe clenched between his teeth – 'You'll like this,' he would assure non-smokers around him as he lit up, 'it's a meerschaum' – and usually had a couple more in his pockets, in case of emergency.

When in 1995 Network SouthEast introduced a smoking ban on the London to Brighton route, a group of commuters commandeered a carriage and continued to light up. Harris was tireless in raising the subject in newspapers and in the Lords, and produced a 22-page report urging the company to reinstate a smoking carriage.

He then convened a meeting in a pub near Victoria station and heard evidence from both sides in the debate. 'BR is indicted in my view of skulduggery,' he declared, pouring particular scorn on a survey which purported to show overwhelming support for the ban.

He was equally sceptical of the claims of the medical establishment that passive smoking was a significant threat to health, publicly challenging the chief medical officer to produce any evidence of harm in a piece entitled *Smoking Out the Truth*. In 1998 he produced *Murder a Cigarette* which was devoted both to extolling the joys of tobacco and casting doubt on the scientific evidence of its dangers.

With his centre parting and toothbrush moustache, Harris exuded a gentle, old-fashioned charm which made him excellent company, as well as proving an effective tool for promoting his beliefs. He was an accomplished amateur conjuror and was fond of bathing in the sea (he took regular dips off Eastbourne).

Harris's favourite dinner was lamb chops with roast potatoes, followed by apple pie, and he always travelled with a portable pepper grinder, in case black pepper could not be found on the table.

He also carried a miniature ivory gavel which doubled as a propelling pencil. By tapping it on a glass, he could quickly bring the most unruly student meeting under control. He was remarkably good with undergraduates, and as a result, a generation which had grown up during the years when the Federation of Conservative students looked to the IEA for guidance regarded him as something of an intellectual godfather.

The death of his two sons caused him much sorrow, but he doted on his daughter and was delighted when, for his 80th birthday, the IEA set up a travel fund to allow him to visit her at her home in France.

Ralph Harris married, in 1949, Jose Pauline Jeffery, and she and their daughter survive him.

The Economist

4 November 2006

LORD HARRIS OF HIGH CROSS, ECONOMIST AND FREEDOM-FIGHTER, DIED ON OCTOBER 19TH, AGED 81

On National No-Smoking Day, March 8th 2000, two suspicious figures were seen loitering outside the Houses of Parliament. One, in a loud red coat and louder lipstick, was Baroness Trumpington, with a clay pipe. The other, straight, thin and moustachioed, in a trilby and exotic waistcoat, was Lord Harris of High Cross, with a Meerschaum.

Ralph Harris loved smoking. He kept two more pipes in his pockets, in case one sputtered out. But as the years passed he loved smoking less for the tang of the tobacco, or its stimulus to thought, than for its defiance of the nanny-hand of the state. As smokers were increasingly repressed and made outcasts by the 'authoritarian itch' of governments, so he all the more fiercely took their side.

He too had been out in the cold, like them. When he became general director of the Institute of Economic Affairs ('my little institute', as he fondly thought of it), in 1957, he was pushing ideas that were deeply out of fashion in the Keynesian post-war years. The IEA, set up by Antony Fisher in 1955, promoted deregulation, privatisation, tax cuts, trade union reform and the free market. It attacked the welfare state, incomes policies and – Mr Harris's particular *bête noire* – high public spending that unleashed inflation. These opinions were so outside the bounds that Mr Harris compared the IEA in those years to a band of 30-year-old boys fooling with fireworks. Or, perhaps, lighting up in a non-smoking carriage; for when he went to give talks in universities in the 1960s, most of the audience would walk out.

To critics, the ideas of the IEA were all the worse for, being 'German'. Their source was Friedrich Hayek, in fact an Austrian. Mr Harris, fresh down from Cambridge in 1947, had fallen under the spell of Hayek's *The Road to Serfdom*. Serfdom was all around him then: ration books, travel restrictions, the persistent shadow of wartime central planning, and most of all the depressing disposition of people to do what they were told and to suppose that this was modern life. He never believed it. The way to freedom was to unleash the millions of individual actions that made up a working economy, and never to seek to control them.

Slowly, these ideas caught on. Arthur Seldon, his chief collaborator, made the IEA's papers readable, while Mr Harris proselytised among movers and shakers and, most usefully, raised money. The IEA stayed aloof from party politics – essential, Mr Harris believed, to avoid embroilment in 'vote-getting, lying and cheating' – but sought to change the intellectual climate in which politicians had to operate. Geoffrey Howe and Keith Joseph, the chief brains of the Conservative Party, deeply inhaled the new air; and Joseph passed the IEA's papers to his favourite pupil, saying, 'Here, Margaret, read this'.

The moral science

Mrs Thatcher adored Mr Harris's ideas. He admired her, and was amazed at the vigour with which she took on the unions and defended the free market through the 1980s. He did Thatcherite things, such as chairing the Bruges Group that opposed the European Union (though on grounds of interventionism, not the single market) and founding in 1985 a fan-club called No Turning Back.

Yet he was not a Thatcherite in his bones. From his lowly beginnings, on a council estate in Tottenham in north London, he understood the 'emotional case' for socialism, and worried about minimum levels of spending on the poor. He did not oppose safety nets, only 'hammocks'. When Mrs Thatcher made him a life peer, her first such appointment, he chose to sit on the cross-benches where he could vote as he pleased, as a 'radical reactionary' or, more accurately, a classical liberal. Offered a coat of arms, he refused it because he could not adorn it with Adam Smith's invisible hand.

He sometimes regretted he had not lived in Smith's time. To him, economics – or at least his variety, the economics of freedom – was a religious belief, the 'moral science' that Smith had taught. The law of supply and demand, he once wrote, was the nearest social science approached to the laws that governed the universe. The modern conception of economics was much too small a canvas for him.

Nonetheless, he could use the jargon for all it was worth. Speaking in the House of Lords in July 2005, he railed against 'statistical jiggery-pokery', 'selective surveys' and 'spurious precision to two decimal places'. The numbers he was pulling apart, this time, were not government predictions for economic growth or industrial output – nonsense, he always thought, implying the sort of comprehensive knowledge humans simply didn't have – but figures for deaths by passive smoking, which he refused to credit. He suspected that untruths were being peddled to curb liberty, and he was having none of it.

John Stuart Mill might have disagreed with him; freedom, he wrote, must be limited when it injures others. Even Adam Smith might have found fault with the unhindered working of a smokers' market. But Lord Harris could see priggish tyranny at work. That was the only 'false step' he ever attributed to Hayek; that, during a spell of bad health, he had let other people persuade him to give up smoking.

The Independent

21 October 2006

FOUNDING FATHER OF THE INSTITUTE OF ECONOMIC AFFAIRS

Ralph Harris, economist born London 10 December 1924; Lecturer in Political Economy, St Andrews University 1949–56; leader-writer, *Glasgow Herald* 1956; general director, Institute of Economic Affairs 1957–87, chairman 1987–89, founder president 1990–2006; created 1979 Baron Harris of High Cross; married 1949 Jose Jeffery (one daughter, and two sons deceased); died London 19 October 2006.

Ralph Harris was the most friendly and least lordly of peers. His easy manner, however, concealed his stature as one of the most influential figures of our age. Along with his fellow director of the Institute of Economic Affairs, Arthur Seldon, he was a key figure in the revival of the doctrines of classical liberal economics which inspired the Thatcher revolution.

Harris was born in a working-class part of north London in 1924, and read Economics at Queens' College, Cambridge, where he was influenced by the liberal ideas of his teacher Stanley Dennison, who introduced him to the works of Friedrich von Hayek. After Cambridge, Harris worked for a time in Conservative Central Office for R.A. Butler's Conservative Political Centre (CPC). It was after a speech he gave at a CPC meeting in Sussex in 1949 that a member of the audience came up to congratulate him. This was Antony Fisher, a businessman and admirer of Hayek, who persuaded him that the best way to combat socialism was to found an institute to spread free-market ideas.

Fisher immediately decided that Harris was the man to run it and said he would contact him as soon as he obtained the money. This he did very successfully through his chicken-farming company, Buxted Chicken, which eventually made him millions. However, he had to wait until 1956, during which time Harris had been lecturing at St Andrews University and then working as a leader-writer on the *Glasgow Herald*. Fisher, true to his word, then offered Harris the post of director of the recently formed Institute of Economic Affairs (IEA). Harris took it, even though, to start with, the part-time salary was only £10 per week.

He was joined the following year by another man of working-class background, Arthur Seldon, who became editorial director. Seldon was a graduate of the London School of Economics where he had imbibed free market economics from Hayek, Lionel Robbins and Arnold Plant. It was a perfect partnership. Harris was a most persuasive and witty speaker and had a wonderful way with people. Seldon had high academic standards combined with exceptional gifts of popular exposition. From the first. he insisted that they should recommend policies which were principled and sound, regardless of whether they were politically acceptable.

This was not easy, because it meant arguing against the collectivist political correctness of the time, which was summed up by *The Economist* in the word 'Butskellism' – the ideas on which Butler and Hugh Gaitskell agreed. Undaunted, Harris and Seldon issued a series of 'Hobart' papers and other publications challenging the consensus on taxation, financing pensions, education, health and housing, on transport, exchange rates and much else. One of the early successes was embodied in Ted Heath's abolition of resale price maintenance. Some of the most controversial IEA writings were those opposing the Keynesian theory of unemployment, coming from authors like Alan Walters and Enoch Powell.

All this activity had to be paid for. Fisher provided most of the launching money and then acted as a backstop to be called on when needed. It was Harris's task to raise more and act as salesman and projector of IEA ideas to the public. In all these roles he was superb. He was indefatigable in phoning newspapers to remind them of the next IEA pamphlet coming off the press.

He ran informal luncheons, which mixed up patrons with journalists and academic writers. These always featured a discussion on some current topic or a new publication, all conducted by Harris, good-naturedly encouraging all the company to have their say. He would finish by gently reminding those present that the Institute needed support in its mission of letting markets operate effectively. There were economic conferences too, which featured the big names, such as Gottfried Haberler, Harry Johnson, James Buchanan, Milton Friedman and Hayek, to mention but a few.

Although, under Harris, the IEA strenuously avoided involvement in politics, it became a magnet for many leading Conservatives who were looking for market solutions for problems, especially after the fall of Edward Heath in 1975. These included notably Geoffrey Howe, Keith Joseph and Margaret Thatcher. Other visitors were John Biffen, John Hoskyns, who would be head of the Downing Street Policy Unit after Margaret Thatcher came to power, and Dr Rhodes Boyson (who at one stage seemed to be there more often than not).

All these connections of course bore fruit in the Thatcher years in the policies of privatisation, trade-union reform, liberalisation of shopping hours, abolition of exchange, hire purchase, rent and price controls. It is hard to believe that what we now call the Thatcher revolution would have been so extensive or so complete without Harris. I say 'complete' because, although Labour returned to power, it was only because Blair essentially accepted the Thatcher legacy.

Harris had prodigious energy. That is how he found time for a whole range of other activities. He was a director of The Times under Rupert Murdoch. He founded the Bruges Group, to oppose the federalising tendencies of the Brussels bureaucracy. He was chairman and, in 2003, president of Forest – the Freedom Organisation for the Right to Enjoy Smoking Tobacco.

He was no mere frontman for Forest either. In 2005 he wrote a well-researched refutation of the Chief Medical Officer's pronouncements on passive smoking entitled 'Smoking out the Truth'. In this he declared: 'The imposition of a ban on smoking in so-called public places represents a triumph of prejudice and propaganda masquerading as science'. He added, 'hatred of cancer is no excuse for hatred of smokers nor for stirring up the wholly phantom fear of passive smoking especially by cynical politicians to whip up support for illiberal, intolerant policies of prohibition'.

Ralph Harris was extremely kind-hearted and ready to help any friend in need. For instance, in 1999 he organised a large fund to provide the legal costs of the former Conservative MP Neil Hamilton in his libel action against Mohamed al-Fayed, at no small potential risk, as it turned out, to himself. He helped another friend by finding an industrialist to sponsor his son's concert at the Wigmore Hall.

In my mind's eye I can still see Ralph with his pipe, his blazer and his fancy waistcoat (his one sartorial extravagance), meerschaum pipe and deerstalker hat, always full of good humour and sense of fun. Few would have known that he suffered the terrible grief of the deaths of two grown-up sons. In all this he was sustained by his Christian faith and the support of his charming and devoted wife Jose.

Ralph Harris was a contributor to the richness of British public life. Yet those who knew him personally will remember him also as a wonderful companion, an inspiration and a staunch and generous friend.

Russell Lewis

The *Financial Times*

20 October 2006

A LIBERAL WHO PREPARED THE GROUND FOR THATCHERISM

Lord Harris of High Cross, who died yesterday at the age of 81, played a decisive role in the free-market counter-revolution of the 1980s. The Institute of Economic Affairs, of which Ralph Harris became the founding director in 1957, prepared the ground for what subsequently came to be called Thatcherism, after Margaret (now Baroness) Thatcher, Conservative prime minister between 1979 and 1990. Yet Harris was never a traditional conservative. The creed to which he held throughout his influential career was 19th-century classical liberalism.

John Blundell, current director of the IEA, said last night: 'Ralph Harris was often described as the architect of Thatcherism but he used to tease her that she was an IEA-ite because the IEA had been advocating market economics for 20 years before her time. She replied: 'Ralph, the cock may crow but it's the hen that lays the eggs'.

The late Antony Fisher put up the money to establish the IEA in the highly unfavourable intellectual environment of the 1950s. At that time the 'Butskellite' consensus – named after the Conservatives' R.A. Butler and Labour's Hugh Gaitskell – reigned supreme. Keynesian ideas, public ownership of large parts of industry and the welfare state were nigh-on unchallengeable.

Fisher had, however, been persuaded by the late Friedrich Hayek, the Nobel-laureate proponent of classical liberalism, that the way to overturn the collectivist consensus was through an intellectual counter-attack. The way forward, suggested Hayek, would be through an institution that would publish research aimed at re-establishing the relevance of free-market ideas. That institution, headed by Harris, with the co-operation of the late Arthur Seldon, was to be the IEA.

Harris was the ideal director. After lecturing at St Andrews University in Scotland, already known as a centre of free-market ideas, he became a leader writer on the *Glasgow Herald*. Under his direction, the IEA was to forge close relationships with sympathetic economists.

Of these the most influential, after Hayek himself, was to be Milton Friedman. Other significant influences were the late George Stigler of Chicago University and James Buchanan of the George Mason University in Virginia, one of the founders of the 'public choice school', both winners of the Nobel memorial prize in economics.

The institute's aim was to argue for the superiority of the free market. The principal instrument used by Harris and Seldon was publication of pamphlets and books. Consistently and controversially, these argued against the prevailing orthodoxies of the 1950s, 1960s and 1970s – against macroeconomic fine-tuning, tolerance of inflation, monetary indiscipline, public ownership of industry, the welfare state, incomes policy and the many other forms that collectivist ideas took at the time.

Conventional wisdom thought the IEA eccentric, at best, and dangerous, at worst. Harris was to have the last laugh. The 1970s tested that conventional wisdom to destruction. The late Keith Joseph, the decisive intellectual influence on Lady Thatcher, started to look for an alternative for a future Conservative government. After her election as leader of the party in 1975, she was to be the standard-bearer of these ideas in practical politics. Although Joseph and Lady Thatcher were to found the Centre for Policy Studies, to hone their ideas, it was on the work of the IEA that they built.

The 1980s and 1990s were the apogee of the counter-revolution in ideas and in policy. In the UK, monetarism replaced Keynesianism, privatisation replaced public ownership, deregulation of the labour market replaced the power of trade unions. Similar changes occurred, in different political circumstances, under Ronald Reagan in the US. The tide of liberalisation spread across the world into unlikely places – China, India and, most remarkably, into the Soviet empire.

The IEA played an active role in this wider revolution. It forged close relations, with similarly inclined institutions in the US. Thus Edwin Fuelner, president of the Heritage Foundation in the US, said: 'Ralph defined for so many of us the importance of the world of ideas and showed there was an alternative to the nanny state. He showed that choice was a noble aspiration that brought out the best in men and women in a free society'.

The IEA also played an active role in founding similar think-tanks around the world. Today, there exists a network of more than 100 similar institutions in almost 80 countries. In this way, it has been able to spread classical liberal ideas across the world. The IEA also spawned think-tanks at home: Civitas, which focuses on social policy, the International Policy Network, which concentrates on economic development and global environmental policy, and the Social Affairs Unit are just three of these.

Harris became an active opponent of the European Union. Not long after ceasing to be director of the IEA in 1987, he became chairman of the Bruges

Group between 1989 and 1991, named after the controversial speech delivered by Lady Thatcher in Bruges on September 20 1988. In this capacity, Harris played a significant part in promoting euroscepticism. This issue was to divide not just the Conservative party but even the IEA, where he remained as founder president,

An enthusiastic pipe-smoker, he was also honorary president of Forest, the pro-smoking group, and an active campaigner against increasingly tough restrictions on the freedom to smoke.

Of the success of much of what he argued for over his lifetime there can be no doubt. The intellectual climate in his own country and across the world on the role of free markets is entirely altered. So, too, is the attitude towards the EU of influential people in the UK. It has certainly shifted in a more eurosceptic direction. But his success was also limited: in particular, the IEA achieved little progress in rolling back the welfare state itself, as David Cameron's new Conservative party demonstrates.

Unfailingly kind and humorous, Harris was a pleasure to know. Even his opponents found it hard to dislike him. Sir Geoffrey (now Lord) Howe, the former chancellor who knew Lord Harris from the inception of the IEA, described him as a 'sparkling, energetic personality' adding: 'He was the dynamo and the presentational maestro of the IEA. He made a crucial contribution to the economic liberalisation of Britain'.

In addition to being a successful director of the IEA, Harris was a prolific author. He published a biography of R.A. Butler in 1956 and pamphlets on advertising, choice in welfare, British economic policy, and other subjects. Professor Patrick Minford yesterday praised Lord Harris' skills as a 'great communicator, able to explain the importance of a free-market economy in concrete terms that ordinary people could understand'.

Harris contested parliamentary seats for the Conservatives twice in the 1950s. But politics was not his metier. He was, however, to become legislator in 1979 when Margaret Thatcher raised him to the peerage. His wit and eccentric charm were to make him an adornment of the House of Lords.

Born in London, the son of a tramways inspector, Ralph Harris read economics, at Queens' College, Cambridge before becoming political education officer for the Tory party in the South East. He married Jose Pauline Jeffery in 1949. She survives him, as does their daughter. Two sons predeceased him.

Martin Wolf

Index

Note: RH in the index refers to Ralph Harris.